HOW LITERATURES BEGIN

How Literatures Begin

A GLOBAL HISTORY

EDITED BY

JOEL B. LANDE & DENIS FEENEY

PRINCETON UNIVERSITY PRESS

PRINCETON & OXFORD

Published by Princeton University Press
41 William Street, Princeton, New Jersey 08540
6 Oxford Street, Woodstock, Oxfordshire OX20 1TR

press.princeton.edu

All Rights Reserved

Library of Congress Cataloging-in-Publication Data

Names: Lande, Joel B., editor. | Feeney, D. C., editor.
Title: How literatures begin : a global history / edited by Joel B. Lande and Denis Feeney.
Description: Princeton : Princeton University Press, [2021] | Includes bibliographical references and index.
Identifiers: LCCN 2020044596 (print) | LCCN 2020044597 (ebook) | ISBN 9780691186528 (paperback) | ISBN 9780691186535 (hardback) | ISBN 9780691219844 (ebook)
Subjects: LCSH: Literature—History and criticism.
Classification: LCC PN523 .H69 2021 (print) | LCC PN523 (ebook) | DDC 809—dc23
LC record available at https://lccn.loc.gov/2020044596
LC ebook record available at https://lccn.loc.gov/2020044597

British Library Cataloging-in-Publication Data is available

Editorial: Anne Savarese and James Collier
Production Editorial: Sara Lerner
Text and Cover Design: Chris Ferrante
Production: Erin Suydam
Publicity: Alyssa Sanford and Amy Stewart
Copyeditor: Kathleen Kageff

Cover images (top left to bottom right): Rubbing of the inscription from the Shi Qiang basin (ca. 900 BCE), Western Zhou dynasty (ca. 1046–771 BCE); leaf from *The Record of So Hyŏnsŏng*, undated. Manuscript. Image courtesy of the Kyujanggak Archive; manuscript leaf from one of the oldest copies of the Koran (Sanaa/Yemen; seventh to eighth century CE); detail of manuscript BnF fonds français 854 (Occitan *chansonnier* I), f. 142v. Paris, Bibliothèque nationale de France, Paris

This book has been composed in Adobe Text, Futura PT, and Lydian BT

Printed on acid-free paper. ∞

Printed in the United States of America

10 9 8 7 6 5 4 3 2 1

CONTENTS

ACKNOWLEDGMENTS

The most important beginning of this book on beginnings was a Humanities Council Capstone Seminar, "How Literatures Begin," in spring 2017, cotaught by the editors. We would like to express our warm thanks to the wonderful group of undergraduates and graduates who took part and whose enthusiasm made us feel we wanted to take this project further: James Brown-Kinsella, Allison Fleming, Yitz Landes, Robert Marshall, Alexander Robinson, Lily Xia, Zhuming Yao, Rafail Zoulis. For the funding of the next step, the symposium on April 13, 2018, we thank the Princeton University Departments of Classics, Comparative Literature, East Asian Studies, German, and Slavic, together with the Princeton Humanities Council; we also thank Eileen Robinson for her invaluable assistance. We gladly acknowledge the assistance of the Department of Classics Magie Fund toward the publication of this volume. Many thanks to our editor Anne Savarese and to the two readers for the press, whose comments made a big difference. Finally, we give our warm thanks to Maggie Kurkoski, whose expertise and cheerful energy made it possible to include the images in this volume.

CONTRIBUTORS

Rolena Adorno
Yale University
14. Latin American

Ksenia Chizhova
Princeton University
3. Korean

Wiebke Denecke
Massachusetts Institute of Technology
2. Japanese

Joseph Farrell
University of Pennsylvania
6. Latin

Simon Gaunt
Kings College London
11. Romance Languages

Simon Gikandi
Princeton University
15. African

Douglas Jones
Rutgers University
16. African American

Martin Kern
Princeton University
1. Chinese

Joel Lande
Princeton University
12. German

Ingrid Nelson
Amherst College
10. English

Jane O. Newman
University of California–Irvine
17. World Literature

Sheldon Pollock
Columbia University
4. Indian

Alberto Rigolio
Durham University
8. Syriac

Gregor Schoeler
Universität Basel
9. Arabic

Deborah Steiner
Columbia University
5. Greek

Jacqueline Vayntrub
Yale University
7. Hebrew

Michael Wachtel
Princeton University
13. Russian

HOW LITERATURES BEGIN

INTRODUCTION

Literatures are rather improbable things. While storytelling and myth making seem to be fixtures of human society, literatures are much more rare. After all, very few spoken languages ever developed a script, let alone enduring institutions of the kind surveyed in this volume. And in those instances where a literary tradition does take hold, survival is far from guaranteed. Literatures require technologies for their preservation and circulation, groups interested in their continuing production, audiences invested in their consumption, and so on. Literatures are sustained over time by diverse practices. But much like individual lives or entire cultures, they also experience birth and death, periods of florescence and of decay, migration from one place to another, and transformation from one shape into another.

With all the specialized interest in individual literatures, in addition to the widespread use of big-picture categories like postcolonial and world literature, one can easily lose track of just how strange it is that literatures exist in the first place. This book embraces such strangeness, asking how an array of literatures, extending across time and space, came to be. By examining the factors that have brought forth and kept alive various literary traditions, the case studies presented here provide the occasion to rethink many of our most basic assumptions about literature in the singular and literatures in the plural.

It is not hard to recognize the risks built into such a project. Neither the concept of literature, nor that of a beginning, can be taken for granted. There are, to be sure, intrinsic difficulties in translating the concept of literature from one idiom to another, especially because of the term's modern European provenance. Using the term *literature* universally, that is, runs the risk of projecting a historically and culturally specific set of textual practices and aesthetic values onto times and places that worked very differently. Along the same lines, the search for beginnings can easily be construed as the attempt to uncover a single pattern or a uniform set of enabling conditions, common to each of the case studies included here. In reflecting on processes of literary beginning, it is all too easy to impose a hegemonic mold that all examples either manage or fail to live up to.

This book began with the realization that these risks are real. As scholars trained in ancient and modern European literature, with a specialized focus on the German and Latin traditions respectively, we wondered whether the emergence of the two literary traditions we know best had any common factors. This narrow question quickly gave way to a more encompassing, but also more puzzling, one: is it possible, in general, to ask how literatures begin? Are there developmental processes, technological conditions, or institutional structures that must be in place as literary traditions come about? Any serious attempt to respond to this question, we quickly realized, required knowledge of languages and regions about which we lacked the requisite knowledge, such as the Far and Near East, the Indian subcontinent, Eastern Europe, and postcolonial settings. More concreteness, not greater abstraction, was essential—and this could be achieved only by a group with a broader set of specializations than the two of us possess alone. Beyond wanting to avoid the eurocentrism that a Germanist and a Latinist, left to their own devices, might well fall into, we also came to believe that the problem of literary beginnings called for a more richly comparative approach.

To this end, we organized a small workshop in April 2018 at Princeton University, loosely building on an advanced undergraduate seminar we had recently offered on the subject. As the invited scholars presented informal papers on literary beginnings in their respective fields, it became clear that our straightforward-enough question, in fact, raised wildly divergent issues and solicited surprisingly heterogeneous responses, depending on the field under consideration. We were left with the strong impression that the topic of literary beginnings presented an exceptional chance to engage in comparative inquiry, and we began to develop a plan for this book. Thanks to the clearly defined nature of the conceptual problem, it would be possible to commission chapters that would place traditions from vastly different times and places, with pronounced cultural-historical differences, alongside one another in a productive way. We came to see that beginnings provide a powerful framework for comparison, a *tertium comparationis*, that can remain respectful of specific contexts and also strengthen our grasp of the similarities among different traditions.

As this project developed, it became clear that beginnings are not themselves "literary units of value," akin to commodities, circulating within a global literary system.[1] In other words, beginnings cannot be equated with a genre like the novel that may (or may not) have sprouted up across the globe from Korea to England and throughout time from late Greek antiquity to the present day.[2] Rather, beginnings are processes that unfold over time in unforeseeable, contingent, and often chaotic ways. Differences among beginnings are also especially revealing of the factors that shape the paths respectively taken by literary traditions, clustering the factors that lend literatures their unique signature. By recognizing commonalities among the contributing factors, one does not thereby erase differences among literatures but rather shows how, to borrow a chemical metaphor, a single element can produce radically different compounds, depending on the other contributing elements and environing circumstances. Just because a single factor like the invention of script or, relatedly, the dissemination of written language, plays a prominent role in many of the literary historical narratives present here does not mean that its impact can be uniformly accounted for.

In order to meet these demands, this volume proceeds as a series of case studies. As a glance at the table of contents makes clear, the contributions do not provide exhaustive coverage—inevitably, readers will find a lamentable absence or two. Our goal was not to create an encyclopedia or handbook of literary beginnings, but instead to offer a representative sample of responses to the conceptually robust question laid out in the book's title. In so doing, we have sought to create opportunities for, without overtly determining, comparative axes to emerge: ancient and modern, East and West, European and colonial, cosmopolitan and national, to name some of the most obvious categories. The sheer heterogeneity of literary traditions also brought with it stylistic and argumentative constraints. If one zooms in too closely on a historical moment or individual problematic, one risks losing readers unfamiliar with the broader historical and cultural context. And if one views a historical landscape only from afar, one may not get a granulated picture of the tradition under discussion. Thus all the chapters included here try to strike a balance between the sort of detailed precision that experts cherish and the broad-brushstroke narratives that grant newcomers access.

The following chapters lay the groundwork for comparison by framing their historical discussions in terms of institutions, processes, and structures that are potentially common to more than one example. Doing so makes it clear that, while the cases are far from identical, there are threads connecting them. These points of convergence among some literatures—which simultaneously mark out points of divergence from others—can provide a fresh perspective on this apparently natural mode of human expression and societal institution. The rubrics included below surely do not exhaust the points of overlap among the seventeen literatures discussed here, but they should facilitate the reader's appreciation of the individual traditions as well as the similarities that emerge when they are placed next to one another.

While it is important to use comparison of this kind to bring similarities into view, any act of comparison highlights difference as much as it does similarity, and this acknowledgment of difference is to be embraced. One of the main contributions of this volume is precisely to reveal how varied the origins and development of literary traditions have been. This comparative exercise can enable students of any one literary tradition to undergo the surprise of defamiliarization that the editors experienced in exploring the subset of possibilities on display in the following pages. For someone working within one tradition, or even at the interface between traditions, it can be all too easy to take the terms of debate for granted. We hope that it will be as salutary for our readers as it has been for us to take stock of the tremendous variations within different societies' ways of constructing and working with literary traditions. Family resemblances certainly present themselves, and we are confident that the term "literature" continues to have heuristic value in transhistorical and transcultural analysis; yet in the sustained act of comparison involved in working on this volume, we have learned as much about our own disciplines as we have learned about others. We hope other readers will have the same experience.

Single and Multiple Beginnings

Counterintuitive though it may sound, literatures do not necessarily have a single beginning or even a single epoch of beginning. Depending on how one frames the literature under consideration, a different beginning can come into view. Consider the example of Chinese literature. Although contemporary disciplinary conventions lend immediate plausibility to the divisions of ancient, medieval, modern, and contemporary Chinese literature, these categories do not mark out contiguous segments along a single line. Instead, the different periods of Chinese history are characterized by such far-reaching changes that the factors shaping the literary tradition of the Han dynasty around 200 BCE are irreducibly different from the ones that gave life to a cosmopolitan literature in the early twentieth century. The question of how Chinese literature begins, in other words, demands further specification, since there is no single beginning that can possibly illuminate all its richly varied phases. Something similar could be said of German literature, with its historically consequential gaps between the epics, romances, and lyric poetry that exploded onto the scene around 1200 and the literary reform movements of the eighteenth century. In the case of Russia, we see numerous "false starts," as imperial attempts to foster a literature repeatedly fail to gain traction. While the concept of an origin points to a singular event (or sequence of events) that remains definitive for everything that came after, beginnings are often multiple and disjointed.

Moreover, not everything now recognized as an early work within a literary lineage contributed, in a meaningful way, to the formation of that tradition.

One good example of this is *Beowulf* in Old English, which was lost, only to be rediscovered and inserted into a lineage it did not give rise to. The same is true of the Old Russian *Lay of Igor*, which was probably written not long after a disastrous military defeat in 1185, but remained unknown until the turn of the eighteenth century. The fifteenth-century Korean poem *The Songs of Flying Dragons* is yet another example of an individual work that, while widely recognized today as an early, even the earliest, instantiation of a literature, did not launch a broader movement. The poem was, in fact, commissioned as part of an effort to wrest Korea free from Chinese cultural and political hegemony. But the project ultimately proved unsuccessful; it was two centuries before a practice of writing and reading literary works in the Korean vernacular gained traction. These two examples highlight the way that literary traditions, like so many other traditions, are formed in hindsight, retrospectively seen as emergent in ways that were often completely unavailable to the participants at the time (as Simon Gaunt argues in chapter 11). The interests and perspectives of those who "create" traditions in this way will always condition their choices, inclining some toward a more nativist position (as with *Beowulf* or the *Lay of Igor*), and others favoring more international moments of translation and cross-fertilization (focusing on Chaucer, for example).

Orality and Literacy

"Oral literature" is not necessarily an oxymoron, and many oral traditions of song, storytelling, and oratory across the world have been intensively studied.[3] All our case studies are of literatures in textually transmitted form, and the question of how written literatures emerge from or interact with oral forms of expression is regularly of crucial importance, as may be seen especially in chapters 5 ("Greek"), 9 ("Arabic"), 11 ("Romance Languages"), and 15 ("African").[4] Because of the continuing special prominence of ancient Greece in discussions of the beginnings of literature and in European-centered university literature courses, it is easy to be misled into thinking of the Greek case as paradigmatic. In Greece we see written texts coming into view after long traditions of oral composition and performance, but we should guard against thinking of such a development as normal. A wider perspective—taking in China, for example, or Latin, Syriac, or Russian literature, and many other cases—makes it clear that there is nothing natural or inevitable about an oral phase as a precursor to a written literature.

It is always worth paying attention to the nature of the writing system that is used for any given literature, for writing is not just speech on a material surface, and literature is never a matter of just writing down what people are saying. The distinctive nature of different scripts can have a significant impact on their literatures, as we see particularly clearly in the case of Japan, which developed its literature from within the penumbra of Chinese literature (chapter 2). The remarkable Chinese script, unlike the alphabet, is not phonetically based, and it could be read by people outside China who could not speak any of the various languages of the Chinese empire: the distinctive nature of this script made it possible for the Japanese to make adaptations and develop their own literature in dialogue with Literary Sinitic, even though very few people in Japan before the modern period could actually speak Chinese.

Writing systems have very seldom been invented ex nihilo, independently of other writing systems, and writing therefore almost invariably spreads from one region to another. Ancient Mesopotamia and China are obvious counter-examples, where the unique scripts remained in use for millennia, contributing—in the case of China—to the comparatively self-generating and enclosed nature of the literary system for so long. Elsewhere one regularly sees scripts taken over or adapted from neighboring or interpenetrating cultures, as in the case of Swahili, which first took over Arabic script but then developed its own writing system, based on the Latin alphabet, as a result of the perception that many Swahili sounds could not be captured in Arabic script (chapter 15).

Although we may instinctively think of literacy as enabling communication, scripts can create barriers. The Greek alphabet is a clear example. This extraordinary invention, an innovation based on the Phoenician version of the West Semitic writing system, had a dynamic effect on the production of literature in early Greece (chapter 5). At the same time, the alphabet isolated Greek literature from its deep original contacts with a more cosmopolitan hinterland in the Near East: in its oral phase, one could see Greek literature as a vernacular of Near Eastern literature, but the alphabetic revolution had the effect of propelling Greek literature in a different and separate direction, eventually becoming a new cosmopolitan literature in its turn.

The attainment of written form for any particular language by no means entails any necessary progression to its being a literary language (from "literization" to "literarization," as Sheldon Pollock puts it in chapter 4; cf. Alberto Rigolio in chapter 8 on Syriac and Ksenia Chizhova in chapter 3 on Korean). Conversely, it is not always true that written languages are first devised for practical or administrative purposes before they come to serve literary purposes. Although it is regularly assumed that the Greek alphabet, for example, was first used for administration or commerce before it became the vehicle for transcribing oral song, a case can be made that its first use was precisely to capture the sound of the bards' unique poetic language (see chapter 5 by

Deborah Steiner). Further, the mere fact of being encoded in script does not in itself dictate any necessary specific consequences for how literatures operate, and we have to allow for a wide variety of conditions in the larger literary culture when we consider written literatures. Some literary traditions might insist on a high degree of fidelity in copying and transmission, for example, while others might have such fluid patterns of circulation that the terminology of "original text" or "variation" is irrelevant. Again, European-derived traditions regularly show a heavy investment in the figure of the author, with sustained discussions of attribution and authenticity, and with authors such as Euripides, Vergil, or Dante becoming celebrities in their own day; but ancient Hebrew or early Chinese literature operate on entirely different principles, and literary texts in these systems circulate for prolonged periods without any necessary attribution to an originary "author."

Nationhood and Cosmopolitanism

Sheldon Pollock introduced the concept of "the literary cosmopolis" to describe the preeminence of Sanskrit as a literary vehicle from Afghanistan to Java during the first millennium CE, and he develops it here in chapter 4.[5] It is possible to pick out a small number of literatures, each in a particularly dominant and prestigious language, that have covered wide expanses of space and time, not coextensive with any particular imperial power or political center. Alexander Beecroft identifies a number of such "cosmopolitan literatures," and we could add Sanskrit to his list: "Sumerian, Akkadian, Greek, Latin, Arabic, New Persian, and classical Chinese."[6] From the point of view of literary beginnings, as Beecroft stresses, the fascinating aspect of these cosmopolitan literatures is the way that they regularly give rise to vernacular literatures on their peripheries, like glaciers calving icebergs. We saw above that Greek literature itself may be regarded as one such case, emerging from an environment where Akkadian literature had high prestige, only to develop its own distinctive script and literary language. In time, even before the conquests of Alexander, and more sweepingly thereafter, Greek literature itself became a cosmopolitan literature, with participants eventually originating from Babylon, Egypt, Syria, Palestine, and Carthage. This new cosmopolitan literature then provided an environment from which new vernacular literatures, such as Latin in the third century BCE (chapter 6) and, much later, Syriac (chapter 8), split off. Latin literature in turn became the cosmopolitan literature of the western Mediterranean under the Roman Empire and itself became a breeding ground for the vernaculars of the Middle Ages, which distinguished themselves from Latin as vehicles for literary expression in a slow and piecemeal process (chapter 10). Again, we see Japanese and Korean literatures forming themselves in their own vernaculars from within the penumbra of the prestige literature of China (chapters 2 and 3).

In all these cases, complex processes of envy and imitation are at play, as one group homes in on a distinctive cultural feature possessed by another group in order to appropriate it for its own purposes. A range of responses is possible, from a systematic reproduction of models and prototypes belonging to the "parent" culture (Latin's response to Greek is an archetype) to an engagement with models that tracks them while stopping short of reproducing them (Japan and China). These relations of imitation are different still from the birth of literatures in languages that have previously given rise to literary traditions, albeit under very different geographical and social circumstances. African American literature (chapter 16) and Spanish-based Latin American literature (chapter 14) assumed their distinctive shape in large part because of the contexts within which speaking subjects expressed themselves. Regularly, the momentum behind the beginning of a vernacular literature out of a cosmopolitan one is to be found in the crystallization of a new sense of group identity, as when Rome suddenly found itself raised to the status of a Mediterranean Great Power after defeating Carthage and gaining control of Sicily in the mid-third century BCE; or when the newly won independence of the Kingdom of Osrhoene in the mid-second century BCE led Syriac speakers to develop a distinctive script used at first for administrative purposes and ultimately for translation and for literary creation (chapter 8); or when new regional kingdoms emerged in India after the middle of the first millennium (chapter 4). We could find strong analogies with the development of Latin American independence (chapter 14), or with the growing establishment of autonomous free Black communities throughout the nineteenth century in the United States (chapter 15). Such moments are easiest for contemporary readers to recognize when they are linked in the modern period to emergent nationalisms, which arose in a competitive international arena in which it came to feel "natural" that each "nation" of people should have its own literature (along with its own folk music, dress, and so on). Compelling examples abound, and the case of French literature's conscious self-definition as a national project in the sixteenth century formed the starting point for Pascale Casanova's influential study of "the world republic of letters."[7] Russian literature is a fine test case of another variety of nationalism at work in the creation of a literature, as we can observe a conscious and sustained state-directed effort, in tandem with numerous other Europeanizing initiatives, to modernize Russia by means of a "national" literature (chapter 13).

It is more challenging for modern readers to apprehend cases of emergent vernacular literatures that are not linked to the initiative of a state, a people, or a nation, as is normally the situation in the premodern period, before the nationalism that we can too readily take for granted as the default mode of group or ethnic self-identification. Even a case as recent as the German one predates a sense of political and territorial cobelonging: German speakers developed a consciousness of German national identity in the eighteenth century—one that gave rise to a German literature—before a German state, or even the popular desire for one, existed. Even more diffuse senses of identification are the norm in the premodern period in Europe. Dante, for example, clearly was attempting something new for his language as he enlarged its literary reach, but he did so in response to other literary traditions and literary languages, not in the service of any state or political identity. In the ancient world, although a vernacular literature in the Latin language was intimately involved in its origins with a quasi-imperial power's sense of its new stature, in Greece we see nothing of the kind until perhaps the Athenian state's fostering of the dramatic festivals in the fifth century BCE. "Greek" literature had a vital role to play in fostering a sense of communality among people who could call themselves "Greeks" (or "Hellenes"), but there was no Greek superstate whose interests were served by this literature, and anyone prepared to make the considerable effort to perfect his or her command of the Greek language and its canons could become, effectively, a Hellene.

Translation, Transfer, Interstitial Figures

If we focus on the cases where a new literature comes into view in response to new senses of group identity of one kind or another, we need to acknowledge that the petri dish in which this new set of reactions is cultivated almost invariably turns out to be an already multilingual and multicultural environment—cases such as premodern Japan, where virtually no one except immigrants spoke Chinese, are very rare, and even there a crucial factor in the development of the new literature was the arrival of a wave of refugees from the destruction of the Paekche state in Korea (chapter 2). To give just a selection of examples: later medieval Britain had a trilingual textual culture; mid-Republican Rome was home to speakers of Greek, Etruscan, and Oscan; the Swahili classic *Al-Inkishafi* came from a hybridized culture involving Arabic rulers and three competing Swahili dialects.

As a consequence, very strikingly, the beginnings of literatures are regularly venues for the transformative impact of interstitial figures, bilingual or trilingual intercultural actors, who become the catalysts for new forms of cultural expression. These individuals are often able to import into the target culture their expertise in an outside literary tradition (regularly from a cosmopolitan literature). Such entrepreneurial experts shuttling in between cultures are key figures in the beginning of literatures in Rome (Livius Andronicus, Naevius, and Ennius); Russia (Antiokh Kantemir [1709–44]); Japan (the refugees from Korea in the seventh century CE, especially Yamanoue no Okura [660–ca. 733], from a Paekche immigrant family); and India (Maulana Daud, the Muslim who in the 1370s composed the first Hindi work, the *Candāyan*). The bi- or trilingual individuals who must have been crucial in mediating the epics and songs of the Near East into the Greek-speaking sphere in the period before Homer and Hesiod are now lost to history. As with any feature of culture, all literary traditions interact and appropriate to one degree or another: in their initial phases, the splitting off of vernacular literatures from their parental cosmopolitan literatures will provide ready opportunity for such middle men and culture brokers.

Translation is often a key mediating and galvanizing element at these moments, and the culture brokers are regularly the people responsible for such work. Translation—often to be understood in the broadest sense of adaptation and transformation—flourishes at moments of origin in many traditions, often being carried out by individuals who are also composing "original" works in the new literary language: Chaucer and Ennius are obvious examples. Yet translation of literary texts, however common it may be in the modern world, is not something we should take for granted. In the ancient Mediterranean the Romans are outliers and innovators in translating literary texts, and the later European attitude that it is normal to translate literature is one due ultimately to the Romans' peculiar decision to translate large quantities of Greek literature, especially drama (chapter 6). By contrast, the astounding Greek-Arabic translation movement of the ninth and tenth centuries (chapter 9) concentrated on philosophical, medical, and technical writing and barely touched on literary texts at all; similarly, the extensive Syriac translation movement that was so important as a mediator for the later Arabic one did not include classical Greek literature either (chapter 8)—literature in the sense of fiction, poetry, or drama.

Such differences in selection prompt us to reflect on the criteria of categorization. Essentially all the cultures discussed over the following chapters operate with a set of assumptions about the differences between kinds of texts within the larger family of "literature." If "literature" may include any texts that are codified, transmitted, and curated, then capacious definitions will include writings on agriculture or medicine along with love poetry or novels, and this is a state of affairs that obtained in Europe, for example, up until the eighteenth century. Yet subdivisions within that larger family definition always have the potential to become important for whatever reason, and translation is certainly one of the key vectors that we can identify as encouraging or enforcing generic subcategorization, regularly homing in on "imaginative" literature as a category for inclusion or exclusion.

Outside Europe we see important cases where translation is not in play at all. India and Japan provide key examples of new literatures being formed out of intense cultural interaction without translation. Here, once again, script can be crucial. As Wiebke Denecke shows (chapter 2), the nature of the Chinese logographic script meant that translation was unnecessary for the elites of premodern East Asia, who could read Literary Sinitic even though they could not speak Chinese. If, then, heightened interaction between cultures appears to be indispensable for the creation of a new literature, this interaction may take many forms, and translation is by no means a necessary condition.

Criticism, Philology

Literatures do not exist in a vacuum. As we remarked at the beginning of this introduction, they form part of complex cultural practices and institutions. If the social practices that sustain them disappear, then they eventually disappear as well, as we see with the end of the cuneiform literature once the environment of palace and temple culture faded away, in a process that took centuries after the Macedonian conquest. In particular, literatures have a role in education, and they attract self-conscious critical attention, which ranges from oral discussion after group reading or listening all the way up to scholarly apparatuses of curatorship and commentary. What relationships do we find among texts or performances and societal institutions of education and scholarship if we adopt the vantage point of a beginning? Should we expect a time lag between the first productions of a new literary culture and the institution of the societal practices we have considered here?

Although the relationship between literature and literary criticism might seem to unfold as a natural sequence, with the literary works preceding commentary on them, the enclosed chapters reveal a much more nuanced and varied array of possibilities. Consider the case of ancient Greek, which within a European context has long set the analytic paradigm. While it is clear that the Homeric poems first had to be set down in writing before they could assume the prominent role in Greek education that they eventually did, needless to say forming the basis for Aristotle's philosophical poetics, chapter 5 shows that reflection on poetic practices was embedded within poetry from the very start.

From the self-reflexive sections of Homeric poems to hexametric inscriptions on ritual or quotidian objects, critical reflection on literary activity was actually part and parcel of the work itself, not something contributed later. The concept of world literature (chapter 17), meanwhile, has swung between the scholarly and economic frameworks, often seeming more vital to the academy and publishing houses than to modern authors.

Sacred literatures—ones where texts are imbued with divine quality and embedded in ritual practices—illustrate vividly that commentary can promote the formation of an authoritative canon and institutionalize the practice of commentary. In the Hebrew tradition, from the third-century Mishnah through the Gemara approximately three hundred years later and up to the present day, an extraordinarily refined practice of rabbinic commentary has taken shape. Beyond the preservation of a select body of texts, in the Hebrew tradition—or the Arabic one discussed in chapter 9—such practices of commentary also provide a model for how the reading of literature often depends on the ascription of profound significance to the object under discussion. There is, in other words, a decisive link between literature and the sacred, insofar as the ennobled status of literature within culture is so often bound up with the belief that the texts deal with issues of ultimate importance.

As counterpole to the Arabic or Hebrew tradition, one might consider the modern German tradition, which, as chapter 12 argues, got its start only after a substantive body of criticism emerged. As early modern rhetorical handbooks gave way to new methods of reflection that express awareness of recent trends in European poetics (thus also an awareness that literatures change according to time and place), the mid-eighteenth century gave rise to a swell of critical commentary, which bemoaned the absence of a German literature of rank and stridently called for new authors to step forward. As in a number of other cases, including Latin, Japanese, and Russian, the knowledge of other literatures and the body of philological writing surrounding them proved essential to the formation of a new literary tradition: the prototypical case will be the formation of Akkadian literature, the earliest case in world history, which is inextricable from Sumerian literature and its apparatus (see part 2).

If one were to ask after the broader function of commentary, one might say that its purpose is to ensure rereading. This is the definition provided by Friedrich Schlegel in his landmark essay on the naturalist and revolutionary Georg Forster.[8] Schlegel argues that attaining the status of a classical text does not depend on its preservation in manuscript or print, but instead on its being read and reread, included in school curricula, and circulated among the reading public through the form of reviews, second-order commentaries, and literary histories. Roland Barthes's definition may be brusque, but it catches something crucial about this aspect of literature as an institution: "Literature is what is taught, period, that's all."[9] Literature depends on circulation for its survival, and the various forms of commentary and criticism form an indispensable element of that circulation.

Literary Language

Perhaps one of the most recognizable features of literature is its specialized use of language—so much so that the linguist and philologist Roman Jakobson famously identified a distinctive poetic function available in all languages. Jakobson claimed that there are forms of expression squarely focused on the "message for its own sake," drawing the individual linguistic formulation into the foreground and giving it a life independent of the world of things.[10] One familiar way to describe literary language, with terminological roots in ancient Rome, relies on the distinction between poetry and prose. While bookstores today are filled with prose novels, many of which are interspersed with colloquial language, which offer a window onto the ordinariness of everyday life, this is a recent and unusual development. The earliest literary texts in European literature paint a different picture. Consider the two Homeric poems, which are written in hexametric verse, built on a centuries-long heritage of extemporized performance. Accompanied by a four-string lyre, the bard that sang the Homeric poems relied on a repertoire of standardized scenes and used a highly artificial, aesthetically charged language. Homer's idiom was, in fact, never spoken by ordinary Greeks. It was a composite of different regional forms, full of antiquated language as well as newly minted terms. Essential genres of ancient Greek literature—lyric poetry, tragedy, epic—used strict and often intricate metrical structures in order to set off their works from ordinary communication.

While the primacy of verse is common to a number of different literary beginnings—Sanskrit, Arabic, ancient Chinese, Russian, the Romance languages, to give a few examples discussed here—it is not universal. Ancient Hebrew, for example, blends together prose and verse, often using poetry to create emphasis or to give an oration a final flourish. Syriac stands out as another literature from antiquity that begins with prose. Korean similarly first got off the ground in prose genres. And among modern literatures, African American literature is unique for the fact while its very earliest works are written in verse, its nineteenth-century efflorescence—both before and after the Civil War—relied heavily on prose genres from the novel to journalism and autobiography. Latin American literature in Spanish, meanwhile, was at home primarily in prose and not poetry, in no small part because of the genres employed in the earliest phases of Spanish colonial writing. Any literature born in the nineteenth century encountered a radically new literary universe, particularly because of the rise of the novel and the acceleration of printing through the invention of the rotary printing press. In this respect and many others, the comparison of an ancient literary beginning and a modern one confronts us with fascinating questions that would not readily occur to us otherwise.

Such questions emerge out of attention to the context specificity of literary expression. Literary languages, that is, are deeply rooted in the life world within which they emerge, including institutional environments and ritual practices as well as political and social hierarchies. The tradition of Chinese verse that first began to take shape in the tenth century BCE was influenced as much by hieratic rituals as by the conventions of court culture. As chapter 1 shows, the beginnings of Chinese literature cannot be understood independently of how ritual vessels were used in ancestral rites, or of the patterns of social and political stratification that characterized the Western Zhou dynasty. The beginnings of Chinese literature are, in other words, profoundly informed by the contexts within which the responsible scribes lived and worked. If the Chinese tradition was shaped by its hegemonic status and rigid monolingualism, the exact opposite holds true for western European literatures. As the discussions of the multilingual situation in post-Norman England in chapter 10 and of the similarly fluid linguistic milieu of the troubadours in chapter 11 show, literary languages often emerge from the confluence of multiple different streams, just as they can be shaped in isolation. What ultimately differs, from one case to the next, is the resulting language and literature. By attending to the processes that lend literatures their distinctive patterns of development, the following seventeen case studies enrich our appreciation of the diverse range of phenomena that we call literary. At the same time, the attention to historical and cultural specificity cultivated here is meant to spur on the search for commonalities across time and space.

We have provided short introductions to each part of this book to underscore common themes of the volume—such as script, translation, social function—that are especially significant for each individual part. Since parts 1 and 2 concentrate on traditions from the ancient world, whose distant writing cultures are less familiar to most readers, we provide historical and philological context. In particular, the introduction to part 2 gives a brief account of Mesopotamian literature, the literature that begins all literatures, with particular attention to the streams that feed into ancient Hebrew and Greek literature. The volume is bookended by brief reflections on the value we recognize in arraying the seventeen case studies that follow.

PART I

East and South Asia

We begin with China, the oldest continuously surviving culture in the world, with the oldest continuously surviving literature—Chinese literature was already eighteen hundred years old when the Japanese began the project of developing their own literature in response to it. The ancient world saw the development of a number of logographic scripts in addition to Chinese (Egyptian hieroglyphs, Mesopotamian cuneiform, Mayan). These scripts all had phonetic elements, but they were all based, as Wiebke Denecke puts it (chapter 2), on "writing meaning ('words' = *logos*) rather than transcribing sound ('phono'graphic)." Astonishingly, one of those ancient logographic scripts, Chinese, is still with us, and its accompanying script-based cosmopolitan literary culture, akin to that of Akkadian or Sanskrit, endured from antiquity until only a hundred years ago. The "Sinographic sphere" extended from central Asia to Taiwan, Vietnam, and Japan: the core of this sphere was obviously generated and sustained by Chinese military and commercial power, but Chinese cultural power held sway even in regions never under Chinese imperial control. Within this sphere educated people could communicate with each other on paper even without the ability to converse in any of the Chinese languages, and Chinese is therefore the original cosmopolitan literary culture, from whose penumbra emerged numerous vernacular literatures, two of which (Japanese and Korean) are discussed in this section. Chinese and Sanskrit provide the first examples in this book of Sheldon Pollock's now classic model of cosmopolitan literatures as the environment from which vernacular literatures can take their origin.[1]

Yet Chinese literature, too, had its own origin—or, rather, origins. In common with most of our case studies, Chinese literature has numerous moments of innovation and departure that may claim to be "beginnings." If we go back to antiquity, we find that the Chinese script is extremely unusual in being "invented independent of any known influence from the outside" (Martin Kern), sharing this distinction only with Sumerian cuneiform and Mesoamerican glyphs (and possibly with Egyptian hieroglyphs, whose inspiration from Sumerian script remains controversial). As a result, the very first Chinese literature is "monocultural and monolingual." This is a highly unusual state of affairs in world literatures, and it is one that did not endure even in China, where monoculturalism is clearly irrelevant in many later new "beginnings," as with the impact of Buddhist writings during the first millennium CE.

The first recoverable literature in China is not regarded as occupying a personal or private domain but is embedded in ritual and societal structures. The inscribed bronze basin from circa 900 BCE discussed in chapter 1 displays deliberate aesthetic choices, yet the text is intimately linked to "specific, local performances." The "Confucian" classics were also deployed in socially significant performance contexts, even if one of the most striking features of these texts is their deliberate removal from their original performance and political context, a process by which they became true "classics"—transferable, appropriable, and requiring interpretation. Tradition located the key moment of organization of these classics as occurring at the initiative of Kongzi (Confucius) within one of the least significant states of the Spring and Autumn period (771–476 BCE). These classics, then, were not tied to an origin that was associated with hegemonic political or military power, nor were they tied to named authors or even pinned down to a fixed form; they were available to all users of Chinese.

The very earliest Chinese writing may have been "monocultural," but Chinese writing did not remain exclusively so. Certainly the literatures we observe evolving from within China's cosmopolitan reach are of necessity intertwined with the Sinographic sphere, and we observe key moments of transcultural impact at formative moments of a new literature's development throughout part 1. Modern nationalist narratives are not accommodating to such moments of cultural appropriation and cross-fertilization, and the case of Japan shows how unhelpful and misleading modern nationalism is in understanding premodern contexts. The modern Japanese understanding of their literary history is a prime example of how "national origins" are created retrospectively, since Japanese authorities, from the late nineteenth century on, used European models to forge nationalist narratives about their literary tradition just as the country as a whole was adopting European models in other areas. These perspectives will tend to occlude the cultural importance of such kinetic moments as the arrival of Buddhism in Japan from around 600 CE, or the influx of refugees from the Paekche kingdom in Korea from 1650 CE on.

The chapters on Japan and Korea illustrate the cardinal significance of script in any literary history. Japanese authors could not speak Chinese, yet they could read Chinese script, and Japan shows a remarkable range of responses to Sinitic writing, developing vernacular scripts to complement the Sinitic variety: socially embedded performance occasions carried a high degree of generic self-consciousness, involving choice of script as well.

The relationship with Sinitic writing continued to be important in Japan and Korea, for it is not at all the case that on the fringes of the Sinographic sphere the Chinese classics were simply supplanted by a "native" replacement.[2] Japan maintained Sinitic writing alongside its own vernacular writing forms. Korea, in fact, particularly the court realm, remained considerably more Sinitic than Japan, even after the remarkable invention of a Korean vernacular script, promulgated by the king in 1446 CE. In the following year there appeared the poem *The Songs of Flying Dragons*, a hybrid production, first written in literary Chinese, then translated into the vernacular language and script, along with a scholarly exegetical apparatus that was also in literary Chinese. This is one of those false starts one regularly sees in literary history, where apparently promising new ventures do not attain escape velocity. One could be forgiven for expecting this innovation to be the precursor to a new genre of vernacular court literature in Korea. But this did not happen. The gravitational pull of the court's conventional Sinitic literature was too strong, and *The Songs of Flying Dragons* remained a "dead branch," as Ksenia Chizhova puts it, while the vernacular language with its new script went underground for centuries, then to thrive "among the domestic, women-centered audiences," without the ability to read literary Chinese, who were the consumers of the privately circulating lineage novels; in the public sphere it was used only for auxiliary, technical publications.

Sanskrit is another fascinating case of a cosmopolitan language that had an extensive reach independent of "hard" power. Sanskrit, like Chinese or Greek or Persian—and unlike Latin—did not depend for its pervasive cultural power on direct military conquest and imperial rule; rather, Sanskrit and Chinese exercised their diffuse influence beyond any political borders through trade, cultural exchange, and prestige. Within the Sanskrit orbit, decisive innovations occurred under the impetus of outsiders with their own agenda, for example the Indo-Scythian groups discussed by Sheldon Pollock in chapter 4, who are the first on record (around 150 CE) to harness the sacred language of Sanskrit for "secular" and political inscriptions. Indian vernacular literatures develop as regional kingdoms consolidate by a process Pollock calls "superposition," as the aesthetic of Sanskrit is transposed to a world that is regional, and self-consciously regional.

Strikingly, translation of literature was a significant factor in the beginnings of new vernacular literary cultures in neither India nor the Sinographic sphere. Imitation was conscious and foregrounded, yet in the formative stages under investigation in the chapters in this section we do not find literary translation playing a role in a new literature's self-definition. In part 2 we shall see how different the situation could be elsewhere.

1

Chinese

MARTIN KERN

To think about the beginning of Chinese literature raises a simple question: which beginning? The one in high antiquity? The one around 200 BCE, following the initial formation of the empire, when China's "first poet" Qu Yuan (ca. 340–278 BCE) came into view as the model that has since been embraced by public intellectuals and literati for more than two millennia? The medieval period, from, roughly, the third through the ninth century, that gave us "classical Chinese poetry"? The early twentieth century with its conspicuous break with tradition and the promotion of modern, vernacular literature in response to both the collapse of the empire and the full experience of foreign—Japanese and "Western"—literature? Sometime in between, when particular genres came to flourish, such as Chinese theater and opera under Mongol rule (1279–1368) or the Chinese novel soon thereafter? All these are legitimate choices, some perhaps slightly more so than others. They can be based on language, literary forms, political institutions, exposure to the world beyond China, the concept of modernity, and other factors. What follows is an essay on antiquity: the time that is at once discontinuous with all later periods and yet its constant point of reference.

Mythologies of Writing and Orality

For most ancient traditions, the modern notion of "literature" does not map well onto the nature, purposes, functions, aesthetics, and social practices involved in the creation and exchange of texts. In pre-imperial China, the term *wen* originated as broadly denoting "cultural patterns," including those of textile ornament, musical melodies, the various formal aspects of ritual performances or any other aesthetic forms; it also was often used to refer to ancestors as "cultured" or "accomplished." It was only over the course of the Han dynasty (202 BCE–220 CE) that the idea of "literature"—at that point just one of the many forms of aesthetic expression—was gradually privileged above all others to the extent that *wen*, together with its extension *wenzhang* (patterned brilliance), came to refer primarily to the well-developed written text.[1] In other words, there was no early Chinese term for "literature" until *wen*, perhaps some fifteen centuries after its first appearance, began to be used primarily in that sense.

When labeled as *wen* or *wenzhang*, early Chinese texts comprise genres that we recognize as "poetry," "prose," or a combination of both, also including compositions in the service of political communication and administration. Cao Pi (187–226), the first emperor of the Wei dynasty (220–65) after the collapse of the Han, called *wenzhang* "the great business in organizing the state" and listed petitions and discussions, letters and discourses, inscriptions and dirges, and songs and poetic expositions as its principal genres—all of them as forms of public discourse. In short, the production and consumption of Chinese writing in antiquity—from its first evidence in the thirteenth century BCE well through the end of the Han dynasty in the third century CE—was always social and political. Whether in the service of the state or in opposition and deliberate distance to it, ancient Chinese literature was not regarded as a private or primarily personal affair. Early discussions of writing were devoted to cosmological, moral, and political concerns.[2]

Literature (as opposed to utilitarian writing narrowly conceived) emerged first during the Western Zhou dynasty (ca. 1046–771 BCE) and developed from there over the long centuries of Chinese political division. In 771 BCE, Zhou rule, initially in the west, collapsed under foreign invasion; as it was reconstituted further east, multiple independent regional states formed across the vast Chinese-speaking realm—largely today's northern China from Shaanxi Province to the eastern shore—that only nominally remained under the increasingly powerless Zhou suzerainty. Toward the end of the Warring States period (453–221 BCE), these states had consolidated into just seven more or less major powers. One of them was Qin, which completed its conquest of the other six in 221 BCE; yet Qin imperial rule (221–207 BCE) soon went up in flames and gave way to China's first great imperium, the Han.

Around 120 CE, a learned scholar at the Han imperial court, Xu Shen (ca. 55–ca. 149), composed the postface to his *Explanation of Simple Graphs and Analysis of Composite Characters* (*Shuowen jiezi*), the first comprehensive dictionary of more than ten thousand Chinese graphs. In the postface, he relied on a much earlier (fourth-century BCE) mythological account of how the sages had created the foundations of civilization. Xu, however, now focused on the invention of writing:

When in antiquity Bao Xi ruled the world as king, he looked up and perceived the images in the skies, looked down and perceived the model order on the earth. He observed how the patterns of the birds and beasts were adapted to the earth. Nearby he took [his insights] from himself; further away he took them from the things of the world. Thereupon he first created the eight trigrams of the *Classic of Changes* in order to transmit the models and images. . . . When Cang Jie, the scribe of the Yellow Emperor, saw the claw and hoof traces of birds and beasts, he recognized that these could be distinguished in their forms and differentiated from one another. [Thus] he first created incised writing.

In this account, gazing from the early Chinese empire back to the dawn of history, Xu Shen traces the origins of writing to both the natural cosmos and the origins of civilization: the Chinese script, while invented by the sages, is at its base "found" in nature. What is more, Xu makes a direct connection to the *Classic of Changes* (*Zhou Yi*, or *Yijing*), which in Xu's own time was regarded as both the origin and the cosmological pinnacle of the *Five Confucian Classics*. For Xu, the creation of the script is coterminous with the creation of the first and still most important Chinese text.

Xu's mythological narrative is correct in one important respect: the creation of Chinese graphs is one of but a handful of instances in human history where writing was invented independent of any known influence from the outside— and so the beginning of Chinese literature is monocultural and monolingual. But neither writing nor literature were nearly as old as was imagined in Xu's time, nor did they emerge hand in hand.

Chinese graphs are first documented in the oracle bone and bronze inscriptions from the site of the Late Shang (also called Yin, ca. 1250–ca. 1046 BCE) royal capital near modern Anyang (Henan Province). While the forms of Chinese graphs changed over time and became only gradually unified in the Qin and Han empires, their forms at Anyang are ancestral to how Chinese is still written today, and they do write the language that we recognize as Chinese.[3] Scratched into bovine shoulder bones and turtle plastrons—the material carriers used to communicate with the ancestral and cosmic spirits—the inscriptions recorded royal divinations on a wide range of sociopolitical matters, including those of the king's physical body politic (see figures 1.1 and 1.2).

The more than 150,000 Late Shang fragments of inscribed bones and plastrons discovered since 1899 point not only to the detailed recording of divination, but also to an impressive management of economic and social resources. Thus, writing may not have originated with these inscriptions but may also have had a prehistory in economic and administrative matters similar to how writing was first deployed in Mesopotamia.[4] But whatever the motivations behind the invention of writing in China, Shang divination records, each running from a few to several dozen graphs, do not constitute "literature" in any meaningful sense of

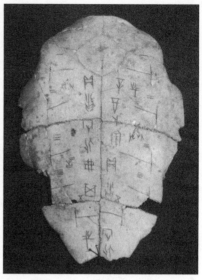

1.1. Inscribed bovine shoulder bone, Late Shang dynasty (ca. 1250–ca. 1046 BCE). Image courtesy of the Metropolitan Museum of Art.

1.2. Inscribed turtle plastron, Late Shang dynasty (ca. 1250–ca. 1046 BCE). Photo © Agefotostock.

the word: on the oracle bones, language is not inflected by aesthetic concerns, be they narrative or poetic. The oracle records are momentary; even in their accumulation, they do not aim to tell a story. The same is true of the much smaller number of inscriptions—usually maxing out at five or fewer graphs—that were cast into bronze vessels at the Shang court: all they do is name a vessel's donor or mark its purpose for the ancestral sacrifice. The first written artifacts that show literary features—aesthetic efforts beyond the purposes of recording or conveying information—postdate the earliest evidence of writing by about three centuries and can be found in Western Zhou bronze inscriptions.

Before turning to artifacts of *literary writing*, something must be said about the prehistory of literature before writing, or rather, the absence of any evidence for such a prehistory in ancient China. In contrast to, say, Greece, India, or Mesopotamia, there is no trace of a grand Chinese narrative or epic that may first have existed orally before finally being committed to writing, nor can we point to an early culture of song that preceded the arrival of writing and was then continued in written form. This does not mean that such things did not exist; in China just as everywhere else, people would have told their stories and sung their songs long before they knew or cared about how to write them. But none of these songs and stories is visible in the early documented stages of Chinese writing. Instead, the known traces of mythical narratives—all of them small fragments and often contradictory—that point to the dawn of history postdate the emergence of writing by several centuries and hence may not reflect that ancient oral culture at all.

The literary teleology from orality to writing, perhaps still a valid paradigm elsewhere, thus does not apply to early China. Nothing in the historical or archaeological record suggests such an idealizing linearity or the beginning of literature "with the common people." There is a body of short songs that, with their charming simplicity, sincerity, and imagery, appear to reflect the daily joys, worries, and utterances of the common, presumably illiterate folk: the 160 "Airs of the States" included in the *Classic of Poetry* (*Shijing*). Already by Han times, legend had it that the ancient kings had dispatched messengers to the "lanes and alleys" to collect the ditties of the commoners in order to learn about their sentiments and well-being, and hence about the condition of the polity. Yet this legend was perhaps an invention in the service of court scholars themselves: songs thus collected were by definition innocent and truthful; they appeared spontaneously like natural omens and could be deployed for political critique.

The second time this paradigm of ancient folk songs became important was in the twentieth century, in the wake of the collapse of the empire in 1912 and the emergence of the modern Chinese nation-state. Here, not unlike in Johann Gottfried Herder's (1744–1803) imagination about German folk songs, the ancient "Airs" were reimagined as the original language of the common people. Yet whether during the Han dynasty or in the twentieth century, the valorization of ancient Chinese folk song was but an ideological construction.

The Royal Voice and the Voice of Ritual:
The Ancestral Temple and Its Sacrifices

By the time of their fall in circa 1046 BCE, the Shang kings had created genealogical records that extended back for twenty-one generations of ancestors, all of whom were served with regular sacrifices. It is in the institution of the ancestral sacrifice, guided by a deep sense of the past, where we find the earliest traces of literature in a narrower sense. These traces appear in the inscribed bronze vessels of the subsequent Western Zhou dynasty,[5] thousands of which have been discovered. Even with just the known artifacts, one arrives at an average of at least one inscribed bronze object for every ten-day period over the 275 years of Western Zhou rule.

Initially, Western Zhou bronze inscriptions were short, just like their Shang predecessors. But within two or three generations, they routinely ran well beyond a hundred graphs; the longest Western Zhou inscription known extends to 498 graphs. Most of the longer inscriptions date from the mid-tenth century BCE onward, a hundred years after the Zhou had established their reign (see figures 1.3 and 1.4).

Often, these texts are concerned with royal appointments presented in the royal palace structure that was both the king's ancestral temple and his administrative center. Here, an official was given an important military or administrative appointment, received gifts and insignia, and was handed a written copy of his appointment, inscribed on a roll of bamboo slips. This text then served as the basis for casting an inscribed bronze vessel that the appointee could use

1.3. The Song Hu vessel, Western Zhou dynasty (ca. 1046–771 BCE), late ninth century BCE. Bronze. Image courtesy of the Taiwan Palace Museum.

1.4. Rubbing of the inscription from the Song Hu vessel.

for sacrifices in his lineage temple. Such inscriptions were typically in prose, though their closing prayer was often rhythmical and rhymed, suggesting that the text was not merely to be read by the ancestors but also to be announced in an oral performance. In the more extensive inscriptions, both the king and the appointee are presented as speakers in the appointment ceremony; their original speech was now repeated in the performance of the bronze text. In thus presenting himself, the appointee spoke to both his ancestors and his future descendants, whom the inscription, in its concluding formula, admonished to "forever use and treasure" the bronze vessel. In short, a bronze inscription marked the pivot between past and future and prospectively created the future memory of the appointee, of his ancestors, and of his own performance as the original rememberer. Its language was the solemn, exalted, and formulaic idiom of ritual, commemoration, and exhortation.

Such texts performed in the lineage temples of the king and the Zhou sociopolitical elite were fundamentally religious in purpose. They were individualized in identifying their donor and sometimes the ancestor to whom the vessel was dedicated. But they were not individual in their expression: the inscription, strictly adhering to the idiom of court ritual, inscribed the individual into the sociopolitical world of his time; its phrasing was shared with any number of similar texts that all followed the same model over generations. The agency of such vessels rested ultimately with the institution of Zhou kingship, its archives, and its foundries, where the craftsmen of historical memory, literary expression, and material production created what must have been the most prized objects of their time.

And yet, at least one exceptional inscription from circa 900 BCE may reveal the beginning of something else. This is the inscription under the name of Scribe Qiang, cast into a flat, wide-open water basin of 47.3 centimeters in diameter and 16.2 centimeters in height. Its base carries on the outside the repetitive and standardized ornamental bands common to countless other vessels. Less common however is the vessel's inside, in this case its most conspicuous surface: here, two columns of altogether 275 Chinese graphs (including a number of ligatures) contain in near-perfect symmetry a genealogy of Zhou kings on the right and a matching genealogy of Scribe Qiang's ancestors as royal scribes on the left. Following the pattern of bamboo manuscripts, the text is written in vertical columns from top to bottom and arranged from right to left (see figure 1.5).

1.5. Rubbing of the inscription from the Shi Qiang basin (ca. 900 BCE), Western Zhou dynasty (ca. 1046–771 BCE).

The designation "scribe" (*shi*) does not suggest that Qiang personally composed his inscription or carved it into the mold from which the vessel was cast; *shi* denoted a ritual and political functionary at the highest level of the Zhou court who oversaw court records but also served as chief ritualist, as spokesperson for the king (including on diplomatic missions), and probably as the principal expert on the movement of the celestial bodies and on the calendar. The scribe was a preeminent official who had mastered the memory of the past and knew how to divine the future.

The following excerpts make up the beginning, part of the middle, and then the end of the text:

> Ah! Ancient-minded was King Wen!
> He first harmonized government.
> God-on-high bestowed excellent virtue and great stability.
> Broadly possessive of the realms above and below,
> He conjoined and accepted the ten thousand states.
> Forceful and martial was King Wu!
> He proceeded and campaigned against the states of the four quarters,
> Assumed [the power] of Yin and governed their people.
> . . .
> Still and secluded was the High Ancestor!
> He resided in the numinous place of Wei.
> When King Wu had inflicted destruction on Yin,
> The Wei scribes, brilliant ancestors,
> Came to present themselves to King Wu.
> King Wu thereupon commanded the Duke of Zhou
> To dispense a domicile in the lowlands of Zhou.
> Penetrating and thoughtful was Ancestor Yi!
> He was brought here to serve his ruler,
> Far into the future he planned with heart and belly.
> . . .
> Filial and kind is Scribe Qiang!
> From morning to night he does not drop his duties.
> May his merits be daily recognized!
> Qiang does not dare to stop.

He requites by extolling the Son of Heaven's greatly illustrious and blessed command. On this account, he has made a precious sacrificial vessel. May the brilliant ancestors and the accomplished father grant him favors, give Qiang rich happiness, fortunate peace, sprouting wealth, yellowing longevity, and fulfilled years, so that he is able to serve his lord! May [Qiang's successors] for ten thousand years and forever treasure and use this vessel!

The 275 graphs, in eighteen lines of fifteen graphs each, are evenly spaced; only the final line contains twenty graphs. This slight deviation at the end suggests the existence of a preexisting text that could not be shortened by even five graphs, but it also suggests a keen commitment to visual symmetry. Whoever carved the text into the mold chose not to let it run into another vertical line. Instead, he squeezed the remaining graphs in the final line of the left column and thus managed to attain both textual and visual integrity. The inscription was to be read, but it was also to be seen; it carried the text while also presenting it as the vessel's principal ornamental feature. Yet the visual appeal is only one dimension of this text: as Scribe Qiang eulogized the former kings together with their scribes, his ancestors, he wrote in tetrasyllabic, rhymed verse, evidently the most prevalent rhythm of early Chinese poetry. The text was not only to be seen but also to be heard in a communal performance that recalled both kings and ancestors. In yet another striking feature, its vocabulary significantly exceeded the shared idiom of other bronze inscriptions.

In this powerful self-representation of a high-ranking official at the Zhou court we may thus detect a particularly conspicuous—and for its time extremely rare, if not indeed unique—manifestation of Chinese "literature": the explicit and even self-referential formation of text in its semantic, visual, and aural dimensions, whose deliberate aesthetic choices distinguished it from any other inscription. However, its place was still in the synesthetic, multimedia performance of the ancestral sacrifice where textual expression was integrated with visual display, music, pantomimic dance, song, and the fragrance of the offerings. Its audience was the lineage members and their guests. Its materiality and use tied it to specific, local performances. Scribe Qiang's inscription was known to his immediate family and descendants, who could further draw on it for their own bronze texts, but it did not enter the later literary tradition. The text's primary reception was thus undistinguishable from its first production: the family that sponsored the casting of the vessel for its own ancestral temple was also its principal community of addressees. It almost certainly had never traveled by the time when it was carefully buried, together with 102 other family bronzes (seventy-four of which were inscribed), in a pit in today's northwestern Shaanxi Province, presumably when the family left the area in the ninth century BCE, hoping to return at some later time. That time never came, and the vessel was unknown for nearly three millennia until its excavation in 1976.

Alongside the bronze inscriptions, there arose, however, two other genres of texts within the same ritual contexts: Western Zhou dynastic hymns and royal speeches.[6] Both genres have survived in collections that became officially canonized in the early empire, yet only after centuries of considerable textual changes, sometimes including their wholesale reimagination. In their majority, they represent a single narrative, albeit told, sung, mimetically danced, and recited in a smattering of texts that are closely interrelated both linguistically and in their contents. This narrative is the story of the origins, rise, establishment, and early glory of the Western Zhou. Within that narrative, particular attention is devoted to the founding Zhou leader, King Wen (also named in Scribe Qiang's inscription above), who had died shortly before Zhou's conquest of Shang.[7] Reaching backward from King Wen to the dawn of history, the Zhou dynastic hymns extend their story to the moment when a woman named Jiang Yuan, after having performed the correct sacrifices, "stepped into the footprint of the Deity" and became pregnant with Hou Ji, or Lord Millet, the inventor of agriculture and progenitor of Zhou.

The Zhou foundational narrative is preserved in two anthologies. The first is the *Classic of Poetry*, a body of 305 songs—including the 160 "Airs" mentioned above—that was purportedly compiled by Kongzi (Confucius; 551–479 BCE)[8] out of originally some three thousand. Within the "three hundred songs," the Zhou narrative is enshrined in thirty-one short pieces of "Zhou Sacrificial Hymns" (*Zhou song*) as well as in thirty-one much longer "Major Court Hymns" (*Daya*) that offer extensive historical narratives. Like Western Zhou bronze inscriptions, the longest "Major Court Hymns" reach close to five hundred graphs. By the fourth century BCE, we have abundant evidence for the canonical status of a circumscribed collection of poetry, though the received version of the anthology, the richly annotated *Mao Poetry*, is a Western Han (202 BCE–9 CE) compilation that, in its glosses and commentary, seems to reflect Qin and Han imperial concerns.

The second canonical collection is the *Classic of Documents*, whose early textual history is impossible to reconstruct; the accepted edition is a heterogeneous anthology of twenty-eight (or twenty-nine) chapters, once again of Qin-Han times. At its core are a dozen speeches attributed to the early Western Zhou rulers; all other chapters—some of them speeches attributed to sovereigns from times immemorial—are clearly of later origin: figments that serve to create a single linear, teleological history where "Heaven" granted its "mandate" to rule "All under Heaven" to dynasty after dynasty, and finally to King Wen. Like the early hymns, the Zhou speeches must have undergone very substantial changes before becoming part of the canonical anthology; but in some version, they must have had their place in the Zhou ancestral sacrifices, where their performances may have mimetically enacted the early Zhou kings in their own voice.

Both the hymns and the speeches are powerful representations of oral performances. Whether they were the actual words of the early rulers or their idealized representations created by later court ritualists and scholars, in the Chinese cultural memory they stand as the original royal utterances from the first golden age in Chinese history. Zhou bronze inscriptions, as noted above, expressed demands on future generations to continue the ancestral rituals and maintain the memory of those enshrined in the temple. In turn, Zhou hymns and speeches repeatedly present their own ritual context as inherited from earlier times. The remembered speakers from the early Western Zhou were themselves rememberers, as in the first of the "Zhou Sacrificial Hymns" dedicated to King Wen:

> Ah! Solemn is the clear temple,
>> reverent and concordant the illustrious assistants.
>> Dignified, dignified are the many officers,
>> holding fast to the virtue of King Wen.
>> Responding in praise to the one in Heaven,
>> they hurry swiftly within the temple.
>> Greatly illustrious, greatly honored,
>> may [King Wen] never be weary of [us] men!

As in some of the bronze inscriptions, the hymn does not merely recall what must not be forgotten. It also self-referentially points to the very ritual in which such a text was presumably performed, thus doubling the ritual performance in the performance of its own words: "the many officers," while emulating the virtue of the Zhou founder King Wen, respond "in praise" to him as they "hurry swiftly within the temple." Other court hymns ask, "Since times of old, what have we done?" or "Truly, our sacrifices are like what?" to introduce a formulaic recital of the practices claimed to have been inherited from time immemorial: "It is not [merely] here what we have here; / it is not [merely] now what is now; / since ancient times, it has been like this."

Is this how the ancient rituals unfolded? And is this the literature at the beginning of literature? Or are we looking at much later textualizations of political and religious memory, created over the many centuries of decline, loss, and disunion, idealizations in the service of invented tradition and imagined community from an experience of deficiency and inadequacy? Here it is useful to recall the purported role of Kongzi in the creation of the anthology of the *Poetry*, an attribution that may or may not be historically accurate but that fully accords with how Kongzi is presented across texts as early as the fourth century BCE. If Chinese literature originated in the religious and political rituals of the Western Zhou court, it was with the figure of Kongzi— however idealized over subsequent generations—that it became conceptualized in new terms and gained entirely new significance. Fundamentally, it was now understood as inherited, removed from its original context, adaptable to an infinite number of specific occasions and arguments, and in need of interpretation.

Following the rise of regional states after the end of the Western Zhou in 771 BCE, the process of political disintegration accelerated rapidly from the fifth century onward, when the old hereditary aristocracy order was challenged by economic and military change. By the time of Kongzi, the ancient social order was already in decline. If the ancient poems and speeches had once been performed and perpetuated in Zhou ritual, they were now the only surviving traces that embodied the memory of such ritual itself. By the time the historiographic and philosophical texts from the Warring States period invoked the ancient hymns and speeches, they were the shared remnants of the past.

Beyond Authorship: The Rise of Literature as Reception and Interpretation

Thus began the rise of Chinese literature as *literary tradition*, when antiquity was experienced as not only past but also lost, and hence, at least in part, an artifact more of imagination than of actual memory. Old texts were recalled and reconstituted in a secondary reception, now reaching those who in time, space, and social milieu were far removed from their first occasion. This conceptual turn both demanded and generated a new hermeneutic engagement that proved transformative: what mattered now was not where a text came from, or to whom it had once belonged, but how it was to be enacted, reactivated, interpreted, and further reproduced. Its core principle is attributed to Kongzi in the iconic phrase "I transmit but do not create."

In this rupture between old and new, the texts from the past attained a significance they had not possessed before, and the agency of literature shifted from the royal voice to that of the royal subject. In the subsequent imagination, this shift is embodied in the figure of Kongzi in multiple ways: he is the uncrowned philosopher king (*suwang*) who failed to gain a position of power but whose supreme judgment put him above the rulers of his time; he is the compiler and interpreter of the *Poetry*, just as he organizes and comments on the *Classic of Documents* and the *Classic of Changes*. And finally, he is, according to the fourth-century BCE *Mengzi*, the creator of the *Springs and Autumns Annals* (*Chunqiu*):

> When the world declined and the Way fell into obscurity, heresies and violence arose. There were instances of regicides and patricides. Kongzi was apprehensive and made (*zuo*) the *Springs and Autumns*. The *Springs and Autumns* is the business of the Son of Heaven. Thus, Kongzi said, "Those who recognize me will do so for the *Springs and Autumns*; those who condemn me will do so for the *Springs and Autumns*."

Elsewhere, the *Mengzi* offers this teleology of literature:

> When the traces of the [ancient] kings were extinguished, the *Poetry* vanished. After the *Poetry* had vanished, the *Springs and Autumns* arose (*zuo*).

The *Springs and Autumns* is a terse chronicle, presumably going back to generations of anonymous scribes, that covers the reigns of the lords of Lu from 722 to 481 BCE (479 in one version). Lu was the small home state of Kongzi in the east. Insignificant in military, economic, and political terms, its singular distinction vis-à-vis its much more powerful neighbors was its unique connection to antiquity: it was purportedly the place where the old "rituals of Zhou" were still preserved. Both Lu and its most famous son, Kongzi, were marginal and out of place: the real powers of the time had little use for the "rituals of Zhou," and even less for someone like Kongzi. It is in this figure, and in this place, that the Chinese tradition located the memory of its lost antiquity.

The ambivalence of Kongzi's position is captured well in the *Mengzi*. It is clear that Kongzi, in fact, did not "create" or "make" (*zuo*) the text in the sense of an original composition. What he is believed to have done, instead, is to have edited the existing annals of Lu in such a way that his "subtle phrasing" (*weiyan*) expressed the "great principles" (*dayi*) of political critique, thus "initiating" or "raising" (other meanings of *zuo*) the text with an entirely new import. (Note that in the second quotation from the *Mengzi* above, *zuo* is used intransitively as "arose.") Through Kongzi's "subtle phrasing," the *Springs and Autumns* thus attained a veiled meaning, and a need for interpretation, as his political criticism was purposefully encoded to render moral and political judgment. While the original *Springs and Autumns* would have represented the deeds of the rulers of Lu, Kongzi is believed to have transformed the text into one of remonstrance and critique.

By Han times, Kongzi's textual agency—derivative and yet primary—was conceptualized in new terms; some texts now saw Kongzi as having "fashioned" (*zhi*), "made" (*wei*), "organized" (*zhi*), "arranged in sequence" (*ci*), "transmitted" (*shu*), "brought to completion" (*cheng*), or "perfected" (*xiu*) the *Springs and Autumns*. While each term still denoted Kongzi's principal responsibility for the text in its final form, it located this responsibility in the adaptation and transformation of a preexisting text. The original, anonymous compilers of the *Springs and Autumns* were long forgotten; their agency had been transferred to the interpreter. Yet when the *Mengzi* spoke of Kongzi as having *zuo*-ed the text, it also, obliquely, called him a "sage" (*sheng*) on par with the creators of culture: only the sages at the beginning of time were true creators, while those who came later, now in historical time, were mere "worthies" (*xian*) who would "follow" or "transmit."[9]

Poetry and Its Contexts

From no later than the fourth century BCE, one finds the expression *shi yan zhi* (poetry expresses intent) or *shi yi yan zhi* (poetry is used to express intent) in transmitted texts. The final graph, *zhi*, in these phrases has two meanings: "record" and "intent." The word *zhi* is probably cognate with several others, including *shi* (to remember, memory), *chi* (to hold, to contain), but also *shi* (poetry). In fact, the formula *shi yan zhi* (poetry expresses intent) may be a mere pun on the three graphs involved: the graph *shi* (poetry) is itself the combination of the graphs *yan* (to express, speech) and *zhi* (record, intent).[10] Yet more important than etymology is how words such as *zhi* (record/intent), *shi* (memory), and *shi* (poetry) are used in early texts. In Zhou bronze inscriptions, *zhi* appears exclusively as "record," never as "intent." Meanwhile, in various transmitted Warring States texts, *zhi* is used interchangeably with *shi* (memory; which in a secondary pronunciation *zhi* also means "record"). On this basis, the notion of *shi yan zhi* appears derived from the function of poetry to perpetuate a "record": poetry contains what is inscribed into the mind, and it is the very form—stabilized by mnemonic devices such as rhyme and meter—to preserve what must not be forgotten. Poetry, as elsewhere in the ancient world, is a principal form in which cultural memory is stored, performed, and transmitted.

When the formula *shi (yi) yan zhi* appeared in texts of the fourth and third centuries BCE, it was with this vestige of profound commitment to the past. As "poetry expresses intent," it merely extended this commitment to the present: "intent" was conceptualized not as original, personal, or idiosyncratic but as the response to historical circumstance. While expressed by an individual voice, this voice was communal. Arising entirely from social experience, it spoke to shared affections and aspirations and thus—prospectively historicizing itself—produced a "record" of the present. Throughout Warring States times, this "intent/record" was rarely if ever associated with authorship. The communal voice was that of the performer who skillfully presented not his own inventions but, instead, poetry that was explicitly inherited. For centuries, *shi yan zhi* remained the only definition of poetry in early China: there is no discussion of the technical aspects of poetry, of the making of poetry, of its forms or genres, or of its aesthetic qualities. There also is no passage, in any preimperial Chinese text, that speaks of the writing or reading of poetry.

By the time of Kongzi, the ancient hymns and speeches—the texts of cultural memory—were still known, or partly known, or retrospectively imagined, as expressions of traditional authority but now became used in political debate and philosophical argument. Especially the "Major Court Hymns" were quotable without the need for explanation; because of their semantic clarity and unquestionable status, they could be applied as proof text to assert "what the [foregoing argument] is about" (*ci zhi wei ye*), a formula repeatedly encountered in philosophical treatises from the fourth century BCE onward. Perhaps the hymns differed from their texts in the received anthology of the *Poetry*; considerable evidence suggests that at least some of the transmitted poems are composite artifacts whose arrangement may date to as late as the early imperial state. Their highly formulaic and tightly circumscribed linguistic register and vocabulary, nevertheless, is much more ancient, whether original or retrospectively compiled from familiar archaisms.

Meanwhile, the "Airs of the States" were mostly invoked in a different fashion, namely, as coded communication or as evocative performances of shared cultural heritage, often in the diplomatic intercourse among representatives from different regional states, suggesting that by no later than the fifth or fourth century BCE, they had become pan-Chinese. We know nothing about how, when, why, and by whom these songs were composed originally; unlike the hymns, they do not have an obvious institutional background. But we do know how they were used. Our richest source for the circulation and use of the "Airs" is the *Zuo Tradition* (*Zuozhuan*), the largest text of historical narrative in preimperial China, that is part commentary on the *Springs and Autumns*, part collection of stories, anecdotes, speeches, and historical data all strung along the *Springs and Autumns* chronology. There is much debate on the origins and historical reliability of the text, as it covers the years from 722 through 468 BCE: some of it seems to reflect historical documents from regional court archives; some of it must come from oral lore; some of it is shaped or invented according to the moralistic judgment and concerns that may best be located with the compilers of the text in the fifth/fourth century BCE; but there also is a wealth of vivid stories, imaginative anecdotes, and literary vignettes, whether they span multiple years or appear just fleetingly. No information exists about the compilers of the text, who evidently drew on a flourishing literary culture, both written and oral, among the various political and cultural centers of early China. Some of the court records in *Zuozhuan* may indeed date back to the late eighth / early seventh century BCE. In addition, there appears to have existed a vast, commonly shared repertoire of story, speech, and song, all of it anonymous. Even the speeches attributed to specific historical actors often—though not without some striking exceptions— seem more exemplary than individual. In its dazzling array of literary forms, *Zuozhuan* itself is widely held as the preeminent source and model not only of subsequent Chinese historiography but, just as much, especially in late imperial China, of narrative fiction.

Orally, the narrative, poetic, and oratory repertoire of *Zuozhuan* appears to have transcended any particular dialect, perhaps as "elegant standard speech" (*yayan*) that Kongzi is said to have used for "the *Poetry*, the *Documents*, and in conducting ritual." Written texts, meanwhile, were committed to rolls of bamboo slips: thin slices of less than one centimeter in width and—judging from known discoveries so far—up to about ninety centimeters in length that were cut from bamboo stems. Dried, flattened, and tightly strung together with horizontal strings of hemp or silk, they formed a continuous rollable writing surface of natural vertical columns for brush writing with black ink (see figure 1.6); another, much rarer, early stationery was silk (see figure 1.7). (Chinese paper didn't become widely available until the second and third centuries CE.)

Yet just as dialects must have differed considerably from one another, so did the calligraphic systems of the various polities; in particular, graphs used further south differed strikingly from those in the north. While the beginning of this literature, oral and written, cannot be assigned to any single place or time, the supreme eminence of the notion of *li* (ritual, ceremony, decorum, propriety in conduct, social order) throughout *Zuozhuan*, and its manifestation in well-patterned speech and behavior, unambiguously points to the aristocratic culture of the eighth through fifth centuries BCE. By the time of its compilation in the fifth/fourth century BCE, the *Zuozhuan* already depicted a world of nostalgic imagination.

Within this world of historical anecdotes and speeches, the "Airs" occupy a special place.[11] A famous *Zuozhuan* event dated to 544 BCE contains a concert at the court of Lu that covered royal hymns, dances, and the repertoire of the "Airs" from the different states. The concert was performed for Prince Ji Zha

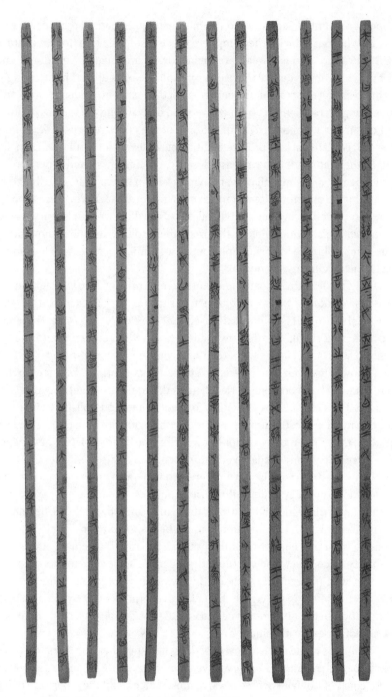

1.6. Section of a Warring States bamboo manuscript (ca. 300 BCE).

1.7. Portion of a Western Han silk manuscript (early second century BCE).

from Wu, a state on the southeastern periphery of the Chinese realm. While hailing from the cultural fringes and descending from speakers of a language other than Chinese, the prince issued perspicacious political judgments in response to the art of performance:

> He asked to observe the music of Zhou. When the musicians were made to sing for him [the "Airs" from] "South of Zhou" and "South of Shao," he said, "How excellent! They have begun to give it a foundation. It is not yet done, yet they are assiduous and uncomplaining."
>
> When they sang [the "Airs" from] "Bei," "Yong," and "Wey" for him, he said, "How excellent! How profound! These are anxious but not hindered by difficulties. I have heard that the virtue of Kang Shu and Duke Wu of Wey was just so; these must be the airs of Wey!"
>
> When they sang [the "Airs" from] "Royal Domain" for him, he said, "How excellent! They are thoughtful but unafraid; these would be from Zhou's move to the east."
>
> When they sang [the "Airs" from] "Zheng" for him, he said, "How excellent! Already they are very trivial, and the people cannot bear it. Surely this [state] will be the first to perish."
>
> . . .

When they sang [the "Airs" from] "Tang" for him, he said, "What profundity of thought! These would be the remaining scions of the Taotang line! Otherwise, how could their concern extend so far? If not the descendants of fine virtue, who would be capable of this?"

When they sang [the "Airs" from] "Chen" for him, he said, "That state is without a master. How can it last long?"

The account (only excerpted here)[12] illustrates the function of poetry and music as omen and symptom: expressions that to a perceptive observer like Ji Zha provide an accurate reflection, or record, of the condition of the polity from which it quasi-naturally emerges, and which it thus embodies. By the first century CE, this cosmology of aesthetic production had become directly transposed to the production of verse and song, according to the "Great Preface" to the *Poetry*:

The affections are moved within and take on form in speech. If speaking them out is not sufficient, one chants them. If chanting them is not sufficient, one draws them out by singing. If drawing them out by singing is not sufficient, unconsciously the hands dance them, and the feet tap them. The affections emerge in sounds. When sounds are patterned, they are called tones. The tones of a well-governed time are at ease and joyful; its government is harmonious. The tones of a time in turmoil are resentful and angry; its government is perverse. The tones of a perishing state are lamenting and longing; its people are in difficulty.[13]

In this reading, as discussed above in the context of *shi yan zhi*, poetry originated not as individual creation but as the quasi-natural, uncontrolled, and therefore always truthful response to the circumstances; it depended on the human voice to emerge, but it was not "made" or manipulated by an individual author. In later (post-Han) China, this notion gradually developed into a theory of individual authorship that prized seemingly authentic, self-expressive, and hence autobiographic poetry above all other forms of literature. But no such emphasis on the person of the poet can be found before the empire.

Much more elliptical, and more typical of dozens of other cases in *Zuozhuan*, is the following account, dated to 612 BCE:

The Liege of Zheng and our lord held a banquet at Fei. Gongzi Guisheng recited "The Wild Goose." Ji Wenzi said, "Our unworthy ruler has himself not escaped this." Wenzi recited "The Fourth Month." Gongzi Guisheng recited the fourth stanza of "Gallop." Wenzi recited the fourth stanza of "Plucking Bracken." The Liege of Zheng bowed, and our lord, in response, bowed.

No received early text outside the *Poetry* anthology itself quotes a poem from the "Airs" in its entirety, and thus we do not know what exactly was recited, even though the titles given here match those of pieces in the *Poetry*. Regardless, the very act of poetry performance is presented as the hallmark of *li*, or ritual propriety. Occasional failures in the hermeneutics of poetry exchange are explicitly noted, and not favorably. Such emphasis on recitation does not necessarily make this early poetry "oral" in the sense of composition or transmission, but it situates its public presence as well as its interpretation firmly in performance contexts. As Kongzi says in the *Analects*, if one can recite the poems but is unable to apply them in the practice of government or in diplomatic speech, "then what use is there for them?"

A recently discovered (looted) manuscript fragment, presumably dating from circa 300 BCE and now held in the Shanghai Museum and titled *Kongzi's Discussion of the Poetry* (*Kongzi shilun*) by its modern editors, may reflect this concern. In its twenty-nine bamboo slips with slightly over one thousand graphs, Kongzi characterizes individual poems with pithy statements that may have served as prompts for how to use them in context. Taking the first of the "Airs" as an example, the text formulates a hermeneutical principle for how to engage the poems:

> It is said: "As [poems] are set in motion, they all surpass what they put forth initially." [The poem] "Fishhawks" uses [the expression of] sexual allure to illustrate ritual propriety. . . . It uses the pleasures [one derives] from zithers as a comparison to lustful desire. It uses the delight [one derives] from bells and drums [to illustrate] the liking of . . . As it guides back toward ritual propriety, is this not indeed transformation?[14]

Here as in *Zuozhuan*, the final emphasis is on *li*, ritual propriety. But most important, poetry is described as going beyond its surface meaning and hence as being in need of interpretation. Moreover, this interpretation is not narrowly defined; as the poem can be applied to various situations, its specific import may change according to the circumstances. Thus, a poem that overtly expresses sexual desire can serve to guide the audience toward ritual propriety; it can be used to offer a moral critique; or, as in one case that on its surface reads as the admonishment of an all-too-impetuous lover ("Please, Zhongzi"), *Zuozhuan* records its performance as a diplomatic plea to have a lord released from imprisonment in another state.

In such performances of inherited poetry, there was no reference to either authorship or the text's original circumstance of composition. Instead, meaning was created through the perceptive application of inherited text in ever-new situations.[15] This hermeneutic fluidity also affected the poems themselves, as they could be reproduced as composition-in-performance in an infinite number of ways. Evidence for this comes once again from recently discovered manuscripts of the time: compared to its received counterpart, a poem could differ in countless variants of individual graphs as well as entire lines; in phrases transposed and recombined; in its roles and perspectives of speech; in its historical contextualization; and in both rhyme and meter.[16] What Stephen Owen has observed about medieval Chinese poetry centuries later is perhaps even truer of the ancient period:

> When we set aside questions of the "original text," authorship, and relative dating, we can think of each extant text as a single realization of many possible poems that might have been composed. What survives is certainly only a small fraction of all the poems actually composed and of different realizations of the texts that survive. We have textual variants, texts given as "variant versions" of the "same" poem, and poems considered "different" but which have lengthy passages in common. When we think of this as a spectrum of variation, we realize there is no absolute boundary separating another version of the "same" poem from a "different" poem. When we imagine the variations that no longer survive and segments combined in different ways, we begin to think of this as "one poetry," as a single continuum rather than as a corpus of texts either canonized or ignored. It has its recurrent themes, its relatively stable passages and line patterns, and its procedures.[17]

Concluding Observations

Chinese literature begins with texts whose aesthetic shaping through rhyme, meter, and evocative images was directed toward performance: literature we call "poetry." The *Classic of Poetry* does not represent the only forms of literature in early China, but certainly the earliest and the most prominent ones: in antiquity, no other text is quoted as inherited authority nearly as often as the *Poetry*. What is more, the boundaries between the *Poetry* and both the speeches in the *Documents* and some of the early bronze inscriptions are fluid in the sense that aesthetic features such as rhyme, poetry, and the use of euphonic (including onomatopoeic) phrases extend to the latter as well. Especially in the fourth-century BCE *Zuozhuan*, the successful performance of poetry is the embodiment of *li*, the ideal of the old—and already lost—aristocratic order. This poetry, however, is without origin or authors; even in those few moments in *Zuozhuan* where a poem might appear as an original, impromptu composition in performance, its scene of creation is indistinguishable from the countless others that record performances of inherited texts.

Such poetry—whether in the ritual language of the hymns that tell the story of Zhou or in the seemingly naïve and simple idiom in which the "Airs" sing of love and loss, toil and suffering, hope and resentment—is the poetry of the past. The hymns speak with authority; the "Airs" need instructions for interpretation and usage. Yet in both cases, their constant citation, performance, and recomposition dissolves the notion of an individual poem as a discrete, reified entity. Instead, any poem, written or oral, may have existed as part of a single instantiation from some particular, shared repertoire that served as a storehouse of ideas and the expressions to communicate them. In the received anthology, no two hymns are the same, but all are similar, and shared phrases and entire lines abound. Likewise, in the "Airs" formulas and images drift easily from one song to the other, let alone between all the "versions" of "a single poem" we no longer know.

Remarkably, this poetry without origin was also a poetry without continuity. Perhaps because of its canonical status, the verses from the *Poetry* could be forever recited and performed, but—as far as our sources tell us—they did not lead to new compositions. The future of the *Poetry* was the Confucian canon, and it ended right there. From the time of Kongzi until the early empire in the early second century BCE, a period of some three hundred years, the Chinese tradition knows of no new poetry except the occasional children's ditty or some short proverbial verses in *Zuozhuan* and elsewhere. Up to the time of the imperial state, when entirely new sociopolitical circumstances generated new texts and, finally, strong ideas about authorship and authorial responsibility, the idea of "poetry expresses intent" remained focused on the performance of inherited text; it did not give rise to new composition. Unlike elsewhere, poetry was not an arena for competition; across all early Chinese states, it was the place of shared commitment to a single cultural tradition.

When, finally, another body of poetry became visible early in the second century BCE, the *Lyrics from Chu* (*Chuci*), it was not a continuation from the *Poetry* but a new beginning with a new meter, a new poetic imagination, a new lexicon of contemporary language, and descriptions of a southern landscape unknown to the *Poetry*. Most important, it was a poetry centered on the political legend of one individual, Qu Yuan, who in the early Han imagination turned from the figure of poetic hero into that of heroic poet: China's first autobiographic author. But this is the story of another beginning, nearly a millennium after the first, and bound up with the creation of the Chinese empire.

Further Reading

Boltz, William G. *The Origins and Early Development of the Chinese Writing System*, 1993.

Bottéro, Françoise, and Redouane Djamouri. *Écriture chinoise: Données, usages et representations*, 2006.

Falkenhausen, Lothar von. "The Concept of Wen in the Ancient Chinese Ancestral Cult," *Chinese Literature: Essays, Articles Reviews* 18 (1996): 1–22.

Kern, Martin. "Early Chinese Literature, Beginnings through Western Han," in *Cambridge History of Chinese Literature*, edited by Stephen Owen and Kang-i Sun Chang, 1–115, 2010.

Kern, Martin. "The Formation of the Classic of Poetry," in *The Homeric Epics and the Chinese Book of Songs: Foundational Texts Compared*, edited by Fritz-Heiner Mutschler, 39–71, 2018.

Kern, Martin. "Ritual, Text, and the Formation of the Canon: Historical Transitions of *Wen* in Early China," *T'oung Pao* 87 (2001): 43–91.

Li, Wai-yee. *The Readability of the Past in Early Chinese Historiography*, 2007.

Liu, James J. Y. *Chinese Theories of Literature*, 1975.

Owen, Stephen. *Readings in Chinese Literary Thought*, 1992.

Shaughnessy, Edward L., ed. *New Sources of Early Chinese History: An Introduction to the Reading of Inscriptions and Manuscripts*, 1997.

Japanese

WIEBKE DENECKE

Telling the beginnings of literary traditions challenges many conventions of national literary historiography of the kind that most people take for granted in contemporary literary traditions. Most literary beginnings in world history have not been monolingual, were not rooted in one particular ethnic community, occurred in courts or urban centers before the nation-state, were not embodied in the spirit of a people, but were rather traces of the activities of emerging ruling elites and fledgling state building. The cardinal categories that allow national literary historiography to tell its story do not hold in premodern contexts: there are no national "masterworks" and great "authors" yet, "genre" concepts are only in the making and highly occasional, concepts of "chronology" and temporal belonging have yet to emerge, and any narratable "zeitgeist" is typically inaccessible because of the sparsity of surviving sources. Textual and oral culture are fluid and polymorphous, making any distinction between the "literary" and "nonliterary" and even "textual" and "oral" premature. Worse yet, if we narrate the earliest phase of any literary tradition we are chasing a moving target that is neither "literature" nor "nonliterature," but a bewildering and rapidly evolving experimentation with applying the usage of signs and writing to various purposes, on various media, and with still unstable social functionality and credibility. This multiplicity of literacies and quite specialized uses of writing in quotidian, political, or religious life stimulates reflections on the power and challenges of the new exciting world of textuality as a human practice.

National literary historiography is strongest at telling the story of modern literatures, the period of its own genesis. But when projected back beyond the nineteenth century, lingering modernist biases unduly prioritize the vernacular and "nationalizable" over the historically far more important cosmopolitan, macroregional dynamics of early literary cultures, severely warping our understanding of literary histories before the modern period.

While the suppression of transregional cosmopolitan languages and their literary cultures is a particular problem of national literary historiography, any narrative of literary history needs a story with its own teleology, as David

Perkins reminds us in his landmark book *Is Literary History Possible?* Thus, narratives of beginnings constitute a much more visceral philosophical and psychological problem. They give us origins, mirror images, explanations of the present. They comfort our sense of self and other, present and future. Yet we are tantalized by the elusiveness of beginnings, because they are typically retrospective, highly underdetermined in historical evidence, but overdetermined in ideological thrust. They give us access to the agendas of the propagators of "origins," not to the beginnings themselves.

If already we are forced to tell a story, what categories can meaningfully stand in for authors, works, genres, chronologies or zeitgeist when writing the beginnings of literary traditions? We need a process-oriented rather than product-oriented notion of the literary. "Literary culture" is now commonly used (e.g., Cornis-Pope and Neubauer's *History of the Literary Cultures of East-Central Europe*) to broaden the notion of "literature" in a functional direction: "literary culture" comprises any practices related to the production of texts and thus gets to the production processes and purposes of the "products" we usually consider literature—works. In this framework the actual life cycle of works and impact of textuality play a crucial role in the beginnings of "literature": the emergence of literacy and reading, inscription, and performance practices; their contemporary purposes and functions; questions of circulation, transmission, and access to knowledge through educational institutions and pedagogical manuals; and lastly, the relationship of texts to memory and acts of remembrance, reproduction, or quotation.

Unlike Perkins, for whom the inevitable teleology of narrative per se precludes any rigorous attempt at literary historiography, I believe we can write literary history with "intellectual conviction" if we are explicit enough about our goals and agendas.[1] Indeed, we can use the issue of teleology to our advantage. Only as long as we tell a single story will teleology be a liability. If we tell multiple stories, the various intersecting teleologies of these multiple "literary histories" will help us relativize, even neutralize some of the biases inherent in each single narrative.

The dominant model of literary historiography in Japan today still remains the national literature model, first sketched in Japan's earliest literary history of 1890 by Mikami Sanji and Takatsu Kuwasaburō, at the time fresh college graduates writing under the influence of Western literary works and national literary histories. They hailed vernacular works as expressions of the Japanese native spirit, excising the large corpus of literature in the cosmopolitan language of Literary Chinese; they upgraded the novel at the expense of the much more prestigious premodern genres of poetry; and dramatic literature, like Noh, Kabuki, and Puppet Theater, which had counted as mere entertainment, was elevated to the status of highbrow literature, all based on nineteenth-century European models.[2]

This view is prevalent in today's Japanese education system and public life and is a good example of how (most) contemporary nation-states project their national pride onto their premodern cultural histories. It is, however, only one perspective, and a rather biased one, onto early Japanese literary culture. To complement this approach, this chapter pinpoints various other histories of literary beginnings that are necessary to understand the why and how of the rapid emergence of literary culture on the archipelago during the seventh and eighth centuries CE. It attempts to grasp the distinctive features of Japanese literary beginnings in the macroregional context at the time, which is shaped by the emergence of the "Sinographic sphere," that came to include polities on the periphery of the Chinese Empire, which adopted and adapted to their purposes the Chinese script, textual canons, institutions, and literary culture. The Sinographic sphere eventually developed into today's East Asia, encompassing the current China and Taiwan, the Koreas, Japan, Vietnam, and a number of now-gone polities in East and Central Asia. By the thirteenth century BCE a mature writing system had emerged in the Yellow River valley in northern China. With the foundation of empire during the Qin and Han dynasties (221 BCE–220 CE) Chinese emperors greatly expanded their territory, making deep inroads into Central Asia and incorporating parts of today's Vietnam and Korea into their realm. Chinese soldiers and administrators brought along Chinese writing and administrative practices based on imperial Confucian ideologies, and the rapid regional spread of Buddhism not the least through the vector of Chinese translations during the earlier part of the first millennium CE created a cultural sphere rooted in shared political and diplomatic hierarchies, technologies, and ideologies. The beginnings of Japanese literary culture were part and parcel of the emergence of the Sinographic sphere. This process of "Sinicization" spread during a time period comparable with "Hellenization" and "Romanization." And although the concept of "Sinicization" has been criticized as focusing too triumphantly on the hegemonic culture (just as with "Hellenization" and "Romanization") it is undeniable that the regional power hierarchy centered around China catalyzed the emergence of literary cultures on the periphery of the Chinese empires during the first millennium CE. Unlike in particular Romanization, which typically spread with military conquest and political domination, "Sinicization" also thrived in territories that either were never conquered by a Chinese empire, like the Japanese islands, or that functioned as independent polities despite longer or briefer periods of Chinese dominance, like Vietnam or Korea.[3]

Literary Histories to Tell

Telling multiple literary histories helps us mitigate the issue of teleological bias. It also helps with another, somewhat counterintuitive problem with beginnings. While poor source preservation makes them elusive and hard to pin down, we struggle in other ways with *too many* "beginnings" that could be constructed, depending on our vantage point and ideological purpose. To alleviate both the epistemological and the ideological problems of a literary historiography of beginnings we divide our account of early literary cultures on the Japanese archipelago into various storylines that need to be considered in order to disentangle the full complexity of the Japanese case. Along the way, I propose a set of models that can be useful in thinking through the emergence of literary traditions in general.

Histories of Literacy and Literate Culture

Although oral composition, transmission, recitation, and performance of songs and stories play important roles in the social life of any community, particularly in the early periods but up to today, literary cultures in all their transtemporal complexity emerge with writing. Scripts are crucial parts of the infrastructure of literary cultures, which builds on various literacies, or "literate culture" as we can call it. They build on the practices of people skilled in reading, writing, and transmitting texts. The writing systems that emerged in antiquity—Egyptian hieroglyphs, Mesopotamian cuneiform writing, the Indus (or Harappan) script, Chinese characters, and Mayan glyphs—were all strongly logographic, writing meaning ("words" = *logos*) rather than transcribing sound ("phono"graphic). Only Chinese characters remain today from the logographic writing systems of antiquity, many centuries after cuneiform writing and the Egyptian scripts vanished during the first centuries CE. All others either disappeared or were gradually replaced with phonographic syllabaries or alphabets.

The technology of writing first reached the shores of the archipelago on inscribed objects from the continent—China and the Korean peninsula.[4] Writing traveled on precious objects, such as coins and mirrors, starting from the first century BCE. They served as status symbols and were placed in tombs. Local chieftains on the archipelago also began to bolster their domestic power against rival leaders through receiving prestigious titles from changing Chinese courts in exchange for "tribute missions." In 1784 a seal was found that probably documents one of these earliest diplomatic exchanges, bestowing a title on a ruler of the small polity of "Wa" 委 (an older name for Japan). Although the authenticity and meaning of the inscription have been hotly debated since, it seems to match the record in the Chinese *Later Han History* (*Hou Hanshu* 後漢書) that mentions the bestowal of such a seal by the Chinese court in 57 CE.[5] The appearance in the third and fourth centuries of the first mirrors produced domestically with garbled inscriptions suggests that written signs on imported objects were no longer "alegible," that is, considered charismatic décor rather than writing. These garbled phrases and "pseudo-inscriptions," imitating writing patterns, show that writing had gained authority as an institution while its practice was not yet fully developed. In the fourth to fifth centuries inscriptions by scribes from the Korean Peninsula start to appear, such as the Seven-Branched Sword held at the Isonokami Shrine in Nara Prefecture that a king of Paekche, one of the "Three Kingdoms" of Korea (ca. 57 BCE to 668 CE), presented to a Japanese ruler during the fourth century. The earliest extant longer texts appear in the early seventh century and are associated with Prince Shōtoku (574–622), an early cultural hero who served as regent to his aunt Empress Suiko and was eventually divinized: he is credited with the so-called *Seventeen-Article Constitution* (*jūshichijō kenpō* 十七条憲法), a statement on the ethics of governance and government service, and commentaries on three Buddhist sutras. Prince Shōtoku was an instrumental figure in the spread of Buddhism into Japan, which constituted an important vector in the transmission of literacy and literate culture from the Korean Peninsula, in particular the southwestern state of Paekche, to the archipelago.

But only with the latter half of the seventh and in the eighth centuries do we see a veritable explosion of textual production and a leap into pervasive uses of literacy. We can grasp this in the archeological record through the troves of inscribed wooden tablets (*mokkan* 木簡) that have been discovered over the past few decades.[6] They had practical uses, as labels and tags or as brief documents used in economic and political administration, but they were also used for writing practice. They give us insights into literacy training: we can see typical mistakes and vernacularizing syntax and get first glimpses of a scribal canon, such as the Confucian *Analects* or vernacular poetry that we find on "poetry tablets." Beyond this only recently discovered epigraphic record we have an unusually large number of substantial texts produced with the surge of literacy unfolding during these one and a half centuries: law codes (the Taihō Code of 703 and the Yōrō Code compiled in 718); local gazetteers (*Fudoki* 風土記, 713–) and two historical chronicles, the three-volume *Record of Ancient Matters* (*Kojiki* 古事記, 712) and the thirty-volume *Chronicles of Japan* (*Nihon shoki* 日本書紀, 720) as well as poetry anthologies, namely the earliest anthology of poetry in Literary Chinese, *Florilegium of Cherished Airs* (*Kaifūsō* 懐風藻, 751; about 120 poems), and the earliest anthology of vernacular poetry, *Collection of Myriad Leaves* (*Man'yōshū* 万葉集, 759; more than forty-five hundred poems), as well as parts of earlier poetry collections anthologized in them; and even, a poetological treatise, *Model Forms for the Canon of [Japanese] Waka Poetry* (*Kakyō hyōshiki* 歌経標式, 772).

Writing styles varied greatly, along a spectrum ranging from logographic, fully comprehensible transregional Literary Chinese (also called "Sino-Japanese" to emphasize its production in Japan and frequent linguistic in-terferences with Japanese vernacular; or "Literary Sinitic" to highlight the standardized cosmopolitan nature of this East Asian lingua franca) all the way to straight phonographic inscription of the Japanese written vernacular, which was recorded using Chinese characters purely for their sound value during the Nara Period (710–94) before the invention of the kana syllabaries. Chi-nese and Japanese are at opposite ends of the spectrum of language families: Chinese and Literary Sinitic is an isolated, monosyllabic, and, syntactically, SPO (subject-predicate-object) language, whereas Japanese and Korean are heavily inflected, polysyllabic (agglutinative), and, syntactically, SOP (subject-object-predicate) languages. From early on Koreans and Japanese developed vernacularizing reading practices, "gloss reading" (*kundoku* 訓読), which al-lowed them to read a Sinitic text in native syntax. That meant glossing the Chinese characters with native pronunciation of the same words and rear-ranging the SPO Sinitic texts into SOP native syntax, placing the object be-fore the verb and adding the rich repertoire of native grammatical elements such as case particles, auxiliary verbs, and honorific, humble, or polite forms. *Kundoku*-style gloss-reading techniques in all likelihood originated on the Korean Peninsula and were brought to Japan by the waves of immigrants settling in Japan in the sixth and seventh centuries. While inscription styles varied greatly from standard Literary Sinitic to the vernacular and included hybrid mixed forms depending on genre and occasion, gloss reading united the great variability of writing into a shared world of vernacularized reading and vocalization. *Kundoku* glossing had become the basis of everyday written communication and also appears in monumental inscriptions from the latter half of the seventh century. Thus, rather than a *bilingual* constellation, where people are able to write and speak two different languages, premodern Japan's literate culture was based on *biliteracy*, the production of texts in inscription styles varying from standard cosmopolitan Sinitic to vernacular forms, which were connected through the vernacularizing reading practice of gloss reading. Japanese speakers of some form of spoken Chinese were extremely rare and basically limited to immigrants during the early period. Instead, elite literacy was based on mastering the gloss-reading techniques that allowed Japanese vocalization of the "grapholect" of Literary Sinitic. Put simply, there were no "Chinese original texts" that were "translated" into Japanese. For early Japanese elites the very act of reading already domesticated and vernacularized them into Japanese.[7]

Japan's biliterate literary culture thrived for more than one and a half millennia into the early twentieth century, when passionate language reformers inspired by European nation-state ideologies fervently promoted the vernacular language in the process of nation building. This led to the death of Literary Sinitic as the cosmopolitan language that had connected East Asia's "Sinographic sphere" for most parts of the past two millennia. The death of the world's last logographic script sphere in the twenty-first century constitutes a world-historical inflection point that can inspire us to think about the distinctive patterns of cross-lingual and cross-cultural communication in logographic script spheres, such as premodern East Asia or, previously, the cuneiform script world. Before the twentieth century, Chinese, Koreans, Japanese, and Vietnamese communicated mainly through "brush talk" (筆談), writing back and forth on paper while facing one's conversation partner, because they could not speak each other's language but could all write in Literary Sinitic. Thus, for the elites East Asia was largely a world without the *need* for translation prior to the early modern period, when much of classical literature was translated into the vernacular for women, commoners, and children.[8] We can appreciate this phenomenon through the sharp contrast with Latin literature (and most literatures relying on alphabetic scripts) that started right away, and rather improbably, as a "translation literature" "beyond Greek," as Denis Feeney has memorably called it.[9]

Collateral Histories of Literary History

The emergence of Japanese literate and literary culture can be understood only through various "collateral histories," namely political and societal developments that catalyzed them in often quite specific historical contexts. We can trace the archipelago's entry into the Chinese world order through chapters in the Chinese official histories, which are the earliest surviving records on Japan. Starting with the Han dynasty Chinese empires built a hierarchical network of vassal states who were invested with prestigious titles and in turn had to send tribute missions that had economic, but—even more importantly—powerful symbolic significance. These missions could be a true financial burden on the vassal states. They could become embarrassing occasions for power struggles vis-à-vis the Chinese court, as we know for a mission in 607 when the Japanese ambassador delivered a letter from Prince Shōtoku to the emperor of the Sui dynasty (581–618) in which he put Japan's "Son of Heaven" on a par with the Chinese "Son of Heaven," greatly enraging the Chinese emperor. Tribute diplomacy also triggered competition between vassal states who ideologically arrogated the hegemonic position of a "little China" at the center of their own subservient vassal states. The *Chronicles of Japan*, our most substantial source on early East Asian diplomacy between Chinese, Korean, and Japanese courts, repeatedly casts Korean states into the role of Japan's vassals, an ideological move with rather little historical substance. Thus, for the peripheral states the China missions became an important theater for self-representation. There were about twenty Japanese missions to the Sui and Tang courts appointed between 607 and 894 (after which the Japanese court abandoned them), and these were the most crucial conduit for Japan's feverish political institution building on continental models during the seventh and eighth centuries, the very period when literacy and literary culture exploded into ever new uses and forms.[10]

Particularly relevant for the emergence of literary culture was the model of a "literate bureaucracy," governance based on a class of scholar-officials, or *literati*, communicating through various genres of governmental prose, adopted from Chinese and Korean precedents. The *Chronicles of Japan* eagerly trace the successive development of the bureaucratic system: the transmission of writing and texts through scholars from the Korean state of Paekche under Emperor Ōjin (trad. fourth/fifth centuries) and the foundation of Korean immigrant scribal lineages serving the Yamato clan, that came to rule Japan, the evolution of the system of ranks and offices, and of various genres of administrative prose. That already the legendary first human emperor, Jinmu, the descendant of the Sun Goddess Amaterasu, speaks in polished and articulate Sinitic prose shows the eagerness of the court officials who compiled the *Chronicles* to anachronistically retroject by several centuries the emergence of sophisticated literary culture on the archipelago. The archeological and transmitted record at least puts many of the benchmarks of the development of literacy much later than the *Chronicles* claim.

But Japan's unusually quick "leap" into literate and literary culture occurred owing to a particular set of events that was so traumatic and transformational that it arguably shaped the fundamental orientations of premodern Japanese culture and literature as a whole, especially in terms of the close interplay between the emperor, court culture, and both vernacular and Sinitic literatures. This set of events was the destruction of Japan's close ally Paekche by Chinese forces and Silla, one of the other Korean "Three Kingdoms," and the subsequent unification of the peninsula under Silla. The regional tensions during the seventh century that accompanied the reunification of China under the Sui and Tang dynasties (after more than three centuries of disunity) had domestic effects in Japan that can hardly be overestimated. In 660 Paekche fell to the Silla-Tang alliance. In 663, during the fateful Battle of Hakusukinoe 白村江 (Battle of Baekgang in Korean and of Baijiangkou in Chinese) Silla and Tang troops extinguished Paekche for good. The end for Koguryŏ, the northernmost of the Three Kingdoms, came in 668. Although it took another eight years for Silla to rid themselves of Tang occupation—their allies had long-standing designs of their own on the peninsula—Silla managed to create a new peninsular political order. In the aftermath of the political showdown on and over the Korean peninsula Paekche refugees washed over Japan. These refugees, expert scribes and craftsmen among them, remade the fate of early Japanese culture with their skills, and religious beliefs and practices.[11] Many of the scholar-officials appearing in the first Sino-Japanese poetry anthology or serving at the State Academy, founded in the late seventh century, were of immigrant stock. The immigrants obviously did not "conquer" Japan, coming instead as vulnerable refugees from a dying state, but their culture did: we might well call this an "internal cultural conquest" of sorts. The politically, culturally, and demographically unusually close intertwinement between Paekche and early Japan is a peculiar case in world history where a chain of brief and fast-paced historical coincidences generated long-lasting, fundamental orientations of Japanese culture, in particular the imperial system and court culture.

The courts of Emperors Tenji (r. 661–72), Tenmu (r. 673–86), and Jitō (r. 690–97) endured the challenges and bore out the fruits of this cultural jump-start by Paekche refugees, who were not always welcome during these also domestically tumultuous times gripped by succession disputes. This is clear from riddle-like "ditties" (*wazauta*) that were put into the mouth of people of low status or limited reason, but whose rhetorical inversion of conventional power hierarchies made their voices all the more prophetic. All poems in the chapter on Tenji in the *Chronicles of Japan* are such ominous ditties, and one under Tenmu expresses the angry envy of Japanese over Korean immigrants receiving prestigious court titles in their new home country. But the *Chronicles* also explicitly spelled out the high-tech cultural capital they brought to Japan: generals with expert military training; officials in the bureau of ceremonies; a chief official of the State Academy; several herbal masters with medical expertise; somebody with Yin-Yang knowledge; or one versed in the Confucian classics.

The Paekche cataclysm and immigrant crisis contributed greatly to a few poignant changes during the last decades of the seventh and the beginning of the eighth century. Under Tenmu large projects of historiography were started, which eventually resulted in the two chronicles. Especially the *Record of Ancient Matters* presents a rich creation mythology that connected the emperor as a living descendant of Amaterasu to the world of the gods. The *Record of*

Ancient Matters focuses on constructing a direct Yamato lineage plus the lineages of officials serving the rulers in various military, civil, and technological functions. Japan had instituted its own first imperial era in 645, a bold statement of independence in the Sinographic sphere, where Chinese-era names were often forced on weaker states. But a real change in self-confidence came during this turn of the eighth century: the powerful term "Tennō" (emperor) was coined under Tenmu (in contrast to the "kings" that stood under the Chinese emperor in the Sinitic world order), and Japan was not any more the barbarian vassal state of Wa but changed its name to "Nihon" 日本 (as documented proudly in the title *Chronicles of Japan/Nihon shoki*) and was now considered a cultivated country (君子之國) with special intermediary status between China and barbarian states. Under Tenmu and his wife and successor, Empress Jitō, a new form of imperial panegyrics in long-verse vernacular poetry (*chōka* 長歌) emerged that divinized the emperor, epitomized by Kakinomoto no Hitomaro (fl. 689–700), the leading poet of *Collection of Myriad Leaves* (who himself eventually became divinized as the god of poetry); and new hybrid forms of Buddhist, Daoist, and Confucian ideas helped build imperial ideology that shaped an imperial court culture like no other in East Asia.

Histories of Letters and Literary Culture

Because our notion of "literature" and the "literary" has drastically shrunk since the nineteenth century and maps even less onto non-Western premodern traditions than it maps onto modern literatures that have developed in dialogue with Western literatures, we need to ask where and how we can capture "literature" in seventh- and eighth-century Japan. A recent revisionary three-volume literary history of Japan has uncovered the drastic shifts of the cultural field in and around "literature" from the early period to the present. Entitled *A New History of Japanese "Letterature,"* it draws attention to the enormous breadth of writing practices and genres, recovers the suppressed Sinitic tradition against the modernist vernacular bias, and shows interconnections between various fields of knowledge and literature. Just like "historiae litterariae" in Europe up to the eighteenth century, which encompassed not the narrow modern notion of poetry, drama, and fiction, but a broad world of "Letters" and knowledge in all arts and sciences,[12] the notion of "bun 文" in Japan was broadly connected to "Letters," highbrow belles lettres, and Sinological and Buddhist scholarship. The coinage "Letterature" captures this combination of humanistic "Letters" and its modern narrowing into "Literature" that characterized the pre-nineteenth-century world in East Asia as well as Europe.[13]

One of the most prominent features of early Japanese literary culture is its biliteracy. Nowhere else in the Sinographic sphere do we have such a rich record of thriving vernacular literature right from the earliest period. With most records before the early modern period destroyed and lost in Korea and, even more so, Vietnam, comparisons with the unusually well-documented early Japanese case are asymmetrical. Yet, as I will argue below, certain ideological and institutional patterns that emerged during the seventh and eighth centuries supported the living transmission of vernacular texts in ways that were clearly absent in, for example, premodern Korea. That this biliteracy was fulfilling important ideological and aesthetic needs is clearly visible in the "doubleness" of the eighth-century textual record, with the two above-mentioned historical chronicles, one in more local hybrid form, the other in cosmopolitan Sinitic, and two poetry anthologies, again one in Sinitic and the other in various forms of written vernacular.

To illustrate this through the chronicles, much research has gone into trying to explain their simultaneous appearance and into showing their significant differences. They do cover the same "reality," Japanese history from its beginnings up to Empress Suiko (593–628), with the *Chronicles of Japan* going further into the reign of Jitō. But they are based on profoundly different compilation principles, narrative logic, rhetoric, and style. Takamitsu Kōnoshi has captured this elegantly in his monograph on the idea of "multiple antiquities" (*Fukusū no kodai* 複数の古代, 2007) within the chronicles and other texts. The *Record of Ancient Matters* boasts a vernacularizing style and is clearly invested in building a continuous imperial Yamato lineage and giving us the stories of its gods and divinized rulers, making it a romantic fictionalized "Tale of the Emperors" of sorts or a "bedroom history of the dynasty."[14] The *Chronicles of Japan*, in Literary Sinitic, preserve story material in multiple variants and is ideologically and rhetorically cast into Sinitic models of rule through writing and literacy. It understands the practice of quoting from texts, features a creative abstract cosmology of Yin and Yang forces (rather than fickle gods), and is conscious of the world around Japan, repeatedly adopting an outside view of the archipelago, *Nihon*, in the context of the larger Sinographic realm of China and the Korean states. Diplomacy within the region is keenly reported, while it is virtually absent in *Record of Ancient Matters*, where the word "Nihon" does not appear.

It is significant that we cannot even speak of "diglossia" here, which would imply the symbiosis of a transregional standard language with dialectal forms of lower status. Although Literary Sinitic was the authoritative language of the court bureaucracy, the Buddhist clergy, scholarship, and highbrow belles lettres into the early twentieth century, the vernacular already had highbrow functions in the seventh and eighth centuries that made it complementary rather than inferior to Literary Sinitic. The vernacular was also the language of gods and emperors, which put it beyond any form of "diglossic" hierarchy. The vernacular poems of imperial panegyrics that came to flourish under Tenmu and Jitō during the last decades of the seventh century develop a hyperbolic, ritualistic, and sacralized written vernacular; vernacular (though still mixed-style) royal proclamations (*senmyō* 宣命) and prayers (*norito* 祝詞) cemented the role of an elevated, irreplaceable written vernacular and greatly helped stabilize vernacular inscription practices (unlike in Korea, which has a significantly more discontinuous history of vernacular inscription practices).

Much of early poetry production was occasional. A ritual calendar of annual festivals emerged during the seventh and eighth centuries that offered occasions for poetry composition, such as the "Winding Stream Festival" in the spring on the third day of the third month of the lunar calendar, the "Lovers' Festival" on the seventh day of the seventh month, or the "Double Ninth" late fall festival celebrated with chrysanthemums on the ninth day of the ninth month. Imperial excursions were a prime occasion for imperial panegyrics, both Sinitic and vernacular. Sinitic poetry thrived during the 720s in the salon of Prince Nagaya, who was framed by the rising Fujiwara family and forced into suicide. But his lavish residence served as a vibrant stage for a fledgling (all-male) literati culture of courtier-scholar-poets and also for hosting embassies of the Korean state of Silla where the hosts and foreign guests graced each other with poems and ornate prefaces on the occasion. The recently founded State Academy trained these courtiers in the Confucian classics and literary composition based on Chinese canonical texts. Although Japan never developed a civil service examination system to recruit the highest echelons of the court bureaucracy, as in China, Korea, and Vietnam, and the status of the academicians remained low and developed into hereditary family privilege rather than meritocratic selection, Chinese knowledge and scholarship had great prestige in premodern Japan. And the Academy afforded occasions for collective poetry composition including lectures on particular texts or the regular rituals for Confucius (*sekiten* 釋奠). While these were places reserved for Chinese-style composition, there was one particular place and occasion that was central in vernacular poetry composition and virtually absent in Literary Sinitic: death and funerals. The Japanese court performed double burial for its royal family members, and the liminal period of "temporary enshrinement," which could last for up to several years, often became the occasion for intense competition and succession disputes. This practice produced some of the most flamboyant imperial panegyrics.[15] One of the three major genre categories of *Collection of Myriad Leaves* are "Coffin-pulling Songs" (*banka* 挽歌), a practically oriented, rather undistinguished genre in China at the time. The hyperbolic language of imperial divinization and ritualistic verbal performance of boundless grief produced sublime vernacular written registers.[16]

Literary production centered on the new capitals built on Chinese models— Fujiwara (694–710) and Nara (710–84). But around the 720s a coterie of local administrators on Japan's southernmost island of Kyushu produced a distinctive, hybrid literature preserved in *Collection of Myriad Leaves*. The "distant capital" of Dazaifu was a major diplomatic stage for exchanges with close-by China and Korea. In this milieu, which was peripheral to the northeastern capital, but central to the latest cultural flows from the continent, Yamanoue no Okura (660–ca. 733) engaged topics far from contemporary court panegyrics, such as the pleasures and pains of family life, Buddhist philosophy and personal suffering, and social injustice and poverty. The Chinese learning he puts on display was partly due to his Paekche immigrant family background and his participation in a mission to the Chinese Tang court. His friend and Dazaifu colleague Ōtomo no Tabito (665–731), from an ancient Japanese military clan, adapted themes of literati recluse poetry and drinking, appreciation for the Chinese trope of plum blossoms (a poetry cycle that recently furnished the new imperial era name of *Reiwa* [2019–] of Japan's ruling emperor Naruhito). His son Yakamochi, the final compiler of *Collection of Myriad Leaves*, engaged in witty exchanges with a kinsman, mixing Chinese-style poetry and prose with vernacular poetic forms. This experimentation with the hybridization of forms, themes, and rhetoric decorum remained quite unique in the Japanese tradition, which after the ninth century settled into a polar divide of Chinese-style versus vernacular modes[17] in occasion, literary composition, anthologization and transmission, and bibliographic description.

Yet we also see recluse and exile poetry resisting the courtly center, in rhetoric and reality. And the peripheries of the realm become palpable in travel and diplomatic poetry composed in the context of the missions to China or Unified Silla; or even in the lowbrow anonymous corpus of "Songs of the Eastland" (*azuma uta* 東歌東歌), which preserves traces of local dialects, or songs of border guards (*sakimori* 防人), both anthologized in *Collection of Myriad Leaves*.

Folkloristic and comparative anthropological research in the twentieth century has connected some of the rich traditions of anonymous vernacular love poetry preserved in *Collection of Myriad Leaves* with erotic harvest and fertility rituals (*utagaki* 歌垣). This is another area where vernacular and Sino-Japanese traditions greatly diverge, as love was a major topic only in the vernacular, not in Sino-Japanese poetry. And the—already in the historical chronicles—amply documented custom of song cycles consisting of erotic exchanges between lovers gives us an unusually high proportion of female authors in the early period, including major poetesses like Princess Nukata

(-690s), jealously pursued by princely brothers, Emperor Tenji and Tenmu, or Lady Ōtomo of Sakanoue (-750s), Yakamochi's aunt. This form also contributed to the prominent vernacular genre of "poetry tales" (*utamonogatari* 歌物語), which flourished with the Heian Period (794–1185) and shaped core works of the Japanese canon like Murasaki Shikibu's *Tale of Genji*.

Despite the wide range of styles from courtified rustic to the most refined elevated registers, early literary culture shows a clear aesthetic interest in putting the complexity of reading and writing practices to work for sophisticated literary effect. For example, in 679 Tenmu, scarred by the succession disputes that had led him to kill his nephew and assume the throne, gathered six princes at the venerable site of Yoshino for a holy oath of loyalty. His poem (*Man'yōshū* I.27) puns on the place name of *"Yoshi" no* ("Good" fields), where he had hidden before the coup, and uses cognates of "good" eight times in the short thirty-one syllables of a *tanka* poem. The incantatory phonetic repetitiveness, certainly fitting for a ritualistic oath verse, stands in suggestive contrast to the logographic variety of inscribing "good": five different characters, all with different connotations, register levels, and connections with the Chinese literary canon. Thus, already in early Japan literary culture thrived on the complexity of literacies.

Latecomer Literary Histories

The overwhelming majority of literatures in world history have in some fashion been what we call here "heterotopic": they adopted and adapted foreign writing systems; foreign textual canons and educational institutions; and foreign rhetorical tropes, topoi and themes, or prosodies and meters. This happened typically through trade, conquest, or diplomacy. But even "idiotopic literatures," such as Chinese, which emerged with its "own" primary writing system and without any traceable influences of adjacent developed literate cultures, could also develop "heterotopic" aspects. This was the case with medieval Chinese literary culture thanks to its intensive linguistic and cultural translation of Buddhist literature during the first millennium CE.

Typically this phenomenon is captured through "reception research" that traces intertextual relationships between the older "mother" culture and the younger heterotopic literature. This is certainly the case for Japan, where modern scholars have produced a wealth of research on the precise intertextual relations between Chinese precedents and Japanese adaptations into their own literature. While it is valuable to research the history of the transmission and canonization of certain texts, this approach is far too narrow to grasp the monumental and visceral impact of an earlier "reference culture" on younger heterotopic literatures.[18] Rather, we need an assessment not only of particular traveling texts or lexical items, but of the cultural adaptation of literary institutions and textual practices in heterotopic literary traditions. Surprisingly, this kind of research has only recently received attention in studies on Japan.

Thus, when we probe the beginnings of literary culture on the archipelago we need to consider another set of beginnings, contained in the records that reached Japan from the continent: the building process of institutions and cultural memory that unfolded symbiotically with the emergence of early Japanese textual production. Early Japanese writers could draw on concepts and conventions that took centuries to develop in its reference culture, China. The earliest texts from seventh-century Japan drew on a literate and literary culture that stretched back some eighteen hundred years to the oracle bones and bronze inscriptions of the Shang (ca. 1300–1046 BCE) and early parts of the Zhou dynasties (ca. 1046–256 BCE). Through many centuries, Chinese communities and writers had developed complex and varied concepts of "authorship"; of text types, "genres" and their conventions; of "poetics," reflections on the cosmic and social function and significance of literature; and of the arts of "allusion."

Unlike with China's earliest scribes, the producers of Japan's fledgling literary culture had a grasp of the meaning of "authorship": they could appreciate the difference between the anonymous early poetry of the *Classic of Poetry* (*Shijing* 詩經, mid-first millennium BCE) and poetry by named authors and the earliest "classical poets" that emerged during the Han (206 BCE–220 CE) and Three Kingdoms Period (220–65) with the poetry gatherings at the Wei court under Cao Cao and his sons Cao Zhi and Cao Pi, the "Seven Masters of Jian'an" (*Jian'an qi zi* 建安七子), and the "Seven Sages of the Bamboo Grove" (*zhulin qixian* 竹林七賢).[19] These poets and the model of court salons played a central role in the early Sinitic poetry in Japan. Although *Collection of Myriad Leaves* contains much anonymous poetry, probably polished and "courtified" versions of songs that were recorded during the seventh and eighth centuries, there is no comparable anonymous tradition of Sino-Japanese poetry. Sinitic poetry in this period is an elite pursuit and required the attribution of an author who is typically referred to by name, court rank, and title.

The Chinese sixth-century literary anthology *Selections of Refined Literature* (*Wenxuan* 文選) was a textbook in the civil service exams in Silla and was known in Japan at least by 735. This model anthology gave early Japanese students a sense of the broad genre spectrum of early and medieval Chinese literature, ranging from the venerable antique four-syllable song meter to medieval "classical" five- and seven-syllable poetry with its many subgenres rooted in particular occasions; to "music bureau poetry" (*yuefu shi* 樂府詩), which supposedly gave voice to commoners—through literate scribes—or was written in the voice of commoners as a literary conceit; to prosimetric genres like rhapsodies (*fu* 賦), a lexically copious genre rooted in Han dynasty court panegyrics and the new natural treasures of a vast empire; and prose genres with specific social functions in the court bureaucracy, in the community of the literati, or in mourning the dead, including edicts (*zhao* 詔), petitions (*biao* 表), examination questions (*cewen* 策問), letters (*shu* 書), prefaces (*xu* 序), eulogies (*song* 頌), encomia (*zan* 贊), treatises (*lun* 論), inscriptions (*ming* 銘), dirges (*lei* 誄), tomb epitaphs (*muzhi* 墓誌), necrologies (*xingzhuang* 行狀), condolences (*diaowen* 吊文), or prayer texts (*jiwen* 祭文), to name but a few of the thirty-some genres appearing in *Wenxuan*.

Genres were strongly bound to particular social needs, and the early Japanese courtiers who produced Sinitic texts picked carefully what their own local culture and the moment demanded. Japanese courtiers began experimenting with a small number of genres. Based on the surviving record, classical five- and seven-syllable poetry, poetry prefaces, and biographies were the first genres they tried their hands at. And banquet poems, "poems stating my feelings" (*jukkai* 述懷), and "poems on things" (*eibutsushi* 詠物詩) were among the first subgenres Japanese courtiers adopted to meet the demands of court life, included eulogizing the emperors and their reigns at banquets, or writing about enjoying a day off from court routine. Gradually, writers would explore a broader spectrum of Chinese-style genres, including rhapsodies, prefaces, and examination essays, as mentioned above. With each genre came a sense of its function and decorum, which Cao Pi, Emperor Wen of the Wei dynasty, had first sketched in his "Discourse on Literature" ("Lun wen" 論文) preserved in *Selections of Refined Literature*.

Cao Pi's treatise provided a practical "genre poetics" very much tuned to the exigencies of court life. It was read alongside other statements about the political, moral, epistemic, psychological, and artistic roles of poetry in society and the cosmos at large. The Confucian *Analects* and the Daoist text *Zhuangzi* in particular provided prominent pronouncements on these various functions. For example, the surprisingly great number of references to *Analects* 6.23, "The wise enjoy waters, the benevolent mountains" (知者樂水, 仁者樂山) (about sixteen times in the ca. 120 poems of the *Kaifūsō*, amounting to an average incidence of once in every seven to eight poems) is typically seen as a statement of political and ethical ideology, namely an "influence" of "Confucianism" (or for *Zhuangzi*, "Daoism"). But they are also poetological statements that highlight the social utility of poetry in Japan's fledgling literary culture: that appreciating nature and writing verse about it during an official excursion is a hallmark of courtiers. It is a polite and, for early eighth-century Japanese, a newly sophisticated compliment to the participants at the banquet, even if Tang Chinese poets at the time or we today might think of it as hackneyed and repetitive. Cao Pi's "Discourse on Literature" would serve as the backbone of the new poetics of "governance through literature" enshrined at the court of Emperor Saga in the early ninth century.

The art of allusion became a central venue for innovation in medieval Chinese poetry. Anonymous four-syllable poetry up to the Han dynasty could be performed and reperformed as part of a repertoire with variation, which persisted into the orally inspired early classical five- and seven-syllable Old Poetry (*gushi* 古詩) and music bureau poetry;[20] similarly, the *Songs of the South* (*Chuci* 楚辭) is a performance repertoire of sorts echoing themes and tropes going back to its earliest texts, the "Nine Songs" ("Jiuge" 九歌) and "Encountering Sorrow" ("Li Sao" 離騷). These texts do not "quote" each other; they echo, replay, reshape central earlier texts in this tradition. With the rise of authorship and the lexical diversification that developed in the early medieval period following the Han dynasty, a sophisticated art of referencing, of twisting through pointed allusion became a major venue of literary innovation. By the sixth century this resulted in criticism of empty flourish and oversophistication by writers such as Pei Ziye (469–530) or Liu Xie, the author of the highly ornate *The Literary Mind and the Carving of Dragons* (*Wenxin diaolong* 文心雕龍), which in turn nourished the various "Return to Antiquity" (*fugu* 復古) agendas that emerged in the seventh through ninth centuries.[21]

The earliest bureaucrats in Japan who wrote the poetry preserved in *Florilegium of Cherished Airs* understood that the art of allusion was a centerpiece of Sinitic poetry composition and put it to more than abundant use: the more the better appears to have been the criterion for late seventh- and early eighth-century writers of Sinitic verse. This stands in strong contrast to contemporary developments in vernacular poetry. Despite its great diversity we can say that the poetry preserved in *Collection of Myriad Leaves* as a whole is hardly allusive (except for the poetry produced by the above-mentioned Sinophile coterie of Dazaifu poets). This quality of primordiality and literary immediacy has allowed the anthology to embody the spirit and heart of the Japanese people for modern national literature scholars. Even in the case of the great poet Hitomaro, who epitomizes the idea of a distinct poetic voice that came to be emulated by later poets (leading, somewhat paradoxically, to an overattribution of poems to him), those later poets do not "quote" Hitomaro. Not unlike with early poetry in the style of the *Classic of Poetry* and *Songs of the South* we have something of a performance repertoire that poets elaborate on and contribute to, which is clearly seen in the "indebtedness" of early court poets such as Kasa no Kanamura (active 715–33) to Hitomaro's voice and artistry. There is emulation rather than allusion, which seems to be a characteristic of strongly oral and song-inspired incipient literary traditions—such as vernacular Japanese poetry, but certainly not Sinitic poetry in Japan.

Parallel Literary Histories

Literary cultures typically unfold in macroregional contexts with complex patterns and interactions of shared scripts, languages, and political, religious, and artistic practices. To fully grasp distinctive characteristics of a literary culture it is helpful to look at parallel cases from the same macroregion. Methodologically, this includes the tracing of historical interactions between adjacent literary cultures, as well as functional comparisons of divergent cases. The study of the reception history of Korean culture in early Japan and the comparative study of early Japanese and Korean literary cultures are notoriously hampered by the extreme scarcity of surviving sources from early Korea, and the aftermath of Japan's colonization of Korea in the twentieth century. Still, from what survives we can infer suggestive differences between early Japanese and early Korean literary cultures. Most importantly, we see a great asymmetry in the relation between Sinitic and vernacular literatures. Whereas thousands of vernacular poems survive from early Japan, only two dozen happen to survive in medieval Korean chronicles. Whereas vernacular literary production thrived from the beginning and throughout premodern Japanese history, the authoritative literary tradition of premodern Korea into the early twentieth century was Sinitic literature. Part of this general pattern is rooted in the early period, where the Japanese court supported the vernacular as the idiom of the gods and emperors and turned vernacular poetry into a tool of imperial panegyrics and divinization. It thus became a central part of Japanese court culture. Its connection with the imperial institution remains unbroken today, as the Japanese emperors still celebrate a "New Year's *Waka* Poetry Reading" in early January (*utakai hajime* 歌会始). Instead, the surviving Korean vernacular poems, *hyangga* 鄉歌, show hardly any connection with the royal institution but were rather supported and practiced by the Hwarang order, aristocratic youths adept in martial skills, Buddhism, and poetry. It died with Silla and the Hwarang after the tenth century.

Instead, Chinese writing and administrative practices reached the Korean Peninsula much earlier than they did Japan: accordingly, the earliest surviving poems from the peninsula in Literary Sinitic are recorded in the archaic four-syllable meter of the venerable *Classic of Poetry*. No such four-syllable poetry survives from early Japan, although early Japanese writers certainly read examples of it in that very classic. But, as part of a later "heterotopic literature" in the Sinographic sphere, they composed only in the "more modern" medieval Chinese five- and seven-syllable meters that gained traction around the end of the Han dynasty. Yet another suggestive difference of the earliest surviving Korean poetry is that many poems are explicitly connected with Buddhist beliefs and practices and could also serve magical purposes as apotropaic objects and function as sacred oaths.

Toward a Comparative History of Beginnings: Distinctive Traits of the Japanese Case

Thanks to the rich survival of archeological artifacts and the unusually well-preserved textual archive, early Japan makes for an exceptionally well-documented case study of the beginnings of a textual culture in comparison to other early literatures, be it Greek, Latin, Persian, Sanskrit, Korean, or Vietnamese. Quite exceptionally, Japan developed a rich vernacular written tradition already during the first two centuries of the emergence of its literate culture. And particular ideological, political, and religious institutions, in addition, certainly, to a good portion of historical coincidences and sheer luck, helped preserve it over the past dozen centuries. Suggestively, poetry composition in the cosmopolitan lingua franca of Literary Sinitic started surprisingly late, only in the 670s, probably catalyzed by the catastrophic defeat of the Korean state of Paekche and the exodus of its ruling elite to Japan. Korean scribal experts, craftsmen, and ritual and administrative specialists shaped early Japanese court culture in ways that can hardly be exaggerated. While lingering views of Korea as a former colony have made it difficult for Japanese scholars to fully acknowledge that debt, recent scholarship has made great strides in reconstructing and recognizing the monumental and transformative scope of this impact.

The creation of the institutional and ideological foundations of Japan's imperial system happened during the transformative last decades of the seventh century and propelled both vernacular poetry—in the form of imperial, divinizing panegyrics—and Sinitic poetry—in the form of literati eulogies and pursuits—to the front stage as tools and accoutrements of state building. The earliest chronicles created a continuous lineage of imperial succession on the Yamato throne and celebrated Japan's civilizational progress in the larger Sinographic sphere. Much of early Japanese court literature served as a vector for ideas and ideologies about governance and the cosmos that helped build and enforce political and social hierarchies on many levels: between Japan and other peripheral states in the Sinographic sphere; between the Yamato court and the provinces, or belligerent border people; and between the court, its courtiers, and the masses of commoners providing for them.

To capture this highly complex process of "literary beginnings" for Japan I proposed a model of complementary types of historiography: history of literacy and literate culture, collateral cultural history, history of letters and literary culture, heterotopic literary history, and parallel literary history. These multiple teleologies intersect and diverge in complicated ways. But they give us a much more nuanced and historically accurate picture, filling in some of the severe blind spots inherent in the modernist anachronisms of national literary historiography. Deploying them in conjunction allows us a clearer glimpse of when, how, why, and with what distinctive traits literatures emerge.

Further Reading

Como, Michael. *Weaving and Binding: Immigrant Gods and Female Immortals in Ancient Japan*, 2009.

Cranston, Edwin A. *A Waka Anthology: The Gem-Glistening Cup*, 1993.

Denecke, Wiebke. *Classical World Literatures: Sino-Japanese and Greco-Roman Comparisons*, 2013.

Denecke, Wiebke. "Sino-Japanese Literature." In *The Oxford Handbook of Classical Chinese Literature*, edited by Wiebke Denecke, Wai-Yee Li, and Xiaofei Tian, 2017.

Duthie, Torquil. *Man'yōshū and the Imperial Imagination in Early Japan*, 2014.

Ebersole, Gary L. *Ritual Poetry and the Politics of Death in Early Japan*, 1989.

Kōno, Kimiko, Wiebke Denecke, Shinkawa Tokio, and Jinno Hidenori, eds. *Nihon "bun"gakushi* 日本「文」学史 [A new history of Japanese "literature"], 3 vols., 2015–19.

Lurie, David B. *Realms of Literacy: Early Japan and the History of Writing*, 2011.

Lurie, David B. "The Subterranean Archives of Early Japan: Recently Discovered Sources for the Study of Writing and Literacy," in *Books in Numbers*, edited by Lucille Chia and Wilt L. Idema, 2007.

Shirane, Haruo, ed. *Traditional Japanese Literature: An Anthology, Beginnings to 1600*, 2007.

Shirane, Haruo, Tomi Suzuki, and David Lurie, eds. *The Cambridge History of Japanese Literature*, 2016.

Korean

KSENIA CHIZHOVA

The beginning of early modern Korean literature—circulation of fictional prose in Chosŏn-dynasty Korea (which itself dates 1392–1910)—falls in the late seventeenth century and is coterminous with the rise of writing in the Korean vernacular. The invention of vernacular Korean script in the mid-fifteenth century prompted a chain of literary developments that resulted in the wide circulation of fictional prose, unseen in earlier times when the Chosŏn society relied on literary Chinese scriptural practices, monopolized by elite men. This chapter connects the beginnings of vernacular literature of Korea to two interrelated phenomena. The first is the rise of elite women's vernacular Korean literacy, which prompted the aestheticization of writing in the Korean vernacular, which until the seventeenth century had mostly technical application. The second is the development of Korea's patrilineal kinship, which provided a narrative momentum to a variety of written forms, including fiction. The two texts discussed in this chapter as representing vernacular literary beginnings are, notably, kinship narratives.

Vernacular Korean script was created by the royal decree of King Sejong (r. 1418–50) and promulgated in 1446 under the title "The Correct Sounds to Instruct the People" (*Hunmin chŏngŭm* 訓民正音). The promulgation edict states that the script was devised with less educated audiences in mind, providing means of expression to those who failed to master the literary language of the time—written Chinese—used in legislature, historiography, and educated men's compositions. Literary Chinese classics and histories captured the fundamental premises of human sociality and culture, which, despite their origin in China, were understood by Koreans to have universal validity. Literary Chinese—a scriptural medium that came with a set of literary conventions—constituted the quintessence of learning and refinement for the elite men of Chosŏn. These men would use vernacular Korean to write to their kinswomen and translate literary Chinese conduct literature for their benefit. They also wrote vernacular Korean fiction, often, according to extant records, to entertain their mothers. But because vernacular Korean fiction added little prestige to these men's literary fame, Korean fiction is mostly anonymous. For women, vernacular Korean literacy was a praiseworthy achievement, and its rise contributed to literarization of vernacular Korean writing, which I discuss below.

This chapter focuses on two texts that mark the beginnings of vernacular Korean literature, one representing a dead branch, and the other the beginning of a literary tradition that flourished through several centuries. *The Songs of Flying Dragons* (*Yongbi ŏch'ŏn ka* 龍飛御天歌; *The Songs* henceforth) was the text created by a group of compilers, who worked under royal auspices. Essentially the first attempt to put the newly devised script to literary use, *The Songs* glorified the legacy of royal ancestral line. This text remains a maverick attempt to link vernacular Korean writing and kinship imagination to the register of monumental state narrative: *The Songs* creates a familial legacy in governance, capturing the historical and ethical foundations of ancestral achievement to secure its generational perpetuity within the dynasty. The discussion below will show that vernacular Korean writing did not survive within the scriptural culture of the state; instead, it thrived among the domestic, women-centered audiences. The second vernacular Korean text discussed here as the harbinger of a flourishing literary tradition is *The Record of So Hyŏnsŏng* (*So Hyŏnsŏng rok* 蘇賢聖錄), one of the earliest known lineage novels (*kamun sosŏl* 家門小說), which circulated in Korea between the late seventeenth and early twentieth centuries. This massive literary tradition comprises dozens of known titles, with individual novels running as long as tens and even hundreds of chapters.[1] Balancing between the normative exposition of kinship values and the unruly details of everyday domestic life, lineage novels became the centerpiece of an elite vernacular Korean culture centered on women. Reflecting on the false beginnings and the ultimate fruition of kinship imagination in vernacular Korean literature, this chapter highlights the productive intersection of vernacular Korean writing with domestic everydayness, both as subject matter for the lineage novel and as the context of women's vernacular Korean literacy.

Family, in the context of Confucian culture that Korea shared with China, is a microcosm of the totality of social relationships, with the hierarchy and affection between father and son serving as a model for the ruler-subject bond. Filial piety, or sincere hierarchized devotion of children to parents, was considered the affective disposition central to relational ordering. Patrilineal succession of the royal line, while imbricated with an extra layer of exigencies of power transmission, was understood in terms of filial reverence for the ancestral moral exemplars, which created foundation for future governance, with uninterrupted generational succession mapping the homogeneity of political time and space. Starting in the late seventeenth century, patrilineal kinship, founded on this moral vision of human bonds, became the social norm for Chosŏn elites, prompting a number of social changes and realigning the affective contours of kinship. Lineage novels, coeval with the emergence of patrilineal kinship in the late seventeenth century, balance between the ideology of kinship and its everydayness; while inculcating fundamental kinship values, they valorize plots of defiance and unruly feelings as integral to personal life stories.

It must be noted that the notion of literature as a separate aesthetic realm, which in its modern Western meaning and academic emplacement often coincides with fictional prose, was nonexistent in Korea before the twentieth century. The expansion of Western colonial empires into East Asia in the nineteenth century respatialized the globe in terms of shared movement toward the unified goal of progress, with Western science, technology, philosophy, and art defining the ultimate criteria of modern development. The Western novel that presented the individual as a self-authoring moral subject of deep interiority became the central agenda for Korean writers at the turn of the twentieth century: this aesthetic program had dimensions of a nation-building project. Traditional fiction was cast as modernity's negative double, which called for literary renewal. At the same time, this very negation singled out traditional fictional prose as a site of immense academic interest, where subsequent postcolonial reformulations of Korean culture in the wake of Korea's liberation from its status of Japan's colony (1910–45) prompted scholars to examine the novel as the repository of national essence and tradition. The lineage novel—a tradition of vernacular Korean fictional prose—marked the first instance of aestheticization and canonization of vernacular Korean writing in elite culture, which then prompted the proliferation of vernacular fiction to broader, non-elite audiences. It is in this capacity—of literarization and proliferation—that fictional prose constitutes an object of interest for the narrative of vernacular Korean literary beginnings.

With this in mind, it is useful to examine the notions of literariness dominant in Chosŏn. Literary Chinese writing was introduced into Korea around the first century BCE, together with the larger system of literary classification. Writing, in this context, belonged to the overarching concept of patterning (K. *mun*; Ch. *wen* 文). Ability to create ordered patterns out of chaos constituted the quintessence of human sociality and culture. In this way, writing, motion through space during ritual performance, and bodily comportment prescribed by social and gender hierarchies were all activities of ordering that manifested cosmological moral fabric in the human realm.[2] This notion of pattern figures as the first semantic element in the modern coinage of the more localized written and academic practice designated as "literature" (K. *munhak*; Ch. *wenxue* 文學), created as an approximation of Western academic classifications.

Traditionally, in Korea and China, writing was subject to rigorous bibliographic classification that distinguished four categories: classics (K. *kyŏng*,

Ch. *jing* 經), masters or knowledge literature (K. *cha*; Ch. *zi* 子), histories (K. *sa*; Ch. *shi* 史), and miscellaneous writings in a variety of genres (K. *chip*; Ch. *ji* 集).[3] Fiction existed outside this canon, which meant it was excluded from literary collections, which compiled educated men's lifetime writings and perpetuated their literary fame. In Korea, where after the fifteenth century both literary Chinese and vernacular Korean script were in use, fictional prose was further stratified along the lines of scriptural medium. Against the prevalently negative view of fiction, literary Chinese prose, especially the texts imported from China, won educated men's favor for the artistry of its style. Vernacular Korean fiction, however, had no such advantage. While traditional vernacular Korean fiction is generally anonymous, male authors of vernacular Korean fiction are known, but until the present not a single female writer has been identified. Also anonymous, lineage novels—balancing between conduct-book moralism and dramatic plots of kinship conflicts—came to occupy an important position in the domestic, women-centered elite culture. In the discussion that follows, I set the fruition of this literary tradition into relief by the abrupt beginnings of vernacular Korean kinship narrative embodied in *The Songs of Flying Dragons* and contextualize it with the history of vernacular Korean script's creation and use, discussed in sequence below.

The Royal Tree: *The Songs of Flying Dragons*

After the promulgation of the Korean alphabet in 1446, its viability was tested in the composition of a text created by the commission of King Sejong (r. 1418–50). *The Songs of Flying Dragons* was then presented to the king in 1447. Before discussing the history of this text's creation and its structure, it is worth taking a closer look at the opening lines of the poem, its first three stanzas:

> Korea's Six Dragons flew in the sky.
> Their every deed was blessed by Heaven,
> Their deeds tallied with those of sage kings.
> The tree that strikes deep root
> Is firm amidst the winds.
> Its flowers are good,
> Its fruit abundant.
> The stream whose source is deep
> Gushes forth even in a drought.
> It forms a river
> And gains a sea.[4]

These lines conjure a powerful picture that streamlines the foundation of the royal dynasty of Chosŏn. The six dragons that sweep through the sky are direct royal ancestors of King Sejong: his father, King T'aejong (r. 1418–22), his grandfather, the founder of the dynasty, King T'aejo (r. 1392–98), and further four direct male ancestors, Hwanjo (d. 1360), Tojo (d. 1342), Ikcho, and Mokcho (d. 1274). The tree and the stream supply vigorous metaphors for the longevity and strength of the royal line. Founded on the moral deeds of the six royal ancestors and leading to Sejong himself, the line has solid foundations that augur future blessings and prosperity.

In terms of its form, *The Songs of Flying Dragons* is a remarkably hybrid text. Its core is composed of verses, where the Korean text is followed by literary Chinese rendition, although scholars believe that the lines were composed in reverse order—first in literary Chinese, which was then translated into Korean. The stanzas that trace the glorious ancestral deeds of dynasty's foundation are set in parallel structure, where the first part describes a moral precedent from Chinese history, and the second establishes a parallel occurrence in the history of the Chosŏn dynasty. The precedence of the Chinese events should not obscure the fact that the narrative of the Chosŏn dynasty's past provides the criteria for their selection. After the 125 stanzas were presented to King Sejong, he requested that a commentary be added in order to explicate the historical context, to which the verses sometimes allude only in very general lines. As a result, each stanza was appended with phonetic and linguistic explications, as well as historical commentary—all of it in literary Chinese (see figure 3.1). The verses and the commentaries are then framed by a preface, presentation, and postface, which describe the intent behind the text's composition and the composition process. While attempts to nationalize traditional culture produced a reading that celebrates this text as the first manifestation of literary Korean vernacular, the very hybridity of the piece speaks against such a reading.

The commentary that follows the first stanza explains that the dragons embody the steadfastness of virtue that harmonizes with the moral laws of the universe. The evidence for the ancestral virtue is captured in the figure of the tally: "Their deeds tallied with those of sage kings." Like the seamless match of the two divided parts of a carved jade tally, the ancestral virtues of the Chosŏn royal ancestors immediately align with the moral precedents established by the sages of ancient China, captured in the Confucian classics and histories. Convergence of pattern between the virtues of the royal ancestors and the revered examples from the past grafts the royal dynasty onto a temporal landscape that surpasses the history of the dynasty and the ancestors' life span. Of note is the extension of the actual dynastic line beyond Kings T'aejo and T'aejong, manipulated to incorporate the four nonreigning ancestors. Timelessness,

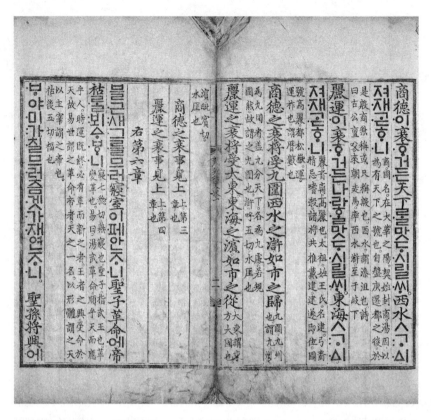

3.1. Leaf from *The Songs of Flying Dragons*, 1447. Woodblock print. Image courtesy of the Kyujanggak Archive.

continuity, and the glorification of the ancestral genealogy—the impeccable bloodline that leads directly into the present of the composition of *The Songs* during King Sejong's reign—are accomplished in the three opening stanzas.

Timelessness was a handy and much-needed resource during the reign of Sejong, who commissioned the creation of the Korean script and the composition of the poem. By mid-fifteenth century, the Chosŏn royal dynasty was slightly over fifty years old, and Sejong, the fourth reigning monarch, was the first to ascend the throne peacefully. The rhetorical figure of seamless continuity and stability that opens *The Songs of Flying Dragons* is set into relief by the actual events of the dynasty's founding by general Yi Sŏnggye, future king T'aejo, at the time of dynastic transition in China. With the Ming dynasty (1368–1644) getting the upper hand over the Mongol Yuan (1279–1368), Yi Sŏnggye's army was sent as a reinforcement to the Yuan, which the then-ruling Koryŏ dynasty recognized as suzerain state. Instead of assisting the Mongols,

Yi Sŏnggye turned his army back on the Koryŏ capital in 1388 and in 1392, after several years of demonstrative pledges of loyalty to the ruling Koryŏ dynasty, founded the new state, backed by the support of Ming China. Just like *The Songs of Flying Dragons*, the historical annals, *The Veritable Records of the Chosŏn Dynasty* (*Chosŏn wangjo sillok* 朝鮮王朝實錄), describe Yi Sŏnggye as an able general excelling at *kyŏkku*, or horseback ball game, killing five deer in succession with just five arrows, and never missing a human target, shooting into people's open mouths, eyes, and faces, sometimes seventy arrows at a time. Although Chosŏn Korea developed into a society that prioritized literary learning, the figure of the founder is depicted in military glory, paying homage to the battlefield prowess that paved his way to the throne.

Instead of going with the principle of primogeniture, Yi Sŏnggye decides to enthrone his fifth son, Yi Pangsŏk, born to his second, beloved consort. Yi Pangwŏn, Yi Sŏnggye's second son by his first queen, who was instrumental to Yi Sŏnggye's ascent to power, begrudges the decision. Alleging to have uncovered a treacherous plot against him, Yi Pangwŏn, future King T'aejong, conducts a military coup, enthroning his elder brother, Yi Panggwa, as King Chŏngjong (r. 1399–1400) in order to maintain the appearance of legitimate succession. The historical annals capture a scene when Yi Sŏnggye, bedridden, signs the enthronement edict and reclines back in a nauseous fit. Just after the edict is signed, the youngest princes Yi Pangsŏk and Yi Pangbŏn are killed, Yi Pangsŏk leaving his father trembling and in tears. Four days after the events, the historical record captures the following scene. Still on his sickbed, Yi Sŏnggye sends a message to the new crown prince: "Since I no longer have my father, I made his portrait to preserve his memory. Though my health has broken down, I am still breathing, which I believe is fortunate for you. While my illness continues I wish for some grapes."[5] Did the historians capture the irony in the words of the withering and disgusted general? Chŏngjong's rule comes to an abrupt end, after a confrontation between Yi Pangwŏn, de facto power holder, and his disgruntled older brother Yi Panggan, after which Chŏngjong abdicates in Yi Pangwŏn's favor. Sejong is thereafter the first to succeed to the throne peacefully after the reigns of his grandfather, uncle, and father.

The first and second strife of the princes, led by T'aejong, hardly conform to the streamlined and powerful picture of a deep-rooted tree and a stream with deep source. The sense of longevity and cohesion conferred on the ruling house of Chosŏn by *The Songs* is also achieved at the expense of the short-lived career of Chŏngjong, T'aejong's brother and Sejong's uncle, who is simply excluded from the family tree. Instead, the efforts of Sejong's own father, T'aejong, are amplified. T'aejong is presented as a faithful aide to his father's pursuits: his political acumen and upright character allow him to uproot treasonous plots at court; he plays an important role within Korea's relationship with China, its suzerain; and he is always able to put the laws of morality and the interests of the state before his own. Indeed, T'aejong is also the only son who bears a striking resemblance to his dignified father's "prominent nose and dragon face."[6] The first use of vernacular Korean script embodies a willful poetical revision of the narrative captured in the historical annals—the objective record called on to act as moral compass for governance. The history of the political strife is supplanted by the royal genealogical tree, grafted onto the landscape of timeless moral pattern and manipulated to suit the articulation of Sejong's direct line of descent.

The willfulness of this gesture is, however, disguised in the vocabulary of paternalistic governance. The compilers of *The Songs of Flying Dragons* model their efforts on of *The Book of Songs* (Ch. *Shijing*; K. *Sigyŏng* 詩經), traditionally attributed to the editorial work of Confucius, who collected people's songs as unmediated reflections on the moral clime of the era. Hence the line in the preface of *The Songs*: "we respectfully gathered the language of the people's joy and praise."[7] Just as the dynasty is validated by its convergence with the established moral pattern, the royal house is firmly embedded in its own time and place. People's praise validates the moral suasion of the royal house of Chosŏn, conceived in the strikingly personal terms of generational bloodline, elaborated through the vocabulary of Confucian governance and moral kinship.

The genealogical tree, in this text, figures as a pattern of generational reinscription: the moral deeds of the ancestors lay the foundation for the future branches of descendants, who, in honoring and commemorating ancestral virtues, settle onto a moral course of action themselves. The poems' postface records the pedagogical, future-oriented goal of the composition:

> When your heirs read these songs, they will inquire into the origin of current prosperity and strive to continue unfailingly the glorious line of our dynasty, and dare not change the norms of preserving the past. When your subjects read them, they will trace in them the cause of current peace, will resolve to perpetuate it to posterity and the irresistible sense of loyalty and admiration will never be ended.[8]

The spatial metaphors in *The Songs* extend in two directions, capturing the firm foundations of the past, and prophesying future-forward continuity. The poem contains admonitions for future rulers, encouraging them to love learning, persevere in good governance, be filial and brotherly, and uphold orthodox foundations of the state. The poem stays faithful to its description in the preface, demonstrating "the remoteness in time of the dynastic foundation and the difficulties of the royal task,"[9] encompassing the past and the future of the state enterprise of Chosŏn.

Kinship imagination is central to the first vernacular Korean text, which appears quite unruly, attempting to arrest the historical narrative and expand the temporal horizons of the dynasty. This is, however, the first and last vernacular Korean text that verges into the space of public state visibility. I discuss the reasons of its singularity shortly below.

The Korean Script and Literature in Korean

King Sejong's edict promulgated the invention of the Korean script in the following terms:

> The sounds of our language differ from those of Chinese and are not easily communicated by using Chinese graphs. Many among the ignorant, therefore, though they wish to express their sentiments in writing, have been unable to communicate. Considering this situation with compassion, I have newly devised twenty-eight letters. I wish only that the people will learn them easily and use them conveniently in daily life.[10]

While twentieth-century postcolonial Korean scholarship inaugurated the creation of vernacular Korean script as a move that valorizes Korea's cultural and linguistic distinctness from China, the script, in fact, was devised as a vehicle for proximity. A Chosŏn official's gaffe at the Ming court provides a case in point. In 1389, during his visit to Ming China, Chosŏn state councilor Yi Saek (1328–96) decides to speak to the Ming emperor in Chinese, in which Yi was fluent, having served in the bureaucracy of the preceding Yuan dynasty. Hongwu Emperor (r. 1368–98), however, having not understood a single word of Yi Saek's speech, laughs him off: "Your Chinese sounds like that of Nahachu," referring to a Mongol warlord who surrendered to the Ming. Hongwu, then, warns: "those [envoys] who cannot speak Chinese will not be allowed to visit."[11]

Diplomatic relationship with Ming China was integral to the legitimacy and identity of the Chosŏn state. Ming China was a powerful political and military ally, and a source of knowledge and culture. Exchanges of the tribute missions and diplomatic correspondence required familiarity with the written and spoken idiom of the Ming standard of Chinese. Hence, among the first publications in vernacular Korean script after its promulgation was the 1449 *Vernacular Manual to the Correct Rhymes of the Hongwu Reign* (*Hongmu chŏngun yŏkhun* 洪武正韻譯訓). *The Correct Rhymes of the Hongwu Reign* (Ch. *Hongwu zhengyun*;

K. *Hongmu chŏngun* 洪武正韻), published in China in 1375, standardized pro-nunciations under the aegis of the newly founded Ming dynasty, repudiating the Mongol pronunciations of the Yuan. Sejong's linguistic project, creating the means of accurate phonetic representation, at once enabled the rendition of the phonetic element of Chinese writing and the speech aspect of the Korean language, which was distinct from the Chinese.

However, it was specifically its distance from the written literary Chinese culture that made the Korean script an object of intense court debate, which is epitomized in Ch'oe Malli's (?–1445) memorial. For Ch'oe, reliance on pronun-ciation rather than graphic meaning distanced Koreans from the civilized realm of culture. In addition, it would introduce a rift between the learned standard of higher civil officials, who studied Confucian classics and literary Chinese compositions, and lower clerks, who could easily gain access to government ranks through the mastery of just twenty-eight vernacular letters, which would obviate the need to learn the classics.[12] While Sejong censored the memo-rial and proceeded with the promulgation of the Korean script, Ch'oe Malli's protestation captured the stratification of power and prestige that continued to distinguish literary Chinese and vernacular Korean writing. Accordingly, throughout the two centuries following its creation, vernacular Korean script is used mainly in auxiliary, technical publication of such texts as interpreter manuals, vernacular glosses to Confucian classics, and medical treatises.

A cultural, political, and civilizational achievement of Sejong's reign, the Korean script found its first use in the glorification of the royal ancestral tree. However, almost immediately after composition, *The Songs of Flying Dragons* fell into oblivion. Just fifty years after the presentation of the verses, hardly any mention of this text can be found in the historical sources. The verses be-came incorporated into the musical state rituals, surviving in this capacity. At times, the historical commentaries of *The Songs* were consulted.[13] Vernacular aspect of *The Songs* hardly drew much attention in the court culture that privi-leged literary Chinese learning. Sejong's attempt to create a vernacular saga of the royal family tree remained incommensurate with the inferior position of vernacular Korean script, which, as Ch'oe Malli's memorial illustrates, was never considered the appropriate scriptural medium for the affairs of the state, remaining in this position until the late nineteenth century.

While the court proved an unlikely place for the flourishing of vernacular Korean writing, it was eventually adopted into elite women's learning curricu-lum; this, in turn, prompted unprecedented development of fictional prose. Starting in the late seventeenth century, when patrilineal kinship took root in Chosŏn Korea, women's lives became gradually domestic, as they lost their freedom to divorce, inherit property, and freely move outside their homes.

Instead of learning, women's productive social identities prescribed embodied, domestic work: child bearing, observing the rules of bodily comportment such as chastity and circumspection in speech, preparing food and clothing for their family. Despite this formal proscription of learning, elite women's vernacular Korean literacy was understood to have a productive social function. Women were expected to send letters of greetings to keep up with the family's immediate kin and social circle. Among the earliest surviving artifacts written in vernacular Korean script are the two letters of Na Sin'gŏl (1461–1524), written to his wife, Madame Maeng of Sinch'ang, around 1490. The letters were included in her coffin and exhumed in 2011. In addition, a variety of other sixteenth-century vernacular Korean letters, dispatched to or by women, testify to the proliferation of vernacular literacy through epistolary networks. Lineage novels—texts that expounded the fundamental values of patrilineal kinship—similarly took central position in elite women's culture. These novels were at once pedagogical and entertaining, and their manuscripts served as first learning primers, with young girls acquiring reading and calligraphic skills by transcribing the volumes that were usually handed down from their elder female kin.

The graphic distinctiveness of vernacular Korean script allowed it to constitute the domain of female literacy with its own connotations of aesthetic and social value. Written in the Korean script and mostly transmitted through kinship networks and through the hands of closest acquaintance, lineage novels occupied a much more circumscribed cultural domain than writings in literary Chinese, the public literary script par excellence. While the authors of lineage novels are unknown, these texts were transcribed and circulated by elite women. The interior, vernacular, women-centered cultural realm of the lineage novel created an alternative narrative space. This privatized dimension of lineage novels' circulation allowed these texts to dwell on the unruly passions of several generations of their protagonists—on the pages of lineage novels, these feelings signal that generational reinscription of the kinship norm is a process fraught with difficulty. Describing the domestic and everyday and circulating among female audiences, Korean lineage novels were coeval with the period when the patrilineal kinship ideology was central to the society and culture of Korea: between the late seventeenth and early twentieth centuries.

The Record of So Hyŏnsŏng

While lineage novels receive very few external references in contemporary sources, *The Record of So Hyŏnsŏng*[14] is the earliest known lineage novel mentioned by title. Kwŏn Sŏp (1671–1759), a late Chosŏn man of letters, records

3.2. Leaf from *The Record of So Hyŏnsŏng*, undated. Manuscript. Image courtesy of the Kyujanggak Archive.

the books that his mother, Madame Yi of Yongin (1652–1712), transcribed in her own hand and then distributed among her descendants (see figure 3.2). Among the numerous volumes is *The Record of So Hyŏnsŏng*. Based on the life span of Madame Yi of Yongin, it appears that *The Record of So Hyŏnsŏng* was in circulation in the late seventeenth century, which places it in the very beginning of the lineage novel tradition.

Lineage novels often aspire to maintain a connection to documentary genres of kinship writing, claiming the veracity and prestige of these texts to add weight to fiction narrative. *The Record of So Hyŏnsŏng* is remarkably reflective of this literary context, this novel being packaged in a number of paratextual references. The main text of the novel is divided into two parts: "The Original Biography of Minister So" (*So sŭngsang ponjŏn* 蘇丞相本傳), which traces the life of So Hyŏnsŏng, and "The Record of the Three Generations of the So Lineage" (*So ssi samdae rok* 蘇氏三代錄), which continues with the lives of his descendants. "The Original Biography," in turn, is appended with a "Separate Preface to the Original Biography of Minister So" (*So sŭngsang ponjŏn pyŏlsŏ* 蘇

丞相本傳別序). These paratexts mimic the organization of documentary narratives. The final, fifteenth, volume of the novel ends with "Yu Munsŏng's Dream Journey to Mount Chaun" (*Yu Munsŏng Chaunsan mongyurok* 劉文成紫雲山夢遊錄), which records an eyewitness encounter with the remaining descendants of So Hyŏnsŏng. This novel's claim to veracity is further underscored, as So Hyŏnsŏng becomes the progenitor of the three famed Song dynasty literary masters: So Sun (Ch. Su Xun 1009–66), and his two sons, So Sik (Ch. Su Shi; 1037–1101) and So Ch'ŏl (Ch. Su Zhe; 1039–1112).

The preface to the biography articulates the main premises of funerary writing. Posthumous biography was a genre with at once personal and historical dimensions; it emplaced the record of a life into the rubric of socially productive ideal and committed the deceased to memory in the form of moral exemplar. Biographies of exemplary persons were included in state histories, and elite families of Chosŏn created their own records, which were transmitted through generations. After an illustrious career at court and having built a household that is prosperous and morally upright, So Hyŏnsŏng, the patriarch of the So lineage, receives highest honors of state. Emperor Injong of Song (Ch. Renzong, r.102–63) then orders P'o Chŭng (Ch. Bao Zheng; 999–1062) and Yŏ Yigan (Ch. Lü Yijian; 979–1044), who were actual historical figures, to compile his life record. While lineage novels are usually set in China, they unmistakably describe the realities of Chosŏn kinship. Claims to historical accuracy, as well as the choice of setting, endowed vernacular Korean lineage novels with attributes of nonfictional literary Chinese writing, lending these texts more prestige and hence making them better suited for the eyes of elite women, their main readers.

The relevance of the account of So Hyŏnsŏng's life proves to extend over centuries. The dream journey that closes the novel depicts Yu Munsŏng (Ch. Liu Wencheng 1311–75), adviser to the founder of the Ming dynasty, the Hongwu emperor, traveling to the old residence of the So lineage roughly three centuries after So Hyŏnsŏng's death. Living the life of a recluse and roaming the mountains, Yu encounters a stele that identifies the location of the So lineage mansion. Discovering So Hyŏnsŏng's gravesite, Yu dozes off and has a dream encounter with So Hyŏnsŏng's son, So Unsŏng. Unsŏng points to the location of the family's buried records, interred in a hurry, as the last descendants were scattering away under the onslaught of Genghis Khan's invasion. Unsŏng's spirit, then, requests that Yu exhume the record and spread the word of his ancestors' deeds. *The Record of So Hyŏnsŏng* is emplaced into an extended historical horizon, as it bridges the centuries that pass between the collapse of the Song dynasty and the rise of the Ming, asserting the timeless relevance of moral virtue.

Returning to the circumstances of the biography compilation, it is worth noting the documents that come into the hands of the compilers: family chronicles, recorded daily at the So mansion by permanently stationed scribes, their presence reminiscent of royal diarists, whose writing would later provide material for historical compilation. This history-like record of the So household becomes pointedly visible in the narrative, as it is often consulted to clarify the course of some domestic events. At one moment, there is a lively exchange between So Hyŏnsŏng and the diarist. One of So Hyŏnsŏng's daughters-in-law practices magic to cast a spell on her husband after protracted dispute. Just when So Hyŏnsŏng discusses this affair with his mother and proposes to put the incident off the record, one diarist stands outside the window. The diarist remonstrates with So Hyŏnsŏng, saying that he never gets to write down anything interesting, while his colleague ends up transcribing all the juicy stories. So Hyŏnsŏng agrees only reluctantly, and the record is made.

To make sure nothing is amiss, the compilers verify the details of the family chronicle during personal conversations with So Hyŏnsŏng's descendants. As a result of these efforts, P'o Chŭng and Yŏ Yigan produce a uniquely accurate account: "People's good and bad deeds are not embellished . . . therefore, this rightful and accurate account is indeed true history."[15] This praise, however, is qualified: "In this text, however, there are very few descriptions of joys and sorrows, laughter and conversations of So Hyŏnsŏng. The readers might get impressed by the lofty conduct of Lord So, but the text has little flourish. Therefore, his descendants created a flowery account,"[16] entitled *The Record of So Hyŏnsŏng*. According to this statement, the novel grows out of the normative biography, itself a result of painstakingly described compilation process. Through this embedded textual account, the lineage novel elaborates the prescriptive moral genre by bringing it closer to the everyday life of kinship community. This domestic everydayness delays and extends the fulfillment of generational teleology: before assuming their prescribed social roles, the novel's protagonists have to come to terms with the unruly feelings that threaten to disarticulate the norm.

The Record of So Hyŏnsŏng itself is divided into two parts, with the first one narrating So Hyŏnsŏng's struggle to establish firm foundations for the lineage, and the second tracing the lives of his descendants. So Hyŏnsŏng comes from a household, "with generations extending like branches of a large tree,"[17] but he is conceived late in his parents' life and born after the death of his father, the latter being the only son in eight generations. From an early age, So Hyŏnsŏng is exceptionally filial, mindful of the precarious position of his family line, and allowing himself no misstep. When So Hyŏnsŏng's friends invite female entertainers, Hyŏnsŏng's mother, Madame Yang, reprimands her son sternly: "extravagant lifestyle does not befit you, bereft of your father, and having to take care of your lonely mother."[18] Upon the first announcement of the civil service examination, which selects talented individuals for service in government bureaucracy, So Hyŏnsŏng's mother immediately encourages him to participate with the following words: "It is not that I am eager about achievement and fame, but you are my only son, and therefore cannot miss the examination without a good reason."[19] Madame Yang's self-vindication highlights the unseemly aspect of unchecked ambition, but the urgent task of lineage building supersedes her reservations. To be sure, once the future of the So lineage is secure, So Hyŏnsŏng does his very best to prevent his own children from early examination success, encouraging them instead to focus on cultivating their moral character.

Apart from the issue of social status, the task of lineage building requires vigilant supervision of domestic affairs to avoid tarnishing the lineage's reputation. So Hyŏnsŏng has two sisters, born to concubine mothers. One of them, Kyoyŏng, takes a lover during her husband's exile. Once the affair transpires, Madame Yang, the de facto head of the So household, orders Kyoyŏng to take poison. Kyoyŏng's birth mother, Matron Sŏk, pleads with Hyŏnsŏng, "How can you only listen to the words of your mother and disregard the emotions that siblings share?"[20] To this, Hyŏnsŏng responds that though it pains him greatly, the situation allows no easy solution. He also advises Matron Sŏk to withhold her grief in front of Madame Yang, who, in her heart, is also devastated by this turn of events. Despite her grief, Matron Sŏk is impressed with the moral uprightness and clarity of Hyŏnsŏng's discourse. This dispensation of domestic justice is strikingly violent. Matron Sŏk's plea with Hyŏnsŏng, moreover, serves to dramatize and underscore the unrelenting moral discipline called on to maintain the uprightness of domestic morals. From this moment on, So Hyŏnsŏng performs loyal service to the country, acquires three wives and numerous descendants, and presides over his household. "The Separate Biography of Minister So," allegedly embellished by his descendants, is a story of austerity, dedication to family fortunes, and absolute moral integrity.

When the novel turns to the lives of So Hyŏnsŏng's descendants, continuing with "The Record of the Three Generations of the So Lineage," the contours of domestic life change significantly: once the So lineage secures social status and multiple descendants, this framework of stability opens space for personal conflicts. It must be noted that So Hyŏnsŏng, having become the head of his own household, does have to deal with a variety of everyday troubles, such as jealousy and discord between his multiple wives. All throughout, he, however, remains rather blameless himself. The ensuing narrative is focused on the life of So Hyŏnsŏng's son, Unsŏng. Notably, Unsŏng is not the first, but the third son of the glorious minister: not being the heir, he is relieved of absolute responsibility for the future of the lineage and his story offsets his father's biography with unruly detail.

It is common for the male protagonists of lineage novels to possess not only extensive learning and moral power, but also extreme physical attractiveness. Unsŏng is not an exception to this rule, and during one of his visits to the palace, Unsŏng's looks come to the attention of Princess Myŏnghyŏn. Having taken an immediate liking to him, the princess requests her father, the emperor, to arrange the marriage, even despite the fact that Unsŏng is already married, and in disregard of the remonstrations offered by the So family. Having entered the So household, the princess reveals her difficult and stubborn nature. She indulges in luxury and demands honors that do not befit her familial rank of daughter-in-law. Despite her continued effort, she fails to win her husband's heart, as Unsŏng bitterly resents this marital arrangement. With her father's power at her side, the princess is often able to get her way at the So mansion. Unsŏng, however, continues to pine for his expelled wife, Miss Hyŏng, expelled to make space for the princess. As Unsŏng's love sickness puts his life in peril, the emperor consents to Miss Hyŏng's return. Even then, disorder persists, as the princess continues to torment her rival for her husband's affection. In one especially violent scene, the princess invites Miss Hyŏng to view lotuses and then attempts to drown her in a pond with the help of her court ladies. Miss Hyŏng is saved accidentally by one of Unsŏng's brothers, who gets a maid's word of the trouble. The plots of violence are frequent on lineage novels' pages, attesting to the strength of passions that play out when the kinship norm disagrees with personal circumstances. The princess's violence can be contextualized in the institutionalized polygyny and the jealousy it produces. A straightforwardly villainous figure, the princess embodies the negativity of female lust. Only males in the lineage novel are allowed to act on their desire, pursuing the objects of their fancy.

It is not only women, however, who embody unruly feelings in the lineage novel. Unsŏng's desperate longing for his expelled wife, similarly, occupies a significant part of the story. Following the incident at the lotus pond, Miss Hyŏng's father grows gradually apprehensive of the princess's hatred toward his daughter. In order to protect Miss Hyŏng, after one of her visits of her parents' home, the family decides to feign her death. Hearing the news of Miss Hyŏng's death, Unsŏng immediately rushes to her parents' house to mourn the corpse. Upon arrival, he, however, encounters barricaded doors, with a servant explaining that Unsŏng is not to be allowed inside, as he was the chief cause of Miss Hyŏng's suffering. After a raucous negotiation, Unsŏng fights his way in, causing great confusion among the domestics, who quickly manufacture a material proof of Miss Hyŏng's expiration. To this purpose, they place a rice chest in the middle of the house, saying that the body of Unsŏng's wife is inside. Unsŏng, however, is not to be fooled. He discovers Miss Hyŏng alive and well inside the house; with the help of his brother Unsŏng tricks her into coming back home with him and hides her in his aunt's house. Unsŏng's behavior hardly fits with the prescription of filiality and respect he owes his elders: his father and father-in-law. He causes a riot at his father-in-law's house and defies the authority of his own father when using his brother's help to trick Miss Hyŏng to return. Receiving a severe flogging from his father, Unsŏng pays the price for his escapades. He grows up to be a moral head of his own household, but the narrative of his youthful mischief inaugurates the contestation of the kinship norm as integral to the narrative of personal life.

All trials of the So lineage come to a happy resolution: So Hyŏnsŏng's descendants are numerous and prosperous, the lineage maintains its good repute and fame through its descendants' renown, and the illustrious ancestor receives an official biography composed by imperial decree. Lineage novels, in this way, prove to be infinitely writeable texts: they extend the generational fabric with the stories of their protagonists' unruly feelings and grow like trees. Individual novels often cover between three and four generations of the central lineage, and it is not uncommon for these texts to have between one and three sequels, often composed by different authors. Much longer than other texts of Korean fictional prose, spanning tens and hundreds of manuscript volumes, lineage novels stand out in the literary space of premodern Korea.

The few external references to these texts that exist suggest that men were proud of their mothers' creation of these novels' manuscripts, which were reverently transmitted among descendants. When these family-held manuscripts were loaned to be copied—by neighbors or kin—and lost, this was recorded as a great disappointment. The novels' margin marks similarly record words of praise for the scribal activity of mothers, aunts, and grandmothers. While men too likely participated in this elite vernacular culture, it did not hold sufficient prestige to be linked with their names. A genre that likely united elite men and women as readers and writers during their pastime in the family compound, the lineage novel shaped a narrative where generational continuity of kinship was crisscrossed with unruly feelings that reflected the personal negotiations of kinship norm. Pedagogical and sophisticated in their nondogmatic presentation of personal life, lineage novels formed a flourishing vernacular Korean literary tradition.

Trees That Grow

The invention of the Korean script in the mid-fifteenth century and the composition of two "first" vernacular Korean texts occurred in the context of a Confucian culture that outlined the principal rules of moral human sociality, holding family and kinship to be the crucial sites for the inculcation of moral hierarchies that grounded the totality of social relations. The affection and hierarchy between father and son was, therefore, a model for ruler-subject relationship. This model constituted the ethical ideal for the relationship between Chosŏn Korea and its suzerain state, Ming China—a crucial ally in matters of military, economy, and culture. This shared civilizational repertoire was captured in the literary Chinese canon of classics and histories, which constituted the core learning curriculum for elite men of Korea. The order of human bonds was to be maintained in the manner of generational reinscription, where descendants' filial reverence for virtuous ancestral exemplars guaranteed that these values be transmitted in perpetuity. Generation, in this cultural framework, was a symbolic form of temporal organization, which received various articulations across a host of literary genres in early modern Korea.

The Songs of Flying Dragons is an attempt to create a vernacular Korean hagiography to the royal Chosŏn bloodline, and this text's narrative idiom and scriptural medium are both grafted onto their literary Chinese counterparts. It is worth noting the linguistic hybridity of *The Songs of Flying Dragons*. While Korean verses retain pride of place within the text, they occupy a small portion, with the commentary, preface, presentation, and postface being composed in literary Chinese. The vernacular Korean of the verses is, furthermore, not self-sufficient, containing large chunks of the transliterated Chinese text, unintelligible without the knowledge of the original. The tree with deep roots that captures the longevity and moral power of the Chosŏn royal house reaches in two directions: its roots converge with the ancient moral examples of Chinese history, and the indefinite expansion of its branches is enabled by the descendants' moral efforts to carry on the ancestral example of good governance.

This tree grows in a space of its own, daringly constituted by the newly devised script, which at the moment of its promulgation was as yet unencoded, without a firm set of literary conventions and audiences of its own. This allowed the narrative of the royal ancestors to tower above the historical record of power struggles and reach beyond the actual time frame of the historical life span of the dynasty. The realm of state narrative in Chosŏn, however, remained dominated by literary Chinese writing, and *The Songs of Flying Dragons*, composed under the orders and careful direction of King Sejong, remains a maverick attempt to introduce vernacular Korean into the realm of state discourse.

The Record of So Hyŏnsŏng, which is among the earliest known examples of the lineage novel tradition, postdates *The Songs* by two centuries. The generational imagination of this text indexes a moment of historical transformation—

the emergence of patrilineal kinship and the spread of vernacular Korean literacy among elite women of Chosŏn, who were excluded from the domain of literary Chinese learning or public social roles. Generational reinscription of the kinship norm, captured in the lineage novels, similarly, makes a clear reference to the literary Chinese canon: fiction is rooted in the moralistic literature of funerary writing. But rather than rising into the epic space, this vernacular tradition takes a trajectory toward the everyday of kinship life, showing that generational reinscription of the norm is a process of practical negotiation between unruly feelings and the kinship norm.

The culture of elite women, of which the lineage novel was part, represented the first attempt in which vernacular Korean writing achieved an aestheticized dimension, forming a cultural domain of its own alongside the literary Chinese culture of elite males. This coalescence of literary energy in the vernacular Korean scriptural realm then paved the way for wider proliferation of fictional prose. The economic developments and the spread of vernacular Korean literacy to wider popular audiences in the eighteenth and nineteenth centuries turned vernacular Korean fiction into a popular pastime. Accessible through rental libraries and cheaply made woodblock imprints, popular vernacular novels were not nearly as long, nor as complex in language, as lineage novels, and their most popular motif was battlefield adventure. Nevertheless, these later vernacular developments are traceable to the constellation of literary energy that produced massive lineage novels, whose narratives of multigenerational lineages circulated in exquisite manuscripts transcribed by elite women's hands.

The Songs of Flying Dragons is a dead branch in vernacular Korean literary development: it reaches into the oxymoronic, impossible space of vernacular Korean state epic, untenable in the court culture dominated by the code of literary Chinese civil learning. The flourishing generational trees of vernacular Korean lineage novels, on the other hand, came to thrive in their localized, domestic domain, as precursors of more extensive vernacular Korean literary realm fleshed out in the popular literature of early modern Korea.

Further Reading

Chizhova, Ksenia. "Bodies of Texts: Women Calligraphers and the Elite Vernacular Culture in Late Chosŏn Korea (1392–1910)," *Journal of Asian Studies* 77, no. 1 (2018): 59–81.

Chizhova, Ksenia, trans. "The Pledge at the Banquet of Moon-Gazing Pavilion: Gender, Fiction and the Discourse of Emotion," in *An Anthology of Premodern*

Korean Prose: Literary Selections from the Tenth to the Nineteenth Centuries, edited by Michael J. Pettid, Gregory N. Evon, and Chan E. Park, 2018.

Cho Hyeran, et al., trans. and ed. *So Hyŏnsŏng rok* [The record of So Hyŏnsŏng], 2010, vols. 1–4.

Deuchler, Martina. *The Confucian Transformation of Korea: A Study of Society and Ideology*, 1992.

Lee, Peter H., trans. and ed. *Songs of Flying Dragons: A Critical Reading*, 1975.

4

Indian

SHELDON POLLOCK

There are two obvious conceptual complexities that all of us face when trying to make sense of the problem of "the beginning of literature." In fact, that problem only becomes one when these complexities are understood to be, well, complex. The first complexity is what we mean by "literature," the second, what we mean by "beginning." We need some agreement about those two categories before we can investigate, as the editors of this volume invited us contributors to do, "the procedures, structures, and institutions that encouraged the development of distinct literatures." As you will see, I take emic, local, or what I call "traditionist," views of both categories, "literature" and "beginning," as seriously as I take "historicist" ones: that is, what people in the tradition believed to have happened, and what we think really happened.

I want to walk you through some elementary aspects of these two categories in precolonial India. With some new clarity, I hope, in our minds about literature and beginnings, I will next address the literary-cultural mechanisms of inauguration, and what I see as the typical social-political context where this inauguration found its ground. Since I have been tasked with accounting for all India (or South Asia; I use the terms synonymously), and since the beginnings of literature in India offer a breathtaking spectacle of literary proliferation without parallel outside western Europe, I will have to generalize shamelessly, though I temper my generalizations by offering detail in several cases that have been the subject of recent scholarly studies. Please remember that mine is only one story among several possible others.

Once this overall picture of vernacular beginnings is sketched, I will turn to the case that lies at the foundation of them all and that nonetheless is the most obscure: how Sanskrit literature itself may be thought to begin. In saying "foundation of them all" I must be clear about the fact that I am making one important omission here, the case of Persian and Arabic. These two literary languages were used for more than a millennium in South Asia, and they also interacted in various ways with Indian vernaculars. But to include them would risk making an already complex story chaotic, and testing my already overstretched abilities.

Literature

I readily acknowledge how usefully Western theory has muddied the question "What is literature?" As others have said and as I myself have often reiterated, the term "literature" needs to be understood as a functional rather than an ontological category. In this it is rather like the category "weed," as Terry Eagleton once put it: for one person a pest, for another a flower, for yet a third, dinner. Any discourse can be read as literature—say, the *Astronomica*, to take an example in honor of our senior editor—or "unread" as literature—the *Aeneid*, for example, as a book of predictions. Precisely as in the case of Manilius and Vergil, in India an astronomical text like the *Bṛhatsaṃhitā* could be read as poetry, and poetry, such as *Rāmāyaṇa*, could be used in a quasi-bibliomantic, or at least magical, fashion (as for example in a *pārāyaṇa*, or daily reading/ recitation, of the *Sundarkāṇḍa*, the fifth book of the *Vālmīki Rāmāyaṇa*).

That the works of the two authors in question, Varahamihira (sixth century CE) and Valmiki (second century BCE?), did cross genres and could lend themselves to literary reading and unreading, suggests strongly that, indeed, function rather than ontology is the key diagnostic of "literature." It is not what the text is, as such—no text, and nothing, is anything *as such*—that makes it literature, but what people do with it: whether—as I will suggest in moment— they seek the rewards of information or those of imagination. Yet, while that may be largely true, readers in India believed, or were encouraged to believe, that there is in fact a clear boundary to be crossed (such that the migration across it, as just described, did not always go uncontested). And at that boundary we can perceive that the functionalist prejudice of Western theory requires supplementation by traditionist knowledge. Such knowledge in the Indian case shows that contemporary arguments against essentializing literature can themselves be unhistorical essentializations. In India, this knowledge is anything but vague. Indeed, we can point to a very carefully theorized conception of the difference between forms of discourse.

There are several typologies dividing up the realm of "discourse," in Sanskrit *vāṅmaya*, "all that is made of language." One typology separates vāṅmaya into two large classes, *śāstra* and *kāvya*, or works of systematic thought, and literature. For our purposes here the two types of discourse may be more generally distinguished, as I have elsewhere tried to distinguish them, as, on the one hand, the "documentary," or informational, constative, contentual, and, on the other, the "workly," or imaginative, performative, expressive (terms, or something like them, first introduced by the intellectual historian Dominick LaCapra, borrowing in turn from Heidegger). A second typology, which I'll adduce in a moment, supports this distinction. Although other traditions may have drawn a similar contrast, I doubt any was as fully conceptualized as in India: there, the *differentia specifica* of the discourse species called *kāvya* within the genus of "what-is-made-of-language" obsessed thinkers for almost two millennia, in their quest to discover what they called the *ātman*, the essence or soul, of kāvya.

I will later return to the historical moment of the constitution of kāvya in practice in the early centuries of the common era. What I want to stress now is that kāvya was constituted and conceptualized for three languages and three only: Sanskrit and two others, called Prakrit and Apabhramsha, that may best be thought of as dialects of Sanskrit, to be used for certain registers, especially the demotic, rustic, and feminine, and genres, such as the pastoral (a crude generalization requiring the nuance of Andrew Ollett's recent work). Note, in passing, that none of these three names is an ethnonym, like "French" or "English," but rather a linguistic descriptor, "perfected," "natural," and "degraded," respectively (and very approximately). More important, Sanskrit along with its two additional literary registers were what we might class as "cosmopolitan" both in their linguistic aspect (where they were strictly regulated in grammar and lexicon) and in the language ideology explicitly argued out by the users of the languages. That is, the three cosmopolitan languages were believed to exist in what could be called a *panchronic* and *panchoric* flatland, where any variation across time and space was denied—and any absence, too: Sanskrit and its two associated dialect-like codes were believed to travel everywhere and to be everywhere the same. In these features they differed radically from those languages, regional or vernacular, that, thanks to the powers that Sanskrit itself conferred, were eventually to become literary and to supplement or even supplant Sanskrit. All these languages were—and all knew themselves to be—restricted in both space and time: that is, they were *epichoric* and *epichronic* (if, in the latter case, we are prepared to coin yet another new term).

This replacement happened through a process of *vernacularization*, which like any process, presupposes a commencement. Here matters get a little complicated, and we need to reflect on how things may in general be thought to begin before we get to vernacular beginnings in particular.

Beginnings

There is a range of conceptual, cognitive, and ideological problems hovering around the idea of beginnings, for which, so far as I can see, we possess no good comprehensive account, as least for the history of culture. Many people, like Michel Foucault, do not like beginnings. You will recall how Foucault (prompted by Nietzsche's shifting use of the terms *Herkunft* and *Ursprung*) came to stress the opposition between his favored historical method of genealogy and the despised "search for 'origins.'" The latter, he told us, is "an attempt to capture the exact essence of things, their purest possibilities," whereas genealogy knows that things have no timeless essences, no essential secret—other than "the secret that they have no essence," that "their essence was fabricated in a piecemeal fashion." When we move from Foucault's vast world of moral philosophy to our small world of literary history, scholars similarly tell us that "discovering the origin of the sonnet," to take that one tiny case explored in Karla Mallette's wonderful book on the history of Sicilian literature, "is a grail that has become less compelling" because "origin studies themselves have come to seem less important" (2005, 77). This despite the fact that thirteenth-century Sicilian literary culture, about which this observation is made, is celebrated for the poets' "keen awareness of the literary history that preceded them" and their "willingness to experiment with received traditions." But how are we even to identify experiment if we are indifferent to knowing, or ready even to deny the possibility of knowing, "origins," that is, how newness enters the literary world? The essence of the sonnet was no doubt "fabricated in a piecemeal fashion," but when Giacomo da Lentini finished his fabrication a poetic form achieved a kind of existence it did not have before. And it made history—or, more important, successive generations of Tuscan poets acted as if it did. If traditionism affirms what historicism denies, that surely counts for something, for it tells us what those historical agents thought and did.

It should be clear that things like sonnets with their "exact essences" do originate and make history, in some hard historicist sense, and we can in principle capture that origin and chart its history of effects. At the same time, actors in a tradition will, in some soft traditionist sense, have various ideas and practices, often discrepant vis-à-vis our hard history, about how things originate and make history, and their ideas must be an equal part of our study of beginnings as well as of "literature," for those ideas and practices have their own effects. I turn now to the process of origins that I will call *vernacularization*.

Vernacularization and Some Other Long Words

To understand the cultural processes of vernacularization I have to introduce two closely linked ideas via terms I find rebarbative but for which I find no suitable alternatives: *literization* and *literarization*. The former is just a translation of the German *Verschriftlichung* and refers to the fact and process of inscribing what, to the degree that we can reconstruct it, had previously been entirely oral. The latter refers to the procedures for turning a "documentary" language into "workly" one: into the expressive, the imaginative, or—in India—into kāvya.

My purpose in introducing these two terms is to provide some analytical language for the beginning of literature in general. They also enable us to chart what for me is one of the most instructive facts of the beginnings of South Asian literature, and what I actually first deployed those two terms to account for: namely, the time lag between the initial inscription of a language, its literization, and its attaining embodiment in kāvya, its literarization. In other words, these two processes are by no means coterminous, and while the former is the necessary condition of the latter, it is not a sufficient condition: Not only can a language exist without literization, but literization does not invariably lead to literarization.

But why is literization essential to the question of literary beginning in any case? One could certainly argue that the category of kāvya itself may have displaced earlier, alternative, forms of literary culture in any given vernacular world. Fair enough, but for one thing, none of those forms is anywhere extant. Consider the case of Kannada, the language spoken today in the modern Indian state of Karnataka.

Those genres mentioned in the first surviving Kannada text, the *Kavirājamārga* (*The Way of the Poet King*), a sort of *de Vulgari Eloquentia* for India, have vanished without trace (I will address in due course the case of Tamil). Second, such an argument would only be substituting one type of beginning for another, and, what is more important, one that the tradition, by its *choice* not to preserve, did not consecrate as a beginning. The same holds for the postulation of "oral literature." However much and however reasonably we philologists may be inclined to find the expressive in the oral texts of South Asia, to which we now have broad access thanks to the work of several generations of anthropologists and folklorists, traditional theorists of kāvya in India never accorded them the status of literature; they never even mentioned them except under the rubric of "song" (*gīti, gāna*, etc.), which itself was never considered kāvya. It was—and let me stress this point—the invention and spread of writing in the last centuries BCE that drew a new boundary between the purely oral and kāvya. You might say, therefore (as I have in fact already said in *Language of the Gods*), that "writing was never essential to Indian literature— until literature became *literature*" (2006, 4) that is, kāvya.

Two points need to be stressed about these processes. First, let me repeat that the attainment of inscription was not inevitable for any given language. Second, if inscription was a necessary condition for literature it was not a sufficient condition. Not all languages attained written form, and not all written languages immediately and ipso facto became literary languages. Nothing about either literization and literarization is natural. Both were slow and uneven developments that occurred under particular and, generally speaking, specifiable conditions, where social-political factors, including imitation and competition among rival polities, were crucial.

It may be illogical to speak of "languages" in the case of codes that never achieved literization, insofar as that process (and even more so literarization) is what enables a language to be known, named, and distinguished from others—to be conceptually constituted as *a language*—in the first place. But we know of numerous cases of what I have to still call languages (or "languages") in South Asia that never found written representation until the colonial or modern era: Kodagu, Konkani, and Tulu are examples in the south, and Dogri in the north; even Panjabi in the northwest was a late (eighteenth-century) participant in the two processes. We also know that the inaugural moment of inscription could be an object of a highly self-conscious awareness that something new and unprecedented was taking place. The author of one of the earliest works, if not the earliest work, of Old Hindi (depending on how one defines "Old Hindi," a question we return to momentarily) was a Sufi romance: the *Story of Chanda* (*Candāyan*), composed in the late fourteenth century by a Muslim, Maulana Daud. The author tells us how (according to Allison Busch) he adapted a love story current in his milieu (he speaks of it as *gāi*, or "sung"), and formalized it into a literary work (2011, 208–9). He did this in part, as again he explicitly reports, by learning to write in "Turki" script under his teacher's tutelage and, having done so, by recording in that same script what he composed. It is all as if this had never been done before for Hindi—as, so far as we can tell, it had likely not.

Why some "languages" were chosen for literization and not others is a question I cannot answer with much confidence, or why and under precisely what circumstances those chosen were first literized. What we can establish securely, however, is the temporal discontinuity—or time lag as I called it earlier—between that process and literarization. The enormous epigraphical record of premodern South Asia allows us to chart this discontinuity with some precision, and it is often vast. Take again the case of Kannada. Our earliest lithic inscriptions date to the early fifth century CE, and from that point on until the end of the ninth century all Kannada writing is documentary: deeds, donations, proclamations, and the like. There is no evidence whatever for literary production until the last quarter of the ninth century, when kāvya and its philological appurtenances (works on rhetoric, prosody, lexicography) began to appear and be preserved at royal courts. The Kannada case is paradigmatic, and it has a lot—though not everything—to tell us about the beginning of literature in India. The two most important things it tells us about are, first, the processes of *culture* at work in this beginning, and, second, the processes of *power*.

Vernacular literatures in India often began via a cultural process I've called *superposition*. To write vernacular literature was to transpose to a given regional world—indeed, a world that thereby became meaningfully "regional" in the first place—the cosmopolitan style and aesthetic of Sanskrit (and, to a lesser extent, Prakrit and Apabhramsha), in both form and content. Here is not the place for detail on these matters (which are fully set forth in my *Language of the Gods*), but briefly, in everything from lexicon to figures of speech to the narratives themselves—often episodes from the Sanskrit epics or even appropriations in their entirety—the vernaculars became literary by being local habitations of translocal literariness. This was never translation, which however variously we might define that term was relatively rare in India before the coming of Islamicate cultures (there is no word for it in South Asian languages until the modern period), but something at once more autonomous and fully recognizable as imitation.

The process of *power* at work in all this pertains to the consolidation of the regional kingdoms that arose with the waning of the great imperial power formations (Maurya, Kushana, Gupta) after the middle of the first millennium. In precisely the same way as Sanskrit had been the vehicle for the political aesthetic of the empire form, so regional language became the vehicle for the political aesthetic of what we might call *faute de mieux*, the vernacular polity form. Notionally at least empire is, if not exactly like Augustine's definition of God—an entity whose circumference is everywhere and center nowhere— defined precisely by its unboundedness. And the cultural vehicle of that political unboundedness had to be itself without boundaries, a language that could travel everywhere: languages like Chinese, Latin, Persian . . . and Sanskrit. But the postimperial form has, or rather creates, boundaries, and its cultural vehicle has to be a language that does not travel far: Korean and Vietnamese, for example; or (precolonial) French and Italian, or Georgian and Uzbek . . . and Kannada, Telugu, Marathi, and the rest of the regional languages of the subcontinent.

Into Some Vernacular Weeds

While it is probably obvious, I should state clearly that not all literary life in premodern South Asia can be fully accommodated by the model I have just sketched, and I want briefly to notice here some of the modifications that might be made.

The most important concerns what I have thought of as a *secondary* vernacular revolution. Here, the high register of the "cosmopolitan vernacular" that characterizes the beginnings of so much regional literature was contested, or rather rejected, by insurgent religious groups beginning from about the twelfth century on, who contested the dominance of the Sanskrit cultural and social order (the Sufi role in the vernacularization process, already noted in the case of the *Candāyan*, is another important strand). Why such groups would reject Sanskrit has to do with a crucial aspect of its sociolinguistics that has so far gone unmentioned: its role in the ideological reproduction of unequal power, in particular the power of caste and untouchability. Caste and Sanskrit are coextensive: there is no caste without Sanskrit, and there is no Sanskrit without caste, and this was the case from the very commencement of caste consciousness in the late Vedic period. It is unquestionably true that earlier groups had fundamentally contested social inequality and, accordingly, explicitly rejected Sanskrit in favor of other languages as the vehicle for their contestation. Preeminent among these were the Buddhists, who favored local idioms such as Gandhari (in today's northwest Pakistan), or fashioned an alternative transregional *Schriftsprach* in the form of Pali. But remarkably, some Buddhists, the Sarvastivadin lineage in particular, would eventually accept that language for their scripture (around the beginning of the Common Era). It is also true that lower caste communities, even untouchables, could and did contribute to Sanskrit literature. Yet, it is also unquestionable, if more difficult to explain, that over the course of the second millennium the social boundaries of Sanskrit began to narrow, and access to the language became more restricted. When Kabir, a celebrated Hindi poet of the fifteenth century, contrasted "the stagnant well water of Sanskrit" with "the fresh running currents of the vernacular," he was contrasting a language that was the voice of oppression with a language that was, or could be, the voice of liberation.

Kabir was an early representative of bhakti, or "devotional," movements, as they are called (for which John Stratton Hawley recently provided a historical overview), which introduced a far more demotic, uncourtly, or even anticourtly, element, in both form and content, into the literary bloodstream. Thus, moraic (or other types of "folk") meters, regional lexemes, and highly localized forms of religious affiliation replaced the quantitative versification, derivative vocabulary, and pan-Indic forms of divinity. Also rejected were the quasi-imperial kingly interests of the earlier literature in favor of the politics of the personal, if I may put it that way. In some places, this movement may not have been "secondary," but rather the only revolution there was: the so-called vernacular polity may not have been the necessary and sufficient condition. This devotional movement was long viewed as the dominant driver of vernacularization, in fact, the only driver. As a hypothesis of cultural change, religious radicalism clearly derived something of its plausibility from its parallels with the vernacular Bible movement of the Reformation; indeed, it was founded on one of those "Protestant presuppositions" that have long shaped Indian historiography. But for some regions parts of the hypothesis may still have purchase.

Christian Novetzke has recently argued that this scenario basically explains the case of Marathi, the language of the modern state of Maharashtra in western India, which I had earlier sought to understand according to my standard, culture-power model. In the Marathi area the principal dynasty in the early centuries of vernacularization was actually a Kannada-speaking one, and political inscription in Marathi was accordingly slow to emerge; even once it did, Marathi remained rare (something easy to perceive in the epigraphical record, but harder to explain). For Novetzke, the court had no direct role to play in the production of literary work in Marathi. Indirectly, however, it created around it and sustained the Brahmanical ecumene that then fed the key creators or producers of the first two major works in Marathi, which pretty clearly emerged in religious rather than political contexts.

In the same way I myself have had doubts about the application of my general model to medieval Bengal. There too, as in Maharashtra, the record of courtly patronage for early Bangla literature is much harder to reconstruct, whether because the data are just too thin or because such patronage was less prominent in a political landscape where Islamic sultanates replaced Hindu little kingdoms.

Aside from the sometimes ambiguous role of the court, two other factors can be identified to complicate my model. One concerns space, the other time. Hindi offers a messier spatial case of vernacularization than any other in South Asia, and Tamil an apparently more disruptive temporal one.

What we today call Hindi offers one of the more complicated puzzles in the history of Indian literary beginnings. Allison Busch, among the few scholars to address this matter directly and authoritatively, begins her study by making the important observation that arguments can readily be offered for multiple beginnings, even if the unit of study, "Hindi," had not itself been multiple and did not comprise a wide range of regional and social (caste) dialects (she lists sixteen varieties off the top of her head), stretching across much of north India, that can reasonably be included in the category. One could easily argue that it was the narrative of the nation in twentieth-century India that synthesized this motley congeries of textual cultures into a homogeneous "Hindi" literary tradition, overlooking or suppressing difference (a typical sleight-of-hand of cultural-nationalist discourse). But if we look comprehensively at this congeries, we can still draw some important and—if measured by India's current nationalist ideology equating Hindi and Hindu—explosive conclusions. In one of these dialects, namely Avadhi (the language of Avadh, or what is today eastern Uttar Pradesh), the first Hindi work, the *Candāyan*, already referred to, was composed by a Muslim, Maulana Daud. Daud represents precisely the kind of interstitial figure shuttling across linguistic and cultural divides whom we can find elsewhere in this book, and who will reappear, in my discussion below, in the figure of the Indo-Scythians located at the center of the origins of Sanskrit kāvya. That is to say, nontraditional agents who appropriated the hieratic language of Sanskrit for political-aesthetic purposes. For Daud's work it is also worth emphasizing Busch's observation that neither Persian nor Sanskrit exclusively provided the superposed model; something else is going on, what she suggestively terms multipolar superposition: several traditions with their particular lexicons, metrics, figures, and themes fed into its creation.

A "major resetting of the dial" of literary culture elevated another dialect, Brajbhasha, into a literary language at the end of the sixteenth century, again, within the power sphere of the Mughals, the Muslim imperial dynasty, and their Rajput (Hindu) vassals. Among the most notable of these Brajbhasha poets, Keshavdas, is celebrated as the *ādi-kavi*, or "primordial poet" in the Braj tradition itself, a kind of vernacular Valmiki, who, we shall see, was thus consecrated in the Sanskrit tradition. One last point: in the case of both Avadhi and Brajbhasha literary cultures, Busch points to the fact that the dividing line between the political and religious is not so easily drawn: works participate in both spheres almost by design, such that (in my terms) primary and secondary vernacularization seem to be copresent.

A last case to consider, one potentially disruptive of my model from a temporal perspective, is presented by Tamil, a language of the far southeast of the subcontinent. Its earliest literature is referred to as the *cankam* (or *sangam*) corpus (the corpus of the "Community," the literary academy associated with early, if not prehistorical, royal courts), which has been the object of extraordinarily divergent dating since rediscovered in the late nineteenth century. Even the concept of rediscovery is up for debate, since the works now are thought not to have totally vanished from literary memory. Part of the puzzle of the historical shape of early Tamil literature is the fact—or it seems to me a fact—that Tamil poets and thinkers themselves seem to have been preoccupied with this historical shape, and invented various archaic origin myths: an academy of poets in an ancient period whose works were washed away by floods, which also took other texts at other times, only to be rediscovered later in this temple or that. In short, Tamil offers a literary culture obsessed—from long before modernity and in ways that seem to me

unprecedented—with the problem of literary history, with antiquity, primordiality, and, in fact, beginnings.

On this very contested terrain, this much can be said, I think, with confidence: A very early date for a *written* body of Tamil "literature" *as defined by
Indians*—in the first or second century CE, as some scholars propose—would
be in massive conflict with the securely dated beginnings more than half a
millennium later for the adjacent literary cultures of Kannada and Telugu,
with which Tamil was closely associated (a point invariably ignored in discussions of dating). A circa eighth-century date—if only for the literization
and codification of an earlier oral corpus, but we cannot know this—is also
suggested by the well-documented and vigorous literary patronage of the period's vernacular polity known as the Pandya. If this setting is the true one, the
culture-power hypothesis I have earlier presented would largely be sustained in
Tamil country, though the jury may still be out as to final dating (David Shulman offers a balanced overview; Eva Wilden supplies much food for thought
to nuance some of the ideas presented here, whereas Hermann Tieken is a
devil's advocate whose views are not easy to dismiss out of court). As for the
role of superposition, it is certainly more muted in the Tamil world, which
possesses an independent system of versification, a unique aesthetic system,
and other highly localized formal features, but it is present nonetheless and
grows increasingly prominent in the later medieval period, especially with
the rise of a commentarial, or more generally philological, culture around the
thirteenth century. Consider that the most ancient book of Tamil literary-and-
grammatical theory is entitled *Tolkappiyam*, "Old kāvya."

Sanskrit Beginnings, Finally

All this brings us, by a commodious vicus of recirculation, back to Sanskrit.
What can I say about how, when, and why Sanskrit literature began? Here too,
of course, even more than everywhere else, it all depends on what we mean by
"literature." Or rather, on what Indians meant by literature. One thing Indians
most decidedly did not mean by literature, once the word for literature, *kāvya*,
was in common use, was what is called Veda, which, with its "ancillary knowledge forms," the *veda-aṅgas* (grammar, prosody, phonetics, and so on) constituted *the whole space of discourse in Sanskrit* before the invention of kāvya.

"Veda" is a cover term used by Indians for a large corpus of very heterogeneous material, only one subset of which concerns us in a discussion of
literature. This is the category of *mantra*, those thought (*man-*) instruments
(*-tra*) said to call to mind the deities, substances, and the like to be used by

participants in the rituals for which the Vedas were used, and in so doing convey mythic or other imaginative content. The remaining materials were categorized by the custodians of the Vedas, the Mimamsakas, or exegetes, into three genres: *commandments*, which are used to prompt the performance of ritual actions; *names* of sacrifices; and "discourses on things," *arthavādas*, accounts of the powers of the sacrifice, and the like. All three are documentary, devoid of any "workly" aspect.

Mantras, however, do have such an aspect. In fact, they are often referred to in the Veda itself and afterward as *sūkta*, "well-spoken," a term often applied directly (or in one of its congeners, such *subhāṣita*, "well-turned") to kāvya itself. Not only that, the persons who composed these sūktas were often called *kavi* in the Vedic corpus and by the exegetes (including the greatest among them, the seventh-century thinker named Kumarila) well into the medieval period. From *kavi*, of course, derives *kāvya*, the "work of the *kavi*," a term not entirely unknown to the Veda but in common currency only very much after the Vedic period. And these mantras are old indeed: the earliest collections (*saṃhitā*) can pretty securely be dated to the last centuries of the second millennium BCE. They were all oral in composition and were transmitted orally over centuries—writing was not to appear in South Asia for another millennium—by a remarkable memory culture that largely arrested textual change, until they were committed to writing first in the early centuries of the *second* millennium *CE*—two thousand years after their composition.

While we philologists and other modern scholars may be inclined to think of this Vedic material as literature (Stephanie Jamison has made strong arguments in this direction), no one in India ever did. Consider the second traditional typology of "things made of language" that I alluded to earlier. This radically differentiates the Veda from the literary: the Veda (i.e., the mantras) were held to be "phonocentric," concerned with sound; śāstra (history, science, scholarship, etc.) "logocentric," concerned with meaning; literature, and literature alone, was said to combine both phonocentric and logocentric features. In fact, the belief that Vedic mantras are purely phonocentric, devoid of meaning, was a very ancient one: their ritual efficacy was held to derive entirely from their enunciation, not from their semantic capacity. In addition, nowhere in the post-Vedic age is a Vedic text ever adduced as an example in any discussion of kāvya; nor is the Veda ever represented in literary anthologies. It was viewed as a radically different, *nonhuman*, form of language. And it is not only typologies and the pragmatics of literary culture that exclude the Veda; Indian thinkers were explicit in their assessment: "The use of the word 'poet' [*kavi*] in the Veda," explained the tenth-century CE scholar Bhatta Tota, "refers to a seer's true insight, but its meaning in everyday life refers to both insight and a gift for description. Valmiki, the primordial sage, however insightful he may have been, did not become a *poet* until he mastered description" (Pollock 2016, 182).

There are two important takeaways here for our understanding of the beginning of Sanskrit literature. The first has to do with the "primordial sage" mentioned here, namely, Valmiki. For all Indian theorists for almost two millennia, Valmiki was the *ādi-kavi*, the "first poet." They had no doubt whatsoever that Sanskrit poetry began (and by the process of superposition mentioned earlier, most vernacular literatures also came to posit a first poet for their own literary cultures). The second takeaway has to do with what it was about Valmiki's work, the *Rāmāyaṇa*, that qualified it for its position of primordiality. For Bhavabhuti, a celebrated eighth-century playwright, it was Valmiki's use of metrical Sanskrit ("the teacher who was the first to use metrical forms") (Pollock 2007, 231) Since formally the *Rāmāyaṇa* does employ many of the same meters as are found in the Veda, the dramatist clearly did not think of the Veda as "metrical" in any comparable sense. What Valmiki invented when he invented *kāvya* was *versified description*, as Tota puts it—a good definition of literature's phono-logo-centric character. And this was, above all, description of *laukika*, "this-worldly," experience—experience of the divine sometimes, to be sure, but human experience nonetheless. In the view of classical Indian thinkers, no text before Valmiki's recorded human experience in metrical language. No text was *literature*.

Leaving the traditionists, what can we say about the historical circumstances for what Indians long acknowledged to have been the beginning of a new form of Sanskrit culture they called *kāvya*? Here things get speculative and dating difficult, but the position I have taken for some time (and which has largely been adopted in the most recent overview, that of Yigal Bronner and his colleagues) is as follows. Written forms of Sanskrit appear for the first time in epigraphs a little before the beginning of the common era. The writing system in use, known as Brahmi (which would eventually be adapted for all South Asian scripts), was invented in India in the middle of the third century BCE in the chancery of the Mauryan emperor Ashoka, for the publication of his edicts. (In my view, this presents another element of imperial imitation beginning with the ancient Persians and descending to the Romans in the west and even to the Angkor kings in the east.) All that early inscriptional material is purely documentary. Workly forms appear only somewhat later, many of them associated with ruling lineages newly immigrant from western Asia, especially Indo-Scythian groups. Our first full-scale expressive text, in Kunstprosa, was produced from within the court of a military governor from one of these groups in 150 CE. This entire epigraphic record had long been believed—given the common prejudice to deny strong beginnings marked by full-formed works—to constitute a *terminus ante quem*: Sanskrit literature must, it was thought, have long preceded these well-formed epigraphs. I find no clear evidence whatever to support such a hypothesis. I therefore interpret the Indo-Scythian and related records as constituting a *terminus post quem*, marking the first experiments in an unprecedented, *public* and so to speak *secular*, use of Sanskrit, the language of the gods, hitherto an exclusively ritual or quasi-ritual language.

One can even argue that this was an experiment that in a real sense was a desecration, which explains why it caught on slowly and why some early examples of the experiment were not in Sanskrit itself but in its less hieratic code, Prakrit. It was obviously those situated outside the old Sanskrit culture who recognized the symbolic value of the language for a new aestheticization of imperial power, of the sort that would be recreated, from Afghanistan to Java, by ruling dynasties (Kushanas, Guptas, and so on) in the coming millennium and transferred thereafter to the regional polity in the vernacular millennium.

Although not associated with these new ruling lineages but participating instead in the new political theology of the emperor Ashoka two centuries or so earlier, the *Vālmīki Rāmāyaṇa* shows evidence of the same historic caesura. It is situated on the very boundary of these new beginnings, composed orally in the last century or so before the start of the Common Era but committed to writing soon thereafter, at the dawn of the new era of literacy. The very idea of commencement is celebrated, highly self-consciously, in the first book of the poem itself, where we find a reflexive representation of orality—and the transformation of an earlier song-like tradition precisely as in the case of Daud's *Candāyan*—that was possible only in a world aware of both literization and literarization.

I leave you with a brisk summary, and a question I have not yet raised and which I think may be the most important for us contributors to this book.

First, both beginnings and "literature," the latter especially, need to be understood at once in a historicist and a "traditionist" sense, and these do not always coincide. Second, in India, the history of literature is a history of cosmopolitan and vernacular literary cultures. The latter inaugurate literature, in the traditionist sense of "literature," on the basis of paradigms established by the former (*superposition*) by a discontinuous process of literization and literarization, in which in many cases so-called vernacular polities were the driving force in progressing from the one, inscription, to the other, literature.

Cosmopolitan literary culture too, again in the traditionist sense, had a beginning (here history and tradition converge, around the figure of Valmiki), where the emergent empire form seemed to grasp the political-cultural possibilities of a secularization of a sacred language, one that seemed to move effortlessly across space and time, for a new aesthetics of imperial power.

My as yet unasked question is what it means to think about the Indian case in a global perspective. What sort of knowledge do we want the comparison of beginnings to produce? Comparative projects typically, if surprisingly, do not thematize comparison itself; what they typically do is abdicate their responsibility to compare, and leave synthesis to the hapless reader. But how do we in fact thematize comparison here in the world of literary studies? There are of course many things we can do: validate a hypothesis over N cases; develop a causal account of big structures and processes; identify the relationship between social or political forms and literary forms; simply (and perhaps not so simply) enrich our individual cases by producing more granular appreciations of their distinctiveness through juxtaposition to others, and so on. This is not a question to be solved before the data are in, of course, but once they are, we must be prepared to try.

Further Reading

Bronner, Yigal, et al. *Innovations and Turning Points: Toward a History of Kavya Literature*, 2014.

Busch, Allison. "Hindi Literary Beginnings," in *South Asian Texts in History*, edited by Whitney Cox, Yigal Bronner, and Lawrence McCrea, 2011.

Novetzke, Christian Lee. *The Quotidian Revolution: Vernacularization, Religion, and Everyday Life in Medieval India*, 2016.

Ollett, Andrew. *Language of the Snakes: Prakrit, Sanskrit, and the Language Order of Premodern India*, 2017.

Pollock, Sheldon. *The Language of the Gods in the World of Men: Sanskrit, Culture, and Power in Premodern India*, 2006.

Pollock, Sheldon, ed. *Literary Cultures in History: Reconstructions from South Asia*, 2003.

Shulman, David. *Tamil: A Biography*, 2016.

Tieken, Hermann. *Kavya in South India: Old Tamil Cankam Poetry*, 2001.

PART II

The Mediterranean

In part 1, with Chinese and Sanskrit, we saw our first studies of how cosmopolitan literatures provide a context for the birthing of new vernaculars. In part 2 we see a churning process underway, as vernaculars emerge from the fringes of Akkadian, the mighty cosmopolitan literature of Mesopotamia. One of those vernaculars, Greek, goes on to attain cosmopolitan status itself, and to breed new vernaculars in its own right. Latin, one of these new vernaculars, in its turn became for western Europe a new cosmopolitan literature that outlived the Roman Empire, with consequences we shall see in part 3. There is no way to predict the relationship between an emerging vernacular literature and its cultural hinterland. Just as Japanese and Korean literature had different ways of innovating within the Sinosphere, so too can we observe a range of responses to the creative environments provided by the interstices of overlapping cultures.

Hebrew and Greek literature both had their origins on the peripheries of an extraordinarily long-lived cosmopolitan literature, known as Akkadian, one of the great literatures of the world, encoded in the cuneiform script that had been invented in Sumer (from the late fourth millennium BCE). Named after the prominent city of Akkad in central Mesopotamia, the hub of the first empire based in that region, "Akkadian" is the name applied to a corpus of literary, ritual, administrative, and technical texts of the diverse empires that in turn held sway with Mesopotamia as their base. The origin of this remarkable corpus is ultimately in Sumer, and the adaptation of the Sumerian corpus into the language of Akkadian is the world's first example of the transcultural and translingual literary appropriation discussed throughout this volume. This process of appropriation lasted for centuries, beginning in the late third millennium, with the canonical Akkadian corpus eventually codified around 1200–1000 BCE. It included such famous texts as the Epic of Gilgamesh, together with hymns, ritual texts, and a body of "wisdom literature" that left its mark on the Hebrew Bible as well as on some of the earliest texts in Greek literature, transmitted under the name of Hesiod.[1] The canonical texts continued to be used even after Aramaic replaced Akkadian as the spoken language of

Mesopotamia and Aramaic script on parchment became the dominant writing technology instead of cuneiform on clay tablets (a process underway already in the eighth century BCE): this new world of Aramaic/West Semitic writing is the immediate crucible for the emergence of Hebrew literature (chapter 7).

For two thousand years, cuneiform was the vehicle for a cosmopolitan logographic sphere, which may be compared to the Sinographic sphere. Like early Chinese script, Sumerian and Akkadian cuneiform had a phonemic element, but—again like Chinese script—its logographic component made it adaptable to a variety of languages of different linguistic families. The script was originally devised for Sumerian, which is a language isolate, with no known relatives, but it was adapted for the East Semitic language spoken by Assyrians and Babylonians, and to the language of the Elamites, another language isolate. The Hittites from Anatolia, whose language belongs to the Indo-European family, and who expanded from Anatolia to control upper Mesopotamia intermittently, took over cuneiform with its apparatus of scribal training in Akkadian literature. Crucially for our story, they adapted cuneiform to their own language as well, writing annals, poetry, and ritual texts in Hittite via the medium of the imported script (ca. 1600–1200 BCE). Another example of innovation on the edges of the cuneiform sphere is to be found in the Syrian city of Ugarit in the thirteenth to twelfth centuries BCE, as discussed by Vayntrub in chapter 7; here we find Akkadian texts alongside texts written in the Ugaritic adaptation of the signs of cuneiform for their own new script.

Egyptian hieroglyphs are also to be found in Ugarit, and we must bear in mind that there was constant exchange between Egypt and the lands to the northeast in the realms of trade, diplomacy, and warfare: in the late Bronze Age Egyptian scribes were trained in Akkadian and used that script to conduct far-flung diplomatic correspondence, with Assyria and Babylon and also the Levant, Anatolia and Cyprus. In comparison with Mesopotamia, Egypt was more self-contained in its script and literature, but there are clear signs of Egyptian scribal practice in the Hebrew Bible: as Vayntrub shows, there are numerous features shared between West Semitic, Mesopotamian, and Egyptian texts. Difficult as it is to analyze these interactions in the formation of what we call the Hebrew Bible, it is a good deal easier than it is to recover the details of how what we now call the first texts of Greek literature were formed within the larger penumbra of Near Eastern literature. Even though it is now almost universally agreed that the illiterate Greek bards were somehow aware of at least the themes and motifs of important classics of the Akkadian canon, the whole subject of their knowledge of and access to this material remains controversial: scholars posit oral communication within a mobile environment, presumably involving bilingual actors, but how this kind of knowledge was transmitted in any case remains hypothetical. The important point is that the first "Greek literature" is not sitting off to the side of Near Eastern literature and drawing on it as it sees fit but is, instead, inextricably involved in that Near Eastern thought world.[2]

As throughout this volume, the script of any new literature repays close attention, and Steiner (chapter 5) brings out clearly the importance of the new writing technology of the Greek alphabet, which appears to have been invented in the early eighth century. This script may well have been invented to make it possible for a non-expert to "play back" the songs of the professional bards. Their specially evolved poetic language was so different from any individual Greek dialect that it was not possible to use the West Semitic scripts to capture its unique sound, since those scripts marked consonants only and presupposed that the reader knew the vowel sounds to supplement—precisely what could not be assumed in the case of the special language of orally composed verse. Unlike so many of the other case studies in this volume, in Greece we observe no time lag between the use of writing and the development of literature: in one of our very first substantially extant pieces of alphabetic writing, the so-called cup of Nestor, "literary consciousness" is already, as Steiner puts it, "incipient."

The Greek alphabet and the script of Hebrew were easy to learn in comparison to cuneiform and hieroglyphic, which required years of special scribal training to master. The literary canons encoded in cuneiform and hieroglyphic appear to have had an extremely limited circulation, within the scribal schools who housed the tiny percentage of the population who were literate (0.1 percent of Middle Kingdom Egypt, it has been estimated). Oral performance is regularly posited for these texts as a way of broadening their reach, yet we are still in a very different world when it comes to Greece (and then Rome): figures are impossible to establish, but we can say that literacy was far more prevalent in the Greco-Roman world, and that education in the literary classics eventually became a sine qua non for well-to-do members of society.

Once Greek was established as a dominant cosmopolitan literature in its own right, especially in the aftermath of the conquests of Alexander the Great (356–323 BCE), we see new literatures emerging in interaction with it: Latin, Syriac, and—much more indirectly—Arabic. As Farrell stresses (chapter 6), very few of the authors of Latin literature were Romans by birth, and many of the first authors were not even native speakers of Latin. From the very start, then, the Latin literature of the growing empire was incipiently cosmopolitan, a project that could be joined by people from other areas who spoke other languages. Cosmopolitan literatures such as Greek may be a fine breeding ground for new literatures in vernaculars that have not developed "literarization," but

Rigolio reminds us that the very ubiquity and prestige of such a dominant literary culture can be—perhaps, ought to be—an impeding factor: as he puts it, "the emergence of Syriac as a literary language was improbable because of the enduring cultural hegemony of Greek in the region."

What can regularly provide the impetus for a departure of this kind is a new sense of group identity, one that finds expression in the appropriation of models from a powerful and familiar literary culture in order to demarcate a new self-consciousness about a group's status. In the case of Latin it seems that a decisive originary moment can be detected in the state festival of thanksgiving in 240 BCE, which celebrated Rome's victory over Carthage in the First Punic War and its conquest of Sicily, a moment that heralded Rome's new status as a great power in the Mediterranean. One might have predicted that the Romans would use Greek as a literary language, and one does indeed see rare cases of Romans doing just that—most famously the emperor Marcus Aurelius, who composed his *Meditations* in Greek, rather than Latin (ca. 170–80 CE). But the *Meditations* was not intended for publication, and for Roman culture in general publishing in Greek was the road not taken. The impetus to make Latin a language of literature had a lot to do with precisely the desire to establish distance between the culture of the new imperial power and the older cosmopolitan environment.

As Vayntrub shows, the development of Hebrew literature (as indeed in the case of Ugaritic) is related to pressures to reflect on the identity of the people. Hebrew literature does not present first-person narratives of the great deeds of individual kings, but "the overarching drama of the people of Israel; the story of their importance in the history of creation; their relationship to their national deity, Yahweh; and the trials and successes of their heroes." Strikingly, it is not possible to find any such momentum behind the sudden emergence of a written literature in Greek, even though Greek literature eventually came to be one of the most important markers of a shared Panhellenic trans-Mediterranean sense of identity.

Syriac literature may also be seen as a response to a felt need to differentiate a group and to foster a sense of their self-consciousness as an ethnic and political entity, with a group identity that was grounded above all in a new Christian identity. The new script of Syriac was, according to Rigolio, "part of a broader effort of differentiation from Greek culture, which had flourished under the Seleucids." Script is once again vital here, for the scribes of the court at Edessa came up with a distinctive innovation, based on "a late version of the Achaemenid Aramaic cursive script." This script, in a familiar pattern, was used by the court for administrative and archival purposes for centuries before it was taken over for literary purposes.

If Greek literature is crucially important as the backdrop for the emergence of Syriac literature, it is not the only element in the mix. We must not overlook the vital significance of the Hebrew Bible to this new movement, while some early Syriac poetry also draws from "ancient Mesopotamian literary forms." We have here a crossroads culture, as a glance at the map will show, one whose intercultural and multicultural environment shares many features with that of other beginning literary cultures. The use of Classical Syriac did not remain confined to the self-expression of its place of origin in the kingdom of Edessa but was used by Mani (the founder of Manicheanism) and "was increasingly adopted as a language of culture by Aramaic-speaking Christians throughout the Middle East." If we turn to Arabic literature, we see that the Koran is also the product of a crossroads culture, at the interstices of Arabic, Jewish, Greek, and Syriac traditions. The Koran did not emerge whole from the intact heart of the Arabian Peninsula but was formed through interaction with Christian and possibly also Jewish liturgical practice, as well as with the poetic and sooth-saying traditions of Arabia. According to Schoeler (chapter 9), the very "idea of a 'scripture' in book form" was formed by Muḥammad in response to the Christian lectionary. It is worth noting how highly anomalous Arabic literature is in beginning with an authoritative text that is overtly religious (even if, as Schoeler shows, the Koran is not the only recoverable presence at the start of what can in retrospect be called "Arabic literature"). As Vayntrub stresses, the texts we call the "Hebrew Bible" or the "Old Testament" were not originally composed or even received as "religious" in anything like the modern sense.

Translation is crucial for the formation of a number of literatures in part 2, in a way that was not true for the literatures of part 1. The cuneiform sphere was marked from the beginning by a high degree of translation from one cuneiform text to another, from Sumerian to Akkadian at the origins and then, for example, from Akkadian to Hittite. Crucially, however, "literature" was not translated out of the cuneiform sphere, as other forms of writing were. When the cuneiform culture began its long process of dissolution after the Macedonian conquest (331 BCE), knowledge of Gilgamesh as a figure survived, but the cuneiform text of the epic was not translated; on the other hand, a mass of nonliterary material was translated into other scripts and languages, particularly Aramaic, and eventually indirectly into Arabic—astrology, divination, astronomy, medicine.[3] These preferences are in themselves testimony to an emic sense of what counted as "literature." This kind of pattern is normative in the ancient Mediterranean: the earliest surviving Greek poets were in no sense translating Near Eastern texts.

It is the Latin case that was extraordinarily anomalous for its time, since the first Latin literature consisted of translations of Greek drama and epic, as

Farrell shows, and there is no evidence that anyone had ever translated such Greek texts before. The Latin example becomes normative in the later European tradition, where translation and adaptation of literary models are generative. Latin literature is also very unlike Greek in that it took on the project of "recapitulat[ing] almost the entire literary history" of its source culture, as Farrell puts it, whereas there was no such emulative comparative dimension to the beginning of Greek literature. Latin literature is bicameral from the start, created by bilingual authors for a bilingual audience: again, this was not the case in Greece, although such bicameral mentalities were to become regular in the later European tradition, very much on the Latin model.

Syriac literature is rather like Latin in its take-off from Greek. Here, too, we have bilingual composers and audiences, and here, too, we see a new literature with its origins in translation, first from the Hebrew Bible and then increasingly from Greek. In Syriac, this translation movement helped create a literary language ("Classical Syriac") out of an existing vernacular, and the generations-long translation of Greek literature into Latin had a similarly transformative effect on the Latin language. In the case of Arabic literature, translation had a dynamically transformative effect at a number of points in its history, though not right at the origins. Before Islam, as Schoeler argues (chapter 9), there might have been some translations into Arabic of portions of the Greek or Syriac Bible, but not in a systematic way. The crucial translation moment for Islam came centuries later, peaking in the ninth century, with the wholesale translation—directly or via Syriac—of virtually all Greek writing apart from "literature." Here again, as in the case of translation out of cuneiform, a translation project sheds revealing light on what a host culture counts as belonging in the category of the "literary," and Schoeler examines the reasons behind the choice to exclude "literature" from translation. Crucial for the literature of Islam, particularly for the development of Arabic literary prose, was the initiative of translating Middle Persian works, as administrators and scholars with originally Persian backgrounds filtered forms that they were at home with (epistles, animal fables, fictive stories, themselves ultimately of Indian origin) into the language of their new masters. Arabic literature is remarkable in its early phases for its ongoing process of amalgamation as it interacted intensively with the cultures of the new subjects of the Arabic conquerors. This dynamically dialogic character was an enduring feature of the culture. Educated readers of Arabic literature ignored the *1001 Nights* for centuries until interaction with European fans of the work in the nineteenth century sent them back to the original with a new zest and appreciation.

In chapter 1 Kern showed that the Greek model of an originally oral literature developing into written form does not obtain in China, and none of the literatures in part 1 follow this pattern. In part 2, both Greece and Arabia are special cases. They began with a special poetic language that was not confined to tribal or dialectical borders, and texts underwent a complicated and controversial transmission history, involving orality and literacy until a period when a fixed text emerged: in the Arabic case, this process took decades with the Koran but centuries with the *ḥadīth*. Although the Greek case has been taken to be normative and typical, in fact it is very much an outlier. Through its enduring prestige as the supposed fountainhead of European literature, Greek literature has mesmerized scholars even of other traditions into searching for Greek-style features that are not, in fact, universal. Just as some scholars assume that all ancient cultures have a systematized mythology, for example, because we find it in Greece, the authoritative Greek model has led many to postulate a phase of transition from oral to written in other cultures, with an assumed background of traditional song that was just waiting to be written down. The great majority of cases in this volume demonstrate that this should not be a default assumption.

In chapter 1 we also saw that there was no need for an author in the literature of Chinese antiquity. In Egypt we do not see a text attributed to a named author before the Hymns of Akhenaten, the works of the Pharaoh himself (ca. 1350 BCE); attribution of texts to identifiable authors becomes regular only from around 1100 BCE. In Mesopotamia we find the first named author in world history very early on in the tradition, as a composer of hymns in Sumerian literature—a woman, Enheduanna (2285–2250 BCE), a priestess who was the daughter of the first ruler of the Akkadian Empire, Sargon. Yet such attestations are rare in later Akkadian literature. We do have a scribe's name attached to the standard Akkadian Epic of Gilgamesh (Sîn-lēqi-unninni, between 1300 and 1100 BCE), but literary texts in Akkadian tend to be transmitted without an ascribed author. The situation is radically different in Greek, Latin, and Syriac literatures. "Homer" is not believed to be a real person's name, but Hesiod is conventionally taken to be a historical individual, writing in the late eighth century; certainly by the time we arrive at figures like Archilochus (active in the middle of the seventh century) we are dealing with actual individuals, and famous ones at that, competing with one another and advancing themselves as described by Steiner in chapter 5. In Rome, from the start, the writers of Latin literature were well-known people who attracted a lot of attention, with Ennius, for example, writing about himself in his poetry and having a statue erected in his honor by his aristocratic patrons, the Cornelii Scipiones. In Syriac literature, poets such as Bardaisan and Ephrem were figures of controversy and interest.

All the literatures in part 2 were the object of the kind of curatorship that so regularly defines the development of a literature. The texts discussed in all five chapters here were preserved and transmitted, and the apparatus of scholarship and education that this process entails is inextricable from what we call "literature" in virtually all the traditions under review in this book. In the Akkadian tradition we see such institutions in place from early on, even though the texts chosen for special attention fall into different patterns: we have lexical lists for Sumerian and Akkadian, and scholarly commentary survives on Akkadian ritual and technical texts, but not to the same extent on the epics or prayers or hymns, although some of these texts certainly did attract commentary. Syriac culture developed its own education system in response to and in competition with the hugely prestigious Greek system of *paideia*, and grammar and philology flourished in Arabic schools.

Finally, we note that the chapters in part 2 all illustrate, in their different ways, that none of this panoply we call "literature" is natural, or predictable, in any given case. Many other cultures in the Mediterranean, on the available evidence, developed strong senses of identity, flourished, and even became regional or international powers without any such apparatus. The Carthaginians, for example, never developed a "literature" so far as we know, while the Romans conquered Italy and Sicily and became a major imperial power before embarking on this strange path. "Literature" retains its alluring dimension of contingency.

5

Greek

DEBORAH STEINER

In 1954, archaeologists excavating at the San Montano necropolis on the island of Pithekoussai in the Bay of Naples disinterred a fragmentary Rhodian drinking cup, a skyphos, dated to circa 735–720 BCE, and found in a grave containing the remains of a young boy some ten to fourteen years of age. Painted in black slip and decorated with black concentric bands, a saw-toothed line around the lower body, and a series of rectangular panels with geometric designs, the cup might go largely unremarked but for a singular feature of its ornamentation: tucked away between its handles runs a three-line inscription, which belongs among the first of extant Greek alphabetic inscriptions of more than a few letters and, as I will suggest, offers among the earliest surviving examples of written literary Greek (see figures 5.1 and 5.2).

The inscription is noteworthy not only for its contents, on which more below, but for its form and arrangement. Incised in the standard Euboean script so as to form an integral part of the larger decorative design on the pot's lower body (note, particularly, the continuity between the letter nu, N, in the inscription and the shape as it reappears in the geometric panels), the lines, uniquely for this period, are written in continuous retrograde, not boustrophedon, where the writing travels first in one direction and then reverses course; lines two and three, both of which form complete hexameters, are divided into two and not, as typically, written continuously; and, this too without precedent, the inscriber has introduced into each of the lines the colon, the two vertical dots that indicate word divisions in the first line and phrase divisions in the second and third. In both latter instances, the colon flags the caesura and diaresis (indications of where breaks occur in lines of verse), and seems designed to help a reader sound out the phrases.

I begin with this object because it neatly encompasses the series of issues that turn about the question of the origins of Greek literature and allows us to witness some of the fundamental characteristics of the early Greek literary tradition that this essay will highlight: the originary and canonical position of Homeric (and Hesiodic) hexameter epic and the reasons for that status, the primacy of sung poetry over prose and the role that the musical character of

5.1. Rhodian black-figure skyphos, ca. 735–720 BCE; Lacco Ameno, Museo Civico Archeologico di Pithecusae in Villa Arbusto, inv. 166788. The Nestor Cup, with poetry inscription, from Pithekoussai, Ischia, Italy. Museo Archeologico di Pithecusae, Villa Arbusto, Ischia, Italy / © Mike Andrews / Bridgeman Images.

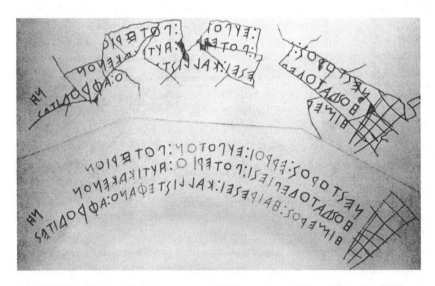

5.2. Detail of inscription on skyphos, ca. 735–720 BCE. Lacco Ameno, Museo Civico Archeologico di Pithecusae in Villa Arbusto. History and Art Collection / Alamy Stock Photo.

poetic composition played in the retention and transmission of a literary work, the passage of orally performed songs into texts, the advent of alphabetic writing and its participation alongside a continuing oral tradition in the preservation and dissemination of archaic and classical Greek poetry, and literature's materiality or the ways in which self-avowedly "literary" works were embedded in and conditioned by their physical form and the contexts for which the objects hosting them were designed. The skyphos together with its inscribed contents also manifests several further properties that go some way to singularizing early Greek literary production: its performative dimensions, whereby poetry, whether in oral or written form, is efficacious, designed to bring about certain ends, and its agonistic character, with each composer/singer seeking to outdo potentially rival works by other poets both past and contemporary and from the first engaging in literary polemic or what would come, at least by the fifth century's second half if not before, to be recognized as "literary criticism." Rather than attempting to present a chronological narrative, with each of these developments plotted along some notional temporal line, the discussion that follows treats the material thematically, using a series of archaic and early classical texts and inscribed artifacts to illustrate its different points.

The Primacy of Hexameter Epic

Time now to turn from the form of the inscription on the skyphos (widely known as "Nestor's cup") to focus on its content, which reads as follows:[1]

Νεστορος : ε[ιμ]ι : ευποτ[ον] : ποτ [[ο]]εριον
hος δ'α⟨ν⟩ τοδεπιεσι : ποτερι[ο] : αυτικα κενον
hιμερος hαιρεσει : καλλιστε[φα]ν̣ο : Αφροδιτες

I am the cup of Nestor, good to drink from. Whoever drinks this cup, straightaway that man the desire for fair-crowned Aphrodite will seize.

What we encounter here, in one commonplace reading of the lines, is a sophisticated joke that assumes its reader/hearers' familiarity with the *Iliad* in more or less the version that we know it today. The humor of the inscription most immediately depends on the patent contrast between this small-scale, workaday, rather crudely decorated terra-cotta vessel and the object so fulsomely described in *Iliad* 11.632–42, where the aged Nestor welcomes Patroclus to his tent while a "lovely-haired" serving maid prepares the exactingly detailed drink for the company in a grandiose vessel:

Beside them was a very lovely cup, which the old man [Nestor] had brought
from home, studded with golden nails; it had four handles, and around each
two golden doves were feeding, and beneath were two supports. Another
man could barely lift it from the table when it was full, for all that he strained
to do it, but aged Nestor could lift it without effort. In it the woman like to
the goddesses mixed them a potion with Pramneian wine and goat's-milk
cheese grated into it with a golden grater, and she scattered into it white
barley and bade them drink when she had prepared the *kykeôn*. Straightaway when they had drunk of it they were rid of parching thirst and began
to take pleasure in conversation, talking with each other.

The disjunction between the fictional and real-world cups extends well
beyond the fact that the Iliadic Nestor's *depas* is golden, has elaborate molded
figurative ornamentation, and is so vast that only this particular hero, his advanced years notwithstanding, could lift it (a paradox that so troubled ancient
audiences that no fewer than three fifth-century sophists would weigh in on the
conundrum). The inscription's language acknowledges the distinctions even
as it claims proximity: the Rhodian cup twice styles itself a *potêrion*, a term
that, in contrast to the epic diction used in much of the remainder of the lines,
is absent from Homer, only to reappear in sixth-century poetry composed for
the symposium, the context for which this skyphos was designed.

But there are relations of likeness as well as difference, apparent only to an
audience fully acquainted with events in this portion of *Iliad* 11 and versed in its
diction and phrasing too. The Pithekoussan inscriber underscores the immediacy of the impact of drinking from this skyphos; even so does Homer signal
how rapidly the draught from Nestor's cup has restored the formerly dispirited
company. And where the epic warriors are moved to enjoy the pleasures of
speech (τέρποντο), the still more powerful desire for lovemaking takes hold
of the skyphos drinker. Further arguing for a nod to the Homeric precedent
is the vocabulary chosen by the inscriber as well as the two hexameters that
complete the declaration; as Oswyn Murray points out,[2] for all the first line's
apparent lack of meter, the ornamental adjective "good to drink from," offers
a variation on the epic *hedupotoio*; Homeric too is the topos of "being seized"
by erotic passion while "fair-crowned" joins together traditional epic epithets
for the love goddess and those used for Demeter, who, in an episode in the
early hexameter *Homeric Hymn* composed in celebration of the goddess, also
drinks a *kykeôn*, the therapeutic cocktail that the attendant mixes up and that
typically includes barley, water, honey, and pharmacological herbs.

In its apparent close engagement and intertextual play with epic precedents, the Nestor inscription seems to stand proof of an incipient "literary

consciousness," of the preexistence of a quasi-canonical and already codified body of hexameter epic poetry on which a sophisticated audience can riff. What then accounts for that poetry's canonicity, and what makes it singularly memorable and worthy of revisionary preservation in the two media apparent on the skyphos, that of oral reperformance (since doubtless the inscription would have been delivered *à haute voix*, a practice to which this discussion returns) and that of inscribed text? This question has several further facets, one concerning the nature of hexameter epic, treated below in this section, another involving the existence of certain criteria ascribing a heightened value to particular types of songs over the many other compositions not considered worthy of such preservation (another issue taken up in the later discussion), and the third the passage of sung poetry to the written text that requires the advent of a writing system (see under "Textualization and the Invention of the Alphabet").

Our earliest extant forms of literary production in archaic Greece, datable on linguistic grounds, were works composed in verse, not prose, and sung or delivered in recitative to the accompaniment of the four-stringed lyre, with the Homeric *Iliad* standing at the outset of a tradition that continued with the *Odyssey*, the two works assigned to Hesiod (the *Theogony* and *Works and Days*), and the thirty-three *Homeric Hymns*, which typically range in date from circa 700 to 500 BCE, although some are considerably later. All are products of an oral tradition of hexameter poetry, a technique of composition-in-performance developed and refined over hundreds of years by illiterate bards who preserved and transmitted their common heritage.[3] This heritage consists of a repertoire of story patterns and motifs (e.g., the wrath of the hero, disguise and recognition, homecoming), themes or "type scenes" (recurring units of action such as a sacrifice, the departure of a ship, or object and place descriptions), and formulaic phrases, whether noun-epithet combinations or repeated phrases that can extend a line or more (treated below). This traditional diction, phraseology, and narrative stock existed for a very specific purpose: thus equipped and schooled through listening from childhood to other bards performing the extant repertoire, the oral poet could compose hexameter epic ex tempore, fashioning an original song each time he performed by using preexisting elements, which he would expand, curtail, reorder, and modify at will and in accordance with audience expectations and demands and the nature of the occasion on which he delivered his song. Since an oral poet performs a new version of his composition each time he raises his voice, the notion of a primary, "original," or fixed text generated by a single individual makes little sense where early Greek literature is concerned.

Two facets of epic poetry further establish the oral nature of Homeric and Hesiodic poetry and their poets' participation in a millennia-old tradition of verse composition, traceable back to Mycenaean and even Indo-European times (certain words, phrases, tropes, and similes attest as much). The first of these is its linguistic medium, the so-called *Kunstsprache*. No Greek ever spoke the language that Homer, Hesiod, and the Homeric hymnists use; instead these poets composed in an artificial idiom, made up of language and forms derived from the different regions of Greece and from the different chronological strata of their language's evolution, with archaisms, neologisms, dialectical composites, and even made-up words standing side by side. The purpose of this vastly expanded dictional and syntactical range (for the infinitive of the verb "to be," the Homeric bard may select among no fewer than five variant forms) was to facilitate hexameter composition, permitting the poet to find the particular word shape that suits a metrical spot in any given six-foot line. No less important to the performer singing his epic lays was the "formula," a basic building block of oral epic song essential for improvisatory composition. Most simply, formulas, chiefly in the form of noun-epithet combinations ("swift-footed Achilles," "horse-taming Hector") and repeated phrases ("when late-born rosy-fingered dawn appeared again," an expression used twenty times in the *Odyssey*) are the means by which the poet articulates a given thought or phenomenon in metrical form. As the work of Milman Parry first demonstrated, these expressions and phrases stand in intimate relations with the line's metrical sequence, with, typically, only one noun-epithet combination existing for each metrical condition and duplication largely avoided, and several different epithets available for each case or form of a name, each designed for a different slot in the line.

If the distinctive nature of the linguistic medium and the existence of a stock repertoire available for deployment by hexameter poets permitted on-the-spot composition, then what made this poetry distinctly memorable and appealing to ancient audiences? Not only, doubtless, its familiarity, with each mention of a well-known name and/or epithet or the poet's embarkation on an episode or story pattern prompting recollections of earlier usages of the same (a sense of *déjà entendu* and the pleasure that affords) but also its aural impact, the distinctive and time-sanctioned rhythm of the hexameter combined with the melodic incantation of the words, this in turn related to the pitch-accents of spoken language.[4] By virtue of its aural appeal, in its earliest manifestations poetic production and performance belonged to the broader world of "song culture," or what the Greeks of the archaic and classical periods styled *mousikê*, a spectrum of activities comprising poetry, music, dance, and their combination, in which all participated on numerous occasions, whether as individuals or as members of their larger communities gathered at private, religious, and/or civic sites.

Notions of Value and Literary Worth

As the Nestor's cup inscription visibly shows, an episode drawn from Homeric poetry enjoyed wide diffusion through the Greek world, deemed worthy of written preservation and reperformance, albeit in humorous form, on an object designed for a drinking party near Naples. What then singularized the *Iliad*, *Odyssey*, Hesiodic epics, and hymnic compositions, distinguishing them from the mass of other hexameter works simultaneously circulating in archaic Greece and that have disappeared virtually without trace? Our extant works already give us some indications of what audiences looked for in a poem and what qualitative properties set one song and its performer over the next.[5]

Perhaps the first of our would-be literary critics-cum-evaluators is none other than Telemachus, who, in the first book of the *Odyssey*, rebukes his mother for asking the bard Phemius to perform a different song: a narrative concerning the ill-fated return of the Achaeans from Troy, Penelope has objected, provokes grief not pleasure in this beleaguered spouse. Countering the critique, her son remarks, "men give greater acclaim to the song which is the newest as it makes the rounds among those who listen" (351–52). But Telemachus's youthful attempts at literary evaluation are shown up as inadequate at best; in an instance of the agonistic spirit underlying Greek poetic production from the first, and to which I return more fully below, the Odyssean poet contrives the exchange so as to remind his audience that Phemius's song is already passé, superseded by the more recent and still ongoing tale that our narrator currently performs, that of Odysseus's successful home return. Innovation remains among the most prized qualities embraced by composers and audiences alike, visible in the seventh-century composer of poetry for performance by maiden choruses, Alcman, who begins a song by asking that the "clear-voiced Muse of many tunes, singer always (*aein aoidê*), begin a new strain (*melos neochmon*) for maidens to sing" (14 *PMG*), through to the early fifth-century choral poet Bacchylides, who similarly petitions his tutelary goddess to "weave out in very lovely blessed Athens something new (*ti kainon*)" (19.8–9), and on to the bold-faced assertions of the late fifth-century musician and dithyrambic poet Timotheus of Miletus, who declares, "I don't sing the old songs (*ouk aeidô ta palaia*), my new (*kaina*) ones are better. Now young (*neos*) Zeus is king; in the old days (*to palai*) Kronos held sway. Go away, ancient Muse" (796 *PMG*). Inviting audiences to hear in the verb *aeidô* the expression *aiei*, "for always," "everlasting," Timotheus reprises the terms used by Alcman for this wholesale rejection of the time-honored in the religious no less than poetic sphere.[6]

Innovation extends to the sound of poetry too and to the especial pleasure that—Plato's later strictures against musical novelty notwithstanding—new modes of instrumentation and developments in melodic modulation seem to have occasioned in audiences from the late sixth century on. Changes in the design of the pipes (the aulos, frequently equipped with double reeds and two pipes) and lyre (through the addition of ever more strings) permitted feats of virtuosity, including the imitation of sounds ranging from snakes' hissing to storms at sea, while the rearrangement of singers in dithyrambic choruses from linear to circular formations improved vocal coordination and sound quality; so too the introduction of an expanded bandwidth of notes, new rhythms, and the transition from a lyre-based to an aulos-based melodic paradigm all seem to have resulted in the creation of novel and sought-out auditory experiences for audiences, prompting the advent of a group of star musicians and composers who enjoyed a high degree of notoriety in late fifth-century Athens.

The particular appeal of sung poetry is already rehearsed in Penelope's remarks to Phemius in the scene cited above; even as she bids the bard change his tune, the queen acknowledges the charm that adheres to his songs, styling them *thelktêria*, "enchantments" (1.337). Cognate terms are used of the impact of desire, creating a link between the bewitchment brought about by speech/song and that caused by eros, an association similarly acknowledged by the inscription on Nestor's cup, where erotic seizure goes hand-in-hand with the lines' performance by the skyphos user. More all-encompassing is a second notion, also sounded by Penelope, concerning the sensations that poetic performances should elicit from auditors and musician-poets alike; even as numerous vase images, those by the early fifth-century Brygos Painter most famously, portray lyre players and singers with their heads tipped back, a gesture that declares their absorption in the sound world of their own creation, visually modelling an audience's response, so Achilles, performing an epic-style heroic narrative while playing on the "shrill-voiced lyre," is engaged in "pleasuring (*terpomenon*) his heart" (*Iliad* 9.186). The *Odyssey* reuses forms of *terpô* on several occasions (Phemius's patronymic is Terpiades, and the evocation of the sensation at 18.305–6 occurs in a sequence of deliberately euphonic phrases), coupling this "delight" together with enchantment (*thelgousin*) in describing the impact of the Sirens' too transfixing song (12.44 and 52). Praising his host Alcinous following the bard Demodocus's performance of a triplet of songs, Odysseus adds a third term to this cluster, noting the *charis*—an expression that encompasses the "grace," refinement, and social orderliness attendant on the best poetic performances—that belongs to the combination of music, song, and sympotic festivity staged by king; so, he declares, "how fine (*kalon*) it is to listen to a bard such as this one is, with his godlike voice. For I maintain that there is no occasion more gracious (*chariesteron*) than when festivity (*euphrosynê*) reigns among the people, and in the halls diners sit in their proper places as they listen to the singer and beside them are tables full of bread and meat while a steward draws wine from the mixing bowl and serves it into the cups" (9.3–10).

Not forgotten in qualitative judgments passed on poetry were the moral and ethical dimensions of songs, and their didactic value. Used in the formal and informal education of the young, poets are charged with producing works conducive to social and political good order (so Odysseus praises Demodocus at *Odyssey* 8.489 for performing one of his songs κατὰ κόσμον, a phrase expressive of such regularity and decorousness) and harmony, religious right-mindedness, and the embrace of civic solidarity. The sixth-century itinerant poet-philosopher Xenophanes of Colophon composed a series of elegiac and hexameter songs promoting these values, from his critiques of anthropomorphic images (B 15 DK), to his strictures against Homer and Hesiod for imputing shameful deeds to the gods (B 11 DK), to his promotion of "reverent speech and purified tales" and avoidance of "profitless" fictions concerning the battles of the Titans and Giants or civil strife, which all run counter to the purity that determines the contents of poetry no less than the state of the room in which it is performed (fr. 1.14, 21–23). The late fifth-century Aristophanes uses Aeschylus as mouthpiece for a similarly ethically and didactically oriented approach to poetry: "Consider how from the first the finest of poets have conferred benefits on us. . . . Hesiod taught us farming, the seasons for crops, times for ploughing, and the divine Homer, where did he get his honor and renown if not from giving good advice about tactics and brave deeds and arming of soldiers?" (*Frogs* 1030–36).

Most striking in this necessarily abbreviated round-up of the qualities that might guarantee a composition preservation and reperformance is the absence of what we might consider purely aesthetic features, whether the property of grandeur, the use of recherché and high-sounding language (or its avoidance), subtlety, polish and refinement, euphony, and other such characteristics. First visible in the *agôn* between "Aeschylus" and "Euripides" that concludes Aristophanes's *Frogs* and that assumes an audience of *readers*, and finding fresh soundings in fourth- and third-century rhetoricians and self-declared literary critics, this novel turn to a more purely literary aesthetic depends on the close study and perusal of songs in the form of texts and receives its most evident statement in Aristotle's contention that a successful tragedy works equally well when read as when seen in performance (*Poetics* 1462a11–12).

Textualization and the Invention of the Alphabet

As the final point in the preceding discussion makes clear, the advent of alphabetic writing and the transformation of orally produced songs into texts play a critical role in these works' transmission and reperformance together with a wholesale shift in mentality. But if the fact of the ever expanding availability of graphic notation remains incontrovertible, then a series of debates surrounds almost every facet of the Greek writing system: when, where, and why was it invented, what distinguished it from forms of writing that preceded it both in Greece and in Near Eastern societies, what was the impact of the spread of the alphabet on Greek daily practices and thought, and what are the chief areas of difference between oral and literate modes of reception and transmission? The discussion that follows does not seek to answer all these cruxes but merely highlights several dimensions of particular pertinence to the question of origins.

We might begin on semisecure ground concerning the invention of alphabetic writing and its distinction from earlier writing systems. Preceding the appearance of the Greek alphabet was Linear B, a syllabic script used in the Mycenaean palace economies of circa 1400–1100 BCE for the purpose of recording the flow of goods and services in and out of the sites. Following the palaces' destruction and the simultaneous loss of knowledge and evidence of Linear B, writing reappears around the middle of the eighth century, now in the very different form of the Greek alphabet, of which several versions existed at the period, each observing slight variations in letter formation from one region to the next. As Herodotus already noted (5.58–59), this novel writing system—perhaps first developed in Cyprus, where Greek and Phoenicians traders existed in close contact, or in Euboia, an area closely connected with the Phoenician Levant—is a modified version of the twenty-two Phoenician syllabic signs, each of which designates a consonant plus an unspecified vowel.

But Greek alphabetic writing nonetheless stands distinct from the Phoenician and other Near Eastern syllabic precedents; by virtue of its inclusion of vowels, this mode of transcription is uniquely capable of recording the sounds of speech, a property that jibes with its earliest usages, where virtually all our oldest inscriptions of more than a few letters or personal names (the first line of the Nestor's cup inscription is the only exception) take the form of hexameters, prompting the (contested) view adopted by several scholars that the Greek alphabet was designed specifically for the purposes of recording hexameter poetry.[7] This privileging of lines of poetic verse goes hand in hand with a second point of departure from other early writing systems. Where these, typically, serve economic, political, and legal ends, with a class of scribes who monopolized this specialized expertise, only in late sixth-century Greece does writing expand from the personal and chiefly amateur realm into the public, political, and commercial spheres, with the first extended prose texts, often recording events of the past or treating natural philosophy, dated to this later period.

In the most radical account of the striking connection between alphabetic writing and hexameter poetry,[8] not only was the invention of the new medium dependent on a single individual, but fueling his innovation was the particularized desire to record the Homeric poems. While this theory lacks support in the evidence, there is no denying the tight link between these monumental epics and the novel form of notation, and it seems probable that the *Iliad* and *Odyssey* assumed written form quite shortly after their date of composition. Since transmission through performance inevitably involves alteration and innovation, poems of such length and complexity could not long have survived in the form in which the Homeric poet composed them unless they were transcribed during or soon after his lifetime. A tabulation of the incidence of various older dictional forms in the poems shows that the songs' linguistic evolution ceased at a very early point, sometime in the eighth century, and well before Hesiod's time.[9] An external stop must have arrested the natural process of modification and change, and a written version readily explains such fixity. As for the process by which the poems were transcribed (dictation,[10] the poet himself as writer?) and the source of the financial wherewithal permitting so costly an endeavor (perhaps a local patron or king seeking cultural capital or more simply that individual's recognition of the poems' superlative worth), here we can only speculate.

What is also evident is the persistence of simultaneous oral transmission. The broad diffusion of the *Iliad* and *Odyssey* throughout the Aegean points to this ongoing performance tradition, as does the presence, attested in sources from the sixth century on, of the professional bands of Homeridae on the island of Chios, whose role it was to recite Homeric poetry. Song contests in which performers of Homeric poetry competed also occurred in early sixth-century Sicyon. Only this continuing composition-in-performance tradition alongside written transmission explains why, when confronted with texts from as far afield as Marseilles, Cyprus, Crete, Chios, and Sinope, the third- and second-century Alexandrian scholars had the daunting task of producing the standardized and stabilized version of the two works standing behind the manuscripts on which our present texts are based.

Before leaving alphabetic writing and textual transmission behind, two further points concerning the medium. As noted in my introduction, the alphabetic lettering on Nestor's cup is all but indistinguishable from the geometric designs used for the remainder of the decoration, a coincidence still more

apparent on a second object hosting another of the earliest examples of literary Greek, the so-called Dipylon oinochoe, a wine jug found northeast of the Dipylon gate in Athens and assumed to have come from one of the numerous graves in the area (see figure 5.3).

Dated to circa 740–730 BCE, the continuous hexameter inscription around the neck, which contains several epigraphic anomalies in its letter formation, declares, "he who now of all dancers dances most delicately, of him this . . ." or, in the Greek original, hοσνυνορχεστονπαντοναταλοταταπαιζειτοτοδε (*IG* I² 919; *IG* I Suppl. 492a), a phrase that allows us to identify the object as a prize awarded to the winner of a dancing competition most probably, again, at a symposium; added on to this declaration are a few more ungainly letters of a different style and hand, κ(μ)μ(ν?)ν, a sequence that straggles upward toward the handle and, in the view of Barry Powell, may form "an incompetent snippet from an abecedarium" scratched on by a tyro writer trying to learn the new letter shapes.[11] Similar to the skyphos, the coherent portion of the inscription takes the form of two hexameters, one complete (ending after the term παίζει, "to dance"), the second partial.

As many discussions point out, the inscription forms an integral element of the larger decorative scheme; for an analphabetic viewer, this would appear a novel form of ornamentation rather than a message-bearing notation.[12] The letters on the wide black stripe of the neck zone maintain the same circularity as the concentric bands of black slip surrounding the body, while the saw-toothed design just below the inscribed shoulder introduces a shape that several of the letter forms echo and that reappears in the decoration on the neck in a somewhat altered form; so too the zigzags below the oinochoe's spout mirror the geometric elements used to construct the letters immediately below.

But the inscription also stands distinct, and not just for the diversity of its graphic signs, which distinguishes them from the regularity and repetition characterizing the other elements, and for the different technique that incising, also used on Nestor's cup, requires.[13] By contextualizing the object through its words, and the νῦν (now) and deictic in the second partial hexameter that firmly anchor the vessel to the occasion, the writing invites the viewer to place its message and other decorations within the prescribed frame of a dance competition. Here form and layout intersect with the message's content so as to engage in a complex form of *mimêsis*: we are witnessing not so much a narrative of an event but the effect of seeing that thing in action. The spidery quality of the letters and thinness of the linear and circular notations, the product of a particularly sharp instrument requiring a skilled inscriber, evoke and match the "delicacy" or "friskiness" the winning dancer displays, the lightness of his trace, grace of his movements, and diversity of his steps. As Jesús Carruesco observes, the inscription circling the vessel, "through the form and direction of the letters and by echoing the movement of the geometric bands below, seems to be trying to imitate the movement of the dance to which it alludes."[14] Here, I suggest, is a distinctive feature of Greek writing from its earliest appearance, and a characteristic simultaneously embedded in the very verb used for the activity, *graphein*, which means both to write and to draw, paint, or inscribe. By virtue of its pictorial quality and role in complementing, enhancing, or even replacing other forms of figurative and nonfigurative representation, Greek writing invites its viewer/reader to engage in what Elizabeth Esrock nicely terms "readerly visuality,"[15] a process whereby we are prompted to attend as much to the look of the letters as to their contents and to witness in these alphabetic assemblages schematized re-evocations of a bygone spectacle.

Further aligning Greek writing with the pictorial medium is a radically different account of the origins of the once orally circulated works subsequently preserved in textual form, and one that looks for Greek literature's origins in artifacts that existed quite independently of and even preceded early poetic performances and their transcription. The giveaway passage occurs when the disguised goddess Iris, our focalizer here, comes down from Olympus to urge Helen to quit her weaving and go as spectator-prize to the duel that Menelaus is preparing to fight with Paris (3.125–35):

> [Iris] found her in the great hall; and she was weaving (ὕφαινε) a great web, double folded and crimson, and working into it (ἐνέπασσεν) the many struggles of the horse-taming Trojans and bronze-corseleted Achaeans (Τρώων θ᾽ ἱπποδάμων καὶ Ἀχαιῶν χαλκοχιτώνων), which they were suffering on her account at the hands of Ares. And standing close, swift-footed Iris spoke to her: "Come hither dear bride, in order that you may see the wondrous deeds of the horse-taming Trojans and bronze-corseleted Achaeans (Τρώων θ᾽ ἱπποδάμων καὶ Ἀχαιῶν χαλκοχιτώνων), who just now were waging very tearful warfare against one another, desirous of destructive battle, on the plain. But now they are sitting in silence, and the battle has ceased; they are leaning on their shields and their long spears are fast fixed beside them (πέπηγεν)."

From the outset, the poet presents Helen as an expert weaver who practices the art of tapestry-like "interweaving" that the term ἐνέπασσεν describes. Her cloth is worked in the costliest of all threads, those colored with the purple dye extracted from the murex shell, and "double" woven so that the textile is two-sided, its back showing the mirror image of the design on the front with the colors reversed. Both the visual and literary records offer parallels for Helen's story cloth; best known is the peplos of Athena, the garment that select Athenian girls, women, and, on occasion, men wove over the course of several months for the tutelary image of the goddess housed on the Akropolis, who received her new gown at the culmination of the annual Panathenaic procession;[16] as our sources attest, displayed on the cloth was the Gigantomachy, the battle between the Olympian gods and the Giants that finds its earliest literary realization in Hesiod's *Theogony*. Although no extant vase shows a textile with this particular episode, archaic and classical images feature many such complex figurative designs; on the early sixth-century François Vase,[17] one of the deities attending the wedding of Peleus and Thetis wears a dress with horizontal friezes of chariots and horses, a motif that reappears on the cloak worn by Demeter on an early fifth-century skyphos by Makron; fantastical winged horses decorate Penelope's unfinished cloth hanging on her loom on a second red-figure skyphos from Chiusi, dated to the fifth century's second half (see figures 5.4 and 5.5).

But most remarkable about the encounter between Iris and Helen is the way in which the scene being woven into the tapestry exactly anticipates the description of events that the goddess goes on to give, as though, looking at Helen's ongoing weaving, Iris finds both the subject matter and diction for her verbal account, which exactly mirrors what the cloth exhibits. The scholia to the passage already flag the originary position accorded the tapestry, observing that "the poet has fashioned a worthy archetype (ἀρχέτυπον) of his own poetry," a view that echoes that of the second-century BCE Alexandrian scholar Aristarchus, who similarly remarked that "from this cloth divine Homer took most of his story of the Trojan war" (scholia on *Iliad* 3.125). The tapestry gives the lead to the narrative in more than its larger content, its state of incompletion that dovetails with the ongoing nature of the struggle, and in the way it furnishes the two epithets, "horse-taming" and "bronze-corseleted," used by Iris for the armies. Rather, it is as though the poem is, for the compass of the episode, compelled to take on the particularized "poetics" of pictorial art,[18] foregoing what distinguishes its verbal medium from what the early fifth-century poet Simonides, comparing poetry and painting, calls "silent poetry" (ποίησιν σιωπῶσαν) in opposition to the "speaking picture" that the verbal artist creates (cited in Plut. *Moralia* 346f). Where typically the Homeric narrator portrays the Greek and Trojan troops loudly vocalizing and in tumultuous motion, here, all but uniquely, both armies are silent and immobile, a stillness underscored by the verb πήγνυμι, "to fix," "freeze," or "make solid," which in the perfect tense rounds out the final phrase of the goddess's speech.

While many commentators, noting that the verb ὑφαίνω used of Helen's weaving is regularly coupled in Homeric verse with nouns for the "fabrication" of verbal and other types of stratagems, readily elide the art of weaving with that of poetic composition, the equation is too simplistic. Neither Homer nor Hesiod ever has recourse to weaving diction when describing poetry's creation and performance nor exploits a possible or supposed etymological link between ὑφαίνω and the ὕμνος (song) on which later lyric sources like to play (e.g., Pind. *Olympian* 1.8, and, more unmistakably, Bacch. fr. 5.9–10, ὑφάνας ὕμνον). Moreover, when epic song does configure itself as a textile, it looks to a later stage in cloth production, the stitching that occurs with the already completed fabrics. So fragment 357 of Pseudo-Hesiod refers to *aoidoi* (bards) as those "stitching song in new *hymnoi*" (ἐν νεαροῖς ὕμνοις ῥάψαντες ἀοιδήν), a representation taken up by Pindar in *Nemean* 2.2, where he names the epic-singing Homeridae the ῥαπτῶν ἐπέων, "singers of stitched-together verses."

5.4. Attic red-figure skyphos by Makron, ca. 490–480; London, British Museum E 140. © The Trustees of the British Museum.

5.5. Attic red-figure skyphos, ca. 450–400; Chiusi, Museo Archeologico Nazionale 1831 Museo Archeologico Nazionale di Chiusi. Photo released by the Polo Museale della Toscana.

So rather than align Helen's weaving art with that practiced by the poet, the Iliadic passage proposes a more startling type of association between the two techniques. If Helen's web stands anterior to Iris's words as transmitted in hexameter verse, then should such story cloths be regarded as among the originators of Greek literature and their collective (and female) weavers as some of the first creators, preservers, and transmitters of what would come to be understood as the literary tradition? Might we even imagine that archaic poets performing in both private and public venues glanced upward toward the textiles, whether suspended on the chamber walls or displayed as dedications, furnishings, and clothing for images at sacred sites, for the matter of their songs, fashioning their narratives after the woven scenes?[19] We might also claim anteriority for the art of weaving in a further regard: following Anthony Tuck's suggestive proposal that the rhythms observed by weavers plying their shuttles through the threads as they moved back and forth across the upright loom gave the cue to the verses' distinctive hexameter meter,[20] then the very sound of epic poetry is grounded in and secondary to the cloth making process. The closing of the subsequent scene in *Iliad* 3, where Helen plays a seemingly omniscient Muse able to supplement Priam's too limited knowledge of events, may reveal the Homeric poet's desire to close down this possible predecessor and rival artist; it is the narrative voice, after all, that ends by correcting and trumping the queen, still ignorant of the fate of her two brothers of which the genuinely Muse-inspired poet is already cognizant.

Poetic One-Upmanship and Agonism

The Homeric poet's "de-authorization" of Helen's rival medium and refusal to allow her to appropriate his narrative role stands testament to one signature property of early Greek literary production, the competitive impetus that frames it from the start. Our earliest evidence for formal poetic competitions belongs to a passage in Hesiod's *Works and Days*, where, after a masterful critique and revisionary version of the Homeric account of the ill-fated Trojan venture, the poet declares that he carried off the prize at the funeral games for one Amphidamas, a Chalcidean king, following his performance of his winning song (654–59), one identified by annotators as his *Theogony*, delivered on the occasion of a song contest with Homer; so too the composer of the shorter Homeric *Hymn to Aphrodite* closes his work by asking the goddess to grant his performance "victory in this contest" (6.19–20). Formal poetic competitions formed part of religious festivals such as the Spartan Karneia (already celebrated on behalf of Apollo in the seventh century, with musical as well as athletic events) and the Pythian games at Delphi where, according to Pausanias's mythologizing account (10.7.2), the winner of the oldest contest, where musicians were charged with singing a hymn to Apollo while playing on the lyre, was the Cretan Chrysothemis, whose father had purified the god after his slaying of the venomous Pytho, the first occupant of what became a principal Apolline cult site. Among later poetic competitions, best known are those that occurred from the sixth century on at the Athenian City Dionysia, where, within a larger festival in celebration of Dionysus, rival poets competed with their actors, choruses, and musicians before carefully selected judges in lavish and high-priced productions jointly funded by private citizens and the polis so as to win the prizes awarded in the tragic, comic, and dithyrambic competitions.

More private bouts of agonism existed alongside these formalized musical contests. Within the more restricted space of the symposium, the seventh-century composer of the poetry of blame and abuse (*iambos*), Archilochus of Paros, trains his sights on Hesiod as well as Homer, famously stripping the Iliadic Hephaestus-forged shield of Achilles of its heroic grandeur in his fragment 5 (here the speaker ignominiously abandons the object in a bush and hopes to get a better one) and upending a dictum pronounced by the Hesiodic voice concerning Zeus's bestowal of justice on men so as to relocate the property among animals instead (fr. 177); in the same set of verses, the Parian poet replaces the nightingale cited in a fable in the *Works and Days*, a patent figure for the bard, with the more wily fox, who avoids the temporary defeat suffered by the weaker Hesiodic creature. In the sixth century, Hipponax, another iambic poet, unmistakably revises the *Odyssey*'s opening line, turning its act of celebration into one of poetic defamation when he opens his fragment 128 by charging his protagonist with gluttony: "Tell me Muse (Μοῦσά μοι . . . ἔννεφ ') of the son of the Wide-Ruler, the sea-swallower, knife-in-the-belly, who eats without limit (οὐ κατὰ κόσμον)."

Polemics could extend to the performance of the lines, and again Nestor's cup exemplifies the dynamics of these competitions, many localized at symposia, where they existed alongside other agonistic events (viz. the dance contest recorded on the Dipylon oinochoe), requiring the increasingly inebriated guests to perform feats of verbal and physical dexterity. With each line on the skyphos conspicuously set off from the next, the tripartite inscription sets up a game of "capping,"[21] whereby the first recipient of the vessel, which circulates from left to right, demonstrates his wit by varying the standard proprietary formula ("I am" plus the object plus the owner's name) so as to introduce the play on the Iliadic precedent that turns about Nestor's name. His neighbor to his right then displays his superior acumen by responding with a perfect hexameter line that additionally appends to this ownership declaration its standard sequel, a curse on the individual who tampers with another's property.[22] It is left to his neighbor and speaker number three to surpass the two previous performers, skillfully deflecting the self-malediction that he would otherwise have to pronounce and turning an unlovely fate into something much more palatable indeed, Aphrodite's visitation.

The Embedded Nature of Greek Literary Production and Its "Performative" Character

Apparent in the exchange of lines that the design of the inscription on Nestor's cup prompts are the penultimate dimensions of early Greek literature treated here, its oral delivery and the interactions between that vocalization and the properties and function of the objects accommodating the words.[23] Just as pronouncing the curse-turned-benefaction as the third symposiast, receiving the skyphos, apprehended the notations between the handles as he lifted the vessel so as to drink, would bring about the consequences it describes, so, very differently, the efficacy of another early artifact, the so-called Mantiklos Apollo, depends on the complex interactions between its physical form and the lines inscribed on its surface (see figure 5.6).

Currently in Boston, this early seventh-century small-scale bronze statuette shows a partly nude male figure wearing a corselet or belt, and variously identified as a generic warrior originally equipped with a helmet, spear, bow, or shield in his left hand, or as a symbolic representation of its donor Mantiklos, or, in a third reading, as a stand-in for Apollo. The inscription, deftly cut using a chisel and punch in Boeotian lettering, announces the object's status as a dedication to the god, perhaps originally an offering at the temple of Apollo in Thebes (*CEG* 326):[24]

ΜΑΝΤΙΚΛΟΣΜΑΝΕΘΕΚΕFΕΚΑΒΟΛΟΙΑΡΓΥΡΟΤΟΧΣΟΙΤΑΣΔΕΚΑ-
ΤΑΣΤΥΔΕΦΟΙΒΕΔΙΔΟΙΧΑΡΙFΕΤΤΑΝΑΜΟΙ

Mantiklos set me up for the far-shooting, silver-bowed (god), out of the tithe as a tenth part [of his spoils]. And do you, Phoebus, grant a *charis*-filled return.

Running boustrophedon and from right to left, the two hexameter lines form a horseshoe pattern that begins at the right knee and travels up the figurine's thigh, where the letters are turned on their side to the left. Continuing down the left thigh, the inscription then bends at the left knee before reversing direction and moving now right to left along the inner thigh.

As in the skyphos and Dipylon oinochoe, and here compounded by the difficulty that reading these diminutive and diversely oriented letters would pose—most are about half a centimeter high, some half of that, and their shifts in position require would-be readers to bend and twist their necks—the inscription again forms part of the larger decorative design, further enhancing this finely crafted statue's visual appeal and display of expertise on its maker's part; the lettering is very much of a piece with the intricately incised fillet around the gleaming figurine's head, which combines a variety of incising techniques, the locks of hair with closely spaced diagonal lines, and the rendering of the torso, whose patterning suggests musculature or a cuirass. Unwilling to leave the lower portions unadorned, the fashioner/inscriber of the statue additionally introduces this particularly complex form of ornamentation, which contributes to making the image into a visible statement of the *charis* (here "gracefulness" and "favor" both, and one among the socio-musical qualities singled out by Odysseus in the passage cited earlier) that the donor aims to stimulate in return.

But also in keeping with the earlier instances, the inscription draws closely on the archaic hexameter corpus, and more specifically on several pivotal scenes in *Iliad* 1. On two occasions, the Trojan prophet Chryses petitions Apollo, first to unleash his plague arrows, and then to restrain them, against the Greeks (*Iliad* 1.37–42, 451–56):

> Hear me, you of the silver bow (ἀργυρότοξ') who walk around Chryse and holy Killa and who are mighty lord over Tenedos, Smintheus, if ever I roofed over a temple for you pleasingly (χαρίεντ') or if ever I burnt for you myriad rich thigh bones of bulls and goats, then accomplish for me this wish: let your arrows make the Danaans pay back my tears.

> Hear me, you of the silver bow, who walk around Chryse and holy Killa and who are mighty lord over Tenedos; if ever you heard me praying on a former occasion and did me honour and struck mightily the host of the Achaeans, still now again accomplish for me this wish: ward off at least the shameful plague from the Danaans.

Among the interfaces between the epigram and the Homeric passages, the donor and inscriber preserve the epithet chosen by Chryses, while the structure of both Iliadic appeals also anticipates that of the inscription, with its more implicit *do ut des* formulation. In further overlaps, forms of *charis* occur in both instances, and the expressions ἑκηβόλος, δέκατος, Φοῖβε, and ἀμοιβή used in the written petition all occupy the same metrical positions as in the standard Homeric hexameter.[25] Mantiklos also frames his request for a pleasing gift in exactly the phrasing that occurs on the occasion of another Homeric petition, this time addressed to Poseidon by the disguised Athena on behalf of Nestor and his sons, in *Odyssey* 3.58 (ἔπειτ' ἄλλοισι δίδου χαρίεσσαν ἀμοιβήν, "but then grant to the others gracious recompense in return for this").

If there is a particularized engagement with *Iliad* 1, then that allusion is highly purposeful: Apollo immediately fulfills his protégé Chryses's request, answering the priest's earlier gifts with his own, first the volley of arrows and then their cessation. Beyond these echoes in diction and form, critical to the efficacious quality of Mantiklos's "Iliadic" appeal is the physical fabric of the statue and its attributes, which not only attract the god by virtue of the gleaming bronze surface and wealth of ornamentation, but make instantly visible the action narrated by the Homeric poet. If, as many assume, the object held in the statuette's left hand were a bow, the weapon so conspicuously wielded by Apollo on Chryses's behalf, then we would witness the god in action. Also spotlighted by the poet and realized by the statue maker is the deity's striding motion as he rapidly descends from Olympus; with his weapons clashing, Apollo "moves in his anger" (χωομένοιο / αὐτοῦ κινηθέντος·, 1.46–7), an enjambed and end-stopped phrase prominently placed at the opening of the hexameter line. Following this, the localization of the inscription on the image's thighs (a placement also determined by the need for a sizable surface to accommodate the extended prayer) carries additional significance: for the archaic Greeks, the thighs are not only a site of erotic delectation likely to draw a viewer's eye, but the locus of motion, the place where a man's vitality concentrates. Positioning the lettering here draws further attention to the god's forward impetus as signaled by the figure's parted legs, promoting the statue's dynamism and capacity for action, as though an epiphany were occurring before our eyes.

In one further respect, the inscription and its Iliadic precedent coincide. There is no mistaking the vocalized nature of Chryses's petition as he addresses his patron god in the vocative and bids him "listen" (κλῦθι) and "accomplish" (κρήηνον) his prayer. So, too, the imperative and vocative reused by the inscriber in formulating the request convey the similarly audible nature of Mantiklos's original appeal, spoken by the donor in the act of dedicating his gift. Rearticulation would be almost de rigueur as the latter-day reader laboriously deciphered the miniscule notations, lending his voice to the absent Mantiklos and guaranteeing that his petition would go on sounding and stimulating a fresh response whenever the inscription were read out loud. Thus the written message proves consubstantial with the statuette as together they both reenact the Iliadic scenes and turn this text-bearing artifact into an autonomous object independent of its donor, capable of restaging a one-off ritual through time and space.

The inscription both functional and decorative on the Mantiklos Apollo promotes its efficacy in one final respect, and here I would observe a different point of continuity between this Theban statuette and the larger class of votives to which it belongs. Dating from circa 700 to the early sixth century, several of the inscriptions found on potsherds from the sanctuary of Zeus on Mount Hymettos and serving as dedications to the god introduce their donors as writers.[26] While some inscriptions simply announce "he wrote (εγραφσε)," another more emphatically spells out the relation between the giver's "writerly" identity and his gift: "I belong to Zeus. X wrote me." In two other instances, the donors foreground the act of inscribing and their "authorial" role: hοσπερ εγραφσεν ("as he wrote") and, with a fresh burst of pride, -αι ταδ' αυτος εγ⟨ρ⟩ αφ[σε ("he wrote this himself"). The same phenomenon occurs elsewhere: the author of the "postscript" to the message on a sixth-century Melian column enhances the value of this already high-price artifact destined for a "child of Zeus" by advertising the donor's scribal skills: Ekphantos "made this vow to you and fulfilled it by writing (ετελεσσε γροπηον)" (*SEG* III 738). The act of writing thus becomes one among the manifestations of technical expertise that elevate objects to the category of *agalmata*, top-rank status goods reserved for dedication and gift exchange, and guarantee texts as well as prestige-bearing artifacts their preservation and perusal in later times.

Poetic Matter

By way of ending, I close with a four-line elegiac fragment that succinctly demonstrates many of the chief "takeaways" of the preceding discussions: the materialist character of very early Greek literature and its context-determined quality, its internal agonism and practice of different forms of evaluation, its functionalism or "performative" impetus, and its awareness of the ongoing process of alphabetic transcription and codification to which it actively contributes. In the brief compass of a work designed for a sympotic gathering, the sixth-century poet-legislator Solon critiques his fellow elegiac composer Mimnermus, taking issue with an assertion in one of that poet's pieces concerning old age (fr. 20 W):

> But if even now you will hearken to me, take this away (ἔξελε τοῦτο)—and do not be offended because the things that I have devised (ἐπεφρασάμην) are better than yours—refashion (μεταποίησον) it, Ligyaistades, and sing as follows: "may my fated death come at eighty."

Even as Solon invites his rival to "sing" the offending line differently—and commentators have been quick to imagine a drinking party where the two poets met and joined in a tuneful game of poetic "capping"—and addresses Mimnermus as the son of the "sonorous" or "clear-voiced" (*ligu-*) one, the diction of his lines envisages this orally delivered and aurally received song as a material artifact from which the offending element can be physically removed. More than this, the verb μεταποιέω, unattested before Solon and later commonly used for marking changes within a text, describes this piece of composition in constructivist terms, something that may be remodeled according to the current singer's superior blueprint or design. A third term, ἐπιφράζω, is similarly oriented, imagining how Solon's "poietic" activity assumes much the same interstitial shape as his rival's: in uncompounded form in archaic and classical texts, the verb describes individuals who apprehend something that stands midway between speech and a visual display and refers to the act of turning sights and visible objects into words and words back into things that are seen.

So finely does Solon hone his attack that it realizes its end even before the performer concludes his song: by virtue of appropriating Mimnermus's now textualized voice in the final phrase, this revisionist has achieved the process of elimination and reconstruction that his words describe, and all that remains for current and future audiences is this newly codified version of the earlier piece. What Solon himself could not, of course, anticipate was the ultimate failure of his stratagem: Mimnermus's offending original line, "would that my fated death might come at sixty" (fr. 6 W), did survive, preserved for us by the imperial author Diogenes Laertius, who cites it together with Solon's *réplique*.

Further Reading

Detienne, Marcel. *The Masters of Truth in Archaic Greece*, 1996.
Gentili, Bruno. *Poetry and Its Public in Ancient Greece: From Homer to the Fifth Century*, 1988.
Griffith, Mark. "Contest and Contradiction in Early Greek Poetry," in *Cabinet of the Muses: Essays on Classical and Comparative Literature in Honor of Thomas G. Rosenmeyer*, edited by Mark Griffith and Donald J. Mastronarde, 1990.
Kurke, Leslie. "The Strangeness of 'Song Culture': Archaic Greek Poetry," in *Literature in the Greek and Roman Worlds: A New Perspective*, edited by Oliver P. Taplin, 2000.
Martin, Richard P. "The Seven Sages as Performers of Wisdom," in *Cultural Poetics in Archaic Greece: Cult, Performance, Politics*, edited by Carol Dougherty and Leslie Kurke, 1993.
Porter, James I. *The Origins of Aesthetic Thought in Ancient Greece: Matter, Sensation, and Experience*, 2010.
Powell, Barry B. *Writing and the Origins of Greek Literature*, 2002.
Svenbro, Jesper. *La parole et le marbre: Aux origines de la poétique grecque* [Word and marble: The origins of Greek poetics], 1976.
West, Martin L. *The East Face of Helicon: West Asiatic Elements in Greek Poetry and Myth*, 1997.
Yunis, Harvey, ed. *Written Texts and the Rise of Literate Culture in Ancient Greece*, 2003.

Latin

JOSEPH FARRELL

One of the key questions in classical studies, and one of the most debated, is how Latin literature began. Even how to understand the question is controversial. We cannot ask "how" without also considering "when." This depends very much, as it does in other settings, on what we mean by "literature." Is it after all a matter of writing, or should we also be thinking about such things as traditional songs that were widely known long before anyone thought to take them down? This in turn bears on the question of "beginnings." If we define literature broadly, then all speakers of Latin will always have been producing it in some form; if we define it narrowly, then we know the exact date when some Romans got the idea of inventing a literary culture of their own, founded on a virtually comprehensive and remarkably intense emulation of Greek precedents. Of course we must reckon with both kinds of "literature," one that had always just been there, and one that entailed a significant departure, even a new "beginning." The two kinds may not have been utterly opposed to one another, perhaps even in respect of Greek influence; but they certainly were and are distinguishable, and the history of our question tends to involve a sharp polarization between them.

Before going any further, it is worth briefly making a second distinction between Latin and Roman literature. Of all the Latin-speaking peoples of Italy, only the Romans left any substantial literary record. They were also successful in establishing their own form of Latin, in contrast to those of older cities in Latium, the home of the Latin peoples, as the standard and most prestigious dialect. As a result, ambitious writers from all over Italy, and then from much farther afield, would for centuries find it necessary to go to Rome. How *that* story began is the subject of this chapter. There would be other beginnings of other stories. Eventually, Rome would stop being the undisputed center of government and culture, but this would not prevent Latin from prospering and expanding during the Middle Ages as a literary and administrative language on an even greater scale than before. The educational reforms of the Carolingian courtier Alcuin of York and the Italian humanists of the fourteenth and fifteenth centuries also marked new beginnings, which are frequently imagined in terms of "rebirth." These are important moments in a larger story that has been told well by Jürgen Leonhardt in particular; but they take us far from the question of how the literature of the ancient Romans as we know it came into being, and if that had not happened, the longer story of Latin literature would have been very different, if it had existed at all.

The Big Bang of Latin literature, the clearly datable beginning that will be my chief subject, occurred in 240 BCE. Before we get to it, however, let me be clear that it is perfectly reasonable for scholars to want to know more about Roman literary culture and its Italian context before this epochal event. By traditional reckoning, in 240 BCE the city of Rome had been in existence for about five hundred years. Having coalesced from a group of settlements at a point where the Tiber River was still navigable, but easily crossed, by the end of the sixth century it had grown from a local to a regional power. Its importance had found substantial expression in the material arts in particular. By this time the city of Rome constituted the largest walled urban environment in Italy, and within it stood the peninsula's largest temple, as well, to Jupiter on the Capitoline hill. By the end of the fourth century, Rome had become the most powerful state of all Italy, and over the next sixty years it would prove itself in wars against two formidable opponents from overseas, first on Italian soil against Pyrrhus, king of Epirus in western Greece, and then mainly by sea against Carthage, previously the chief maritime power in the western Mediterranean. As many have said, it would be amazing if the Romans had accomplished all this without producing *any* literature at all, of any kind.

Of course, they must have done so. What they did not do, however, was to produce a list of identifiable authors. In fact, there is just one solitary figure, the great senator, consul, and censor Appius Claudius Caecus (340–273 BCE), most famous perhaps for building the Appian Way, who is remembered by name as the author of a book: a collection of *Sententiae* ("Opinions" or "Maxims") of which just three specimens happen to survive. The attestation is controversial, however: it is quite possible that in much later times these sayings came to be ascribed to Appius as a wise man, perhaps on the model of the Seven Sages of the Greek world. Indeed, the three surviving sayings themselves seem to be taken directly from the Greek. This is a pattern that will be repeated, many times.

Named authors aside, there were in fact from an early date at Rome and elsewhere in Latium different forms of "literature" in the broadest sense, and actual literacy, in a fairly narrow sense. This much is not in doubt. We have a number of archaic inscriptions, in Latin as well as Greek, that contain texts representing a variety of genres. These include laws, hymns, personal inscriptions, and so forth. A few extremely archaic texts were also quoted by ancient scholars and have been transmitted to us by ancient and medieval scribes. Again these include liturgical and legal texts, but in somewhat greater bulk than the individual inscriptions offer. In addition, a few authors like Cato the Elder (234–149 BCE) quote incantations and prayers, presumably based on actual practice, for use in different situations throughout the agricultural year. It is certainly possible to gain an impression of early Roman literary culture, in the largest sense, with reference solely to these materials. We can go further and imagine this culture in relation to a larger Latin and Italic culture by comparing these texts, along with the social practices that they represent, to similar materials found throughout central Italy. The situation is not unlike that of trying to understand the key figures of Roman religion—gods and goddesses like Jupiter, Juno, Minerva, Saturn, Mars, and Vesta—before they came to be identified with their Greek counterparts, Zeus, Hera, Cronus, Ares, and Hestia. With this process of identification—the so-called *interpretatio Graeca*—came a body of mythological lore, in which Greek literature is so rich. By this means, Jupiter became not just the weather god who lived on top of the Capitoline hill, but the king of the Olympians who put down the rebellious Titans and Giants, as in Hesiod's *Theogony*, as well as the prolific patriarch who would eventually be satirized as a randy adulterer by Ovid. These and other Greek myths found expression in Rome and throughout Italy in a variety of media, which survive in the form of monuments and descriptions of monuments.

Many questions, however, remain. For instance, if early Romans and other Italian peoples were familiar with Greek mythology, in what forms did they experience it? Does familiarity with a myth necessarily entail familiarity with a literary expression of it? Or does a depiction of, say, Hercules or Odysseus imply a tradition of shared or adapted visual representation independent of literary expressions? The Tomba dell'Orco at Tarquinia, built in the fourth century BCE, is an Etruscan tomb built in the form of a dining room and featuring a mural of Odysseus and his men blinding the Cyclops Polyphemus. It is impossible not to infer that those who used that space were capable of telling the story depicted there, teaching it to their young, and discussing it with one another. But what did they find in this story that made it worth teaching and discussing? In the Homeric *Odyssey*, the hero behaves recklessly and transgressively, by slaughtering and feasting on the Cyclops's sheep, and then must defend himself when the Cyclops responds even more outrageously by devouring some of Odysseus's men. Did those who assembled for a meal in this space use the mural in the way that both ancient and modern critics have done, as a prompt to teach and discuss ideals of hospitality and guest friendship, particularly as they relate to dining? Since the meal in question must have been connected with a burial or with the commemoration of the dead, did the users of the room interpret the episode, once again like earlier and later commentators, as an allegorical encounter with, and triumph over, death itself? Whether they did any of these things, how did they tell the story? Did they actually recite passages of Homer in Greek, or summarize them in their own language? We cannot answer any of these questions; but simply by asking them, are we not trying to discern the outlines of a literary culture in archaic Italy?

Here of course is where we run up against the question of what, precisely, one means by "literary." Like "classical," "literary," or even "literate," it is a word that is practically impossible to use in a value-free way. Because literacy is a tool of such basic importance in modern society, illiteracy is treated as, in effect, a disability or even worse, and the most comprehensive, very influential study of ancient Greek and Roman literacy, by William V. Harris, takes a similar view, representing literacy as a "golden gift" (1989, 337) that conferred almost incalculable advantages on those who possessed it, to the enormous disadvantage of everyone else. In the world of near-universal literacy that members of modern "developed" societies inhabit, it is impossible for many people to imagine preliterate societies as attaining anything like the level of complexity and accomplishment that we take for granted in our own, especially, perhaps, where verbal artistry is concerned. But this is so in spite of the fact that anthropologists and folklorists have complied evidence in sufficient abundance to prove otherwise. If we continue our brief visit to the world of ancient Etruscan burial spaces, we may consider the François Tomb in Vulci from the late fourth century BCE, which juxtaposes two paintings. One of them corresponds to an episode of the Homeric *Iliad* (23.175–77) in which Achilles sacrifices Trojan victims to the shade of his friend Patroclus. In the other, a band of Etruscan warriors, including one named Mastarna and a pair of brothers named Vibenna, are shown defeating their enemies. The Etruscan soldiers are thus depicted not as if engaged in generic or routine warfare, but in a pursuit comparable to that of Homer's greatest hero. There may be an irony here, in that some ancient authorities regarded the Etruscans as descended from the Lydians of Asia Minor, whom they identified with Homer's Maeonians, allies of the Trojans. If the artist or his patron shared this belief, then the inversion of allegiance and cultural identity that informs this painting would anticipate by centuries the more celebrated reversal by which Vergil assigns the role of Homer's Achilles to the Trojan and proto-Roman hero Aeneas. In both cases, an Iliadic plot would trump genealogy in determining how Etruscans and Romans understood and represented their own history in terms of Greek myth. Vergil's hyperliterary rendition of the Aeneas legend is widely celebrated for the sophistication of its typological handling of Homeric story patterns, but the essential ingredients may already be in play, four centuries earlier, in paintings alluding to Greek mythology made by a culture that has left, in the narrow sense, no substantial literary record at all.

A point that needs making here is that, in the major examples I have discussed so far, Homer is an unavoidable point of reference. Is it possible to speak of a literary culture, or of any recognizable culture in archaic Italy, that is not to some extent derived from that of the Greeks?

It is certainly not easy. Ancient poets and mythographers traced the foundation of many Italian cities to last generation of heroes who fought on either side in the Trojan War. The earliest written reference to the *Iliad* was found on Ischia (in Greek, Pithekousai), an island not far from Naples, on "Nestor's cup," the drinking vessel discussed in chapter 5. The earliest surviving Greek inscription known to date was actually found in the old Latin city of Gabii, just eleven miles from Rome. The very name of Rome, according to ancient scholars, is from the Greek word *rhōmē*, "strength." The city's development parallels that of a Greek polis to a surprising extent, even in chronological terms. According to legend, Rome was founded in about 750 BCE, when the Greek city-states were emerging from a period known as the "dark ages," which followed the collapse of Mycenaean civilization, and were sending their first colonies to Italy and Sicily. According to tradition the Romans expelled the ruling dynasty of kings and replaced them with a republican government at the end of the sixth century, just when the Athenians were ousting the Peisistratid tyrants and introducing a democracy. In the fifth century, Athens developed rapidly into the leader of a naval defense league against Persian expansion, and then into an imperial power that for a time dominated other Greek cities in the eastern Mediterranean, before their ambition to conquer Sicily as well brought them down. The Romans expanded more slowly, but by the time of Athens's defeat in the Peloponnesian War (404 BCE) they had assumed permanent leadership of the Latin League in central Italy. During the fourth century, as Athens and other Greek cities jockeyed for advantage against one another, they all fell under the sway of the Macedonian Empire, while Rome became the single most powerful city in all Italy. By this time, the Romans had long enjoyed diplomatic relations with more distant powers, such as the Greek colony of Massilia (the modern Marseille) in Gaul and the Phoenician colony of Carthage in the area of northern Africa now known as Tunisia. By 146 BCE, when they destroyed Carthage and converted most of mainland Greece into the senatorial province of Macedonia, the Romans had long since stopped tracking the experience of other successful cities and had surpassed them all, actually achieving the hegemonic position to which Athens had aspired, but never fully attained.

In spite of this general parallelism between Rome and Athens in a political and military sense, we have no comparable record of Roman literary activity. There is no contemporary of Herodotus or Thucydides writing in Latin to inform us about the origins and early development of the Roman Republic. There is good reason to believe that some of the festivals that are featured in the Roman civic calendar were celebrated during these centuries, just as the festivals of the Greater and Lesser Dionysia and the Lenaea were celebrated at Athens. However, while we have over fifty extant plays by Aeschylus, Sophocles, Euripides, and Aristophanes that were performed at the Athenian festivals, and vestigial evidence of many more plays by many other authors, we have only summary accounts of Roman dramatic festivals before the middle of the third century. Like Greek accounts of their own drama before the fifth century, these Roman accounts are not entirely coherent; moreover, unlike the Greek accounts, which are largely based on what seemed to ancient scholars like plausible inference, the Roman accounts look very much as if they were based not on an independent tradition, but on inference from those of the Greeks. We have explicit evidence that by the late second century BCE Roman intellectuals had begun to wonder about the early history of their own culture, and had begun to suggest that it must have developed either in unconscious parallel with that of the Greeks or perhaps in deliberate imitation of it. For instance, the poet and cultural historian Lucius Accius (179–86 BCE) wrote that the consummately Roman festival of the Saturnalia must have been modeled on an Athenian festival, the Cronia—Saturn being an ancient Italic divinity who had come to be seen as analogous to the Titan Cronus of the Greek pantheon. Not much later, in the mid-first century BCE, the orator and intellectual Cicero, who had known Accius personally, suggested that it should be possible to imagine how impressive Latin poetry must have been even in the decades that immediately followed the founding of the city—that is, in the eighth century BCE, seven hundred years before Cicero's time—simply by reading the work of Romulus's Greek contemporary Homer.

Not long after writing this, Cicero revised his opinion, perhaps after the work of his friend Atticus brought it home to him that no Roman poet could be named who was active until *five hundred years after* the time of Romulus. During those five hundred years, the Greeks developed a highly elaborate literary culture, based on the works of certain "canonical" authors, who were specifically recognized as the master practitioners of specific literary genres (history, oratory, tragedy, comedy, lyric poetry, and so on). This culture was institutionally supported by the recitation and reperformance of canonical works in civic and intercity festivals held throughout the Greek world, and by the establishment of official texts of the relevant works by scholars employed

by individual cities, cult sites, and regal courts, some of which operated libraries both as repositories of books and as research centers. This widespread
institutional support encouraged and, to an extent, standardized the system of
education based on canonical literature that had long been in use throughout
the Greek world. There is absolutely no evidence that anything like this existed
at Rome before the middle of the third century BCE. We do, as I noted earlier,
have legal, religious, and other texts in Latin that survive from centuries before
that time. There is no doubt that these texts and others like them were used
for a variety of civic purposes. We also have accounts written by classical authors, such as the aforementioned Cato the Elder and also the historian Livy
(59 BCE–17 CE), that speak of songs sung at banquets in celebration of heroic
exploits, or of rustic festivals that featured dramatic performances, largely improvised, both of which supposedly became more and more professional over
time. None of these accounts, however, refers to a tradition that was still living
at the time when the author in question described it. Indeed, Cato is explicit
that the heroic songs he has in mind were sung at banquets *many generations
before his time*. On the whole, he and other ancient theorists of archaic Roman
culture seem, like Accius, to be extrapolating, from no evidence, on the basis
of what most people believed about Greek cultural history. To be fair, we have
seen that in the realm of political development, as well, the experience of early
Rome has been seen as running parallel to that of a Greek polis, especially
Athens. An important difference is that we have detailed and credible ancient
evidence for these political developments, particularly in the material record,
whereas we have absolutely nothing comparable in the realm of literature.

All this said, I repeat: it is hard to believe there was no literary activity at
all, in the broadest sense, taking place in Rome before 240 BCE. The problem is just that the actual evidence we have of it is vague, confusing, or hard
to credit in crucial respects, and silent on a number of important questions.
For instance, as I mentioned above, Livy states that in 364 BCE professional
theatrical performers were first brought to Rome from Etruria in an effort to
expiate a plague, and that they performed at the Roman Festival (*ludi Romani*),
an annual feature of the state civic and religious calendar. There is nothing at
all implausible about this: the Romans had been importing foreign elements
into their state religion for some time, and they would continue to do so. The
problem is that Livy's account of what these Etruscan performers actually did,
and specifically of how their improvised performances of dance to musical
accompaniment gradually assumed the form of stories based on a script, is difficult to follow with precision and to reconcile with other accounts of Roman
theater prior to 240 BCE. On the other hand, accounts of quite loosely and
variously defined performances, many of which are said to involve mockery

and improvisation, are attested for parts of Italy other than Etruria and Latium and are said to involve other Italic languages, such as Oscan. It is not impossible to imagine a connection between such forms of entertainment as these and the comedies that Plautus (254–184 BCE) and Terence (185–159 BCE) would later produce. Even though these fully canonical Roman authors explicitly based their scripts on the canonical texts of Greek New Comedy, the Roman versions contain elements that correspond to nothing that we know about Menander (342–291 BCE), Diphilus (342–291 BCE), Philemon (362–252 BCE), and other Greek models claimed by authors of the *comoedia palliata*, the Roman comedy in Greek dress. We know further that other dramatic forms, mainly improvisational, continued to be popular for centuries after the Romans began to create their own canonical literature. However, such forms were held to be "subliterary." Only a few authors of "mimes," as such performances were called, tried to turn this form into a genre on the canonical model, and scraps of these texts survive; but most mimes seem to have been truly improvisational affairs that performed traditional stories mainly through music, dancing, boisterous behavior, and erotic spectacle. It is hard to imagine any aficionado going to a bookseller to acquire the script of a mime that he had particularly enjoyed, not least because most of them probably had no actual script, in the way that the comedies of Plautus and Terence did. It may be that in comedy we can find traces of such popular, noncanonical performance traditions that are largely independent of Greek influence, but comedy is a genre that flaunts its relationship to the Greek canon, and we would have not even those traces unless they were embedded in an equivalently canonical Roman genre.

All this leads to the central point on which our sources most decisively converge. Like the importation of Etruscan professionals in 364 BCE, it concerns another theatrical innovation, again specifically dated, but intended as a gesture of thanksgiving rather than as a response to crisis. In 240 BCE, the year that followed the end of the First Punic War, for the very first time a poet we can confidently name, Livius Andronicus, produced one or more plays translated from Greek originals into Latin, again at the Roman Festival. Who was this man?

There were already in antiquity questions about Livius's biography, and some of these remain difficult to answer; but two essential points are quite clear. First, his work as a translator is well attested. To corroborate that notice about 240 BCE, we have the titles of nine tragedies and two comedies that he adapted from Greek originals, along with what may have been his masterpiece, a very close translation of Homer's *Odyssey*. Second, we know of at least one other occasion when the state appealed to Livius for a poem that would be performed on an important occasion. In 207 BCE, during the Second Punic

War, after the Temple of Juno Regina was struck by lightning, Livius composed a hymn to be sung by a chorus of twenty-seven girls in supplication of Juno, whom the Carthaginians worshiped as Tanit, one of the principal deities of their pantheon. The text of the hymn survived at least until the time of Augustus, when Livy once again reported on this entire episode, but decided against quoting the hymn, because its style was too archaic for his taste. For literary historians, this was an extremely frustrating decision! Still, Livy's account is suggestive in important ways. For example, he does not refer to the hymn as a translation from the Greek, and it is widely assumed, because it was so closely tied to contemporary events, that it was not. However, like Livius's attested translations, which corroborate the story that the scripts of 240 were also translations, so too does the story about the hymn support the idea that the state had turned to him before to provide a literary response to events of national importance.

Although Livius Andronicus was remembered as a foundational figure and as Rome's most prominent poet at this time, he was not alone. His near contemporary Gnaeus Naevius (270–201 BCE) also produced tragedies and comedies, together with an epic treatment of the First Punic War. The somewhat younger Plautus, whom I have mentioned above, became famous for his comedies around the turn of the third to the second centuries and is the earliest Latin poet whose work survives in bulk. Other names from this period include Quintus Ennius (239–169 BCE), also famous for dramatic as well as epic poetry (not to mention still other genres), the comic poets Caecilius Statius, Gaius Licinius Imbrex, Marcus Atilius, Sextus Turpilius, Quintus Trabea, and Luscius Lanuvinus. All these playwrights were active during the half century that followed Livius's innovation at the Roman Festival of 240. Whatever poets may have been active before that time, other than the suspect Appius Claudius Caecus, we have no idea of their names or of what specifically their work was like. As I have noted, there must have been some continuities, especially in the comic genres. Livius himself cannot have come from nowhere. Perhaps he produced one kind of play in the years before 240, and only then began translating Greek plays into Latin. Whatever the truth may be about this—and it cannot be stressed too much that we have virtually no concrete evidence—it is impossible not to acknowledge that the Romans themselves viewed the events of 240 as a literary and cultural watershed, and that the surviving evidence strongly supports this point of view. In the first five hundred years of its existence, Rome was not only a functioning polis, but one that rose to great power and achieved notable expression of its cultural prestige in the material arts. Like other cities, it used writing in its legal and political life and used music and poetry in civic and religious ceremonies, including those festivals that offered different forms of entertainment to their participants. What it did not do is develop the habit of identifying any literature produced during that time as the work of particular authors or make any systematic effort to preserve it. With the events of 240, this situation suddenly changed. Texts composed by individual authors began to be preserved. The authors themselves began to be remembered by name. The occasions on which their work was offered to the public were recorded. Eventually these works came to be used in educating the young. Crucially, most of the texts themselves are Latin versions of Greek originals, ranging from very faithful, almost word-for-word translations to free adaptations of particularly effective plots. It is obviously not impossible that some or all these things happened from time to time, or even with some regularity in the years before 240; but again, there is no direct evidence for this, at all. It is true that ancient Roman scholars—who like ancient Greek scholars were in love with the motif of the *prōtos heuretēs*, the "first inventor" of a particular idea, custom, or literary genre—may have exaggerated the importance of Livius to the point of actually ignoring or suppressing what evidence that they had of prior literary activity along similar lines, so that it has been lost. The fact remains, however, that we do not have such evidence; and what evidence we do have, such as the story about the introduction of *ludi scaenici* (theatrical games) in 364, looks very much as if any kernel of truth that it contains might be embedded in an account developed to make that event a convincing precursor to Livius's more decisive intervention a little more than a century later.

The dates of the Roman Festival in 240 and of the Hymn to Juno in 207 are the most reliable fixed points in Livius's life, and they bespeak a long career. His name, too, tells us something important. Livius is a Roman name and Andronicus a Greek one. This pattern usually denotes someone who was born Greek but then enslaved and later freed (or manumitted) by a Roman master, whose name the former slave (*libertus*, "freedman") took as a sign of gratitude and continuing loyalty to his former owner (*patronus*, "patron"). The date of Andronicus's birth and the circumstances of his enslavement and manumission are matters of guesswork. Ancient scholars believed he was from Tarentum in Magna Graecia, a center of Hellenistic culture that was captured by the Romans in 272 BCE. If Livius was taken prisoner then and somehow became the property of M. Livius Salinator, a prominent senator at that time, this would explain both how he got his Roman name and why he is associated with that senator's family in later years. What we cannot answer is how old Livius was in 272—remember that he composed his Hymn to Juno in 207, some sixty-five years later—and so whether it was clear at the time of his capture that he was a man of literary ability, or rather that he was too young for such qualities to have become evident. In either case, we do not know how, when, or at what age he learned Latin so well that he was chosen to write the epoch-making scripts for the Roman Festival of 240. The fact that these scripts were translations from the Greek helps to explain this choice, and it does something more.

The way the Romans told the story of how their national literature began stresses that the first authors were not Roman, but Greek or "half-Greek," as the imperial scholar and biographer Suetonius (69–126 CE) puts it. In fact, over the long history of Latin literature, only a small minority of authors have been native Romans. Most have come from other parts of ancient Italy, where languages other than or in addition to Latin were in use, or from more distant provinces, like Africa (Terence, Apuleius, Tertullian, and Augustine) or Spain (Seneca the Elder and the Younger, their kinsman Lucan, Martial, and Quintilian). Literature was always represented as something that was not native to Rome or to native Romans. This was done deliberately and officially: making a foreigner like Livius Andronicus the star of the Roman Festival in 240 and turning to him again in 207 would have been unthinkable without the initiative of the Roman ruling class. That does not mean that he, or any other poet, enjoyed the status traditionally associated with the poet's calling in the Greek world. We are told that Livius was eventually enrolled in an institution called the Poets' and Writers' Guild (*collegium poetarum et scribarum*), but this was not like being worshipped as a god or hero in the way that Homer and Archilochus were, or joining the staff of the Alexandrian Library as, literally, a priest of the Muses. In later times, Latin prose authors, whatever their origins, were very often of the senatorial class, the highest in Roman society, and had no reason to fret about their social status. Latin poets, on the other hand, would for centuries insist that they deserved the same respect that the Greeks accorded their poets, but they would seldom receive it. In a very real sense, Livius's condition as a foreigner who achieved Roman citizenship through service to the state, and his marginal status as a freedman, were as foundational for Latin literature as his success in adapting Greek texts to Roman purposes. His prestige as the founder of Latin literature went hand in hand with the stigma of his foreign birth and his enslavement.

The remains of Livius's dramatic works are not plentiful, and it is often a matter of guesswork which Greek play he was adapting in any given case. On the other hand, though we do not know when or why he translated the *Odyssey*, what remains of that work is much easier to understand. Because we have the Homeric original in its entirety, and because Livius's translation of it is so close, it is usually not difficult to match even a few surviving words of the Latin version to the corresponding passage of the Greek. What is equally important, precisely because the Latin *Odyssey* follows Homer so closely, is that the places where it diverges stand out in sharp relief; and the way it does so has made Livius's contribution as an interpreter of Greek poetry for Roman audiences one of his most celebrated talents.

Famously, in the first line of the poem—which happens by the merest of chances to survive—where Homer invokes the Muse to inspire his *Odyssey*, Livius instead calls on a Camena. This is a "familiarizing" or "naturalizing" cultural translation. The Greek Muses were, in effect, a sisterhood of nymphs, goddesses who lived on Mount Helicon near the source of the Hippocrene, or "Horse Spring," which gushed from the ground where the winged horse Pegasus first touched hoof to earth. The Roman Camenae, too, were nymphs who inhabited a grove watered by spring that flowed just outside the Porta Capena in the south side of the city walls. These Camenae had different functions from the Muses, but their grove was where the legendary second king of Rome, Numa Pompilius, consorted with his spouse, the water-nymph Egeria, who is associated with these goddesses. For Livius to invoke a Camena, we have been taught, rendered comprehensible to Roman audiences the relationship between Homer and his Muse. In some sense, this has to be true; at the same time, the idea that Livius's Roman audience was radically unprepared to conjure with Homer and his Muses must be exaggerated. In the first place, we have seen that stories from the *Iliad* and the *Odyssey* had been familiar to Italian audiences for centuries. On the other hand, there is evidence that the Muses themselves were not entirely unknown in Rome, although there would be no actual cult of the Muses until around 185 BCE, almost certainly after Livius was dead.

This familiarizing treatment of the Muses as Camenae has been interpreted in two rather different ways. On the one hand, German classicist Friedrich Leo (1851–1914) saw in Livius's act of translation and interpretation the originary impulse and, as it were, the script or algorithm for a series of translations and interpretations by which the creativity, imagination, and civilizing power of Greek literature would be adapted and made available to other peoples. This, Leo believed, was the Roman contribution to the march of civilization, to show later peoples how to profit from the wisdom of earlier ones. Livius's translation of Homer is in every way the essential act in this process. In this sense, as Leo would have it, his *Odyssey* is an indispensable contribution to European literature. Without this act of translation, adaptation, and interpretation, he reasoned, such a thing as European literature could not even exist.

On the other hand, in keeping with the Romans' own insistence that they first felt the civilizing impact of Greek culture at this time, Leo clearly conceived of Livius as a cultivated individual tasked with civilizing barbarians. Indeed, the aforementioned Suetonius remembers Livius as having earned his keep as a teacher, and it is not uncommon for modern scholars to suppose that

Livius translated the *Odyssey* mainly for use as a textbook for young students. This is hardly an unreasonable idea, since Homer himself was put to the same purpose by the Greeks. What is unreasonable, or at least unnecessary, is to suppose that Livius was content to produce a text more rudimentary than the original, or one that would not take advantage of the substantial record of Homeric interpretation that had been building for centuries, and that was being organized and circulated in ever more convenient form thanks to the activities of contemporary scholars, especially in the great research centers of the Hellenistic world. What evidence do we have of this?

Another passage illustrates a conundrum that confronts students of Livius's *Odyssey*. When the hero visits the island of Scheria, his host, Alcinous, king of the Phaeacians, honors him with a festival that features dancing, among other entertainments. The Phaeacians excel in dancing, and Homer describes their movements by using rare words and elaborate syntax to suggest the intricacy of their skillful movements. Such passages are often found in Homer, so that professional grammarians, probably within Livius's own lifetime, began writing commentaries to help contemporary readers understand expressions that were difficult for them. In this case, we have a scholarly gloss on the passage in question; and it just so happens that Livius's Latin translation of it corresponds more closely to the commentator's gloss than it does to Homer's own Greek. The natural inference is that Livius translated the gloss instead of Homer; what to make of this is not so obvious.

It would be perfectly in keeping with the idea that one of Livius's goals as a translator was not just to interpret, but also to simplify Homer, especially where even a Greek reader might find him difficult, for the benefit of a Roman readership. It is not in keeping with the idea that Livius was working in an outpost far from the centers of the civilized world without access to any scholarly assistance apart from his own wits. Sheer availability is the key here, along with Livius's own relationship to contemporary Greek scholarship. A passage like this one suggests that he did have access to interpretive works that had only recently begun to circulate in the Greek world. The very idea of their availability to him in Rome has struck some scholars as astounding, so that they tend to treat this case as anomalous and deny it any larger explanatory power. But what if, instead, we accept the hypothesis that Livius was conversant with Greek literary scholarship and that he used it in his work as a translator. What then would we expect to find?

The passage concerning the dancing of the Phaeacians involves grammatical exegesis, and this is one common kind of scholarship that might prove helpful to the translator. Another kind, which has a grammatical dimension but goes beyond it, is moral and ethical criticism of Homer. Many readers are familiar with those passages in Plato's *Republic* where Socrates criticizes Homer and the tragedians for what he sees as their faulty representation of gods and heroes as morally and ethically defective—philandering, fearing death, and behaving in other ways unworthy even of a reasonable human being, let alone someone more than mortal. Other critics could be equally censorious, but most found in poetry both patterns of behavior to emulate and others to avoid. This sort of evaluation came to be associated with a branch of ethical philosophy known as "kingship theory"—kingship here being broadly defined not just as the business of monarchy, but as the social role assumed by any active citizen under any political economy. Within this discourse, the question of who was the best hero, or king, according to Homer—who best exemplified the behavior of the ideal citizen—assumed a particular salience. During the fifth century, this discussion had been carried on primarily by the tragic poets, who staged episodes of Homeric and other archaic epic in which the greatest of the heroes were closely examined, and often found wanting. Under these conditions, Achilles was generally agreed to be enormously problematic, but indispensable, because his sheer physical prowess so greatly surpassed that of all his nominal peers, and because he was, at least, the most honest and straightforward of them all. Odysseus, on the other hand, came off badly: the trait that Homer celebrates as versatility came to be seen instead as shiftiness, to the point that the Irish scholar W. B. Stanford (1910–84) entitled his treatment of Odysseus in fifth-century tragedy, simply, "The Stage Villain."

The reception of Homer's principal heroes in Greek tragedy was thus starkly divergent. With this in mind, we may ask why it was that Livius Andronicus in the third century chose to translate the *Odyssey* instead of the *Iliad* into Latin. The decision is all the more puzzling if one believes that Livius meant his version to serve as a teaching text, because in Hellenistic Greek schoolrooms the *Iliad* was the more commonly studied of the Homeric poems. It has been suggested that Odysseus's more fantastic adventures had come to be located in various parts of the western Mediterranean, and since the time of Hesiod he had been connected, as was noted above, with the foundation of cities in Italy. Both aspects may indeed have played some role in Livius's decision. It is worth remembering, however, that Greek mythographers had connected Odysseus with the foundation of Rome itself, but that the Romans preferred a story that made their founder none of the Greeks, but the Trojan hero Aeneas, instead. It is also the case that the Romans in all periods tend to emphasize their warlike nature and preference for straightforward valor, while denigrating their opponents, be they Greeks, Carthaginians, Parthians, or what have you, as duplicitous and untrustworthy. Indeed, Livius's immediate successors in Latin epic poetry, Naevius and Ennius, both wrote about the voyage of Aeneas to Italy, and both framed their works to a large extent in terms of battle narra-tive. Why, then, did Livius choose to translate the *Odyssey*, and not the *Iliad*?

The answer may be that in the century and a half before Livius's career as we know it began, the general perception of Achilles and Odysseus among ethically minded Greek critics reversed itself entirely. The process has been traced by Silvia Montiglio, who identifies Socrates and his associates—apart, notably, from Plato—as responsible for the rehabilitation of Odysseus, in par-ticular. In line 1 of the *Odyssey*, Homer calls his hero "a man" (*andra*) "of many turns" (*polytropon*). Since he is talking about Odysseus's defining quality as a hero, Homer must mean that he is "versatile" in some positive sense; but it is partly by virtue of his inconstancy that the tragedians had found Odysseus wanting. By the beginning of the fourth century, however, critics began to examine the meaning of this line in penetrating detail. An ancient note on the word *andra* states that it marks the hero not only as "male," but also as "manly," that is, possessed of *andreia*, "manliness (or) courage." This is a good, simple example of a grammatical comment that has an ethical dimension, as well. A further note on *polytropon* tells us more. It says that Antisthenes (445–365 BCE), who was an associate of Socrates, posed an interpretive problem by observing that Odysseus's versatility can be understood in both favorable and unfavorable ways:

> Antisthenes says that when Homer calls Odysseus *polytropos*, he does not praise him more than he blames him. In fact, he did not make Achilles and Ajax *polytropoi*, but simple and noble; and he certainly did not portray Nestor the wise as crafty and devious in character, but as dealing straight-forwardly with Agamemnon and all the others, and as giving the army whatever good advice he had, without hiding it away. Achilles was so far from accepting that sort of behavior that he considered as hateful as death that man "who hides one thing in his heart, but says another" [cf. *Iliad* 9.313]. (2011, 20–24)

The note continues by giving Antisthenes's solution to this problem, as well. Odysseus is *polytropos* because he commands many *tropoi*, many ways of engaging different interlocutors; as such, he is not "shifty," but *sophos*, "wise." As Montiglio explains, Antisthenes's opinion that Homer praises Odysseus for his wisdom quickly became the dominant interpretation of Odysseus as a paragon of ethical heroism.

Antisthenes's statement of the problem and its solution cannot possibly have been unfamiliar to serious students of Homer at any time after they were first promulgated, more than a century before Livius began his career. One would have to be fanatically committed to the idea that Livius was out of touch with his native culture to believe him ignorant of such issues or uninterested in them. Indeed, his own treatment of the phrase *andra . . . polytropon* places even greater emphasis on it than Homer himself does. Consider the opening of the two poems:

ἄνδρα μοι ἔννεπε, Μοῦσα, **πολύτροπον,** ὃς μάλα πόλλα πλάγχθη . . .

Sing to me, Muse, **the man of many turns,** who suffered very many blows . . .

—HOMER, *Od.* 1.1–2

virum mihi, Camena, insece **versutum**

Sing to me, Camena, **the versatile man**

—LIVIUS, *Od.* fr. 1

Both Homer and Livius emphasize Odysseus's flexibility and adaptability. Homer, by making *andra* the first word of his poem and making *polytropon* stand just before the only major pause within the same line, lends the phrase enormous emphasis. Livius, however, clearly alive to this fact, goes a bit further, making *virum . . . versutum* frame the entire first line of his poem. Some would say that Livius's Saturnian meter, which accommodates fewer syllables than Homer's hexameter, forces him to do this; but I would answer that making an aesthetic virtue out of technical necessity is almost the definition of a poet's art. Equally important is the fact that Livius's *virum* (man) and *versutum* (versatile) resemble one another sonically in a way that Homer's *andra* and *polytropon* do not. To this extent, Livius's Latin reinforces the idea of a connection between "manliness" (*virtus*) and "versatility," drawing on linguistic resources unavailable in Greek. This is more than making a virtue of necessity: it is an instance in which the meaning of the original text actually gains in translation. Finally, it seems appropriate here to mention an observation by Stephen Hinds that Livius's *versutus* is lexically related to *vertere*, "to turn," which is also the usual Latin word for "to translate." If we remember Antisthenes's contention that Odysseus is *polytropos* because he commands many *tropoi*, so many ways of engaging different interlocutors, the relevance of his opinion to the art of translation is obvious. This particular act of translation implicitly links the heroic virtue celebrated by the poem with the expertise of the translator, whose work makes Homer's lessons in heroic ethics accessible to an allophone audience.

These arguments are circumstantial, but so are almost all arguments that can be made about the dawn of Latin literature. The real difference here lies in the assumptions that one brings to the evidence. Instead of assuming that Livius—the founder of Latin literature, after all—was a poet of limited cultural horizons or of modest ambition, whether for himself or his audience, we must come to terms with the possibility, or indeed the likelihood, that these tokens of engagement with the instruments of Greek literary culture, in the work of its first identifiable Latinate imitator, speak to the goal not only of calquing the individual texts of the Greek canon, but of conjuring with the entire apparatus that gave Greek culture its prestige and its staying power, right from the beginning of the Romans' own effort to emulate it. This is an issue that may or may not be related to the question of how unusual the form of Greek literary culture itself was, or how unusual the Romans were in attempting to reproduce it in their own language. Indeed, comparative evidence suggests that the Japanese, in forming their own literary culture in their own language, took advantage not only of canonical Chinese literature itself, but also of the intellectual and institutional apparatus that their predecessors had developed to support the earlier literature. In this sense, however typical or unusual the Greeks and Romans may prove to be in an ancient Mediterranean context, there may well be a sense in which the Romans and the Japanese conform to a distinct pattern of emulation, perhaps experienced by others as well, in which a derivative literary culture at its beginning recapitulates almost the entire literary history of a source culture. This might be just one, but hardly the least interesting, of the ways in which literatures begin.

Further Reading

Bolter, Jay. "Friedrich August Wolf and the Scientific Study of Antiquity," *Greek, Roman, and Byzantine Studies* 21 (1980): 83–99.

Conte, Gian Biagio. *Latin Literature: A History*, translated by Joseph B. Solodow, revised by Don Fowler and Glenn W. Most, 1994.

Denecke, Wiebke. *Classical World Literatures: Sino-Japanese and Greco-Roman Comparisons*, 2013.

Farrell, Joseph. "Roman Homer," in *The Cambridge Companion to Homer*, edited by Robert Fowler, 2004.

Feeney, Denis. *Beyond Greek: The Beginnings of Latin Literature*, 2016.

Habinek, Thomas. *The World of Roman Song*, 2005.

Harris, William V. *Ancient Literacy*, 1989.

Hinds, Stephen. *Allusion and Intertext: The Dynamics of Appropriation in Roman Poetry*, 1998.

Leonhardt, Jürgen. *Latin: Story of a World Language*, translated by Kenneth Kronenberg, 2013.

Montiglio, Silvia. *From Villain to Hero: Odysseus in Ancient Greek Thought*, 2011.

Wiseman, T. P. *The Myths of Rome*, 2004.

Hebrew

JACQUELINE VAYNTRUB

Literature, Not Scripture

For the most part, a study of ancient Hebrew textual culture, its genres, and distinct features, must focus on the written works collected and preserved in the Hebrew Bible, since these twenty-four works[1] account for its largest and most broadly attested corpus. These twenty-four books are generally divided into three sections. The first is the Torah or the Pentateuch, the five books of Moses: Genesis, Exodus, Leviticus, Numbers, and Deuteronomy. Together, they cover a story that begins with the world's creation, the rise of human civilization and its nations, and the particular story of Israel and their god, Yahweh, in the land of Canaan.

Scholars describe this narrative as *compiled* since there is ample evidence in the text to show that multiple narratives telling the same or similar events were spliced and stitched together to make one continuous story. There is wide disagreement among scholars on when any of these stories would have been composed and where their narrative divisions lie, though it is thought that their *compilation* into one overarching story may have taken place after the destruction of the First Temple in Jerusalem by the Babylonians and the exile to Babylon at the end of the sixth century BCE. The second section is known as the Prophets, subdivided into the "Former Prophets" and the "Latter Prophets." The Former Prophets, beginning with the book of Joshua, continue the story of the five books of Moses, which ends in Deuteronomy with the death of Moses before the crossing of the Jordan River into the land of Canaan. The book of Joshua, named for Moses's successor, continues the story with the conquest of Canaan, and this narrative is succeeded by Judges, Samuel (1 and 2), and Kings (1 and 2). These four works, Joshua, Judges, Samuel, and Kings, tell the story of Israel in the land. The Latter Prophets—Isaiah, Jeremiah, Ezekiel, and the Twelve—can be read as speech collections that are attributed to named prophetic figures hailing from various periods. The prophetic collections are not chronologically arranged, and at times, later prophetic speeches can be found attributed to figures who would have lived in periods before the events described would have taken place. The third section of the twenty-four books consists of the Writings, with collections of poetry, such as Psalms, Lamentations, Proverbs, and Song of Songs, wisdom (Job and Ecclesiastes), shorter narratives, such as Ruth and Esther, apocalyptic prophecy (Daniel), and finally, stories that continue and recapitulate the narrative of Israel from the end of the books of Kings, Ezra-Nehemiah, and Chronicles. These works found in the Writings also derive from varied periods that would be difficult to pin down and continue to be hotly debated by scholars.

While these twenty-four books cover a variety of genres, styles, and periods, we should also recognize that the Hebrew Bible does not contain a comprehensive record of ancient Hebrew texts. For its ancient authors, readers, and interpreters, other texts may have been seen as part of the literary tradition. The texts preserved in the Hebrew Bible, as well as the Greek translations of Hebrew texts preserved in the Old Testament (the Septuagint, the Jewish Greek translation that was subsequently adopted by Christians), and those documents found in modern archaeological discoveries, such as the Dead Sea Scrolls, are a significant representation of ancient Hebrew literary traditions. At the same time, they represent but a fragment of the literary traditions— both textually and orally transmitted—that existed in antiquity. The corpus of preserved texts, alongside comparative evidence from the wider ancient Near East, must all be drawn on when one examines Hebrew literature at its beginnings. Because of the long history of the reception of this corpus in Jewish and Christian religious communities as Scripture, and because of the framing of these texts themselves as Israel's story, and the nation's relationship with its god, Yahweh, it would be natural to conclude that ancient Hebrew literature is largely a religious set of texts. When studied in light of its historical intellectual and cultural context, however, it becomes clear that ancient Hebrew texts, while bearing unique local features, emerge from a West Semitic cultural context and have much in common with the literary traditions of its Mesopotamian, Egyptian, and Mediterranean neighbors. The claim that ancient Hebrew literature, including its genres and themes, is somehow more inherently sacred or religious than the literary output of another ancient tradition is anachronistic. All ancient Near Eastern and Mediterranean literary traditions imagine the problems of human life and the unfolding of history in the context of a world of deities that share responsibility with willed human action. We can understand ancient Hebrew literary texts only against the backdrop of the history of West Semitic literary and scribal culture, and more broadly, in its Near Eastern and Mediterranean context.

As a final introductory note, it is worth mentioning that the "canon" of the Hebrew Bible, which does not include the Apocrypha and Pseudepigrapha, much of which is preserved in Greek translation in the Septuagint (whose textual evidence dates it to approximately the mid-second century BCE), and in other texts found in modern discoveries in the Judean desert (such as the Dead Sea Scrolls), while in some ways representative of ancient Hebrew literary traditions, is also a historically contingent collection of texts. If we look beyond a scriptural model and shift toward a more literary model of these texts, and if we recognize that ancient literary cultures are necessarily much wider than the fragments that happen to be available to the modern reader, a fuller understanding of ancient Hebrew notions of textual production, transmission, and reception comes into view. Setting aside theological or canonical models as much as possible allows the ancient Hebrew texts to be considered through the lens of a question that is substantively different from the more conventional one that asks, "How do these stories, poems, and laws contribute to the formation of a later Jewish or Christian perspective?" Instead, such an approach seeks to recover and reconstruct the values and techniques of ancient Hebrew literary culture. How are we to go about recovering and reconstructing ancient Hebrew literary culture? We do so through the various genres native to this text tradition, paying close attention to their distinctiveness vis-à-vis dominant Western genres inherited through the ancient Greek traditions of literary criticism. We also attend to the various social values and practices that are manifested by these native genres and literary techniques. For example, oftentimes composition types found in the biblical texts (and in Hebrew and Aramaic manuscripts found in modern archaeological digs dated between the second century BCE and second century CE) are marked by various terms in the Hebrew that do not match up with inherited Western genre categories, such as lyric, lament, epic, or proverb. The simple observation that the biblical literary tradition operates according to its own aesthetic and cultural categories can also help us see what is unique about these texts, including authorship and attribution of texts to named individuals and the various forms collections can take.

A Focus on Written Texts

In *A Social History of Hebrew*, William Schniedewind shows that a nontheological account of ancient Hebrew textual traditions necessarily leaves us with a gap between the products of a writing system and "the ancient speech community." His study reminds readers that with respect to ancient Hebrew texts, "written artifacts are the products of a *scribal community*, not a *speech community*."[2] Schniedewind speaks here of a "scribal community" in the sense of elite groups in society trained in the scribal arts who transform cultural knowledge and ideals through their textual productions, not only by committing them to written form, but also in light of the sociocultural commitments in these groups, including their exposure to neighboring scribal practices (Mesopotamian and Egyptian) and classical texts. For example, ancient Hebrew epistolography (letters found in archaeological discoveries dating to the Iron Age) makes use of hieratic numerals inherited through the Egyptian scribal traditions. This is an example of how neighboring scribal *practices* are incorporated into ancient Hebrew scribal practice. The repeated reference to Mesopotamian legal genres in the production of biblical texts, meanwhile, reveals one way that ancient Hebrew scribal communities were exposed to neighboring textual cultures. Similarities have also been observed between laws recorded in the stele of Hammurabi, a Mesopotamian literary classic copied over a period of hundreds of years, and the so-called Covenant Code found in the Hebrew Bible in Exodus 20–23. The ancient Hebrew texts available to contemporary readers do not provide a full picture of ancient Hebrew society but rather have been profoundly shaped by the biases and writerly practices within the rarified circle of Hebrew scribes. Without getting mired in the question of what defines "literature," we can begin by acknowledging that the advent of visible language—writing—does not mark the advent of literature.

As in many other cultures, ancient Hebrew literature existed before and after the invention of the technology of writing. Literature before the written word, and likely after its advent as well, was composed, disseminated, and performed orally. Nevertheless, ancient Hebrew literature was shaped in a variety of ways by this technology in the social circles that made use of it.[3] Recent scholarship has attempted to recover knowledge of ancient Hebrew scribal culture and the development of these circles through comparison with the well-attested scribal cultures of Mesopotamia and Egypt, neighbors to the northern and southern kingdoms of Israel and Judah.[4] The dissemination of this technology throughout the two Hebrew-speaking kingdoms of ancient Israel and Judah, the scribal cultures that surrounded its development, and its selective use for various types of linguistic expression, however, remain largely unknown to scholars. The question of the dissemination of these scribal technologies and their developmental trajectory is frequently theologically inflected by scholars. That is to say, it is common for scholars of ancient Hebrew literature to reconstruct high levels of literate activity in earlier periods. This argument is frequently made so that scholars can temporally locate the composition of biblical texts in close proximity to the very events these texts narrate. An example of this might be to attribute, for example, the Song of Deborah in Judges 5 (a song of victory over Canaanite enemies by Israelite tribes) to a very early period in order to claim these texts as fragments of Israel's collective memory of the history of early Israel and the consolidation of various tribes into a national unit. There is a sense among scholars that the question of *when* to locate the composition of a biblical text hinges on an understanding of when and how scribal traditions developed in ancient Israel, and in turn, the relevance of the biblical texts as historical documents hinges on these types of inquiries.

Scholars continue to negotiate the relationship of the biblical texts to the reconstruction of the history and material culture of ancient Israel. And while such questions are of great interest to experts and non-experts alike, there are other considerations that should also concern modern readers. Among these considerations, which will be a dominant focus here, are the literary strategies shared across ancient Hebrew texts that distinguish them from neighboring traditions. Attention to such formal elements allows us to recognize, in particular, these literary strategies' differences from Mesopotamian and Egyptian compositional practices.

One important example is the distinctive way in which ancient Hebrew literary composition attributes authorship. Many compositions, particularly poems, instructions, prophetic speeches, and collections of proverbs, are attributed to legendary figures of a much earlier period, harkening back to the distant past. Sometimes these legendary figures are known as characters in the overarching narrative history of Israel in the Hebrew Bible—for example, King David of the Psalms, or King Solomon of Song of Songs. Other times these figures of prophecy and wisdom remain obscure to the modern reader but are presented so that the reader assumes that the instruction or prophecy is authoritative or important precisely *because* of the significance of its named speaker.

Ancient Near Eastern literary compositions are mostly "unsigned" by their authors. In fact, some scholars argue that the first "signed author" of ancient Near Eastern literary corpora appears in the epilogue of the Wisdom of Ben Sira, where the speaker of the text offers his own name. This too, as will be discussed further, cannot be fully equated with modern authorial practices but rather fits into the broader pattern of "legendary authorship," common to ancient Hebrew and ancient Near Eastern compositional practices. A legendary author is one who lends authority, prestige, and the biographical flavor to the composition that names them, but they could not possibly have been the text's author because they lived long before the text was composed. This practice of attribution, traditionally known as *pseudepigraphy* or "false attribution," is distinct from the self-identification of scribes who at times identify themselves on ancient Near Eastern documents. In some cases, a scribe will be named, but it is clear that the scribe has either copied an older, previously unsigned or oral composition; or, as in the case of a letter, the scribe has transcribed the spoken words of his client, the letter's sender. These words, committed to writing on a clay tablet by a scribe on behalf of the speaker, would be brought to the recipient and read aloud to the recipient by the letter's messenger. In the context of ancient Near Eastern compositional strategies, a frame speaker, such as a psalm attributed to King David or a prophecy attributed to the non-Israelite prophet Balaam, would not have indicated their authorship. Rather, the attribution of a type of speech to a particular named character indicates a very specific literary practice. This compositional practice, not quite "authorship," but something closer to a character-driven mode of genre identification, associates certain types of performed speech (such as certain types of instruction, prophecy, or lament) with characters who were famed for having performed these types of speech according to their broader biographical narrative. This type of practice of naming not *authors* but *legendary characters* is a common feature of ancient Near Eastern texts. Contemporary readers of these texts should take care not to conflate the naming of legendary speakers in ancient Hebrew texts with modern expectations of authorship and historiography. Additionally, these literary practices in the ancient Hebrew textual tradition can be compared and contrasted with those literary practices of their neighbors. One distinctive thread we can identify in ancient Hebrew literary traditions that we might not see in the ancient literary practices of Mesopotamia, Egypt, or Ugarit (an ancient West Semitic city-state of the late Bronze Age) is a modal distinction between unframed and unattributed narrative prose (used for historiography) and framed and attributed law, instruction, wisdom, prophecy, and other forms of poetry. In the overarching biblical narrative, spanning the creation of the world to the Babylonian exile, divine law, wisdom, and prophecy is communicated through Israel's named heroes in poetic performance. Even compendiums of these poetic performances, in works like the books of Psalms, Proverbs, and the collection of speeches of the prophets, are attributed to named and famed speakers. By contrast, the prose narrators remain unnamed, and their documents remain unsigned.

Like all other literatures, ancient Hebrew literature was shaped in dialogue with the formation of other elements of its culture. Their literary traditions took both oral and written form. Today, however, this literary culture can be experienced only in the medium of writing. Western scholarship emphasizes a dominant tradition of the authority of the written word, and as a result, scholars are prone to assume that the surviving texts were more important than ones lost to oblivion. Within the academic community, written evidence may serve as an ideal form for making authoritative claims about the world and its history, and academic conceptions of performed speech may be modeled on this ideal. However, following scholarship in the twentieth century on living oral literary traditions, notably studies by Albert Lord, Ruth Finnegan, and John Foley, scholars today no longer reduce the "written" and the "oral" to a simple dichotomy but instead recognize a complex relationship between the two for the production and transmission of a literary culture.[5] These considerations do not, however, change the nature of evidence available to modern readers encountering ancient Hebrew literary culture. While we must assume that a rich oral background lies behind the composition, transmission, and performance of these texts, our questions are shaped by our access to written evidence. What is the nature of ancient Hebrew literary production? How does ancient Hebrew textuality uniquely reflect its rich cultural traditions, including oral ones? What are its models of knowledge formulation, acquisition, and transmission? How are these models reflected in and reshaped by the texts?

In contradistinction to its neighboring literary cultures, ancient Hebrew literature is characterized by a fascinating paradox: that while all our means for recovering the literary culture are written texts, these texts time and again are characterized by the spoken word in their formulation of authoritative claims. Law, prophecy, wisdom, and testimony are represented in the written texts as being articulated in the *spoken voice* of their transmitters, prophets, sages, and legendary heroes. This particular use of voice in ancient Hebrew texts is connected to the distinction between biblical narrative history, which is given in an anonymous narrator's voice, and those prophetic, legal, and wisdom performances given in the named voices of characters from Israel's overarching story. Even though Israel's literary traditions have been significantly shaped by the intellectual commitments and textual practices of scribes, a value for the extraordinary spoken voices from Israel's past remains in these documents.

Ancient Hebrew Textuality in Its Broader Historical and Cultural Context

The writing system of ancient Hebrew is alphabetic. Sometimes called by scholars "consonantal syllabaries," the West Semitic writing system invented the use of individual symbols to represent consonants, and later, certain vowels. This West Semitic invention from which the ancient Hebrew writing system emerges is also the origin of the Greek and Latin alphabetic writing systems, which in turn, fully integrate the notation of vowels—a process that had already started in ancient Hebrew and Phoenician with the use of *matres lectionis*, or certain consonantal symbols used to mark vowels to aid the disambiguation of multiple otherwise graphically identical terms. The West Semitic consonantal writing system is distinct from Mesopotamian cuneiform and Egyptian hieroglyphic systems, which use logograms and phonograms, and syllabic systems that arose through state-backed institutions. Because West Semitic alphabetic writing emerged from beyond a centralized state or institutional context, unlike Mesopotamian cuneiform and Egyptian hieroglyphic, one should use caution comparing their respective scribal traditions. The alphabetic technology that uses discrete symbols to represent individual consonants and vowels is, originally, a West Semitic invention that arose through cultural contact with ancient Egypt. The earliest traces of this technology known to scholars are inscriptions found in the Sinai (Serabit el-Khadim) and in Wadi el-Hol dating to the Egyptian Middle Kingdom and Second Intermediate Period, sometime around the eighteenth century BCE.[6] The script, known as Proto-Sinaitic, was a West Semitic alphabetic adaptation of the existing Egyptian hieroglyphic and hieratic script system. While the letters of this alphabetic script frequently took the form of Egyptian hieroglyphics, the acrophonic principle behind the association of the name of the letter with its initial phoneme via the Semitic vocabulary—the sound they represented—was the initial consonant of the name for the logogram as it would be in West Semitic, not Egyptian. For example, the form that takes the shape of a bull's head would be used to express the sound of the initial consonant of the word for bull in West Semitic, *'alp*, the / '/ or the glottal stop; likewise, the sign resembling a hand or arm would be used to express the sound of the initial consonant of the word for arm in West Semitic, *yad*, the /y/ sound. Thus the alphabet was born as a technology adapted from an existing, nonalphabetic writing system.

Local Literary Culture and Foreign Influence

Unlike the earliest Mesopotamian or Egyptian written texts, the earliest alphabetic West Semitic texts do not appear to function initially in economic or institutional contexts. Even though this technology for writing came onto the scene within the context of already fully developed centralized scribal systems, it was used for completely different purposes from the ones that mattered in Egypt and Mesopotamia. As Seth Sanders writes in *The Invention of Hebrew*, the earliest alphabetic inscriptions pose

> no threat to the hegemony of Babylonian cuneiform. By contrast with the sophisticated corpus of Sumero-Akkadian, the *Wadi el-Hol* inscriptions are typical graffiti. All we can decipher of [these inscriptions] are short,

unevenly written blessings. . . . These inscriptions suggest the quick and dirty tool of foreign workers, scratched in desolate places: the mines, the gulch of horrors. There is no high culture here.[7]

This social context for the earliest alphabetic inscriptions suggests something rather distinct from the context of existing writing systems. Here we encounter a decentralized, informal technology, used for purposes outside of state-backed institutional interests. It is not until the thirteenth century BCE, at the city-state of Ugarit in coastal Syria, as Sanders insightfully notes, that the alphabetic writing system became a component of statecraft for a native West Semitic culture. The native West Semitic language of Ugaritic thus systematized an alphabetic script, one very similar to the Proto-Sinaitic script in its form and function, against the backdrop of cultural contact with long-standing traditions of cuneiform culture, rendering its inherited alphabetic forms in cuneiform-style wedges.[8]

Ugaritic scribes developed their own local writing system on the basis of Akkadian models. Ugaritic's alphabet (in the long form) consisted of a repertoire of thirty graphemes. It adapted a phonemic inventory into a graphical rendering inspired by the wedge shapes of Sumero-Akkadian syllabic cuneiform, written left to right as normative in those cuneiform logographic systems. This alphabetic script was used for three kinds of text production: national narrative poetry, epistolary communication with local polities, and ritual texts. Those texts that fell within the Mesopotamian literary tradition continued to be produced according to the cuneiform script practices. Based on the earliest-attested consonantal forms in the Proto-Sinaitic inscriptions discussed above, this new West Semitic scribal practice seems to have been devised at Ugarit itself and for the purpose of writing the Ugaritic language.[9] Local scribes developed their script on inherited West Semitic alphabetic models but also borrowed the wedge-shaped forms for their consonants, clay tablet technology, and other elements of established Akkadian scribal practices. While some have viewed the development of this script as marking independence from neighboring polities, it was still in a certain sense inspired by the writing systems of Mesopotamia.

Regardless of the origin of their script and the extent to which Ugaritic literary traditions were local and native, the fact remains that these scribes communicated ideas common to the ancient Near East in their own language and writing system. The translation of foreign cultural ideas into a local idiom was also at work in some of the word lists that have been found at ancient Ugarit. One such text attests three parallel columns of deity names in Sumero-Akkadian, Hurrian, and Ugaritic, which belong to a larger group of polyglot lists consisting of common words. It becomes clear then that we do not see merely the translation of words in lexical lists, but at times, cultural concepts as well.[10] So while some have understood the development of Ugaritic script as part of the ambition to develop local vernacular identity in the face of a foreign one, one might alternatively think of this development as a form of translation from a dominant foreign literary culture into a vernacular local one.[11] The seemingly polarized alternatives of the local vernacular versus the foreign imperial seem to be, in fact, two components of a shared cultural experience. At Ugarit, scribes were conversant in the dominant culture, even as they strove to relate it to their own traditions and language.

What, then, is shared between Ugaritic and ancient Hebrew literature, beyond its related languages (both West Semitic), literary forms (poetic techniques and genres), and broader social, religious, and cultural norms? What can we learn about ancient Hebrew literature through its comparison to other related West Semitic literary traditions? It seems that in both cases, homegrown literary traditions that may have continued to be transmitted and performed orally—those literary traditions that encode social and cultural values—have been transformed in the written record through overarching narratives that focus on the fate of a people. In the case of Ugaritic literature, which comes to us chiefly in the form of narrative poetry and ritual texts, along with snippets to be found in letters, this consolidation of literary traditions seems to serve the interests of those in power at the highest level of government, central state actors who negotiated notions of legitimacy and inheritance through stories of mortals (*Aqhat* and *Kirta*) and gods (*The Baal Cycle*). In the case of ancient Hebrew texts including the Hebrew Bible, inscriptions, and materials found among the Dead Sea Scrolls, literary traditions and compositional strategies were consolidated through the overarching drama of the people of Israel; the story of their importance in the history of creation; their relationship to their national deity, Yahweh; and the trials and successes of their heroes. The role of writing technology in this story of ancient identify formation, then, has less to do with a culture reaching a particular "stage" in their development along a predetermined trajectory but instead more to do with the various functions served by storytelling on a grand scale. As we know from those monumental inscriptions that mark the achievements of great kings and rulers dating back to the second millennium BCE, a literary form discussed below, writing in the West Semitic tradition can serve a memorializing function, expressing an "I was here" type of statement. The commitment of well-known literary traditions to a more durable and static medium, both in the Ugaritic and ancient Hebrew tradition, might follow a similar set of values in their production: "We were here; this is our story."

While the Hebrew Bible is the largest attested corpus of ancient Hebrew literary traditions, there are other texts that should be considered as well to fill out a wider picture of what shapes core concepts of text production, transmission, and reception. Earlier West Semitic, Mesopotamian, and Egyptian texts share a number of general features with biblical texts. An important feature common to both West Semitic memorial inscriptions and biblical law, instruction, prophecy, and testimony (such as laments and victory songs) is that these discourses are all framed in a first-person voice. This is a remarkable yet frequently overlooked feature shared by these supposedly distinct genres.

The Voice and Body of West Semitic Literary Texts

West Semitic memorial texts are frequently inscribed on stone and often feature visual representations of the speaker's body and face.[12] These texts often open with the speaker naming himself in the first person with his patronymic ("I am so-and-so, son of so-and-so"), followed by a description of his title. Sometimes the speaker adds a justification of the legitimacy of his rule (inheritance of the position and/or being named by a deity to the position) and a longer description of his accomplishments in life. These inscriptions are written in a variety of Semitic dialects (chiefly West Semitic) over a period of at least two thousand years, particularly if you count within this corpus Hammurabi's so-called law code (from eighteenth-century BCE Babylon) and the Idrimi statue (from fifteenth-century BCE Syria). The West Semitic instances of these monumental inscriptions date to the Iron Age, located in Aramaic- and Phoenician-speaking city-states.

The aim of these inscriptions seems to be preservation of the speaker's name, voice, and deeds. The inscriptions accomplish this rhetorically through its first-person framing as well as through threats to its readers. Hypothetical future readers are warned not to remove the object from its location or damage the inscription in such a way that the speaker's name might be altered or erased. A typical example can be found in the Phoenician Kilamuwa stele, "Whoever of my sons who will sit in my place and damages this inscription . . . and whoever strikes out this inscription, may [multiple deities listed] strike his head," and the Azatiwada stele, "If a king . . . prince . . . man of renown . . . shall erase the name of Azatiwada from this gate and shall place [his] name [on it] . . . then may [multiple deities listed] erase that kingdom, and that king, and that man who is of renown. Only may the name of Azatiwada be forever like the name of the sun and the moon."[13] In these texts, the speakers' names along with their embedded voice and their accomplishments in life stand in for their person. The continuation of their voice, through the inscription, in a memorial or mortuary context and in a monumental medium, is both a rhetorical and a material strategy for the individual's perpetuation beyond death. The erasure of the speaker's name is treated as the erasure of the person and his or her memory. The recently discovered West Semitic inscription memorializing Katumuwa, an eighth-century BCE royal official in southeastern Anatolia, seems to rhetorically embed the speaker within the stone monument itself: "I am Katumuwa, servant of Panamuwa, who commissioned for myself [this] stele while still living. I placed it in my eternal chamber . . . a ram for my 'soul' (*nbšy*) that [will be] in this stele."[14]

We might compare two significant points found in these inscriptions to features of the Hebrew Bible. The first is the warning in these memorial inscriptions to future readers that they not erase or otherwise alter the name of the speaker in the inscription or the content of the inscription, or move the inscribed object itself. Deuteronomy, as well as several other works, warns readers or listeners to maintain the text (written or oral) in the manner in which they received it. The formula of the command is to neither add nor subtract from the words of the text. For example, in Deuteronomy 4:2, the Israelites are told to keep God's commandments as transmitted, and similar statements can be found in Deuteronomy 13:1 and in the book of Ecclesiastes, a wisdom text focused on the stability and transmission of instruction.

A similar set of expressions, intended to maintain the integrity of the words inscribed in texts, is also encountered in ancient Near Eastern treaties and instructions. These treaties and instructions warn readers to neither subtract from nor add to the words of the text. In the Late Babylonian Erra epic, the scribe claims that he had received the words of his text in a dream, and that "he did not leave out a single line, nor did he add one to it."[15] Ben Sira, a second-century BCE instruction text, originally written in Hebrew but best preserved in the Greek Septuagint, uses this formula of "do not add, do not subtract" to praise the extent to which God's wisdom is complete. There, the expression seems to reflect the fullness of revelation, that nothing needs to be added nor subtracted (Ben Sira 42:21). Beyond a statement on revelation, these texts relate to the scribe's faithful copying of the received text and the process of textual transmission as a whole. In this sense, ancient Hebrew literary culture relates the production and transmission of texts to the dynamic relationship between the one giving instruction (usually the father) and the one receiving instruction (usually the son). The performance narrative of instruction that can be found not only in the book of Proverbs in the Hebrew Bible but also in the context of law giving and death-bed testament shares elements with the ancient Egyptian genre of instruction. Instruction as a genre with a particular constellation of features is not unique to ancient Hebrew literary traditions, as it has its antecedents in ancient Mesopotamian and Egyptian textual traditions.

However, the consolidation of this genre in the book of Proverbs as a collection of the best of ancient wisdom (and differently, in the book of Ecclesiastes), attached to the paradigmatic surpassing wisdom of King Solomon recounted in his biography according to the overarching story of ancient Israel, *is* unique to the ancient Hebrew literary tradition.

Biblical Narrative and Its Speech

Since both function as a kind of historiography, West Semitic memorial inscriptions might be linked loosely to biblical narrative. However, their framing is distinct. Memorial inscriptions, like biblical law, prophecy, and instruction, are framed in a first-person voice, even when embedded in a broader, third-person narrated frame. Biblical narrative, both in the overarching history of Israel and Judah from creation to exile spanning Genesis through 2 Kings *and* in self-contained tales of Ruth and Esther, is framed by a prose narrator.

Those first-person compositions can therefore be categorized into two distinct modes of presentation: (1) stories framed by a third-person narrator that frame the speech of characters and (2) anthologies that collect these speeches. Of the anthologies of nonnarrative works like song and instruction, there are various types of frames. Sometimes these frames are only attributive, linking the anthology to a figure from Israel's past (such as King David), and sometimes the frames are minimally narrated, as is frequently the case in prophetic collections, where the narrator will say that such-and-such famed prophet uttered these prophecies. In biblical narrative, poetry is represented in the text as the speech performance of characters, but the narration is in prose. By contrast, Ugaritic narrative is entirely in poetic form at both the level of the narrator and character speech. Unlike metered poetic traditions, ancient Hebrew is not metered but rather is characterized by parallelism. The basic poetic unit is therefore a pair of parallel lines, known as a "bicolon" or "couplet," whose elements in the first line find their parallel complement in the second. For example, in Genesis 4:23, Lemech opens his speech addressed to his wives saying, "Adah and Zillah, hear my voice; O wives of Lemech, lend an ear to my speech." Here, Adah and Zillah are addressed, and in the second line they are again addressed but in collective terms: "wives of Lemech." Likewise, the command to which they listen, "hear my voice," is complemented in the second line with a parallel sentiment, "Lend an ear to my speech." This type of symmetry—in varying degrees and in many different permutations beyond the synonymous pattern, usually notated as ABA'B'—is a characteristic feature that gives Hebrew verse its character and rhythm. Some have described the literary convention of parallelism in ancient Hebrew poetry as a continuation of dramatic speech from early Canaanite epic, as evidenced by the much earlier Ugaritic narrative corpus.[16]

In the Hebrew Bible, poetry that is presented as character speech often concludes narrative episodes. Such is the case in Exodus 15, Genesis 49, and Moses's final speech in Deuteronomy 33, as well as the song of Deborah in Judges 5, Hannah's prayer in 1 Samuel 2, and David's lament in 2 Samuel 1. Biblical law is also framed as character speech: the laws in Exodus 20–23 (the "Covenant Code") are in the voice of the deity. Likewise, all the narratives in Deuteronomy are presented as the instructions of Moses, spoken on the other side of the Jordan. Why is the Hebrew Bible's narrative form—specifically its form as the recounting of the deeds of ancestors—important for understanding biblical poetry and its framing? What we actually encounter when we read the songs, laments, prayers, prophecies, and instructions of the Hebrew Bible are the spoken words of legendary characters of Israel's story. These ancient speeches derive their rhetorical power from their presentation as voices of named heroes, whose deeds preceded their words in the story.

But, in fact, the reverse is the case in the first creation story in Genesis 1:1–2:4a. Scholars identify this creation story as separate and distinct from the narrative in Genesis 2:4b–3:24, the famous story in the garden. In the first creation story, God is quoted as speaking aloud his deeds, in an incantatory manner, and then the narrator reports that they have been accomplished. In God's first act of creation, in Genesis 1:3, God speaks, "Let there be light," and the narrator reports its fulfilment using the same words, "And there was light." This pattern continues throughout the narrative that follows this creation story, at first with repetition of God's words in the narrator's reporting, and later with a simple report, "And it was so." The order of deeds and speech is reversed, but the principle is in some sense the same: speech validates, authenticates, affects, or actualizes the deeds. While the prose narrator can make claims for the audience, the story requires the quoted speech of characters, the presentation of their voices, making the biblical narrative tradition in this sense comparable to how instruction and prophecy are presented.

Anthology and Attribution

While biblical narratives in the Pentateuch and the Former Prophets are structured by the chronological ordering of event sequences, there are also anthologies that collect multiple, self-contained compositions generally (with the exception of the book of Job) without a narrated frame. These collections are, instead, attributed in their titles or speech performance frames to a well-known figure (for example, Solomon or David) whose narrative biographies are attested elsewhere. The biblical book of Proverbs, a compilation of multiple, smaller collections of sayings and instructions, is an interesting example through which to study anthology in the Hebrew Bible. As previously mentioned, poetry in the Hebrew Bible either is presented within a narrative, through the voice of speaking characters, or else is organized into collections.

Like Psalms, Song of Songs, and Lamentations, the book of Proverbs is a collection of self-contained poetic units. Somewhat distinctly, however, Proverbs presents itself as a compendium of self-contained collections, themselves collections of individual poems, aphorisms, or instructions. These minicollections are attributed to individuals (e.g., "The Wise" in 24:23 and "King Lemuel" in 30:1) other than the titular figure to whom Proverbs is attributed in 1:1, King Solomon. One might be inclined to compare Proverbs and its anthological features to Psalms, which collects 150 more or less self-contained poems, many with titles that attribute and dedicate them to a variety of figures, such as David, Solomon, Sons of Korah, and Asaph. The book of Psalms, in its version received through the Masoretes (the early medieval Jewish scholars who added vowels and extensive annotations to the biblical texts), seems to show a clear organization of the book, dividing it into five books (Psalms 1–41, 42–72, 73–89, 90–106, 107–50). But beneath the surface, it becomes clear that there is little other than the closing doxological statements of each "book" within the Hebrew Psalter (for example, at 41:13, 72:19, etc.) to identify these as independent collections. By contrast, in the case of the collections brought together in the book of Proverbs, whether or not these were in fact originally independent collections, the titles and distinct attributions framing these sections give the sense that Proverbs includes multiple preexisting collections. This is because while each "book" of the Hebrew Psalter indicates a division between sections, the individual psalms are still self-contained and delimited poems with their own individual titles and attributions. The entire Hebrew Psalter, its book divisions notwithstanding, is a collection in the true sense. The various proposed reasons for the collection of the Psalter remain a matter of scholarly debate and are beyond the scope of the present discussion.

Both the books of Proverbs and Psalms are collections that contain multiple titles and attributions. These two compilations can help us better understand the compositional strategies available to authors in the ancient Hebrew tradition and the expectations audiences might have had for how poems, prophecies, and proverbs are transmitted through the medium of text. Such collections are nearly always attached to named and known figures from a larger story, whose trials and triumphs bring context to nonnarrative texts. When seen alongside ancient Near Eastern and Mediterranean practices of text production, it becomes clear that attributions like that to King Solomon in Proverbs 1:1 do not mark authorship in the modern sense. Rather, these attributions situate nonnarrative texts—texts without a context in the overarching narrative history—in the voice of a known, named character from literary lore.

Speech Collections: Prophecy, Instruction, and Poetry

As previously mentioned, poetry is often encountered in biblical narrative as the speech of characters at the conclusion of an episode or episode cycle. The direct speech of individual figures comes in two basic forms as a backward-looking review of past events or as a forward-looking command or prediction. Both backward-looking and forward-looking speech rely on the integrated authority of the speaking character, his name and reputation, and his legendary biography—in short, the character's voice. Prophecy moves between these two valences, using past deeds to predict or account for future ones. Prophecy also relies on a more complicated concept of the speaker's voice, where the human speaker becomes a medium for relating the words of God. This makes the prophetic speech event more complex than human performances of praise, lament, instruction, or petition.

The three "major" prophets (the prophetic collections of Isaiah, Jeremiah, Ezekiel) and the twelve minor prophetic works (Hosea, Joel, Amos, Obadiah, Jonah, Micah, Nahum, Habakkuk, Zephaniah, Haggai, Zachariah, and Malachi—but counted as one single "book") are collections of speeches attributed in their frames to these figures. Isaiah contains both those speeches attributed to an Isaiah figure in Judah from the eighth to seventh centuries BCE as well as speeches attributed to a figure who would have prophesied in the sixth century BCE, and a third collection of speeches are set when a return to Persian-controlled Judah had already taken place. The prophets to whom these speeches are attributed, as with those headings found in Proverbs and Psalms, do not claim authorship. Rather, these headings mark a particular type of speech or set of themes associated with the named legendary figure. Some scholars connect the headings of prophetic books to a phrase found in the West Semitic Deir 'Alla plaster inscription, a text discovered in an archaeological excavation in Jordan. This inscription describes the activities of a seer named Balaam—the same name as the foreign prophet who gives speech performances in Numbers 22–24. The plaster inscription reads, "The scroll/inscription of [Balaam, son of Be]or," thus employing a well-known term used in the headings of other works, *sefer* or "scroll," to identify the words of a known prophet.[17] But the precise term used in the Deir 'Alla inscription that marks the recording of a *prophetic* speech is found only in the book of Nahum (1:1). Otherwise, the titling strategies of biblical prophetic texts prefer to characterize their discourse as specifically performed speech: for example, the self-designation of the book of Jeremiah is in its opening, the "[spoken] words of Jeremiah," and this trend is consistent with other prophetic and wisdom texts in the Hebrew Bible.

The collected speeches in Jeremiah, which are set in seventh- to sixth-century BCE Judah, demonstrate a relationship to Deuteronomy. By contrast, Ezekiel's material, set in sixth-century BCE Babylon, is presented in the first-person voice of the speaker. The twelve "minor" prophets are anthologized as the "book of the Twelve," though they recount the prophetic speeches of prophets from a variety of times and places. The editorial history that led to the compilation of these twelve works into a single collection remains unknown to the modern reader, though we know from other ancient Hebrew texts like the Wisdom of Ben Sira, that this collection of "twelve" discrete prophetic works from much earlier periods was established as early as the second century BCE. Like other nonnarrative collections in the Hebrew Bible, distinct organizational strategies take the place of a temporally driven plot. One such strategy is to organize an anthology into a specific, often meaningful number of subcollections. For example, at some point in its editorial history, the book of Psalms was organized into five books. One recalls a similar division of the books of Moses into five as well (i.e., the Pentateuch). Like other biblical anthologies, the collection of minor prophets was at some point gathered into one single work with its own framing attributions.

As previously mentioned, another form of ancient Hebrew speechmaking that relates to ancient Near Eastern genres is instruction, usually configured as advice transmitted from a father (usually of high rank and/or legendary character) to a silent son who receives the instruction. This type of transmission, from one generation to the next, can be compared in some ways to the performance and transmission of prophetic speech that moves from the deity to the prophet elected to receive the divine message and serve as its mouthpiece. In addition to the fact that both instruction and prophecy share the phenomenon of speech transmission in their presentation in biblical literature, both genres appear to have pedagogical aims. Instruction aims to preserve and extend the life of the attentive son, who will benefit materially from the father's advice and is warned of punishment if the wrong choices are made (see Proverbs 1–9); prophecy aims to warn of impending divine punishment for improper behavior. Both instruction and prophecy take the form of a speech performance and are authorized by the relationships and deeds implicated in the particular voice who animates its words.

Ancient Hebrew literature—as represented by the tradition of literature spanning the Hebrew Bible, the Apocrypha and Pseudepigrapha in the Old Testament, texts found among the Dead Sea Scrolls, and other manuscripts and inscriptions—reflects a number of important social values in its genres and literary strategies. One such value that the genres of ancient Hebrew literature share can be seen through the social dynamics of the instruction. In ancient Hebrew instruction, the authoritative voice of the speaking father transmits principles for correct living to the passive, obedient son. The transmission of instruction, with its values for an enduring voice and memory of generations past, animates much of ancient Hebrew wisdom, prophecy, law, and testament. A second concept that shapes ancient Hebrew literature is its naming strategies in collections of nonnarrative work. Poems, prayers, and prophetic speeches are frequently attached to famed individuals—heroes of Israel—who are praised through their deeds in the narrative tradition. Moving beyond modern concepts of authorship, we can see how Hebrew authors named works not after themselves or in their own names. Instead, they endowed these works with authority and the richness of tradition by naming works after great voices of Israel's past whose wondrous deeds speak in perpetuity.

Further Reading

Berlin, Adele. *Poetics and Interpretation of Biblical Narrative*, 1983.

Bolin, Thomas M. *Ecclesiastes and the Riddle of Authorship*, 2017.

Lambert, David A. *How Repentance Became Biblical: Judaism, Christianity, and the Interpretation of Scripture*, 2016.

Mroczek, Eva. *The Literary Imagination in Jewish Antiquity*, 2016.

Pardee, Dennis. *The Ugaritic Texts and the Origins of West-Semitic Literary Composition*, 2012.

Reed, Annette Yoshiko. "Pseudepigraphy, Authorship and the Reception of 'the Bible' in Late Antiquity," in *The Reception and Interpretation of the Bible in Late Antiquity: Proceedings of the Montréal Colloquium in Honour of Charles Kannengiesser* 11–13, October 2006, edited by Charles Kannengiesser, Lorenzo DiTommaso, and Lucian Turcescu, 467–90, 2008.

Rollston, Chris A. *Writing and Literacy in the World of Ancient Israel: Epigraphic Evidence from the Iron Age*, 2010.

Sanders, Seth L. *The Invention of Hebrew*, 2009.

Vayntrub, Jacqueline. *Beyond Orality: Biblical Poetry on Its Own Terms*, 2019.

8

Syriac

ALBERTO RIGOLIO

When the sixteenth-century linguist Johannes Goropius argued that the primordial language spoken in Paradise was Brabantic (the Dutch dialect used in his hometown of Antwerp), there is no doubt that several of his contemporaries found this argument ridiculously chauvinistic. When, however, fifth-century Christian Greek scholars made a case for Syriac, the Aramaic dialect originating in the ancient city Edessa (modern Urfa in Turkey), as the language from which all others had derived, they initiated a tradition that found eminent followers over the centuries. For instance, in ninth-century Spain, a case for Arabic as the primordial language was made by reinterpreting Syriac as a corrupted version of the Arabic that Adam truly spoke when he left the garden of Eden.[1] The emergence of a literature in the local Aramaic dialect of Edessa and its remarkable growth over few centuries was an extraordinary historical development; the present chapter addresses the question of how a local variety of Middle Aramaic became the vehicle of one of the richest and most prestigious literatures of late antiquity.

The surviving body of Syriac literature is monumental and diverse and is especially notable for its poetry, its historiography, its hagiography, and its theological writings, but also for a huge corpus of Syriac translations from Greek that made Syriac a fundamental intermediary language in the transmission to the Arabic-speaking world of Greek philosophy and science, as well as Christian theology. Here, I will focus on how Syriac literature began, and I will address four major moments: the development of a distinctive Syriac script, the standardization of the language as classical Syriac, Syriac's attainment of literary status, and the emergence of Syriac versification. I argue that it is possible to understand the emergence of Syriac literature in terms of vernacularization, and it can be helpful to make use of the concepts of "literization," namely the introduction and use of a vernacular language in written form in everyday contexts, and subsequently "literarization," the process connected with the creation of a written literature.[2]

"Literization"

The process by which spoken Syriac was recorded in written form and was used in the composition of literature can be linked to major historical developments. The origins of the Syriac language, and in turn its literature, are inextricably connected with the ancient history of the city of Edessa and its surrounding region, Osrhoene (delimited by the river Euphrates in the west and by one of its tributaries, the Khabur, in the east), in the broader context of the Greco-Roman, Parthian, and Arab Near East (see figure 8.1).

The region of Osrhoene (a territory currently divided between Turkey and Syria) had been part of the Achaemenid (Persian) Empire, where Aramaic had gained the status of a lingua franca. After Alexander the Great's conquest of the Achaemenids and his death, however, Osrhoene came to be ruled by the Greek dynasty of the Seleucids, who instead promoted the use of the Greek language in the public sphere and the spread of Greek culture. The city of Edessa was in fact a Seleucid foundation, established by Seleucus I Nicator in 303/2 BCE on an older settlement, Adme, which was renamed Edessa after the ancient capital city of Macedonia, Seleucus's homeland.

Between the second and first centuries BCE, however, the fragmentation of the Seleucid Empire gave rise to independent kingdoms ruled by dynasts under whom Hellenism and Near Eastern customs and traditions could acquire new meanings. Perhaps the most well-known example of these new dynasts was the Hasmonaean dynasty, which asserted to have repossessed a region unduly occupied by the Seleucids that originally belonged to Judean ancestors.[3] Similarly, from around 140–30 BCE, the Abgarid dynasty took power in Osrhoene. The Abgarids eventually ruled over Osrhoene for three and a half centuries, skillfully safeguarding their power from the Parthians and the Romans almost without interruption until the eventual annexation of their territory by the Roman Empire in the third century CE.[4] It was as a response to the administrative and cultural needs of this new independent Kingdom of Osrhoene that the local dialect of Aramaic (later known as "Syriac," from the Greek adjective *syriakos*, "Syrian") was first put into writing, using a distinctive script adapted for this purpose; this enterprise, which entailed the end of the use of Greek language in the Edessene public sphere, was part of a broader effort of differentiation from Greek culture, which had flourished under the Seleucids. Modern historians are not aware of any foundation story for the origin of the Syriac script (in fact derived from a late version of the Achaemenid Aramaic cursive script) that would link its introduction to the administration of the small kingdom; by contrast, there is an early Armenian foundational myth that identifies Mesrop Mashtots (d. 440), the inventor of

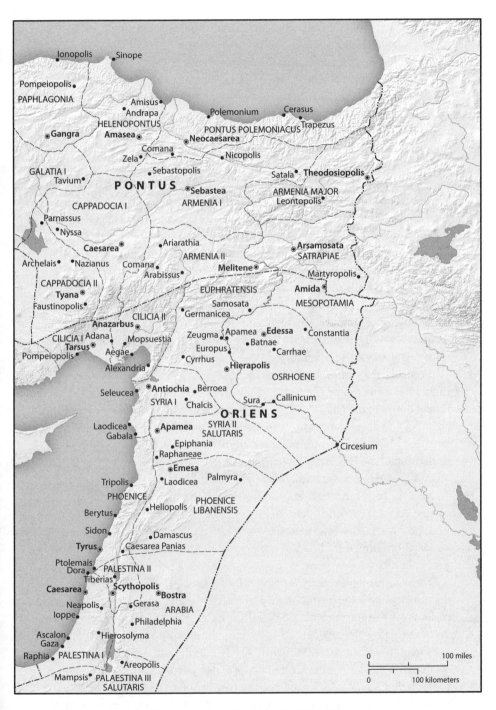

8.1. The Roman province of Osrhoene at the end of the fourth century CE.

the Armenian alphabet, as a bureaucrat and administrator employed by the local Armenian king.[5]

Like other Aramaic dialects in the Near and Middle East, such as Palmyrene (used in Palmyra), Nabataean (used in the Nabataean kingdom), and Hatran (used in Hatra), in Osrhoene Syriac was commonly employed in inscriptions and official documents, of which more than a hundred survive. Surprisingly, Syriac did not cease to be written after the Roman conquest but instead continued to flourish, alongside Greek and later Arabic. Several early Syriac inscriptions (such as the earliest dated one, possibly from the year 6 CE) are funerary, commemorating the burial place of members of the Edessene elites and often emphasizing their bonds with the royal family. Others have a marked religious and votive character and reflect a local variety of the ancient Near Eastern pantheon. At the same time, the royal status of the Syriac language can be gauged from its use on coins and from official dedicatory inscriptions, such as the one identifying the statue of an Edessene queen or princess on a column still standing on the citadel of Edessa. The city also possessed an important royal archive managed by trained officials and scribes, which contained not only private documents such as the copy of the Syriac deed of sale found in Dura Europos (*P.Dura.28*), but also annalistic records on the Abgarid dynasty, such as those later used in the compilation of the Syriac *Chronicle of Edessa* (sixth century).[6]

Arguably, the earliest known instance of Syriac outside a documentary setting comes from around the middle of the second century CE, with the translation of books of the Hebrew Bible into Syriac (later known as the "Peshitta"), an important development that paved the way for the use of Syriac as a literary language.[7] It was in the aftermath, or, perhaps, even at the same time as the translation of the Bible, that Syriac literature began to be produced, at first in Osrhoene, then also spreading throughout the Middle East, and eventually arriving, in later centuries, in central Asia and the Indian subcontinent. The earliest dated manuscript, written in 411 CE in Edessa (and now at the British Library, Add. 12150), is an extremely fine artifact that reveals a long-standing and well-developed tradition of calligraphy and manuscript production certainly dating back centuries.

The transformation of Syriac from a local dialect used for inscriptions and documents into a successful literary language was an extraordinary development. From the fourth century onward, both Greek and Syriac sources offered accounts of how Syriac poetry, and Syriac culture more broadly, had come to the fore, but unfortunately very little survives of the earliest Syriac literature for us to test and accept these often fictional narratives, such as those found in the *Doctrina Addai*, which predated the conversion of Edessa to Christianity to the time of Jesus, and in the *Vita* tradition of Ephrem, which presented the emergence of Syriac poetry as a spinoff of Greek versification and music. In the words of Sebastian Brock, "all that can be said with certainty is that by the end of the second century Christianity was well established in Edessa (probably in various forms) . . . ; with the fourth century one particular form of Christianity emerges as 'orthodox' and from that date on we become much better informed, since later generations were only concerned to transmit literature of this particular provenance."[8]

The acquisition of a literary status was not an obvious development for Syriac, which, like Palmyrene, Nabatean, and Hatran, had until then been used, in written form, as a documentary language; in particular, the emergence of Syriac as a literary language was improbable because of the enduring cultural hegemony of Greek in the region. Although Syriac was not the only Aramaic dialect to acquire a literary status, and other Aramaic dialects also produced literatures within specific religious communities (most notably Jewish, Samaritan, Mandaean, and Christian Palestinian Aramaic), it is necessary not to take this development for granted; one must recognize that only under rather specific historical circumstances did Aramaic dialects give birth to literatures. Second-century speakers of Aramaic could indeed write literature in Greek, as is exemplified by the rhetorician and satirist Lucian (born in ca. 125 CE just north of Edessa), the Christian apologist Tatian (ca. 120 CE–after 172 CE), and, although with less certainty, the novelist Iamblichus (fl. 165–80 CE). While these authors no doubt received the best Greek education available at the time and could have accessed Greek literature in the original language, epigraphic evidence as well as recent linguistic analysis of early Syriac texts show that language contact between Greek and Syriac was widespread, and that a degree of bilingualism, not limited to the upper classes and with considerable geographical variation, can be assumed.[9]

In many of the instances that we can study today, the use of Syriac must have been the result of deliberate choices. Archeological evidence in particular, largely in the form of mosaics, confirms that in the second and third centuries CE Syriac speakers from the Edessa region were familiar with aspects of Greek literature and culture more broadly. Syriac mosaics depicting Greek mythological scenes reveal not only the circulation of Greco-Roman figurative motifs and techniques but also some knowledge of Greek literature. Especially remarkable in this respect are the following examples: a mosaic representing the mythological creation of humankind by Prometheus, funerary mosaics representing Orpheus playing the lyre, and an impressive circle of mosaics representing selected scenes from the *Iliad*, all of them labelled in Syriac despite the fact that no known Syriac translation of the *Iliad* (or of any other piece of Greek classical literature for that matter) was available at the time (see figures 8.2, 8.3, 8.4, 8.5, and 8.6).[10]

8.2.
Mosaic representing
Prometheus and
the creation of
humankind, second
or third century CE.
Private collection.

8.3.
Funerary mosaic
representing
Orpheus playing
the lyre, 194 CE.
Haleplibahçe Mosaic
Museum, Urfa.
Image courtesy of
the Dallas Museum
of Art.

8.4. Mosaic representing Briseis as in *Iliad* 1.318–38, second or third century CE. Courtesy of the Bible Lands Museum Jerusalem. Photo: M. Amar and M. Greyevsky.

8.5. Mosaic representing Achilles and Patroclus as in *Iliad* 9.182–98, second or third century CE. Courtesy of the Bible Lands Museum Jerusalem. Photo: M. Amar and M. Greyevsky.

8.6.
Mosaic representing Troilus, second or third century CE. Photo: Françoise Briquel Chatonnet.

A silver jug with a grapevine decoration found in Dura Europos, not far from Edessa, was in all likelihood used for symposiastic practices and, as the Syriac inscription on its bottom rim makes clear, belonged to a person who could read Syriac. Its rich decoration with bunches of grapes indicates that the vessel was used to pour wine: like similar items manufactured in third-century Syria, this jug instantiates the local adoption of the Greco-Roman custom of the symposium, a customary setting for the performance of literature (see figures 8.7 and 8.8).[11]

"Literarization"

A necessary step for the emergence of a literature *in Syriac*, and therefore the use of Syriac, in written form, outside documentary and epigraphic settings, was the acquisition of a literary status by the Syriac language, the kind of transformation that Sheldon Pollock refers to as "literarization." A tangible change that was concurrent with this transformation may be historically reflected in the differentiation between the language used for early Syriac inscriptions and documents, known as "Old Syriac," and the increasingly standardized type of Syriac used in

8.7. Silver jug from Dura Europos, second or third century CE. Yale University Art Gallery. Dura-Europos Collection.

8.8. Silver jug from Dura Europos, bottom, showing a Syriac inscription on the rim, created by punching the metal, second or third century CE. Yale University Art Gallery. Dura-Europos Collection.

the production of literature, known as "Classical Syriac." Important linguistic features set the two languages apart, both orthographically (most notably in the rendering of the proto-Semitic *ś) and morphologically (most notably in the use of different prefixes to mark the masculine third-person singular imperfect), even if a moderate degree of internal variation should be recognized within both languages.[12] Scholars are divided on the origins of the linguistic peculiarities of Classical Syriac, which they explain either as a chronological development of Old Syriac or as a reflection of a different register or variety in the spoken language; nonetheless, this variation could be exploited in order to mark off the use of Classical Syriac as a new cultural enterprise.[13]

The emergence of Classical Syriac may well have taken place gradually, and earlier texts could easily be updated at a later stage, but it is generally accepted that the translation of the Bible into Syriac played a vital role in the standardization of Classical Syriac. From about the middle of the second century CE, books from the Hebrew Bible began to be translated into Syriac from the Hebrew, rather than the Greek, a project presumably supported by the religious interests of the Jewish community in Edessa. Inscriptions marking burial sites just outside the city of Edessa give good reason to believe that Jews adopted Syriac in a way comparable to the use of Greek by the Jewish community in Alexandria that produced the Septuagint (the language of the inscriptions was in all likelihood Syriac, rather than any other dialect of Aramaic, even if such inscriptions may be too scant to allow for certainty). Similarly, the earliest translation of the Gospels in circa 170 CE, from Greek and at times associated with the name of Tatian, responded to Christian religious interests. The text took the form of a narrative merging the four Gospels, a "harmony" that became widely used as a liturgical text until it fell in disuse in the fifth century and was replaced by a translation of the individual Gospels, carried out during the third century. These translations were integrated into instructional and liturgical settings and had important repercussions for the standardization of Classical Syriac.[14]

In addition to the emergence of a standardized language, however, the impact of the translation of the Bible on later Syriac literature can hardly be overestimated. In the same decades as the translation was being carried out, there circulated a collection of forty-two odes attributed to the biblical king Solomon (known as *Odes of Solomon*) and Christian in subject matter and themes; they were either translated from Greek or originally composed in Syriac. The *Odes* do not follow the conventions of later Syriac versification (more on this below), and, as Sebastian Brock writes, they were not "in any recognizable Syriac poetic form, yet they are clearly intended as poetry." Another text, the *Acts of Thomas* (ca. early third century), is an instance of Acts of the Apostles composed in Syriac and narrating the missionary travels of the apostle Thomas to India, at the same time offering important glimpses into the Edessenes' perceptions of Roman and Parthian imperial powers. Biblical themes were also recurrent in later Syriac poetry; for instance, the imagery of the siege and fall of a city, common in Syriac historical poetry from the fourth century onward, owed much to biblical models of the siege of Jerusalem. Another peculiar strand of Syriac poetry from the fourth century, the dialogue and dispute poems, in which two protagonists speak in alternating verse (e.g., the Death and Satan; body and soul; Cain and Abel), drew from ancient Mesopotamian literary forms repurposed to include biblical and theological characters and themes.[15]

In later Syriac historiography, not only was the Bible mined for historio-graphical and chronographical material, but it could also be used for the pre-sentation of the Syriac people as one ethnic entity characterized by a common language (Aramaic) and a shared geography as described in the Biblical text. As will be discussed below, an early attempt to write the Syriac past in biblical terms comes from one of the most influential Syriac poets, Ephrem the Syrian, living in the fourth century. Not unlike later Syriac historians, Ephrem used the Old Testament to support the case for the cultural superiority not only of the Jews over the Greeks, but also, and especially, of the Syrians over the Jews, on account of the greater antiquity of Aram over Abraham and his descendants, a cultural exercise that Eviatar Zerubavel would describe as "outpasting." In addition, the book of Daniel (with its articulation of world history as a suc-cession of empires) offered a suitable model for Syriac historians writing on the post-Roman succession of the Sasanians, Arabs, Mongols, and Turks in the Middle East and Asia.[16]

There is, however, also a trace of another strand of literature that circu-lated during the second century that was not obviously related to the Bible or to the religious interests of the Jewish and Christian communities in Osrhoene. This literature was likely to cater primarily to the interests of the class of scribes, administrators, and diplomats of the kingdom of Edessa, and it is best attested in the *Story of Aḥiqar*, a long-lived piece of ancient Aramaic literature that was received into Syriac and then was consider-ably expanded. This fictional narrative centered on the legendary career of Aḥiqar, an Aramaean minister working at the court of the Assyrian king Sennacherib, who, although long distinguished for his wisdom and royal service, was slandered by his own adoptive son and apprentice Nādin and consequently sentenced to death. The official in charge of carrying out the sentence, however, secretly spared such a respected colleague and helped Aḥiqar go into hiding. When the king eventually discovered the slanderous plot and wished Aḥiqar were still alive to help in a delicate diplomatic mis-sion with the Egyptian pharaoh, Aḥiqar was "rediscovered" and reinstated at court, whereas his adoptive son received a miraculous death as a just retribution for his offence. The narrative stands as an important reminder of the potential connections between Syriac and ancient Aramaic literature; and in its expanded Syriac version, it includes much moralizing and instruc-tional material that reveals a strong interest on part of the Syriac-speaking elite in moral education and etiquette. This instructional drive was a recur-ring aspect of the earliest Syriac literature; at the same time, teaching and instruction became a basic part of the Syrians's religious imagery in their pedagogical understanding of Christianity.[17]

The Emergence of Syriac Versification

Classical Syriac presents a peculiar and well-developed system of versification that sets it apart from other Semitic lyric traditions such as those of Hebrew and Arabic. Syriac versification is based on meter and is usually described as "isosyllabic," in that each verse or stanza is constituted by a fixed number of syllables, while rhyme occurs rarely and is not a necessary feature. More problematic is the question of whether any additional rhythmic device (such as stress, caesurae, or accompanying music) played a role in versification—an especially pressing question given that the Syriac language cannot effectively create a rhythmic sequence by alternating long and short syllables (in Classical Syriac, short vowels are seldom retained in an open syllable, thus largely resulting in sequences of syllables that are all long). In the past, scholars have made a case for stress as an additional rhythmic device, and so a Syriac verse was such only if it conformed to particular accentual patterns (it has also been suggested that either the appearance of Greek accentual poetry received an impulse from Syriac models, or vice versa); however, our poor knowledge of the functioning of the accent in early Syriac has complicated this line of analysis. Unfortunately, the earliest surviving Syriac treatise on meter was written considerably later, by Antony of Tagrit, probably in the ninth century (and published only recently); Antony took the occurrence of the divisions between words within a verse, which he described in terms of "segments of verse," as the fundamental rhythmic feature in Syriac versification, in addition to syllable count.[18]

The origin of Syriac versification has been the subject of heated academic debate, and it is best to concentrate here on those points where near consensus currently exists. The earliest known stages of Syriac versification roughly coincide with the decades of the translation of the Bible into Syriac, during the second half of the second century, but how Syriac versification looked before this time (if, indeed, there was any Syriac versification) remains the subject of speculation. An important role in the development of Syriac poetry is usually credited to a man named Bardaisan, a philosopher and polymath who lived at the court of Edessa (ca. 154–ca. 222 CE), and who was singled out as an important player in the development of early Syriac poetry by one of the most influential Syriac poets, Ephrem the Syrian (d. 373 CE), himself well informed about earlier traditions. It is of course not possible to rule out that others before Bardaisan wrote Syriac verse and that, at the same time, Ephrem had a particular agenda in dealing at length with Bardaisan, who was one of his doctrinal opponents. In fact, anonymous poems that can be dated to this early period survive (notably two poems included in the *Acts of Thomas*: the *Hymn of the*

Pearl and the *Hymn of the Bride*), but their uncertain chronology makes their assessment in the emergence of Syriac versification especially problematic. None of them can be dated earlier than Bardaisan with certainty, and we do not have names of any other poet before him.

At any rate, Ephrem's engagement with Bardaisan's poetry attests to a search for etiology in Syriac versification and implies Ephrem's awareness that Syriac poetry was a new literary phenomenon in need of explanation. By singling out Bardaisan, Ephrem seems to imply a link between the origins of Syriac poetry and the courtly culture of Edessa, with which Bardaisan was affiliated: Bardaisan, whose name means "son of the Daisan," the river by Edessa, was an Edessene nobleman born from a pagan family who certainly received the best education available in town; he was well informed about post-Hellenistic Roman philosophy and early Christianity, but he also had astrological interests that linked him to Mesopotamian and Parthian intellectual traditions. Bardaisan's other interests, such as archery and horse riding, attest to his full participation in the aristocratic circles of the city. Anecdotes about him were narrated by his contemporary Sextus Africanus, an erudite scholar writing in Greek who was at the time attached to the court of Edessa, possibly in the position of a royal tutor. Unfortunately, posthumous accusations of heresy (because of the philosophical form of Christianity to which Bardaisan adhered) and the eventual disappearance of the Bardaisanite community resulted in the loss of most of his works and those of his followers, and only quotations now survive; there is no other option than to rely only on secondary sources, which were written later and are mostly polemic.[19]

As the fourth-century Greek historian Eusebius of Caesarea reports, that Bardaisan wrote original texts in Syriac was well known outside Syriac circles, but the best source for his verse is Ephrem the Syrian, who, in one of his hymns, first described the metrical character of Bardaisan's poetry, in a polemical passage that has been much discussed:

> He [Bardaisan] wrote hymns (*madrāšē*) and mixed them with music;
> he composed songs and put them into metrical form;
> by means of measures and balances he distributed the words;
> he offered to the guileless bitter things in sweet guise,
> in order that, though feeble, they might not choose the food that heals.[20]

According to Ephrem, Bardaisan composed *madrāšē*, often translated as "hymns" but in fact a form of stanzaic poem in which each stanza follows the same syllabic pattern. The *madrāšā* (pl. *madrāšē*) was soon to become one of the two main forms of Syriac poetry, the other one being the *memrā*, the

PLATE 1. Rhodian black-figure skyphos, ca. 735–720 BCE; Lacco Ameno, Museo Civico Archeologico di Pithecusae in Villa Arbusto, inv. 166788. The Nestor Cup, with poetry inscription, from Pithekoussai, Ischia, Italy. Museo Archeologico di Pithecusae, Villa Arbusto, Ischia, Italy / © Mike Andrews / Bridgeman Images.

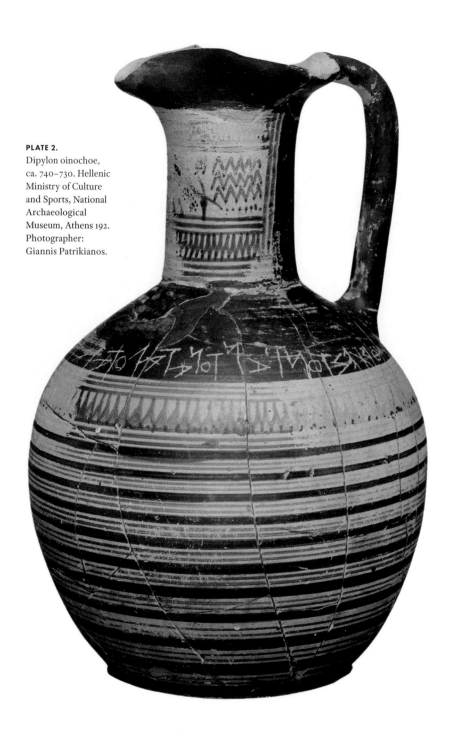

PLATE 2.
Dipylon oinochoe, ca. 740–730. Hellenic Ministry of Culture and Sports, National Archaeological Museum, Athens 192. Photographer: Giannis Patrikianos.

PLATE 3. Attic red-figure skyphos by Makron, ca. 490–480; London, British Museum E 140. © The Trustees of the British Museum.

PLATE 4. Mantiklos Apollo, ca. 700–675; Boston, Museum of Fine Arts 03.997. Photograph © 2021 Museum of Fine Arts, Boston.

PLATE 5. Funerary mosaic representing Orpheus playing the lyre, 194 CE. Haleplibahçe Mosaic Museum, Urfa. Image courtesy of the Dallas Museum of Art.

PLATE 6. Mosaic representing Briseis as in *Iliad* 1.318–38, second or third century CE. Courtesy of the Bible Lands Museum Jerusalem. Photo: M. Amar and M. Greyevsky.

PLATE 7. Mosaic representing Achilles and Patroclus as in *Iliad* 9.182–98, second or third century CE. Courtesy of the Bible Lands Museum Jerusalem. Photo: M. Amar and M. Greyevsky.

PLATE 8. Silver jug from Dura Europos, second or third century CE. Yale University Art Gallery. Dura-Europos Collection.

PLATE 9. Bronze coin from Edessa. Laureate head of Septimius Severus (193–211) and diademed and draped bust of Abgar VIII (177–212) wearing tiara decorated with stars and crescent. Leu Numismatik AG Web Auction 3, 25 February 2018, 749.

PLATE 10. Bronze coin from Edessa. Obverse: Gordian III (238–44). Reverse: Gordian III, sitting, receiving Abgar X (239–42), standing and wearing a tiara, in the act of offering Victory with his right hand to Gordian. Photo: Nomos AG.

"narrative poem," or "homiletic poem."[21] The name *madrāšā*—derived from a root with meanings such as "to teach, to explain, to thrash out, to argue"—may imply an originally didactic and potentially polemic purpose for this form, although the ways and the settings in which it was initially performed remain the subject of speculation, and we are much better informed of its later use in Christian liturgy.[22] This passage by Ephrem has also been used to argue that the introduction of music in the madrāšā was itself Bardaisan's innovation, a fact that may help explain not only the longevity of Bardaisan's own poetry (which was still performed in the fifth century, if we trust later sources), but also the fact that later manuscripts contain ancient indications of the particular melody according to which each madrāšā had to be sung.[23]

A crucial issue of discussion has been whether Ephrem intended to say that Bardaisan arranged his own material according to existing Syriac meters, or whether he played the more important role of introducing syllabic meter into Syriac poetry. Too little is known of Syriac versification before Bardaisan to corroborate either scenario (and very few lines survive even from Bardaisan's own poetry, quoted by later authors); it is nevertheless generally agreed that Bardaisan did indeed write madrāšē in isosyllabic meter as Ephrem would have understood this poetic form, and it is accepted that this form, in isosyllabic meter, may have already been in use at this time despite the lack of evidence. Conversely, a different account of the introduction of meter into Syriac comes from a Greek source, the fifth-century historian Sozomen of Constantinople, who similarly connected the emergence of Syriac versification with the circle of Bardaisan but who singled out a son of Bardaisan, who wrote under the name of Harmonius, as the author who "was the first to subdue his native tongue to meters and musical laws." Sozomen also implied that the influence of Greek versification and music shaped the emergence of Syriac meter and poetry more broadly; yet, his account, repeated in later sources such the *Ecclesiastical History* by Theodoret of Cyrrhus and the Syriac *Vita* tradition of Ephrem, is usually taken as nothing more than an exercise in Greek chauvinism (perhaps evidenced by the implausible Greek name of Bardaisan's son). Be it as it may, Sozomen's account may ultimately originate from a factual notion, since Ephrem did indeed quote from a madrāšā composed by a son of Bardaisan.[24]

The fact that, through the figure of Bardaisan and his son, both Ephrem and Sozomen linked the origins of Syriac versification, or at the very least an important moment in its emergence, to the court of Edessa may indeed imply that this setting played a role not only in the development of the Syriac language as shown above, but also in the emergence of Syriac versification, and, more broadly, in the acquisition of a literary status for Classical Syriac. It may be a useful exercise to compare the birth of Syriac literature with the model of "vernacularization"—in the words of Sheldon Pollock, "the historical process of choosing to create a written literature, along with its complement, a political discourse, in local languages according to models supplied by a superordinate, usually cosmopolitan, literary culture." The absence of early Syriac texts that would help study the political rhetoric of the Edessene court, however, makes us reliant on the archeological, epigraphic, and numismatic evidence. Local coinage in particular provides a taste of Edessene royal rhetoric in the late second and early third centuries; here, the Edessene king's association with the Roman emperor stands out as a badge of political legitimacy, as in the bronze coins portraying the king of Edessa and the Roman emperor on opposite faces without any apparent attempt to distinguish between obverse or reverse, therefore associating the two figures; or in the remarkable "presentation coinage," in which the local king is represented as being received by the seated Roman emperor in a similar way as other "investiture" scenes, with the notable difference that the king of Edessa does not adopt a pose of submission and rather stands in a position of power, his height equal to or even exceeding that of the emperor, augmented by an exaggeratedly tall tiara—at the same time, these portraits of Edessene kings show their clear debt to Parthian iconography and stand as a problematic reminder of the eastward-looking political and cultural allegiances by the earlier Abgarids (see figures 8.9 and 8.10).[25]

Unfortunately, there survive no dictionaries, lexica, and grammars, which often accompany the process of vernacularization, with the exception of a curious interest in etymology and Aramaic "linguistics" found in an indirect account of Bardaisan's doctrine.[26] The composition of vernacular works of literature emulating the cosmopolitan tradition (in this case the Greek), as is common in the early stages of vernacularization, is perhaps instantiated in the *Book of the Laws of the Countries*, a dialogue on free will composed by a follower of Bardaisan and clearly aware of Platonic models, in which Bardaisan plays the role of a teacher of philosophy in conversation with his students.[27]

Most surviving Syriac poetry has a Christian religious character, and the same consideration applies to Syriac literature as a whole, but it is necessary to emphasize that what survives of the earliest Syriac literature was selected and transmitted according to the interests of Syriac Christianity as it became institutionalized from the fourth century onward, and it is possible that there existed other strands of Syriac poetry that instead left little trace. For instance, a case was made for a strand of Syriac poetry, possibly in rhymed seven-syllable verse, that was secular in character, as is instantiated by a mournful quotation within an early text, the *Letter of Mara Bar Serapion*, and by a quotation from the mouth of a "secular (or lay) poet," as reported by the poet Isaac of Antioch in the fifth century. A rhymed verse epigram included in a third-century fu-

8.9. Bronze coin from Edessa. Laureate head of Septimius Severus (193–211) and diademed and draped bust of Abgar VIII (177–212) wearing tiara decorated with stars and crescent. Leu Numismatik AG Web Auction 3, 25 February 2018, 749.

8.10. Bronze coin from Edessa. Obverse: Gordian III (238–44). Reverse: Gordian III, sitting, receiving Abgar X (239–42), standing and wearing a tiara, in the act of offering Victory with his right hand to Gordian. Photo: Nomos AG.

nerary mosaic inscription laments the mortal condition of humans and might also be added to these.[28] A close study of the earliest phases of Syriac poetry that would do justice to the role of Bardaisan and to the recently studied fragmentary material does complicate any teleological narrative of the emergence of Syriac poetry; it becomes therefore necessary to reconsider, or at least to further qualify, the inherited view of a purely ecclesiastical origin of Syriac poetry, as famously expressed by Rubens Duval in his 1907 history of Syriac literature: "Syriac poetry, purely ecclesiastic, was born and developed among the clergy; it was the best suited instrument to instruct the people in religion and to endow the liturgy with the solemnity that is fitting to it."[29]

The continuation of Syriac poetry after Bardaisan and before the major authors of the fourth century, Ephrem and Aphrahat, reveals in full some of the peculiarities that accompanied the emergence of Syriac literature. The Roman annexation of the Kingdom of Osrhoene did not result in the demise of written Syriac (as was the case for the Aramaic dialects of Nabataea, Palmyra, and Hatra); this is evidence for the special status Syriac had attained by this period. Syriac documents continued to be written in Edessa in the third century; and Syriac was also still used in works of literature, even if the Syriac poetry written during the third century (presumably influenced by Bardesanism and certainly by Manichaeism) did not survive the institutionalization of Nicene Christianity in the fourth and fifth centuries. During the third century, followers of Bardaisan kept this tradition alive by performing poetry with music;[30] but the most spectacular and unforeseeable development took place in Mesopotamia, thanks to the activity of Mani (216–77), a singularly successful religious leader who soon had followers stretching from the western Mediterranean to central Asia. Perhaps unexpectedly, Mani, emerging in Sasanian Iraq, chose Syriac as the main language in which to record his teaching; and he thus became the first known author to write madrāšē after Bardaisan (at least according to our best source, once again Ephrem the Syrian).[31] These works are mostly lost; yet a passage quoted by Ephrem appears to be written in six-syllable verse (as the ancient *Hymn of the Pearl* was) and likely indicates that Mani's poetry was also isosyllabic in nature.[32]

The fact that Mani, born in southern Babylonia, chose Syriac as the language in which to record his teaching (although he also wrote in Middle Persian) attests to the literary status and the prestige that Syriac had gained by this time, as it was recognized outside Osrhoene. Unlike what might have been the foreseeable course of events, Mani and his followers did not write in any known Aramaic dialect used in southern Mesopotamia, such as Mandaean or Jewish Babylonian Aramaic. As far as it is possible to reconstruct, they adopted the orthography and morphology of Classical Syriac, although at the same time allowing for occasional idiosyncratic features, perhaps under the influence of local spoken Aramaic (and possibly ancient Aramaic literature as well). Their choice attests to the status of Syriac after the turn of the third century, at a time when it was increasingly adopted as a language of culture by Aramaic-speaking Christians throughout the Middle East. Mani's choice must have been dictated by the strong proselytizing drive of Manichaeism, the texts of which were intended for—and eventually enjoyed—wide circulation from the western Mediterranean to central Asia, and were translated into several languages including Latin, Greek, Coptic, and Sogdian. The use of Syriac by the Manichaeans shows that, by the third century, Syriac had acquired a literary status and could be used for the production of literature outside the local context of the kingdom of Edessa; the peculiar features of Manichaean language and its characteristic script may even be read as an effort to establish a Manichaean Syriac in opposition to (Edessene) Classical Syriac. While Syriac was emerging as a Christian language of culture in the third-century Middle East, Mani's religion was intended to incorporate and supersede Christianity.[33]

Given the almost complete loss of Manichaean poetry, however, it is difficult to take stock of it and, more importantly, to assess its impact on Syriac literature more broadly.[34] It seems unlikely that Manichaean poetry was simply dismissed without leaving any trace in subsequent Syriac literature: although this must of course remain a speculative exercise, aspects of Manichaean poetry that might have affected later Syriac literature (or, at the very least, paralleled its developments) are its universal, or at least "supranational," ambitions (as shown, for instance, by a Syriac-Coptic dictionary found in Egypt); the role of religious teaching as the fundamental component of Manichaean literature; and, last but not least, a strong argumentative drive in matters of religious doctrine.[35] After Mani, Aphrahat, a Syriac author flourishing in the first decades of the fourth century, provides excellent evidence for an enduring tradition of Syriac literature in Sasanian Mesopotamia.

Ephrem and the Fourth-Century "Clash" of Madrāšē

As will have become clear by now, Ephrem the Syrian (d. 373 CE) is our most important source for the beginnings of Syriac literature, but we should not ignore the fact that he was also a fundamental player in the emergence of this literature. In fact, Ephrem's poetry—Christian in content and pro-Nicene in theological orientation—was in direct competition with at least two other established strands of Syriac literature, the Bardaisanite and the Manichaean. Like Bardaisan and Mani, Ephrem (who lived entirely under the Roman Empire, first in Nisibis and then in Edessa) chose to write in the Syriac language and to use the madrāšā form for many of his literary texts. Yet his stance in favor of Nicene theology, which built on the first ecumenical council of the church held in Nicaea in 325 CE, gave his poetry an edge in its later transmission and, coupled with Ephrem's extraordinary poetic talent, marked a radical turn in Syriac literature (if not even a new beginning, as Ephrem might even have wanted to argue). Ephrem eventually succeeded in

eclipsing his non-Nicene competitors; he replaced Bardaisan's and Mani's
madrāšē with his own compositions in the memory of his audience. His
eventual success, however, was all but certain at the time he was writing,
and he deployed a wide range of strategies in his competition with Bardesanite and Manichaean literatures—an authentic "clash of madrāšē" to use
the words of Sidney Griffith.[36]

As a by-product of this engagement with earlier literature, Ephrem's poetry
reached a level of self-consciousness that was yet to be seen in Syriac; in addition, as mentioned above, the biblical text played a fundamental role in the
development of this new consciousness. First and foremost, Ephrem set up a
geographical framework for this (theological as much as literary) clash with
earlier literature: this territory was, quite simply, "our country, our land," *'ar'an*
in Syriac, understood as the land of Aram of biblical memory—most importantly, the region connected to the origin of the Aramaic language. This was
therefore a competition on an epic scale for the hearts of all Aramaic speakers
beyond their current religious differences; for instance, they included those
"brothers of ours" who still followed Bardaisan. With the help of biblical material, Ephrem defined "our country" as the region "in which Abraham and his
son Jacob walked, / Sarah, Rebecca, Leah, and Rachel too, / even the eleven
chiefs of the tribes." Ephrem pointed out that Old Testament patriarchs originated in the land of Aram, which, for this reason, was culturally and religiously
superior to the land of the Jews.[37]

An element of competition with Judaism (and, in turn, with Hellenism) was
intrinsic to Syriac identity as this was articulated in Ephrem. The poet wrote
that "our country's name [i.e., Aram] is greater than her companion's name
[i.e., the Holy Land], / for in her Levi, the chief of the priests, was born; / Judah
too, the chief of the royals, / and Joseph, the child who went on to become
/ the lord of Egypt." The biblical narrative provided Ephrem with not only a
geography, but also with a convincing ground for the historical precedence
(and therefore the cultural superiority) of Aram over the land of Israel, and,
in turn, over the land of the Greeks. The scope of Ephrem's poetry had clearly
moved beyond the philosophically oriented aristocratic circles of the court of
Edessa that Bardaisan frequented and, in his hands, had grown considerably
in scale and ambition; Ephrem was later celebrated as "the crown of the Syrian nation," "the master orator of the Syrians," and "a divine philosopher who
vanquished the Greeks in his speech" by Jacob of Serugh (d. 521; *Homily on
Ephrem* 65). At the same time, Ephrem's use of the biblical text as a source for
his historical understanding of Syriac opened up the possibility of exploiting
ancient Mesopotamian and biblical literature as suitable literary models, as
instantiated, for instance, by Ephrem's introduction into Syriac of the dispute

poem, shaped on the ancient Mesopotamian precedence dispute and enriched with the introduction of biblical themes.[38]

As a Christian teacher serving local bishops (first in Nisibis and later in Edessa), Ephrem also exploited the instructional and apologetic facets of the madrāšā, possibly two of its original features indicated by its etymology; he employed this form as a tool for religious teaching as much as for theological controversy. At the same time, Ephrem's criticism of Bardaisan's madrāšē ended up producing a range of unprecedented second-order observations on this literary genre. Ephrem used sexual imagery to denounce the deceiving seduction emanating from Bardaisan's poetry, which, although it "outwardly displays chastity[,] inwardly it is perverted into the very emblem of blasphemy. It is a stealthy woman; she commits adultery in the inner room."[39] Ephrem went further in critiquing and deconstructing Bardaisan's poetry, for instance when he countered Bardaisan's view that "the senses of the soul do not have the capacity to attain anything that pertains to 'existence'" by arguing instead that the human soul indeed had the capacity to deconstruct Bardaisan's madrāšē, "to unravel their composition, to pull down their structure, to reveal their secrets, and to reprove their teaching." Here, the critique of Bardaisan's poetry seems to reflect the sort of textual work that Ephrem would have wanted to carry out with his theologically minded students, for he soon moved on to argue that the artificial and affected character of Bardaisan's poetry was an inescapable consequence of the concocted and made-up nature of his entire philosophical system.[40] Elsewhere, Ephrem brought to the fore the contrast between the form of Bardaisan's poetry and its contents: in Ephrem's view, Bardaisan's poetry aimed at emulating the beauty of the Psalms, but its contents ultimately revealed his tacit acceptance of paganism.[41] Obviously, none of these shortcomings affected Ephrem's own poetry, either in form or content; the audience would come away with the sense that there had been a genuine clash with earlier non-Orthodox poetry, a clash that had been comfortably won. The almost complete disappearance of Bardaisan's and Mani's poetry, and the immense popularity of Ephrem's poetry in both Syriac original and Greek translation, speak for the success of this narrative.

The facts that Ephrem was a teacher and that the madrāšā, a form that he used for instruction and controversy, dominated his production stand as a reminder of the important and long-standing connections between teaching practice and the emergence of Syriac literature (and some of Ephrem's own pupils were later known as successful Syriac authors). From the earliest stages, Syriac language and literature developed against the backdrop of a lively educational system in the Syriac language, which, unfortunately, can be reconstructed only indirectly. The adoption of Syriac as an administrative language in the Kingdom of Edessa could be feasible only by suitably training aspiring Edessene bureaucrats and administrators, and such training, or some form of it, was unlikely to have subsided with the Roman conquest of the kingdom, given the abiding vitality of the archive of Edessa and the production of Syriac legal documents well into the third century. Early Syriac manuscripts (dated from the early fifth century onward) also reveal a long-standing and well-developed scribal tradition that was intertwined with existing administrative practices; these archival, administrative, and scribal habits kept on developing in the Greco-Roman context and could even be used to express, in Syriac, integration and membership in a larger Roman "commonwealth."[42] In addition, the interest in etiquette and moral education by the Edessene elites, as is revealed in the *Story of Aḥiqar*, seems to imply a sort of education that was not limited to scribes, but rather catered to the demands of a broader social group; at the same time, the use of Old Syriac as a religious and royal language could be successful only by assuming some degree of alphabetization by the broader population. The Edessene aristocracy, of which Bardaisan was a representative, had absorbed aspects of Greco-Roman culture but was also engaged in the development of a philosophical and intellectual tradition in the Syriac language. In the only Bardesanite text that survives extensively, the dialogue known as *The Book of the Laws of the Countries*, Bardaisan is depicted as instructing philosophically minded students, and later accusations against him condemn the grip of his doctrine on the minds of young nobles in Edessa.[43] In the religious sphere, the Syriac translation of the Bible, and therefore the use of Syriac as a religious language possibly within the Jewish but certainly within the Christian communities, must have gone hand in hand with the instruction of the clergy: the instruction of the clergy, and, in turn, of the broader Christian community, was the sort of activity, sponsored by the local bishops, that Ephrem was involved in during the fourth century.

Ephrem attacked Bardaisan's poetry as deceiving the minds of the young,[44] but Bardaisan was not alone in catering to the instructional demands of younger generations in Edessa. There survives an especially rich, and still understudied, strand of early Syriac literature consisting of instructional texts such as wisdom and moralizing literature that reflect an educational drive that was not limited to instruction in the Christian religion such as that represented by Ephrem's poetry. These texts include Syriac translations of the early Christian apologists Pseudo–Justin Martyr (*Exhortation to the Greeks*) and Aristides (*Apology*), which effectively provided an elementary introduction to Greek philosophy and Greek mythology respectively from a safe Christian perspective; but they also included non-Christian literature, such as moralizing and philosophical texts by Plutarch, Lucian, and Themistius, and wisdom collections containing material circulating under the name of Plato or ancient Greek philosophers. The *Letter of Mara Bar Serapion* was written by a self-styled philosopher who collected moral precepts for his son, possibly in a similar way to Isocrates collecting a series of precepts for his nephew in the speech *To Demonicus* (this was in fact a pseudepigraphic instructional text that circulated widely in Greek schools during the Roman imperial period and was soon translated into Syriac). Whether or not members of the Christian clergy were the teachers who used these texts in classroom settings, these instructional materials reveal the interests of a lively culture endorsing, through translation and on its own terms, Greco-Roman educational traditions.[45]

Conclusion

The present chapter has sketched the emergence of Syriac literature by tracking the transformation of the Syriac language from a local dialect of Middle Aramaic in the region of Edessa into the primary literary language of the Aramaic-speaking Christian communities throughout the Middle East, ultimately becoming the vehicle for one of the most prestigious literatures of late antiquity. I have attempted to understand the beginnings of Syriac literature in terms of vernacularization, on account of the complex and fertile connections between indigenous culture and a superordinate culture, here the Greco-Roman, and in consideration of the extraordinary cultural efforts that went into the development of a new literary, political, and religious discourse in the Syriac language. Key stages in this process were (i) the development of a distinctive Syriac script, designed to respond to the practical and ideological needs of the local Kingdom of Edessa; (ii) the orthographic and morphologic standardization as Classical Syriac, which likely resulted from efforts connected to biblical translations and their use by local communities; (iii) and Syriac's attainment of literary status, particularly owing to the efforts of authors such as Bardaisan, possibly Mani, and certainly Ephrem. With the last of them, Syriac poetry reached a degree of literary self-awareness that had not yet been seen in this tradition.[46]

Further Reading

Briquel Chatonnet, Françoise. "Syriac as a Language of Eastern Christianity," in *The Semitic Languages: An International Handbook*, edited by Stefan Weninger, 2012.

Brock, Sebastian P. "The Earliest Syriac Literature," in *The Cambridge History of Early Christian Literature*, edited by Frances Young, Lewis Ayres, and Andrew Louth, 2004.

Brock, Sebastian P. "Poetry and Hymnography (3): Syriac," in *The Oxford Handbook of Early Christian Studies*, edited by Susan Ashbrook Harvey and David G. Hunter, 2008.

Debié, Muriel. *L'écriture de l'histoire en syriaque: Transmissions interculturelles et constructions identitaires entre hellénisme et islam; Avec des répertoires des textes historiographiques en annexe*, 2015.

Griffith, Sidney H. "St. Ephraem, Bar Dayṣān and the Clash of Madrāshê in Aram," *Harp* 21 (2006): 447–72.

Healey, John F. "Syriac," in *The Semitic Languages: An International Handbook*, edited by Stefan Weninger, 2012.

Healey, John F. "Variety in Early Syriac: The Context in Contemporary Aramaic," in *Aramaic in Its Historical and Linguistic Setting*, edited by Holger Gzella and Margaretha L. Folmer, 2008.

Possekel, Ute. "The Emergence of Syriac Literature to AD 400," in *The Syriac World*, edited by Daniel King, 2019.

Van Rompay, Lucas. "Early Christianity in the Near East," in *Blackwell Companion to the Hellenistic and Roman Near East*, edited by Ted Kaizer, 2021.

Witakowski, Witold. "Syriac," in *The Oxford Handbook of the Literatures of the Roman Empire*, edited by Daniel L. Selden and Piroze Vasunia, 2017.

Wood, Philip. "Syriac and the 'Syrians,'" in *The Oxford Handbook of Late Antiquity*, edited by Scott F. Johnson, 2012.

9

Arabic

GREGOR SCHOELER

The seat of the Arabic language (and literature as well) is the Arabian Peninsula; Arabic was first carried into the surrounding countries and ultimately the Near East and North Africa during the Islamic expansion after the death of the prophet Muḥammad (ca. 570–632). In the course of less than a century, Arab "fighters in the way of God" under the first caliphs (the successors of the Prophet as political and religious leaders of the Muslims) imposed the rule of Islam from Persia in the east (642) to the Maghrib in the west (670), followed by Spain in 711. Medina, the home of the Prophet, was the center of power of the new empire for only a few decades; the capital cities soon shifted to the conquered provinces (Kufa, Damascus, later Bagdad). With time, the Arabic language expanded into these subjugated lands (except for Persia), though the native languages were not completely displaced.

Along with their language, the Arabs brought their literature to the conquered lands. This literature comprised initially only the Koran and a highly developed poetry that had likely originated already around 500 CE with the Bedouins (the nomads of the Arabian Peninsula) but had not yet been redacted in written form. The Koran, the Holy Writ of Islam revealed to the prophet Muḥammad according to Muslim belief, became the most important book in Arabic literature. The old Arabic poetry, though not the only cultural achievement of the pre-Islamic Arabs, was nonetheless their greatest. Through the Koran and the old Arabic poetry the Arabic literary language was placed on a firm foundation.

The problems posed by research of early Arabic literature are many. One of the main problems is the peculiar (mixed written and oral) transmission and the late redaction of the texts: the Koran didn't receive its definitive form, around 650 through production of an official collection and edition, until some twenty-five years after the death of the Prophet; poetry not until some two to three centuries after its inception (in the sixth and seventh centuries) through the work of philologists (in the eighth and ninth centuries). This makes the question of the authenticity of the texts often impossible to resolve.

As the texts had no definitive written form for a long period, the question also arises as to whether they can be considered "literature" at all. That is why the following explanations should begin with a definition of what is to be understood as "literature."

I suggest the following definition:

Literature is the body of finalized, published written works belonging to a language or a people. "Finalized" means that those written works constituting "literature" were definitively redacted and edited by their authors, and "published" means that they were produced with a public readership or audience in mind.[1]

There was no Arabic literature before Islam; but there are several phenomena that eventually *became* literature. In the following we will treat the most important of these phenomena, sometimes paradoxically called "oral literature," but perhaps better deemed "preliterary." In doing so we shall attempt to pin down the beginnings of the "preliterary" phenomena. But it should be said at the outset that these attempts will generally not go beyond hypotheses. The genres treated here didn't become literature as such until the Islamic period, following a long process of transmission. We shall treat in detail this process, which culminates in the beginning of the "literary" genre.

Pre- and Early Islamic Tribal Poetry and Tribal Reports in Prose

Pre- and early Islamic, or "Old Arabic" poetry, is a genuine creation of the Bedouin Arab, that is, the nomadic Arab of the desert. It was originally tribal poetry and purely oral. It did not arise from the pre-Islamic polytheistic religion whose contents had for the most part dissipated long before Muḥammad's time and had survived only in cultic usage, for example, in pilgrim rites in Mecca. There are Christian Arabic religious poems, purportedly from the early Islamic time (content: the Creation, the Flood, the birth of Jesus, etc.), the authenticity of which, however, is questionable.

The language of the poets was a high-level language differing from the common speech, a *koinē* comprehensible beyond tribal and dialectical borders and, like the poet himself, of high social prestige. Formally, the poetic language is distinguished from the prosaic in that it has quantitative meters and end rhyme. These two formal elements, monometer and monorhyme, remain constant throughout the entire poem; they are already developed in the oldest extant poems. One theory is that the meters developed from a rhythmized rhymed prose (*sajʿ*) to the simplest meter, the iambic *rajaz* (x x ‿–), and that it is from the latter that the complicated meters derive.

The contents of the Old Arabic poetry reflect the material life and ideals of the Bedouins. Yet courtly and urban influences were current already
quite early; they emanated mainly from the courts of the Lakhmids in al-
Ḥīra (an Arab tribal dynasty allied with the Persian Sassanids) in Iraq and
the Ghassānids (a tribal dynasty allied with Byzantium) in Syria (both sixth
century) as well as Yathrib, the later Medina.

Let us now turn to the name and function of the pre-Islamic poet. The word
for "poet," *shāʿir*, means "one who knows." This suggests that the original prevailing notion was that the poet, like the diviner or soothsayer (*kāhin*) (for this
figure, see below), received his knowledge through superhuman inspiration, that
is, genies (demons) or *shayṭān*s (devils). And as a matter of fact, there are indications that lampoon poetry (*hijāʾ*) derives from the magical cursing of the enemy.
However, the oldest extant literary texts are not magical curses, but invectives;
the "magical" derivation thus remains a hypothesis that might perhaps be drawn
on to explain some curse formulas, but not to explain the origin of Arabic poetry.[2]

The poet was spokesman and standard-bearer for his tribe. His talent with
words found use in all matters pertaining to the tribe, for example, in tribal
councils and in disputes with the enemy. Of much fame is an ode in which
the poet Zuhayr (d. ca. 609) lauds two peacemakers in an intertribal war.

The poetry of lamentation had a special function: it was to express the grief
of the family and the tribal group, to commemorate the noble qualities and
exploits of the deceased, and to preserve his renown for future generations.[3]
Initially, the dirge was mainly a domain of women. Precursor of this dirge was
the rhythmic and rhymed lament accompanying the funeral rites performed by
female relatives of the deceased. The ritual character of this genre is apparent
in early examples at hand.

One of the primordial functions of the Old Arabic poetry is its—often
polemic—stance on a personal situation or a "political" event: lamenting a
suffered plague, objections to reproaches because of a neglected duty, warnings, threats, invectives, calls to blood vengeance, assurance of forgiveness
when the accused accedes to the demands, triumph, and so on.[4] Since this
group of poems primarily concerns disputes with distant opponents, many
are formulated as messages ("Announce to x that . . ."); others are presented as
reactions to incoming messages. This pertains also to the dirges of the women
(mentioned above): many of them begin with the reaction to an incoming
death message or the request to deliver or to disseminate one.

The messages served in the broadest sense the safeguarding of honor and
self-assertion. This "occasional poetry" makes the Old Arabic poetry especially
valuable within the framework of world literature, in that such poetry borne
of everyday experience is rare, except in Iceland (skaldic poetry).

There is also a genre of poetry in which the poet, rather than taking a position on a specific event, expresses a sentiment of life or remembrance, often of the joys of youth (amorous adventure, hunt, wine-drinking binge, heroic deeds). These themes are then developed into detailed descriptions, framed as self-praise ("It is often that I have . . ."). The poet can also bring forth aphorisms on the transience of the world and other types of wisdom. This poetry has no immediately effective function; it is not occasional.

A verse group of both mentioned genres (message; expression of a sentiment of life or remembrance) or also a praise of a tribal head or a prince can form the final section of a *qaṣīda* (ode).[5] Correspondingly, there are three types of qaṣīdas: message qaṣīdas, remembrance qaṣīdas, and praise qaṣīdas.

The qaṣīda is the most important and most artistic genre of Old Arabic poetry. It varies in length from about thirty to about one hundred verses. The most commonly occurring type is the message qaṣīda, the most developed type the praise qaṣīda. The starting section in all types is a love poem (*nasīb*). This theme is almost always introduced with a stereotype frame motif, the most common of these motifs being the lamenting of the poet at the abandoned camp of the beloved who set forth with her tribe. Love poems, but also portrayals of the wine binge and the hunt (mentioned above), never appear in the older Arabic poetry independently, but only in the framework of a qaṣīda. As a rule, between the love passage and the final section a more or less detailed description of the poet's mount, the camel, is to be found. (The camel is of utmost importance for the Bedouins.) In the final section of the praise qaṣīda, but occasionally also in self-praise passages of the remembrance qaṣīda, the peaceful social virtues (mainly hospitality and generosity) and martial merits (chiefly bravery) are highlighted. The transitions between the individual parts can use a stereotypical connective motif or also happen abruptly.

The emergence of this highly artistic and composite genre of poetry occupied researchers for quite some time; and several theories have been put forth. The latest and most plausible[6] suggests that the underlying idea was that the messages—objections to reproaches, warnings, threats, and so on, and, more than ever, the praise of a benefactor—were afforded more weight when expressed in the framework of an artistic qaṣīda, comprising several themes. For only by that means, even if such messages were originally occasional poetry, could they be deemed a full-fledged work of art.

Of the peculiarities of imagery (comparisons, metaphors) and rhetorical devices (metonymy, iteration, paronomasia, antithesis) employed by the qaṣīda poet, one deserves special mention: the so-called independent comparison. As in the Homeric simile, the *secundum comparationis* is developed further, whereby the comparative function of the comparison gets lost and the *secundum* takes on a life of its own as a small scene or complete episode. In this way the poet can compare the fragrance of his beloved to a meadow in blossom and while away several verses describing the meadow and its flowers. The most artistic independent simile is to be found in the camel section of the qaṣīda: it is the comparison of the camel, because of its speed and endurance, to an onager stallion.[7] This comparison develops into a longer episode relating one or more "stories" concerning the characteristic behavior of the onager and his mares. The independent simile affords the poet the opportunity to introduce new themes into the poem.

Originally, this poetry was purely *oral*, but it was not the *impromptu* oral-formulaic epic poetry Milman Parry and Albert Lord have described in the Balkans and (*ex hypothesi*) ancient Greece.[8] For one, the Old Arabic poetry is not narrative (epic); it deals with different issues, primarily those gauged for immediate effect (rebuke, invective, praise, etc.). Also, unlike popular epic poetry, the poems are almost always transmitted under the name of a composer. Furthermore, the longer poems—mainly the qaṣīdas whose length does not exceed some dozens of verses and thus can easily be memorized—that adherents of the theory of oral formulaic composition consider comparable to the Homeric epic poetry are not improvised; on the contrary, some poets, for example the famous Zuhayr (mentioned above), needed a considerable amount of time, even up to one year, to prepare a substantial qaṣīda. Accordingly, the formulas occurring in Old Arabic poetry do not serve to facilitate improvisation but have a completely different function: They are "a stylistic device based on intertextuality (a device) which is consciously implemented by the poet in a calculated and often very sophisticated manner."[9]

In the following, we will have to take a look at an additional form of speech from the early period: the utterances of the (male and female) soothsayer or diviner (*kāhin* [m.], *kāhina* [(f.)]). This will help us to understand certain forms of speech and style of the Koran.

The soothsayers were regarded as inspired by genies (demons) or *shayṭāns* (devils); they were consulted before every important undertaking, raids in particular. In everyday life they served as arbitrators yet also interpreted dreams, predicted the future, and solved past mysteries. Their oracle sayings, often cryptic, consist of short sentences in rhythmic prose with monorhyme or the alternation of short rhyme sequences (*saj'*). Soothsayer utterances were introduced with a series of oaths by the heaven, earth, sun, moon and stars, and flora and fauna. We will see that the same form of speech—rhyme prose (*saj'*)—and similar oath formulas introduce numerous suras of the Koran (for this see below).

Among the furthest developed narrative genres is the *Ayyām al-ʿArab* (The [decisive] days, i.e., the Battle days of the Arabs). These are semihistorical accounts of tribal disputes of pre-Islamic Bedouins. They were recounted at tribal gatherings in the evening. The stories are composed in a succinct, vivid, dialogical, sometimes metaphorical prose; the portrayal is often realistic; the sequence of events stereotypic: A tribe encamped at a watering place is suddenly attacked by an enemy tribe. Fighting ensues; the attackers prevail and withdraw with the booty; negotiations follow over the release of prisoners and payment of blood money for the fallen fighters. Prose is almost always supplemented with poetry (*prosimetrum*). The style of the Ayyām lived on in the biography of the Prophet.

Poetry (like also the genres of prose described above) was initially and for a long time not literary. It did, however, eventually *become* literature. This came about in a protracted process of transmission. The poems were memorized, recited, and disseminated at first by the poet himself, or by a special transmitter (*rāwī*), and after his death by transmitters from his tribe. Tribal elders or chiefs, but also other male and female members of the poet's tribe, were involved in this transmission. Reciting, making public (henceforth: "publishing"), and transmitting, all coincided in one single act. This action ensued orally; yet, perhaps from the end of the seventh century on, or even earlier, the transmitters used written notes in order to bolster their memories.

Beginning in the second quarter of the eighth century, this poetry was collected by a new kind of transmitter: learned transmitters (sing. *rāwiya*), who compiled collections on a large scale, not confining themselves to poems from a single tribe. These collections were recorded in writing; nevertheless, they were still "published" and transmitted by recitation. Transmission is thus seen to have occurred in a form in which orality and literacy were mutually supplementary; writing backed up the oral transmission. The edited compilation of the poems of an individual poet or a whole tribe was named "Dīwān." Eventually, in the ninth century, all this material was redacted and edited by philologists. Only then did it become "literature."

The Use of Script in the Pre- and Early Islamic Period

Arabic culture in its very early period was not purely oral. The use of writing is attested through inscriptions and graffiti already long before the emergence of Islam. While not used for literature, it was used for political and practical purposes (commemorative inscriptions; building inscriptions). The oldest extant papyri, serving practical purposes, come from the early Islamic period.

The use of writing for the pre- and early Islamic period is also attested by later literary sources, which mention official letters, contracts, treaties, and so on. Unlike the inscriptions, which are direct, contemporary evidence, the authenticity of the literary sources is almost always open to question. There are numerous letters that are ascribed to the prophet Muḥammad that he is thought to have sent to diverse tribes; many include the demand to accept Islam. Their authenticity is often questionable, but it can be taken as certain that the reports on the dispatching of letters reflects a genuine practice. One document of great significance from Muḥammad's time that is generally assumed to be genuine is the famous "Constitution of Medina."[10] This is a contract of alliance concluded by the Prophet between the Meccan refugees and Muḥammad's "supporters" in Medina who converted to Islam, a contract that also regulated the relations of the Muslims with the Jews of Medina.

The publication of important documents had to meet special requirements: such documents had to be deposited in prominent places (e.g., the Ka'ba or the house of council in Mecca). The purpose of depositing an important document in a revered site is clear: it directs attention to the nature and character of its content, and, more importantly, it confers on the document the status of an authentic, enduring, reproducible original. This is evidently a form of publication, or something that anticipates it.

A Christian Literature before Islam?
The Recitation and Dissemination of Religious Texts

It is almost certain that no official Arabic translation of the Bible existed before the advent of Islam. Because neither Syriac nor Greek, the main liturgical languages of Arab Christians, was understood by the majority of native Arabic speakers, the priests had to produce, or use, ad hoc translations of the sacred texts for the liturgy. There is some evidence that these translations were written down for private use and even had a limited circulation.

As to the religious texts in liturgy: they were not read out from the Bible, but from lectionaries, that is, books containing selected scripture readings (pericopes) prearranged for worship on a given day or occasion. The liturgical tradition was, so to speak, a mixed one, both oral and written.

We are now equipped with the background to understand the context in which the Koran, the first actual book in Arabic, materialized.

The Koran

The Koran (Ar. *al-qur'ān*) is a unique work within Arabic literature: it is what Muslims believe to be the word of God, borne by the archangel Gabriel, revealed to the prophet Muḥammad. Muḥammad belonged originally to the old Arabian polytheism holding sway in his hometown of Mecca in Arabia. There were also Christians there and, in Medina, Jewish tribes as well.

The Koran, revealed in the period between circa 610, the approximate time of Muḥammad's call to prophethood, and 632, the year of his death, is primarily a prophetic oration and recitation text. But it is also a literary work of a very special sort: it is not only the first, but also the most important work of Arabic literature. Nonetheless: even the Koran was not literature from the start; it became so only after a process of some twenty-five years: the official redaction of the Koran was done under the rule of 'Uthmān (644–56), the third caliph.

Koran, actually *al-qur'ān*, means "recitation," "reading" (inf. from Ar. *qara'a*, "to read"), but also "lectionary, pericope" (from Syriac *qəryānā*). The word is used for the whole book and also for the individual revelations compiled therein. The language of the Koran is the elevated language of Old Arabic poetry. Certain graphic features of the consonantal text (like the Hebrew Bible, the Koran was originally written only with consonants; signs for vowels and marks for distinguishing consonants written in the same way were added only later) could, however, indicate that it had been influenced by the dialect of Mecca, Muḥammad's hometown, yet these dialectical influences were not strong enough to cast doubt on its high-level character.

The Koran consists of chapters called suras (Ar. sing. *sūra*, pl. *suwar*); these in turn comprise "verses" (sing. *āya*, pl. *āyāt*), which, however, since they have no meter, are not identical with poetic verses (*buyūt*; sing. *bayt*). They are rather written in a more or less rhythmized, rhymed prose (*saj'*). The rhyme that closes the verses (*fāṣila*) differs from that of poetic verse (*qāfiya*): it is subject to considerably fewer rules than the other. Accordingly, it corresponds rather to the rhyme in the oracle sayings of the soothsayer.

The suras from the official edition of the Koran, compiled under the caliph 'Uthmān, are arranged according to length, not chronologically. Already the indigenous Koran scholars strove to detect a chronological order and had already distinguished between suras revealed in Mecca, Muḥammad's hometown, until his emigration to Medina (*hijra*) in 622, and suras revealed in Medina, his residence after the hijra. Nonetheless, it was first European scholars, Theodor Nöldeke (1836–1930) in particular, who grounded and documented the prevailing contemporary theory according to which it makes sense to assume four periods: three successive Meccan and one Medinan. The most important criterion for chronological ordering is, apart from allusions to dateable events, the length of the verses. According to this—generally accepted—theory, the revelations with the shorter verses are the older, those with the longer the younger.

Muḥammad was emphatically opposed to being seen as a soothsayer or poet (sura 52:29). The individual suras are divine revelations received by the

Prophet on certain occasions, delivered to him by the archangel Gabriel. The revelations emanate from a celestial template out of which parts thereof, "pericopes," were sent down to the Prophet in batches.[11]

Muḥammad, for his part, recited them to the believers. Later on, these sacred texts, subsequent to being compiled in the Koran, were (and are until now still) themselves divided into pericopes and recited in worship to and by the believers. In this way, they tie in with the Christian tradition of scripture readings (pericopes); and the book containing the collected suras, the Koran, is something like the lectionaries of the Christians.

As a prophetic oration, "the Koran is oriented in its diction towards biblical models," yet it must be understood that it is "never really similar to biblical scriptures."[12] Found in its language and style are also elements of older, original Arabic genres of speech (for these, see below). As for content, the Koran deals with much material from the canonical and apocryphal scriptures of the Jews and Christians, or also from the oral Torah of the Jews. This material, for example, stories about the earlier prophets, must have been familiar to Muḥammad through participation in religious services and/or through personal connections. Since the Prophet could assume audience familiarity with the material, the stories are often only alluded to. In cases where they are given a detailed recounting in the Koran—an especially attractive example is the account of the Old Testament Joseph in the sura of that name (sura 12)—the narrative structure is found to be unique enough to be deemed "creative appropriation."

That the suras, like the recitational units in the neighboring religions, were conceived as pericopes was explained above. What is evident here is the influence of Christian and possibly also Jewish liturgical practice. In form, content, and structure, the tenor of the Koran in the different phases of its development approaches individual biblical forms of speech and liturgical texts.

Many early Meccan suras can be likened to the Psalms, based on form (they are mostly short, the early suras monothematic), language (short rhythmic verse), and content (praise of God, consolation and encouragement, prayers, laments, warnings, threats) (for example, suras 87, 92 93, 94, 104, 107, 113, 114). A true innovation is the introduction of eschatological prophesies, often followed by polemics against the unbelievers, and of portrayals of the joys of paradise and the horrors of hell (for example, suras 81, 84, 99.) What is also conspicuous in these early suras, however, is a pre-Islamic, Old Arabian influence, namely, in the rhyme prose and the oath series with which numerous suras in this period are introduced. The oaths, mostly by phenomena and forces of nature and sacred places (for example, suras 77, 85, 90, 92, 93, 95), remind us of the oracle sayings of the soothsayers.

The middle and late Meccan suras are longer and have longer, more thematically complex verses than the early Meccan suras; they contain adaptations of numerous biblical stories. As scripture read aloud in worship, they are more comparable to liturgical than biblical text ensembles. Of outstanding significance here is a certain number of middle Meccan suras that exhibit a tripartite structure. They are often introduced with an oath, but now no longer by phenomena and forces of nature, as in the earlier suras, but mostly by the holy book, the Koran (suras 36, 38, 43, 44, 50; 26). The subsequent first part is appellative, that is, it includes themes like warnings and the call to accept Islam; it can also embrace polemics, like threats addressed to the disbelievers. The second part is narrative; it is shaped by "punishment legends." These stories are primarily biblical (e.g., Noah and the flood); others, however, are also of Old Arabian origin (the fall of the godless tribes 'Ād and Thamūd): they tell of punishments suffered by folk in earlier times who failed to heed the warnings of their prophets. The third part, or close of the sura, is again appellative; it often refers back to the theme of the first part.

The "verses" of the late suras already from the late Meccan period on are extremely long. They no longer have an intrinsic rhythm and are still recognizable as such only by the rhymed verse end. In the late suras, biblical models are again recognizable. And this is evident mainly in the so-called speech suras of the Medinan period (for example, suras 22, 33, 49, 60), which are reminiscent of the biblical prophet orations. These suras can begin with a hymnic formula reminiscent of the Psalms (suras 61, 62, 64). The following is an address to the community or also to the Prophet (the speaker is God or the archangel Gabriel). In the main segment, orders and laws are proclaimed that possess temporary or eternal validity, or matters pertaining to the young community are dealt with.

Even though the Koran became Islam's first book, it did not exist in that form during the lifetime of the prophet Muḥammad. We do not know precisely when the project of producing a "book" or "scripture" became a priority in Muḥammad's mind. In the Koran itself the term *kitāb* (book) was increasingly used to describe the sum total of the revelation, effectively replacing the term *qur'ān*, "recitation." This gradual replacement shows that the idea of a "scripture" in book form akin to the Christian lectionary gained increased prominence in Muḥammad's mind.

We do not know with certainty if the Prophet himself could write; reports in this regard are contradictory; most Muslims assume that he was illiterate. Yet we are told that he had scribes to whom he dictated the revelations. Nevertheless, no compiled book or "scripture" existed at the time of Muḥammad's death. It was only as a result of a process that lasted some twenty-five years that the Koran acquired the form it has today.

As to the history of the collection and codification of the revelations, suffice it to say that it started, during the lifetime of the Prophet, with scattered writings on various materials (fragments of papyrus and parchment, palm stalks, sheets, etc.). It then led to private copies in the possession of family members and companions of Muḥammad, and came to a first end with the codification and official edition of the entire text at the behest of the third caliph, ʿUthmān (r. 644–56). He is said to have ordered the task of codifying the revelations because of the fact that disputes regarding the correct text of the sacred book arose in the army, threatening the unity of Islam. The collection took place in Medina, now the first capital city in the Islamic empire.

The "publication" of the sacred book was initially realized by depositing a copy in Medina and sending other exemplar copies to the provincial capitals: Damascus, Basra, Kufa, and so on. This method of publication reminds us of the earlier practice of depositing important documents in prominent places.

The Koran had now become an actual book, a work of literature. Yet, even after its codification, it remained a collection of texts to be recited (*qurʾān*) and to be used in instruction. This proved necessary because the official text was still only a consonantal structure without any signs for vowels or marks for distinguishing consonants written in the same way (see figure 9.1).

Those who initiated its collection and promoted its written dissemination were state officials, at their head the caliph. On the other hand, the custodians of

9.1. Manuscript leaf from one of the oldest copies of the Koran, sura 42:49-43:13 and sura 43:13-43:32 (Yemen; seventh or early eighth century CE). Sanaa, Dār al-Makhṭūṭāt.

its oral dissemination and transmission were the Koran reciters (*qurrā'*). Their way of "publishing" the sacred book was *recitation*, which included teaching and transmission—a method reminiscent of that of the transmitters of poetry (*ruwāt*).

The Muslim Tradition (Ḥadīth)

Ḥadīth, literally "news, information; story" is the sum total of the transmitted reports on the words and deeds of Muḥammad—the Muslim Tradition per se. This term (*ḥadīth*) is also used for the individual tradition traced back to Muḥammad or to one or more of his companions. Ḥadīth is, after the Koran, the second important literary phenomenon of Islam. While, nowadays, the Ḥadīth is a vast genre of Arabic literature available in many multivolume collections, it was originally, as the word implies, information recited and then passed on orally. To become "literature," Ḥadīth needed considerably more time than the Koran: 200 years or even more.

How the structure of an individual tradition presents itself is exemplified in the following definition: "A complete *ḥadīth* consists of a text (*matn*) and information about its path of transmission (*isnād*, literally 'support'), i.e. a chain of transmitters through which the report is traced back to an eyewitness or at least to an earlier authority."[13] In time, the accounts developed into a "highly standardized account of the normative behavior of the Prophet, comprising his sayings and deeds as well as his tacit approval of the practices of others."[14]

The Ḥadith emerged in the last third of the first Islamic century (seventh century CE) in Medina, the Prophet's city, and soon spread throughout the Islamic world. In the first and second generations after Muḥammad, inquisitive people, especially the children and grandchildren of the first believers who had themselves never met the Prophet, began to collect information about his words and deeds. They gathered this information from various informants, in particular from living companions of Muḥammad, and grouped these accounts, and then transmitted them to believers ("students") following a special method. They are also said to have already made private notes. The "students" then passed the received information on in the same way. This oral transmission, often based on written notes, created a form of systematic teaching. Thus arose the Ḥadīth scholarship represented by "Ḥadīth scholars" or "traditionists."

The instruction took place within scholarly "sessions" (*majālis*, sing. *majlis*) and "circles of students studying under a master" (*ḥalaqāt*, sing. *ḥalqa*, or *ḥalaqa*) (see figure 9.2).

9.2. *Study Circle in a Public Library.* From a manuscript (Iraq; thirteenth century CE) of the *Maqāmāt* ("Assemblies") of al-Ḥarīrī. Paris, Bibliothèque nationale de France. Ms. Arabe 5847, fol. 5 verso.

From the very start, those who transmitted an account would name their informant(s), as follows: "A said, B told (or transmitted to) me from C." This was the beginning of the notion of the *isnād* (chain of transmitters). In this system, reciting, teaching, and transmission were identical, reminding us of the method of the transmitters of poetry (*ruwāt*), but also of that of the Koran readers (*qurrā'*).

Ḥadīth exhibits a wide variety of themes. Indigenous scholarship distinguishes between three genres: 1. edifying reports (*tarhīb wa-targīb*; lit. "inspiring awe and arousing desire"); 2. reports containing the merits of certain people or institutions (*faḍā'il*); and 3. legal traditions (*ḥalāl wa-ḥarām*; lit. [precepts about] the permissible and the forbidden). The latter include regulations concerning human behavior and way of life of every sort, from laws on corporal punishments and cultic-ritualistic rules (e.g., on the exact orientation of the daily prayer and on the pilgrimage to Mecca) all the way to regulations regarding personal hygiene. The most important Ḥadīth genre concerns legal traditions.

This division does not incorporate the entire thematic pallet of Ḥadīth. In particular, it ignores the traditions about the historical events from the life of the Prophet, his contemporaries, and his successors. They are the most important component of the *Sīra*-works (biographies of Muḥammad), which form an independent literary genre. In addition, there are also ḥadīths with theological opinion as their subject (dogmatic ḥadīths) and those in which prophecies about the end of the world and on the situation of the blessed and damned in paradise and hell are pronounced (eschatological ḥadīths).

The path from orally transmitted report to written tradition in a redacted work, organized in chapters, was already recognized and described by indigenous ḥadīth scholars. The following scheme[15] is based on their perceptions: 1. unsystematic records (*kitāba*) at the time of the Prophet's companions and earliest successors (as of ca. 630) on tablets, on leaves, and in notebooks; 2. deliberate collections (*tadwīn*) (ca. 690–740 CE); 3. compilations arranged systematically according to chapter content (*taṣnīf*) as of around 740 on into the ninth century CE and beyond; more or less finalized redacted works since the ninth century.

The entire codification process of Muslim Tradition was accompanied by a vehement discussion among the Ḥadīth scholars about whether it was legitimate at all to write down ḥadīths or not. Opposing the proponents of the written recording of traditions were scholars who took the position that the Koran was the only book in Islam and should remain so and that the Ḥadīth should be retained in memory alone and accompany the "Scripture" as an oral teaching. They based their position on ḥadīths in which the Prophet is alleged to have said: "No other book than the Koran!" These scholars thus lectured their collected traditions from memory and forbade their students to write them down in class.

This discussion among the traditionists was, however, purely theoretical, because even the opponents of the recording of traditions almost always had written notes, which they kept at home or hidden. On the other hand, it is crucial to note that, before the ninth century, all this written material, including greater and systematic collections of traditions, were devices to bolster the memory, not edited books.

From the ninth century on, more or less finally redacted collections, among them the canonical Ḥadīth works, for example, al-Bukhārī's (d. 870) and Muslim ibn al-Ḥajjāj's (d. 875) *Ṣaḥīḥs* (The authentic [collections]), were produced. Thus, the Ḥadīth became "literature" approximately 200 to 250 years after the advent of Islam. Yet even after its codification, the oral tradition of the Ḥadīth survived, more as a postulate than in practice. The student was supposed to have "read" or "heard" the relevant book or text under the aegis of an authoritative master. Only upon having "audited" was he authorized to teach and transmit it further.

The development from the oral to the written, or the edited text, demonstrated so far using the example of the Ḥadīth, also holds more or less true for a wide range of "Islamic" sciences using the methodology of Ḥadīth: the biography of the prophet Muḥammad, Koran exegesis, history, also some philological disciplines. These sciences, too, became "literature" only 200–250 years after the advent of Islam.

Here, a few remarks on two works containing the biography of the Prophet should suffice. In al-Bukhārī's *al-Ṣaḥīḥ*, for the majority of Muslims the most venerated book after the Koran, there are two long chapters on the biography of the Prophet comprising more or less chronologically ordered historical ḥadīths. In the most significant biographical work on Muḥammad, Ibn Isḥāq's (d. 767) *Kitāb al-Maghāzī rasūl Allāh* (Book of the campaigns of the messenger of God), such ḥadīths accompany a wealth of other material: legends about earlier prophets; speeches and sermons of Muḥammad; contracts and other documents; poems. Besides serious traditions, the author also draws amply on material from professional storytellers and popular preachers (*quṣṣāṣ*) who embellished their accounts with miracle stories. The book's style, above all in the longer narratives on Muḥammad's military campaigns, evidences influences of the style of the Old Arabian *Ayyām al-'Arab* (Battle days of the Arabs; see above).

The entirety of the material of the *Kitāb al-Maghāzī* is arranged so as to generate a cohesive narration. Unique in its time, this work stands out as such in that it is conceived under a guiding idea: the story of Muḥammad and his faith is arranged in the history of divine revelation since the beginning of the world. Ibn Isḥāq is said to have received the impetus to produce such a well-organized work from the court of the caliph: The Abbasid caliph al-Manṣūr

(r. 754–75) is to have commissioned him with the task of compiling and editing his material for the crown prince.

This caliphal commissioning of a scholar to redact a foundational religious work reminds us that the definitive text of the Koran was also compiled by order and under supervision of a caliph, ʿUthmān. He was compelled in this regard by the well-founded fear that the previous polymorphism of the Koranic text represented a danger to the unity of belief and cohesion of the empire; for al-Manṣūr (who also decisively promoted the translation of antique books, see below), a political agenda likewise stood behind the project. He too felt a book of such supreme importance should have a uniform and official text. It is possible that the endeavor to prevent the recurrent rise of new sects, perilous to the empire, also played a role.

This edited version of the *Kitāb al-Maghāzī* is not extant, however. What we have are large parts of what Ibn Isḥāq transmitted "orally" through lectures and dictations to his students, and it is on hand only in later, rather diverse recensions. The most famous is Ibn Hishām's (d. 834) *Sīrat Rasūl Allāh* (The life of God's messenger).

Can a book like Ibn Isḥāq's *Kitāb al-Maghāzī* already be deemed "literature"? It clearly fulfills many, but not all of the conditions given in our definition of the term. For works of this type, I have chosen the term originating in classical studies: "literature of the school for the school, meant to be published through lectures."[16] A further example for this category of works is the Corpus iuris *Kitāb al-Muwaṭṭaʾ* (The well-trodden path) of Mālik b. Anas (d. 796) that was compiled relatively simultaneously with Ibn Isḥāq's book.

It is first with Ibn Hishām's *Sīra* that Ibn Isḥāq's work became "literature" in the strict sense of the word.

The Epistle (Risāla)

Arabic scholarly literature did not exhaust itself in material that was originally transmitted orally, then collected and eventually edited in written form. The first scholarly and literary writings after the Koran took the form of epistles. They were originally private communications intended for specific individuals and were not given the form of books intended for a wider readership (perhaps a consequence of the commandment "No other book than the Koran"?). They drew on the tradition of official letters and documents. These texts were the result of an impetus that came from the court: high-ranking individuals, even the caliph (see above, on Ibn Isḥāq), used to write letters to experts (legal scholars, or state secretaries) asking for information about a specific theme or issue, and the experts, in turn, responded in an epistle, referring back to the commission by an appropriate formula at the beginning of the letter. Though commissioned by, and addressed to, a specific person, epistles of literary value were recopied and disseminated.

There are two genres of epistles: letters of scholarly content and letters of literary content. The authors of the first category were mostly legal scholars, those of the second category state secretaries, initially all of them of non-Arabic, mostly of Iranian origin. We will return to the latter theme below.

The First Systematic Book in Arabic Literature: Sībawayhi's al-Kitāb ("The Book")

The study of linguistics, in particular grammar and lexicography, began in the seventh century, probably in Medina, and then flourished in the towns of Basra and Kufa in the eighth century. There, Arabic grammar schools were established. What stimulated this great interest in grammar was "the need to establish a definitive text of the Qur'ān [the official binding edition was only consonantal] and to preserve the language as a whole from the corrupting influence of an ever-increasing number of non-Arabic speaking Muslims."[17] Thus, grammar had from the outset very close ties to Koran sciences. It took shape in the first half of the eighth century alongside Koran exegesis and jurisprudence. It cannot be excluded that Greek, in lexicography also Indian, influences played a role, Greek influence in particular in the formulation of terminology. There is, however, no documentary proof of this. If such influences obtained at all, then they proceeded via the so-called *voie diffuse*, that is, through direct, difficult-to-determine contacts with non-Muslims. The influences could have emanated from Christian academies and cloister schools whose teachings were permeated with ancient bodies of thought; such schools continued to exist subsequent to the Islamic conquest. In contrast, influences from neighboring disciplines developing in parallel are clearly documented; in part, the same termini and methods are employed as in the earliest Koran commentaries[18] and in Islamic jurisprudence.[19]

Grammatical speculation took place until around the middle of the eighth century exclusively, or at any rate mainly, orally in the discussions of grammarians of the school of Basra. The earliest surviving book in the field of grammar is al-Kitāb (The book) of Sībawayhi (d. ca. 180/798). It is also the very first book, properly speaking, in all Islamic scholarship. Muslim scholars were quick to recognize its uniqueness, dubbing it "the Koran of grammar."

In his Kitāb, Sībawayhi was the first to undertake "a complete description of Arabic on all three levels of syntax, morphology and phonology . . . in the framework of a unified grammatical model."[20] The "Book" was consciously drafted with a large readership in mind. It is systematically subdivided into chapters and even contains internal cross-references in the text. Thus, it is unmistakably an actual book, a work of literature, although it is still devoid of an introduction and (presumably) a title chosen by the author himself; the name *al-Kitāb* may have been applied by later scholars and means "The Book" per se.

Sībawayhi's *Kitāb* subsequently attracted the lion's share of attention of all subsequent scholarly activity in the field of grammar. Like the Koran, the first actual Arabic book quite generally, it garnered abundant commentaries and subcommentaries. Many other works were devoted henceforth to extending and supplementing the *Kitāb*—it was as if the whole tradition, or "literature," rested on this one text, subjecting it to a constant and continuous process of commentary and explication.[21]

Works Originating from the Translation Movement "From Greek into Arabic"

Arabs distinguish between Arabic or indigenous sciences (*ulūm al-ʿArab*) (Koran and Ḥadīth scholarship, jurisprudence, grammar, lexicography, etc.) and foreign sciences (*ʿulūm al-awāʾil*) (natural sciences, mathematics, medicine, philosophy). The indigenous sciences embrace above all those that serve to explain the Koran and Ḥadīth; they often have the form of commentaries. Included in this genre are also grammar, lexicography, philology, and historiography. Muslims consider the most important of these sciences to be Islamic jurisprudence (*fiqh*), which developed simultaneously with grammar orally, in academic discussion circles; the first legal text that was given an edited form was an epistle authored by order of the caliph Hārūn al-Rashīd (r. 786–809), Abū Yūsuf Yaʿqūb's (d. 798) *Kitāb al-kharāj* (Book of land tax).

The foreign sciences came into the sphere of Islamic culture through the appropriation of ancient knowledge by the Arabs in the course of a sweeping translation movement. Unlike the emergence of many indigenous sciences, this was a purely written tradition; the originals and the translated works were "books" or "literature" from the outset.

The enterprise to translate a huge amount of Greek works, mostly of scientific, medical and philosophical content—to a lesser extent also Middle Persian and Indian works—into Arabic in a systematic way represents one of the great cultural movements in history: In the twelfth and thirteenth centuries these translated works were passed on to Europe, shaped by the Arabs; this means, for example, that translators had corrected errors on hand in the originals. The works were often accompanied by commentaries and adaptations (paraphrases, epitomes). It is noteworthy that, in the earliest stage, translations of Greek scientific works passed through the intermediary of Middle Persian versions, later, and much more often and much more importantly, in a second stage, via Syriac versions. The Middle Persian works under discussion included philosophical and astrological books, mostly of Greek origin, but, more importantly, also books of belletristic content, mostly of Persian or Indian origin (for these, see below).

Regarding the beginnings of this translation movement and the motives, there are diverse theories. The most recent, from George Saliba, has the movement beginning already in the Umayyad period (661–750), following the administrative reform of the caliph ʿAbd al-Malik (r. 685–705). Since for this reform of the Dīwān (the public administration), Arabic instead of the previously used Greek language (in the west, Syria) and Persian (in the east, Iraq) was introduced, the non-Arab, non-Muslim bureaucrats (state secretaries) lost their privileged positions to Arabs. According to Saliba, the translation movement is "generated by the desire [of the descendants of the non-Muslim bureaucrats] . . . to re-acquire jobs. . . . And in order to do that . . . they aimed to become indispensable to the government by their sheer possession of highly specialized knowledge."[22] By reviving academic activities, non-Muslim translators as well as bureaucrats, who were their patrons, were able to rise to yet higher official positions, like personal physicians and councilors to the caliph.

According to another theory, from Dimitri Gutas, which places the beginning of the deliberate translation movement later, under the Abbasid caliph al-Manṣūr (r. 754–75), its inception can be explained in that the Iranophile Abbasids "considered themselves not only successors of the Prophet Muḥammad but also heirs of the Sassanid emperors," and accordingly were also out to continue a certain "cultural policy" prevailing in Sassanid Persia.[23] In line with the underlying ideology of this policy, science, which was purported to be of Persian origin, was forcibly transferred to Greece by Alexander the Great and returned home only thanks to Sassanid translations.

The Greek-to-Arabic translation movement reached its apogee in the ninth century. Most translators were now Aramaean and Arab Christians, usually Nestorians; this explains why they initially had recourse to Syriac versions of the works of the great Greek thinkers and scholars. It was not until the middle of the ninth century that Greek works were translated directly from the Greek originals. The most important translator was the Nestorian Christian Ḥunayn b. Isḥāq (d. 873), a physician who rose to become personal doctor of the caliph. It is mainly owing to Ḥunayn's reliable translations of Hippocrates and Galen that the Arab physicians became worthy successors of the Greeks (see figure 9.3).

9.3. *Dioscorides and a Student.* From a manuscript of the *Materia Medica* (Iraq or northern Syria; thirteenth century CE). Istanbul, Topkapı Saray-Museum, Ahmet III, 2127, fol. 2 verso. Photo: akg-images.

The question naturally arises why the Arabs did not also translate major works of Greek poetry and historiography. The reason is that the late antique scientific tradition of the Alexandrian school, which was appropriated by the Syriac Christians and—in their wake—the Arabs, had already failed to incorporate those Greek literary genres. Moreover, the Arabs had their own highly developed poetry and historiography, and they may have felt that their own poetic and historiographical traditions were sufficient.

The Emergence of Arabic Literary Prose: Translations from Persian and the Writings of the State Secretaries

We now turn to the activities of the state secretaries (*kuttāb*; sing. *kātib*) and their initiative to translate Middle Persian works. This movement was significantly involved in the emergence of Arabic literary prose.

Ever since the period of the first Islamic conquest (ca. 634–44 CE), secretaries had worked in the administrative offices of the state. In the chanceries (sing. *dīwān al-rasā'il*) of the caliphs and governors (extant as of the beginning of the Umayyad period, ca. 660 CE), their job was to draft the official correspondences of state. Of non-Arab descent—in Iraq recruited mainly from families of Persian origin—these Zoroastrians and new Muslims had ideas and ideals completely different from those of the Muslim scholars engaged in religious and linguistic scholarship. "Their aim was . . . to remold . . . [the] political and social institutions [of the Islamic empire] and the inner spirit of Islamic culture on the model of the Sassanid institutions and values,"[24] and in accordance with this effort, they borrowed their material from the cultural heritage of the fallen Sassanid empire.

The original works composed by the state secretaries often took the form of epistles (sing. *risālah*, pl. *rasā'il*) and were consequently addressed to a specific person, the caliph, a prince, other secretaries and the like. This holds true for all the works of ʿAbd al-Ḥamīd al-Kātib (d. 132/750), among them *Letter to the secretaries* and a *Letter of advice to the Crown prince*. The latter is a precursor to the "mirrors for princes" genre (see below). ʿAbd al-Ḥamīd was in all likelihood of Iranian or Aramaean origin.

With certainty of Iranian extraction was the most famous translator from Middle Persian, Ibn al-Muqaffaʿ (d. 139/757). Like ʿAbd al-Ḥamīd, he authored epistles; but one of his translated works, *Kalīla wa-Dimna* is of special importance. It is a "mirror for princes" of Indian origin, in which by means of fables the young prince is to be taught correct behavior and political savvy. Kalīla and Dimna are two jackals; Kalila is the good, Dimna the evil councilor of the king, the lion (see figure 9.4).

9.4. *The Lion and the Jackal Dimna.* From a manuscript of *Kalīla and Dimna* (probably Syria; ca. 1200 CE). Paris, Bibliothèque Nationale, Ms. Arabe 3465, fol. 49 verso.

The original Sanskrit work, composed likely about the year 300 CE in Kashmir, was translated into Middle Persian in the sixth century. (Both the original Sanskrit work and the Middle Persian translation are lost.) Ibn al-Muqaffaʻ translated, that is, adapted, enlarged, and embellished the Middle Persian version and in so doing gave the Arabic language its first prose masterpiece. The Arabic version is the basis of numerous translations in both Orient and Occident.

Through *Kalīla and Dimna*, two prose genres originating in Indian literature, and likewise an Indian literary technique, were introduced into Arabic literature:

1. the mirrors for princes genre;
2. the animal fable genre (even though fable-like elements are extant in Old Arabic poetry and in the Koran); animals that act and speak like people were something highly unusual for the Arabic audience;
3. the structure of the frame technique.

With *Kalīla and Dimna*, the totally fabricated story, fiction, entered into Arabic literature. In native literary criticism, this is hardly discussed; an exception is an Arab critic, Ḥāzim al-Qarṭajannī (d. 1285), who terms fiction "invention of impossibility" and goes on to note that it played a big role in classical Greek poetry.[25] In the prose where it was able to hold its own, there had till then been only feeble attempts at fiction; it was initially completely foreign to poetry, and even later, up to the European influence (in the nineteenth century), there was hardly any fiction in Arabic poetry—unlike Persian, which had a rich and great fictional epic tradition. Of the few exceptions, significantly, are Arabic versifications of *Kalīla and Dimna*.

Not much later than *Kalīla wa-Dimna*, another Middle Persian work of Indian origin that likewise employed the frame technique and contains fictive stories was translated into Arabic: A book in Persian called *Hazār Afsāna* (Thousand tales), and in Arabic originally *Ḥadīth Alf layla* (The story of the thousand nights). The frame story goes as follows: "An ingenious female storyteller [called Shahrazād] manages to escape the impending threat; she tells stories so as to attract the ruler's attention and to distract him from his previous habits."[26] The earliest testimony is a fragment of one of the oldest existing Arabic paper manuscripts, from the second half of the ninth century. The work that after the entering of much new material later received the title *Alf layla wa-layla* (*1001 Nights*), notoriously had, in world literature, even more success than *Kalīla and Dimna*. This is mainly because of the many varied and exciting stories it contains, fairy tales and other tales, fictional but also realistic (see figure 9.5). Their influence on Western literature almost approaches that of the Bible.

9.5. *The Blind Man and the Cripple.* From a manuscript containing a tale from the *1001 Nights* (Egypt; sixteenth or seventeenth century CE). Staatsbibliothek zu Berlin, Orientabteilung, Ms. or. fol. 2564, fol. 19 recto.

During a continuous development through many centuries, mainly in Baghdad and later in Egypt, stories from the most diverse of genres and origin were added to the original Indian-Persian corpus. In the entirety of its long development, the *1001 Nights* remained "folk literature," "middle literature," penned by anonymous writers and orally recited by folk storytellers. For the learned in the Orient, the prestige of the *1001 Nights* was minimal; it was considered entertainment for children and women. From the start of the eighteenth century there was a great show of European enthusiasm for this work, and it was this that attracted the attention of Arabic intellectuals and scholars— whose estimation of fictional literature had in the meantime changed under Western influence—to "their" *1001 Nights*.

The importation of fiction into the Arabic literary tradition provides a point of orientation for looking back on the path taken by Arabic literature from its beginnings to the goal we have set. Pre-Islamic Arabic poetry is a domestic growth despite evident influences from the ambient cultures. These influences, however, concern phenomena like habits and customs, not literary borrowings; for instance, the reflection of Persian customs in Persian names of flowers and musical instruments in Old Arabic portrayals of wine and binges. In the Koran, the conscious engagement with non-Arab religions and cultures, particularly with Judaism and Christianity, begins. This engagement comes to the fore after the Islamic expansion and Muslim contact with the literary and scientific traditions of the surrounding Hellenized cultural landscape, in the aftermath of which Syriac and Greek works are translated into Arabic by Christian Arab scholars. Translations and adaptations of Persian works partly of Indian origin subsequently enriched Arabic culture, inter alia through masterpieces of fictional literature that later became models for Arabic works of this type. And so it is that Arabic literature, in whose creation and development both Muslims and non-Muslims participated, became the fascinating cultural phenomenon that it is. The volume and versatility of Arabic literature can be readily compared with that of China and India.

Further Reading

Beeston, A.F.L., and T. M. Johnstone et al., eds. *Arabic Literature to the End of the Umayyad Period*, 1983 (see especially chapters "Background Topics" by A.F.L. Beeston; "Early Arabic Prose" by R. B. Serjeant; "The Maghāzī-Literature" by J.M.B. Jones; "The Beginnings of the Arabic Prose Literature: The Epistolary Genre" by J. D. Latham; "The Qur'ān -I" by R. Paret).
Brown, Daniel W., ed. *The Hadith*, 2020.

Carter, M. "Arabic Grammar," in *Religion, Learning and Science in the 'Abbasid Period*, edited by M.J.L. Young, J. D. Latham, et al., 1990.

Cook, Michael. *The Koran: A Very Short Introduction*, 2000.

Irwin, Robert. *The Arabian Nights: A Companion*, 1994.

Latham, J. D. "Ibn al-Muqaffa' and Early 'Abbasid Prose," in *'Abbasid Belles-Lettres*, edited by Julia Ashtiany, T. M. Johnston, et al., 1990.

Versteegh, C.H.M. *Arabic Grammar and Qur'ānic Exegesis in Early Islam*, 1993.

Wagner, Ewald. *Grundzüge der klassischen arabischen Dichtung*, 1987–88.

PART III

European Vernaculars

A study of European vernacular literatures might be thought of as an accordion: depending how compressed or expanded the articulation is, the instrument will produce different sounds. It is not difficult to imagine dozens of chapters beyond the four that follow. Alongside a chapter on the most familiar Romance languages, one could imagine one on the neglected youngest sibling in the family, Romanian, or on a distant cousin like Catalan. So, too, one might wish for a chapter on the Celtic literatures of the British Isles, or one on the literatures of the Low Countries, Yiddish, or Austrian—each of these a venerable tradition in its own right. And this is to say nothing of the, broadly speaking, eastern European literatures, some closely connected to Russian (Polish, Czech), some more removed (Serbian), some entirely other (Georgian). The coming chapters cover only a small sampling of the European vernaculars but gesture repeatedly toward the many literatures that ramified across Europe over the last millennium.

In so doing, these chapters do not claim to identify the roots from which all other literatures have sprung. Instead, they do much to complicate the straightforward idea of a root and its branches. The vision of literary tradition that emerges over the next four chapters is one of creative appropriation. A guiding thesis that underlies these case studies is that literary beginnings cannot be recognized *ab ovo* but instead take place as a process of consistent remaking, of taking up preexisting forms from local culture (oral song and storytelling) or of established practices of literary writing found elsewhere. Invention turns out to be less important than transfer, innovation less powerful than emulation. Indeed, these chapters force the question whether invention and innovation are best regarded as independent categories from transfer and emulation, or if literary innovation is not equally backward and forward facing.

Viewed against the backdrop of the first two sections, one might suppose that this one should begin with a lengthy discussion of the cosmopolitan root, followed by individual chapters addressing the ramification of the European. There is a vantage point from which something similar is visible. Literatures in the English (chapter 10) and Romance languages (chapter 11) were, indeed, fruits of the Latin-based culture that at the end of the Middle Ages still dominated the life of the religious, political, and military elite. But their process of emergence was distinctive from the ones we saw in parts 1 and 2. For one, the lexicons of the Romance languages were organic outgrowths of Latin—hence the onomastic reference to Rome—and all the literatures discussed in the following chapters used some modification of the Greek and Roman alphabets. While there is good reason to think of the first three literatures discussed in this part as products of bicameral cultures, as we have seen repeatedly in this volume, we also see that vernacular literatures quickly began to circulate beyond territorial boundaries and that the hegemonic role of Latin became increasingly ambiguous. As Simon Gaunt points out in chapter 11, the earliest surviving manuscript of the *Song of Roland* may be written in Old French, but it was actually recorded in the British Isles. And the rise of English literature was deeply informed by knowledge of earlier and contemporary texts in the Romance languages. Before Geoffrey Chaucer wrote his *Canterbury Tales*, he wrote an epic poem entitled *Troilus and Criseyda*, which relied heavily on French and Italian sources, notably the great Giovanni Boccaccio.

Polyglotism was rather the norm than the exception for the European vernaculars, as the later cases of German (chapter 12) and Russian (chapter 13) attest. These two literatures differ from almost all the others in this book insofar as they were born of top-down efforts to establish a literature of rank. As Michael Wachtel shows, Peter the Great found his inspiration for a theater on Red Square during his travels in western Europe, but his efforts ultimately suffered from the absence of a public interested in such performances. It took time and generations of writers and readers for the idea of a Russian-based literature to get off the ground. Joel Lande tracks a similar set of developments around the same time in the German-speaking world. What these two literatures share is that their births were not exclusively—or even predominately—products of a Latin hegemony. Instead, the pioneers of German and Russian literature drew on multiple different linguistic traditions, participating in a Europe-wide literary cosmopolitanism that included the ancient literatures of Greece and Rome, but crucially informed by earlier innovations in English, French, and Italian.

The accounts of literary beginnings that unfold over the following four chapters rely, perhaps somewhat counterintuitively in this day and age, on the role of the signal genius in the construction of literary history. At least since the 1980s, a deep uncertainty has emerged whether it is still permissible to, as Nietzsche once put it, leap from mountaintop to mountaintop indifferent to the valleys populated by ostensibly countless middling authors. Notably, each of the four literary traditions discussed in this section assigns the towering literary writer or text a prominent place. Although the authors of these four chapters are not so cynical as to doubt the greatness of the *Song of Roland* or Guilhem's poems (chapter 11), nor of Chaucer (chapter 10), Goethe (chapter 12), and Pushkin (chapter 13), they emphasize that such aesthetic judgements tell only a partial story. The significance of such texts and authors consists not only in the perceived quality of the texts they produced but also in the pathways they open up to other literary cultures. What is more, exemplary authors become points of orientation for subsequent generations of writers, who draw inspiration from and measure themselves against the landmark achievements of earlier generations. A synoptic view of the literatures discussed here reveals that the formation of tradition is not a continuous evolutionary arc, but instead a process of fits and starts, with nonuniform pacing, at times leaping forward and at times plugging along. What is more, the literary mountaintops are not freestanding; they draw on preestablished conditions and translation activities for their unique ingenuity. To study chaotic moments of beginning is to recognize that the precedent for the unprecedented lies in the inchoate preconditions recognizable only after the fact.

The following chapters devoted to the emergence of four European vernacular literatures cover, roughly, two different periods. While the chapters on the Romance languages and English are devoted to the late Middle Ages, the ones on German and Russian concentrate especially on events in the eighteenth century. Although it would be a mistake to suppose that just because these literatures arose around the same time they assumed an identical shape, their juxtaposition reveals important commonalities. For example, the earliest phases of literature in the Romance languages and in English were equally shaped by the costliness of parchment, the difficulties of hand-copying manuscripts, and the low rate of literacy. The rise of German and Russian literature, by contrast, was connected with a growing literacy rate, the increased circulation of texts thanks to new printing technologies, and changing attitudes toward the freedom of literary expression to operate independently of religious censorship. In addition, German and Russian drew energy from overt attempts by elites to establish a literary tradition of rank, even if both also discovered that a literature cannot be created by fiat.

In the course of the following chapters, it becomes clear that the one hallmark of literary beginning is the establishment of a literary language. The challenge was two-pronged: Developing the linguistic and stylistic resources for literary expression, it became clear, depended on the achievement of the sort of stability that characterizes an independent language. Although we tend to think of the case studies that follow as national languages and literatures, each of the chapters here is devoted to a phase of historical development before the modern nation-state, before the educational tools and institutional structures existed for the promulgation of essentially consistent practices of linguistic expression and textual composition. The seeming inertness of categories like English or French literature can easily obscure the fluid magma out of which relatively stable linguistic systems are built. It is only by means of institutional structures aimed at achieving standardization that European vernaculars became substantively differentiated and, in due course, molded into literary languages. The state of literatures *in statu nascendi* is, in fact, more hybrid and polylingual, with crossover zones in which agents shuttle back and forth between different languages and even literary traditions. It is this very porousness of languages and literatures that lends the European vernaculars their persistently accordion-like shape.

English

INGRID NELSON

English literature has many beginnings. Anthologies and survey courses traditionally start with the first recorded Old English poem, the seventh-century "Caedmon's Hymn." The fourteenth-century poet Geoffrey Chaucer has been called the "Father of English literature" for expanding the literary possibilities of the English language in the *Canterbury Tales*, a collection of stories told by pilgrims of all social classes. Poets and literary theorists of the sixteenth and seventeenth centuries are the first to claim for English the prestige previously accorded to classical literatures in the West, with Shakespeare still the preeminent English writer in many minds and curricula. If we think of "English literature" not simply as a body of texts but as a coherent field of study, its origins come even later, with the nineteenth-century philology that edits many of these texts and locates their historical contexts, or with the twentieth-century invention of "English" as an academic discipline centered on literature.

How, then, to choose among these beginnings? Answering this question puts pressure on the idea of a vernacular literary "tradition" that for much of its early history has only a loose relationship to a sense of nationhood and has expanded in the past century to a global scope. If Old English owes as much to Germanic and Scandinavian language and culture as to insular traditions, the Anglophone literatures of modernity demonstrate the flexibility of Global Englishes in making new literary cultures across political and geographical borders. Much of this has to do with England's (and later America's) history and geography. In the Middle Ages, Britain's insularity and central location on maritime routes rendered its culture at once permeable to other influences and separate from them, while the two major Anglophone powers in modernity have been primary engines of colonization: military, political, and cultural.

Given the spatial, temporal, and linguistic range of English literatures, finding a direct lineage among them is difficult at best, futile at worst. This is because at every beginning English literature is marked by its *relation* to other cultures and languages. These relations can be linguistic, reflecting the Germanic, Latinate, and Romantic influences on the early development of the English language, not to mention postcolonial creolizations. These relations are cultural, as peoples from English-speaking lands encounter others both at home and abroad through conquest, trade, and pilgrimage. And finally, these relations are formal, as English writers assimilate and innovate on the literary genres and poetic forms they find in the literature of other cultures. Thinking relationally of English literature counters a narrative of cultural purity or creation ex nihilo: Chaucer does not invent the idea of writing literature in English against a backdrop of French cultural imperialism in late fourteenth-century England; neither does Shakespeare (or Thomas Wyatt) overthrow a literary tradition clouded by religiosity and moralism by introducing neoclassicism into sixteenth-century England. Instead, English literature throughout its history proves creatively permeable with respect to other literary languages, textual cultures, and forms, adapting and assimilating them while extending their possibilities.

One of the most trenchant (if difficult) writers on the concept of cultural relation and its effect on literature is Édouard Glissant (1928–2011), the French Caribbean writer and philosopher. The "poetics of relation" that Glissant identifies in modern Antillean culture is grounded in very different historical circumstances than those of the medieval England that will be the focus of this essay, and it would be facile to draw too close a parallel between the sources of Caribbean creolization and England's premodern culture, not to mention out of the scope of this essay to fully account for the subtleties of Glissant's thought. Nonetheless, Glissant's extended exploration of "relation" as a literary theoretical term offers some insights that resonate with medieval English culture. In particular, he distinguishes between two kinds of identity: "root identity," which "is founded in the distant past in a vision, a myth of the creation of the world," and "relation identity," which "is linked not to the creation of a world but to the conscious and contradictory experience of *contact* among cultures" (emphasis mine).[1] While Glissant draws a hard boundary between these two identities, for our purposes it makes better sense to think of them as opposite ends of a spectrum. As we will see, English literature begins in England amid a historical period in which a root identity based in origin myths is not distinct from cultural and literary relation. I suggest that these conditions inaugurate English literature as a permeable tradition readily adaptable to later cultural contacts.

This essay concerns the emergence of English literature within the multilingual culture that followed the Norman Conquest of England in 1066. The literature written in the thirteenth and fourteenth centuries in the language known as "Middle English" marks an important beginning of English literature that at once demonstrates its contact points with European textual cultures and lays the foundation for a linguistically and culturally distinct English literature.

The prior Old English literary corpus, as we will see, constitutes a singular and dormant tradition during this period. While English continues as a written (and of course, spoken) language across the pre- and post-Conquest periods, an English literature emerges in the thirteenth century that lays a foundation for the masterworks of poets like Chaucer, Gower, and Langland in the late fourteenth century as well as for much later literary innovations in the language across cultures. Thus, we cannot consider the beginning of literature in English without accounting for the multilingual textual culture of later medieval Britain. In this period, especially in the thirteenth and fourteenth centuries, English imaginative writing does not mark a distinct cultural awareness of emerging nationhood linked to language.[2] Instead, literature in English becomes a distinct, marked category in dialogue with the contemporary literatures of the British Isles. The manuscripts that preserve the thirteenth-century corpus show that it is highly relational with respect to other languages and genres, including practical, didactic, and devotional writings. Indeed, these categories are not distinct in early English literature but imbue the imaginative writing of this period. The literature of the period spanning roughly 1270 to 1400 thus lays claim to important innovations in the literary culture of England, which in turn emerge from lively and creative interests in literary relations.

The history of the British Isles is at once insular and European: marked, in the Middle Ages as today, by its geography as a set of islands separated on all sides from continental Europe. These islands attracted conquest by and trade with mainland Europeans (who in turn transmitted mediated aspects of Arabic literature and culture) even as they held a set of cultures slightly apart from them. Following the collapse of the Roman Empire's rule in Britain in 410 CE, Angle, Saxon, and Jute mercenaries from northern Europe poured into the British Isles in the fifth and sixth centuries, eventually establishing regional kingdoms. "Old English," a Germanic language that evolved with Anglo-Saxon settlement, is the native vernacular of the British Isles until the twelfth century. Of course, most Anglo-Saxon authors wrote in Latin, as did most Europeans. Nonetheless, a body of Old English literature composed in the seventh to eleventh centuries survives that comprises narrative and lyric poetry, devotional and homiletic verse and prose, chronicles, practical treatises, and much more; Gaelic and Celtic literatures, though weakly attested in this period, likely go back even further.[3] The first extant Old English poem, "Caedmon's Hymn," is recorded in the Venerable Bede's *Ecclesiastical History of the English People* (731 CE). According to Bede's tale, this poem was composed orally in the seventh century by a divinely inspired illiterate novice. The poem itself is a masterful string of appositives praising God within a concise Creation narrative of nine four-stress alliterative lines. The Old English literary corpus also includes an extraordinary body of elegies—lyrical poems of lament—that intersect with another significant component of the tradition, battle epics, in the masterwork *Beowulf*. The date of this poem is still debated; it was composed between the eighth and tenth centuries, with the sole surviving copy recorded in the eleventh century.

Yet the Old English texts we now most esteem as literature were largely overlooked until two broad cultural trends of modernity brought them prominence. The first of these was the antiquarianism that began in the sixteenth century and persists today, in which medieval manuscripts gained economic and cultural value as secular relics. Collectors such as Robert Bruce Cotton (1571–1631) and Kenelm Digby (1603–65) sought out manuscripts of English writing; their libraries contain many of the earliest copies of medieval English literature. Old English literature survives only in manuscript until the first printed edition of *Beowulf* in 1815, edited by an Icelandic scholar. By contrast, post-Conquest English literature, such as Chaucer's writings, were among the earliest texts printed in England by William Caxton in the late fifteenth century. The second factor was the twentieth-century establishment of "English" as an academic discipline focused on the study of literature. The formation of this discipline occurred amid methodological differences that at once created and segmented the English literary tradition. Medieval literature, long the subject of philological and historical scholarship, was set apart from "humanistic" literature like the plays of Shakespeare, imagined to speak universally; at the same time, it was enshrined in curricula through a model of historical coverage and nationalizing unity that assimilated all literatures in "English."[4] For this reason, it is helpful to decouple the history of English *literature* from the history of English as an academic discipline, whose twentieth-century canons and anthologies inaugurate a literary history that might seem unfamiliar to the composers and audiences of English imaginative texts near their times of creation. Old English literature, in short, enjoys a vibrant cultural presence during the currency of its language, fades into obscurity for centuries, returns to prominence as an object of antiquarian and philological interest, and enters the academic curriculum of English literary studies thanks to the dual impulses of historical coverage and national cultural hegemony. This account is not intended to undermine the extraordinary literary corpus of Old English literature, but rather to suggest that in searching for English literary beginnings, this corpus's unusual history of study renders it at once singular and belated.

The culture of Anglo-Saxon England bore the imprint of its contacts with Germanic and Nordic cultures as well as its native Celtic and Breton heritage. But an eleventh-century event brought a new cultural relation to the British Isles, one that would have far-reaching implications for its literature: the

Norman Conquest of 1066. Following the Norman habitation of England, Old French and Old English combined to form "Middle English," a language dated roughly 1100–1500 CE, from a generation following the Conquest until the beginning of English early modernity. Following the Conquest, the eleventh and twelfth centuries see the continued production of manuscripts containing "English," from new copies of Old English devotional and homiletic texts, to extensive English glossing in trilingual texts like the Eadwine Psalter, to new English compositions like the Peterborough Chronicle, to the extraordinary compendium of Gospel translations in idiosyncratic English spellings known as the *Ormulum.* These compositions demonstrate the continuing use of a form of the English language in certain institutional contexts: namely, the Benedictine monasteries in which most were produced.[5] But these English texts are not "imaginative literature," an admittedly constructed category that attempts to mark out for special attention writings in which the resources of fictional narrative and aesthetic style dominate the purpose of the work.

Instead, with French monarchs and nobles dominating English courtly culture following the Conquest, the imaginative literature of England in the twelfth and early thirteenth centuries is largely written in Latin and an English-inflected French, known as Anglo-French. The new genre of "romance," named for the term that describes the French language, *Romanz,* originated on the continent. These fictional, extensive verse narratives frequently drew on historical sources, such as chronicles, peopling them with real or (more often) apocryphal characters caught up in courtly intrigues, dramatic battles, and complicated love affairs. In England and in France, many courtly romances were inspired by Geoffrey of Monmouth's fictional account of King Arthur and his court in the Latin *History of the Kings of Britain* (completed by 1139), as well as in insular Gaelic and Celtic literature. These Arthurian romances offered a powerful fiction of origins uniting French and English cultures in a shared Celtic heritage spanning Wales and Cornwall in the British Isles, and Brittany on the continent. English Arthurian romances pursued these cultural relations in Anglo-French writings such as the *Lais* of Marie de France, written in the Angevin court of Henry II and Eleanor of Aquitaine, which purports to collect and translate into French several short Celtic tales that include many French romance conventions: star-crossed lovers, political exile, and magical transformations.

These English and French writings lay the groundwork for a thirteenth-century emergence, at least in the manuscript record, of English literature. In this sense, English literature begins again after the Conquest in relation to other literary traditions, especially French and Latin. The Middle English literature that develops in the thirteenth and fourteenth centuries represents an important beginning, in Said's sense of "the first step in the intentional production of meaning," for the many English literatures that will follow.[6] But this corpus is largely devoid of "originals," either in the conventional sense of innovative, new literary expression or in Said's sense of passive foundational sites. Instead, the corpus is defined by relational textual practices; in particular, *borrowing* and *translation*, two terms that have the potential to illuminate the relational, innovative quality of English literature's beginnings. This corpus is expansive in its use of genres, comprising lyric poetry (e.g., "The Cuckoo Song"), romance (*Havelok the Dane*), saints' lives (the *South English Legendary*), debate poems (*The Debate between Body and Soul*), and collections of exempla (Robert Mannyng's *Handlyng Synne*). None of these genres is original to English, and many English writings in this period are translations or adaptations from other languages. The *South English Legendary*, for example, freely borrows from Jacob of Voragine's Latin *Legenda Aurea*; Mannyng's exempla largely draw on French and Latin sources. Compendiums of stories, a genre that is wildly popular in medieval England as in much of Europe, owe much to the influence of the Arabic *maqâma*. Other borrowings are more complex and attenuated than the translation or adaptation of a single source. For example, many English lyrics begin with a "reverdie" opening celebrating the arrival of spring: "Lenten is come with love to town." They borrow the phrase from each other and from French lyrics going back to the twelfth- and thirteenth-century troubadours, but it can as easily initiate a secular love lyric as well as a devotional meditation. Within this culture of borrowing, innovation takes on a different shade of meaning than it has in contemporary literary reading. It is less about original phrasing or material, and more about the embellishment and artful arrangement of such material, as well as the networks created by borrowed and adapted language. Indeed, this was a principle of medieval rhetoric, the discipline that underlies both poetry and oration: a writer first finds a topic (*inventio*), arranges his material, and decorates it using the resources of rhetoric.[7]

Before examining some of the English literary texts and their manuscript contexts more closely, it is essential to understand the multilingual culture of the British Isles in the thirteenth century. Although a language such as English, unlike Latin or French, had limited readership, texts did not circulate strictly within the bounds of the modern nation-state of England. Instead, textual production and audience was at once highly localized, as household books attest, yet also mobile along established commercial routes. In the Middle Ages "England begins at Calais and not at Dover or Canterbury; the English Channel or *La Manche* is a much-traveled highway rather than (as by Shakespeare's time) a defensive moat."[8] Moreover, formal education revolved around Latin literacy, from the earliest "song schools" housed in cathedrals, where young children learned Latin hymns, through secondary schools that taught Latin "grammar," the reading and writing of texts, through the universities where the scholastic art of *disputatio* involved Latin orations and dialogue. Education of this sort was reserved for a narrow slice of the population, but even unschooled medieval English people were acquainted with liturgical and biblical Latin through church attendance. Wealthy laypeople, especially women, might commission Latin psalters and books of hours that they would work through with the assistance of dedicated clergy, giving them familiarity with these texts even if they did not "read" Latin. This kind of language knowledge, distinct from literacy or fluency, is highly invested in beginnings, as its mainly aural reception ensured that listeners were most familiar with the "incipits," or beginnings, that frequently served as titles and identifying phrases for medieval texts. Such Latin formulas served as a kind of shared cultural text, available for literary elaboration and play.[9]

Thus, churches and schools were the primary institutions of Latin usage in Britain, while French literacy and fluency signified social standing. A thirteenth-century verse grammar, the *Tretiz* of Walter de Bibbesworth, instructs native English speakers in French by demonstrating the correct usage of homonyms and near homonyms in context. Most versions of the *Tretiz* circulate with English glosses, and its rhyming octameter form aids its mnemonic function. The poem's structure makes clear its social purpose. The prologue announces that a primary reason for learning the finer points of French diction is to avoid social shaming, and the treatise is organized, in part, around the domains of a wealthy landowner's estate: the fields, bakery, brewery, orchards. French was the language of the courts into the fourteenth century, and the social climbing Geoffrey Chaucer, who was in royal service as a page by 1357, is recorded as speaking French in historical records and may have written his earliest poetry in French. He was certainly a prolific translator from French: in his lyrics, his English *Romaunt of the Rose*, and several Canterbury Tales. French may well have been known in England primarily as a spoken language, even in the reception of its literature. A common form of entertainment in noble households was "prelection," listening to romances being read aloud from a book to an assembled audience. At the same time, the languages we now identify as "French" and "English" were less strictly delineated in later medieval England, as both practical affairs like trade and personal matters like love affairs were conducted in a layered "international language" drawing on both vernaculars.[10]

At the same time, the British Isles were home to multiple native vernaculars with their own flourishing literatures. A Gaelic oral tradition dating to the sixth century gives Ireland perhaps the oldest vernacular literature in Europe. After the Norman Conquest, aristocratic patronage encouraged a strong Irish bardic tradition, as well as the production of Gaelic and non-Gaelic literary manuscripts. In Wales, post-Conquest literary vitality is attested by vernacular Arthurian legends, Celtic translations and adaptations of French literature, and a bardic class of court poets that arose following Edward I's reconquest of the region in 1282. The lyrics of the most esteemed poet of this group, Dafydd ap Gwilym (ca. 1330–ca. 1360), bring the Welsh language to new literary heights while also revitalizing the conventions of the European lyric tradition. These regions not only are home to native oral literatures but also participate energetically in manuscript culture, producing books ranging from glossed scriptures to secular compilations.[11]

Within this multilingual landscape of overlapping contact zones, pre-Chaucerian English writings more often signal their participation in textual culture than avow the intention of establishing an "English literature" defined by language. That is, these writings are not transcriptions from folk orality but are composed as written texts. To some extent, this culture is linguistic, as English texts translate, adapt, or write back to popular literatures in Latin and French. But more saliently, it reflects a number of the writing cultures within and adjacent to its production. One of these cultures is clerical. With the emergence of universities in later medieval Europe, a new educated class of clerks, secular and religious, became responsible for much of the production and circulation of written texts. English literary writing in this period frequently takes the form of clerical debates, like the thirteenth-century poem *The Owl and the Nightingale*, in which the titular birds debate personal, social, and devotional topics with reference to learned authors from the curriculum. A trilingual poem in Latin, French, and English, *Dum ludis floribus*, begins with the convention of celebrating the spring and concludes with a description of the writer's life as a university student in Paris. Another textual culture is curial, buoyed by the thirteenth century's increasing focus on pastoral care. The Fourth Lateran Council of 1215 promoted yearly confession by the laity, necessitating increased spiritual education, and fraternal orders founded in this century, the Franciscans and the Dominicans, stressed the importance of lay preaching. English preachers used a number of literary strategies to reach their lay audiences, including the performance of dramatic "interludes" and the inclusion of French or English verses to summarize key points of a sermon. In 1372, the friar John of Grimestone copied an anthology of such verses organized by topic, from *Abstinencia* to *Voluntate*. A robust corpus of pastoral literature emerged that presented doctrine in popular, accessible forms, from debates to allegorical narratives. Finally, English textual culture was legal and administrative. Following the Magna Carta (1215), English law relied increasingly on documentary proof, supplanting a prior system of communal memory and personal warrant. As a result, English bureaucracy flourished throughout the thirteenth through fifteenth centuries, developing an extensive system of written record keeping that employed many poets for their clerical skills.[12]

In short, post-Conquest medieval England enjoys a robust textual culture marked by multilingual writings from a number of institutional contexts. The corpus of English literature that emerges in the thirteenth and fourteenth centuries often speaks to these contexts, incorporating their specific lexicons and concerns. Yet notwithstanding the vibrant textual culture of later medieval England, its literature largely lacks the kind of interpretive and authorizing apparatus that marked other European literatures in the later Middle Ages. Many contemporary European textual cultures had well-developed conventions of production and commentary that bear some resemblance to the philology of the nineteenth and twentieth centuries, if lacking the later period's interest in historicizing texts. These textual cultures focused on compiling and glossing the works of *auctores*, a Latin word meaning both "author" and "authority," including biblical and patristic texts, the writings of prominent theologians such as Thomas Aquinas, and classical writings by Ovid, Vergil, and Aristotle. During the period of our interest, methods we would now recognize as philological had come to be applied to literature in other European vernaculars. Most notably, Dante (1265–1321) served as his own philologist. His *Vita Nuova* (1294), a kind of spiritual and erotic autobiography of alternating prose and verse, compiles and explicates its own poetic compositions. Dante's masterpiece, the *Divine Comedy*, was recognized from the outset as a text demanding commentary; two of its earliest glossators were Dante's own sons. But English literature was not until much later subject to this kind of commentary. Instead, what we might call its "literary theory"—its interpretive and authorizing structures—were implicit, embedded in the texts themselves or in their relations to the texts they cited, adapted, or accompanied.[13]

Another mark of the emergence of a single-language literature is its anthologizing. Textual production of the Middle Ages involved four agents, elegantly summarized by St. Bonaventure (in his own commentary on Peter Lombard's *Sentences*): scribe, compiler, commentator, and "author," who writes primarily his own materials. Compilers are a kind of philologist, in that they assemble and curate collections of texts, sometimes based on a patron's request but also, as bookshops emerged in early fourteenth-century England, according to their own sense of the marketplace.[14] During this period, however, English literature is not exclusively anthologized according to language. More commonly, English texts, literary and otherwise, appear in books along with French and

Latin texts. Multilingual anthologies of this sort decrease in number toward the end of the fourteenth century, and by the fifteenth century English literature largely appears in manuscripts containing only English texts. Further, English literature was not anthologized by genre. Unlike, for instance, the elaborate French troubadour manuscripts of the thirteenth century, which collect lyric poetry organized by author and accompanied by authorial vitae, English lyric poems tend to appear alongside thematically similar material in a variety of genres and language and are generally unattributed until the fifteenth century.

Nonetheless, describing the beginning of English literature as belated with respect to contemporary European literary cultures misses the point. Manuscript evidence demonstrates that imaginative writing in English flourished in the late thirteenth and early fourteenth century, surviving in books that present it quite differently than its continental counterparts, and thereby create a concept of "English literature" that is not autonomous but relational. In general, such manuscript books include texts in all three English languages, and display (from a modern perspective) a fluid approach to genre, combining practical, didactic, and recreational texts. Yet each one also emphasizes particular concerns along these axes, often with respect to the conditions of its production and intended audience. We will consider four such books, produced between 1270 and 1340, in order to understand how English literature begins during this period as a relational phenomenon.

One of these, now known as Oxford University, Jesus College, MS 29/2 (hereafter "Jesus 29"), was compiled as a planned collection in the English West Midlands between 1270 and 1300, probably for a bishop who accumulated its texts on his official travels. The manuscript primarily contains texts in English on religious and moral themes, with additional French and Latin compositions. It includes the aforementioned debate poem *The Owl and the Nightingale*, Middle English devotional lyric poems, two Anglo-French saints' lives in verse, and a Latin table of the relative prices and weights of bread and corn. Many of the didactic texts approach their subjects with literary craft and imagination. The author of the French saints' lives concludes one poem by comparing it favorably to medieval romances and the tales of Ovid. *The Owl and the Nightingale* includes several literary techniques in its quasi-scholastic debate. The birds are characters with emotions: the owl's heart swells, and his breath quickens at the nightingale's insults, which themselves observe the conventions of literary invective. The debate includes arguments concerning rhetoric—is it deceptive, politically exigent, or truthful?—and the relative merits of joyful and melancholy songs. Arguments over what we would today call literary values shade into devotional arguments in the poem, concerning which type of language and song best aids human salvation. Yet the moral program does not overshadow the poem's evident care in its craft. In a passage where the nightingale defends his preference for England, he offers a striking description of the wilderness elsewhere, from landscape to the savagery of other people (lines 999–1014). Jesus 29 also contains a series of lyric poems on devotional themes, including a number of Marian hymns, *contemptus mundi* poems, and the "Love-Ron" of Friar Thomas of Hales, a moral poem extolling virginity. One of these, now known as the "Little Sooth [True] Sermon," paints a vivid picture of village life and its temptations: bakers and brewers who cheat their customers with false measurements, women and men flirting in the market while their mass books remain at home in locked boxes. Overall, while the book takes devotion as a foundation of imaginative writing, it understands religious precepts very much within the scope of quotidian activities and secular concerns.[15]

Another book also compiled in the last quarter of the thirteenth century, Oxford, Bodleian Library MS Digby 86 (hereafter "Digby 86"), circulated among a small group of lay families as a "commonplace book," that is, a collection of material assembled over a period of several years that would be useful and enjoyable for a small coterie of readers. The first half of the book is dominated by practical prose texts, including medical recipes, charms, an alphabetical interpretation of dreams, and a manual for the care of hunting birds, as well as useful religious material, such as common prayers in Latin and French. The other half contains primarily verse texts in English and French that could be described as literary or at least recreational.

A common thread in many of the texts is what we might call "practical magic": instructions for managing the seemingly uncontrollable forces in one's world, rendered with literary interest. These include healing "charms" that instruct the reader to perform incantations, prognostications based on which day of the week Christmas occurs, and a copy of the French verse text known as the "Ragman Roll," a game of chance in which players blindly chose a stanza in order to hear their "fortunes." One section of Digby 86 deserves special notice with regard to the beginning of English literature. This is an unusually short quire, consisting primarily of two English texts, that probably originated as an autonomous "booklet" intended for independent circulation. Its first text, *Dame Sirith*, is a verse dialogue about a man who coercively seduces a married woman. This is the sole extant English fabliau, or raunchy comic tale, until Chaucer's "Miller's Tale" in the late fourteenth century, and its plot relies on a simple physical trick that is represented as clerical "magic" in the tale, thought to result from extensive book learning. The second text is the "Names of a Hare," a verse charm of seventy-seven English epithets for the animal that the user must recite when encountering it, in order to forestall the bad luck hares were supposed to bring. The magic of this text is incantatory, relying on a belief in the supernatural power of words that is a feature of oral cultures and is documented in a philosophical tradition going back to Plato. The booklet concludes with a third text, copied later than the first two by the same scribe, that is a French text of unlucky days of the year, "Les dolorous jours del an" (The unlucky days of the year), that also appears in a section of the manuscript that seems designed to "bridge" the two main sequences that were put together when the book was first assembled. Presumably, the scribe-compiler would not have recopied this text here had he intended the booklet to be part of this codex. If this is the case, the texts here are meant to stand apart, perhaps for their language but, given the French text, perhaps also for their magical qualities and allusions. Taken together—as their compilation suggests they were meant to be—*Dame Sirith* and "The Names of a Hare" suggest that the Digby scribe-compiler is experimenting with an idea of English literature.[16]

Half a century later, two significant manuscript collections demonstrate different approaches to English literature. The first of these, British Library MS Harley 2253 ("Harley 2253"; ca. 1330–40), bears many resemblances to Digby 86. It, too, was produced in the west of England by a single scribe-compiler, contains texts in Latin, French, and English and was likely used by a wealthy lay household. The manuscript shares texts with Digby 86, including the verse drama "The Harrowing of Hell." It contains a collection of poems now known as the "Harley Lyrics" that have been identified as the earliest lyric "anthology" in Middle English. Like Digby 86, its contents serve practical, devotional, and entertaining ends. The lyric poems move between secular and devotional topics, freely interchanging language to express devotion to a human or sacred love interest. These poems demonstrate a particularly English literary aesthetic, combining earthy erotic imagery with rhetorical elegance. For example, a mournful lover describes his suffering against the backdrop of animal sexuality: "Woo these wild drakes / Animals delight their mates / . . . Worms woo under clod, / Women grow wonderfully proud." The Harley scribe-compiler emphasizes a continuity between sacred and secular love. On one folio, he copies two lyrics, both beginning with the phrase "Lutel wot hit any mon" (Little does anyone know); one concerns secular love longing, the other devotion to Jesus Christ. Harley 2253 also contains poems on a number of other subjects: the regrets of an old man, the distress of farmers under new laws of taxation. Its texts are entirely untitled and unattributed, like most surviving English literature before the late fourteenth century. Instead, the compiler's focus appears to be on collecting aesthetically striking poetry that addresses the joys and sorrows of everyday life.

The final manuscript book, known as the "Auchinleck Manuscript" (ca. 1330–40), differs significantly from the three other compilations discussed. Compiled around the same time as Harley 2253, it contains exclusively English texts: romances, hagiographies, a chronicle, and didactic poetry. Copied by six different scribes, the manuscript may have been created for a specific patron, or on speculation for a London "bookshop." Even as many of the Auchinleck romances emphasize English nationhood, they also embrace a kind of medieval globalism. France is a primary site of relation for these romances: tales of French heroes from the Charlemagne cycle, *Otuel* and *Roland and Vernagu*, appear, as do English versions of French romances, including *Amis and Amaloun* and *Floris and Blancheflour*. Many of the romances in the book are English adaptations of earlier French romances concerning fictional English knights: *King Horn*, *Beves of Hampton*, and three versions of *Guy of Warwick*. As with the Carolingian romances, crusade and conversion are a frequent theme of the romances that locate England as a cosmopolitan power in the medieval world. *The King of Tars* begins with a coerced marriage between the Christian princess of "Tars," an indeterminate Eastern country, and the Muslim sultan of Damascus; its climax concerns the sultan's conversion and holy war against other Muslims. *King Richard*, also known as *Richard Coer de Lion*, is an assertively English heroic story of the Crusader king Richard I. From the outset, this romance places itself within a French literary tradition, listing many of the heroes of these tales, before explaining that its author will write in English to appeal to the uneducated, and speak of English knights. The gruesome tale sees Richard perverting many of the codes of chivalry, frequently resorting to trickery to win contests and cannibalizing his Muslim opponents, yet it ends on a jingoistic note celebrating English prowess. Within the corpus of surviving manuscripts containing English literature from this period, the Auchinleck manuscript is unique for its exclusively English contents as well as its large collection of romances. If a concept of English nationhood and English literature is emerging in this book as witnessed by content and language, it emerges as relation to other cultures of contact, Western and Eastern.[17]

These four compilations demonstrate the emergence of English literature within a textual culture of relations that are linguistic and discursive. Texts written in English with features we would today describe as literary (fictional narrative, poetic rhetoric) appear alongside practical, mnemonic, and didactic works and often incorporate these features. We cannot, then, segregate "English literature" from these contexts, but neither can we overlook the attention to and interest in preserving and circulating a corpus of imaginative literature that these manuscripts reveal. Such compilations make an implicit claim that English texts belong with French and Latin, and that their uses include the practical, the didactic, and the pleasurable. Without diminishing the aesthetic appeal of many of these texts, we can see that aesthetic enjoyment was only one reason for preserving these texts. The Auchinleck manuscript offers a different kind of relation, creating a linguistically singular literary corpus that understands English literature within a medieval global context. In short, the manuscripts of English literature produced between 1270 and 1340 indicate that English literature does not emerge as a linguistically or generically autonomous corpus, but instead draws on the full scope of the written textual culture of the British Isles and of the medieval world.

The weight of evidence for an important beginning of English literature in the late fourteenth century is strong. The European plague years 1348–49 decimated the English population, creating a historical rupture whose wide-ranging consequences include a literary history that would seem to begin anew following the crisis. A group of English poets once called the "Ricardian Poets" (Chaucer, Gower, Langland, and the Gawain poet) after the English king Richard II (1377–99) produced ambitious literary works that inspired a subsequent generation of writers (Lydgate, Hoccleve) to mark their own works within a lineage of "English literature." This body of secular literature is contemporary with a corpus of "vernacular theology," English works that, while often literary in their rhetoric, are unabashedly theological in content. Such writings include the spiritual visions of Julian of Norwich, known as the *Revelations of Divine Love*, and the anonymous *Cloud of Unknowing*, a mystic prose text that seeks to bring its reader closer to God through an apophatic process of "unknowing." All these writings contribute to the confident recognition of the rhetorical strengths of the English language. But Chaucer, Gower, and Langland emphasized the instructive as much as the literary purposes of their works; and all used the kinds of linguistic, textual, and formal relations we have observed in the manuscript compilations discussed above within the scope of their extended literary works. What began as manuscript compilation has become fictional compilation, as literary writers of the late fourteenth century translate, adapt, and combine into single, extensive poems the kinds of texts that were previously copied and compiled in manuscript books. Although the scope of this essay does not permit examining each of these at length, a sense of the relationality of the most significant work of each poet demonstrates how they innovate on the relations already established in English literature over the previous century.[18]

The late fourteenth century was a time of literary ambition among English writers, even if we judge only by the lengths of their compositions. Gower's *Confessio Amantis* (*Confession of a Lover*) is an English poem of approximately thirty-three thousand lines in eight books. In its framing romance plot, the goddess Venus orders the allegorical lover Amans to make a secular "confession" of his woes to "Genius," who takes up the task of educating Amans in philosophy, ethics, and politics by retelling much of the literature of antiquity. Gower's corpus also includes extensive writings in French and Latin: the French *Mirour de l'Omne* (*Mirror of Man*) is about thirty-two thousand lines long, and *Vox Clamantis* (*Voice of One Crying*) is a seven-book moral poem in Latin elegiac verses. Gower himself recognizes particular and distinct uses of each literary language in a Latin colophon that distinguishes the purposes of each of his three major works. The French *Mirror of Man* is intended to remind people to return to God after sinning; the Latin *Voice of One Crying* to document the political event of the English Peasants' Rebellion of 1381; and the English *Confession of a Lover* to accomplish three aims, to relate biblical world history, provide instruction in governance, and describe the experience of lovers. Although we might expect the Latin work to be devotional, the French amatory, and the English political, following the most widespread uses of each language, Gower's colophon indicates that English multilingualism is more nuanced. Each of these three languages has strategic uses that vary depending on context, location, and time. As the colophon also reveals, Gower understood his English masterwork in relation to his long French and Latin works. Within the *Confession* itself, classical tales are translated and recontextualized, organized by the frame story and edited to fit an ethical agenda. As a compendium, the *Confession* relies on the availability of a broad range of sources, but its specific literary technique is to put those sources into relation to each other.[19]

William Langland's *Piers Plowman* also puts a number of sources in conjunction with each other to create an ethical narrative. The book-length poem survives in three versions ("A," "B," and "C") ranging from about twenty-five hundred lines to over seven thousand lines. It follows the dreams of "Will," who encounters a number of allegorical figures (Holy Church, Lady Mede, Dame Study) in a quest for moral guidance. The poem is famously macaronic, with its English alliterative verses interspersed with Latin citations from scripture and other authoritative sources. These linguistic relations undergird relational ways of knowing that Will encounters throughout the poem. Even as each figure imparts some specific knowledge to the dreamer, he or she produces more questions that lead Will to the next step in his quest for guidance on how to "do well," "do better," and "do best." The poem reaches an ecstatic apex when Will has a vision of the Passion and the Harrowing of Hell, and it ultimately concludes with an apocalyptic institutional satire, pitting the church against the fraternal orders. As this extremely abbreviated description suggests, the poem is an intricate exploration of the conflict between internal ethical and external political structures, rendered poetically as an intersection of authoritative maxims, allegory, and quest narrative. Langland's literary relations are not sequential, like Gower's, but dialectical. Authoritative Latin verses punctuate Will's quest rather than conclude it; each allegorical figure addresses one aspect of Will's questions that lead him to another.

Finally, we come to the poet whose work makes an obvious beginning for English literature: Geoffrey Chaucer. Poets who wrote in the generations after Chaucer's death in 1400 identified him as the origin and apotheosis of English literature: Thomas Hoccleve calls Chaucer the "first fyndere [founder] of our language"; John Lydgate, "fayrest in our tonge"; William Dunbar, "of makaris flour" [flower of poets.][20] But Chaucer understood himself as much in relation to his European and English contemporaries—for example, Petrarch, Machaut, Gower—as to a lineage of poets including Statius, Lucan, and Dante, all of whom he names within his corpus. He traveled to France and Italy during his life and read voraciously in contemporary as well as older literatures. Even as he rendered in English many of the works that inspired him—French lyric poetry, Dante's *Divine Comedy*, Boccaccio's *Teseida*—he rarely "translated" directly. Rather, he permuted, adjusted, spliced, and invented. His poem *The House of Fame*, which Lydgate called "Dante in Inglissh,"[21] bears some resemblance to the Christian allegory, in that it includes a seeking first-person narrator and a giant eagle who carries him to another realm, but also elaborates on Ovid's description of the palace of Fama, retells the Dido and Aeneas story, and includes an excursus on the science of sound. The structure of *The Canterbury Tales* is profoundly relational, a compendium of adaptations and translations put in various pilgrims' mouths. This important English work includes ecclesiastical Latin—as a satirical element in the Pardoner's sermon theme, for example—as well as a number of French cognates that have become English words but also reflect Chaucer's fluency in the continental language. Indeed, Chaucer has fun with the paucity of English as a literary language, apologizing that "rhyme in English has such scarcity," and noting that his English translations of ancient lovers' speech seems "wonder nice [weird] and strange" to modern ears. What is not happening here is a lineal or hierarchical movement, either with English triumphing over other literatures or subordinating itself to them. Rather, as we have seen, the English absorption of cultural contacts that had gone on for centuries continues in the structure of these works. And if Chaucer as a point of origin of English literature made a convenient narrative in the fifteenth century, his nascent canonization embeds relation into its beginning.

This abbreviated discussion of three important writers of the late fourteenth century suggests how rich the literary possibilities of relation proved for later medieval poets. Characterized throughout the Middle Ages by its permeability and its insularity, England developed a literature that at once absorbed and expanded a number of cultural, poetic, and linguistic points of contact. The literary culture of England in the thirteenth and fourteenth centuries was marked by material texts that rarely anthologized and authorized literature in its native language according to the conventions common in, for example, French and Italian manuscript production. Even as poets began producing book-length English works, they continued to imagine the scope of English literature by means of its relations to other languages, institutions, and cultures. Examining the beginning of Middle English literature, we find that it displays a remarkable openness to absorbing and reimagining textual "others." The literary history outlined here suggests that the cultural hegemony responsible for delimiting English literature at certain historical moments in modernity has not lessened the fundamentally relational nature of this language and corpus. As English literature continues to travel beyond its insular origins, this distant lineage reminds us of its foundation in cultural contacts and relations.

Further Reading

Ashe, Laura. *Conquest and Transformation*, 2017.

Butterfield, Ardis. *The Familiar Enemy: Chaucer, Language and Nation in the Hundred Years War*, 2009.

Cannon, Christopher. *The Grounds of English Literature*, 2004.

Gikandi, Simon. *Maps of Englishness: Writing Identity in the Culture of Colonialism*, 1996.

Graff, Gerald. *Professing Literature: An Institutional History*, 1987.

Matthews, David. *The Making of Middle English: 1765–1910*, 1999.

Simpson, James. *Reform and Cultural Revolution*, in *The Oxford English Literary History*, 2002.

Treharne, Elaine. *Living through Conquest: The Politics of Early English, 1020–1220*, 2012.

Wallace, David. "Calais to London," in *Europe: A Literary History 1348–1418*, 2016.

Wallace, David, ed. *The Cambridge History of Medieval English Literature*, 1999.

Romance Languages

SIMON GAUNT

The simple and straightforward image that delivered the real never actually existed. It was only ever visible from a vantage point inside a later image, which worried about its own crafted and mediated nature. The later work is inhabited by imagined earlier modes of art making that were imagined precisely to be uninhabited, independent; imagined to be not yet art but simply images.

—NAGEL AND WOOD, *ANACHRONIC RENAISSANCE*, 28

The question of when and why the different languages deriving from Latin were sufficiently distinct both from Latin and from each other so as to be mutually unintelligible has long exercised Romance philologists (scholars devoted to the comparative study of these languages), as has the conundrum as to when and why literate elites started not just to write things down in Romance languages, but to write things down that may be considered literature, since Latin remained widely used for written texts throughout the Middle Ages. Furthermore, what constitutes "a language" within a "family" of languages such as the Romance languages is contentious, and while it is possible to identify more, the following is a relatively uncontroversial, if not comprehensive, list of Romance languages with significant numbers of speakers in the Middle Ages: Catalan, French, Italian, Occitan (the language spoken in roughly the southern third of modern-day France until the early twentieth century), Portuguese, Romanian, and Spanish. All these languages were to different degrees further atomized into dialects to a much greater extent than is the case today, where national education systems, national literary traditions, and print culture have exercised considerable pressure to standardize how people write and how educated people speak. While Latin offered a model of relative lexical and grammatical stability (even if this stability had continually to be reasserted through education), Romance languages were fluid and subject to change over time, sometimes quite rapid change.

For traditional literary histories of the Romance languages, the turn of the eleventh and twelfth centuries is a key period. The two Romance languages of what we now call France (French and Occitan) are precocious when it comes to developing a literature compared to the languages of the Italian and Iberian peninsulas. Whereas snippets of Italian and Iberian languages survive from the eleventh century onward, either in the margins of Latin manuscripts or embedded in other texts, more sustained literary endeavors in Italian or Iberian languages do not survive in the written record from before the thirteenth century (and in Romanian far later still). In French, however, the famous Strasbourg Oaths (I will return in my conclusion to the question of whether these are "literature") date from the early ninth century while the *Séquence de Sainte Eulalie*, a brief hagiographical poem, dates from the late ninth century. After this a small number of (mainly hagiographical) texts in French and Occitan survive in single manuscripts from the late tenth and eleventh centuries: in French the *Vie de Saint Léger* and the *Vie de Saint Alexis*, as well as a fragment of an epic poem, *Gormont et Isembard*; in Occitan a fragment of a free translation of Boethius and the *Vida de Santa Fe* (or *Chanson de Sainte Foi*).

There are also a number of lyric and prose fragments dating from the tenth and eleventh centuries embedded in longer texts or in Latin manuscripts that seem to have been composed either in Latin with vernacular elements, or in some intermediate form of French and Occitan (see Asperti 2006 and Paden 2005 for further details). But in modern scholarship French and Occitan literary history tends to cast these beginnings as tentative and embryonic precursors to two decisive and more properly literary interventions around 1100, which predate the subsequent proliferation of literary texts in both languages from around 1150 onward by a good fifty years, with French in the second half of the twelfth century then dominated by narrative texts, and Occitan by lyric. This precociousness of French and Occitan is further underscored by the fact that texts in both languages circulated in both the Iberian and Italian peninsulas well before they developed an indigenous literature of their own, and indeed well after.

Histories of French literature invariably stress the foundational status of the *Chanson de Roland*, a four-thousand-line epic poem (at least in the form in which it is usually read today), concerning the heroic deeds of Roland, Charlemagne's (fictitious) favorite nephew, composed around 1100. Histories of Occitan (and indeed European) literature proclaim Guilhem IX, Duke of Aquitaine and Count of Poitiers (d. 1126), to be the "first troubadour," a troubadour being a composer of lyric poems (often, but not exclusively, love poems) set to music and performed in a court setting. The vast, perhaps disproportionate, amount of critical attention afforded the *Roland* and Guilhem's lyrics, precisely because of their supposed inaugural status, is nonetheless also a measure of the fascination they elicit as literary masterpieces: French and Occitan literatures begin, apparently, with material that dazzles with its brilliance.

Yet these beginnings of literatures in Romance are not truly beginnings. Even setting aside the earlier surviving texts I have already mentioned, the *Roland* must have been preceded by an oral tradition and may well also have been preceded by a lost written tradition in Latin and Romance; Guilhem IX's ten surviving lyrics include jewel-like love lyrics, scabrous but deeply witty and well-crafted comic songs, a hilarious but nonetheless serious philosophical meditation on nothingness, and a moving *congé* (farewell to the world), but, as we shall see, they make sense only if it is assumed that they are embedded in and emerge from a poetic tradition of which the other witnesses have been lost.

This chapter considers the inaugural status of the *Roland* and the lyrics of Guilhem IX both in relation to what precedes (how are they different and why are they seen as a beginning?) and what follows (do they found a tradition?), while also offering some conjecture as to what makes them "literary." My main point will be a simple one: beginnings are only perceptible as such in retrospect and with hindsight. In some senses, literatures begin only when an activity that seems literary is taken up and imitated by others, then commemorated as such.

The straightforward chronological account I have just evoked may be inflected differently depending on the framework used to tell the story. Three such frameworks are particularly pertinent: vernacularity and orality as opposed to Latinity and writing; the related question of language; and then the manuscript culture through which we know these texts in the first place and which projects the texts into the future. First, are we measuring what these texts bring into being against a learned postclassical Latin tradition—always already literary—that had been mediated through writing for centuries, or a vernacular and oral popular tradition that also went back centuries, but for which we have only indirect and fragmentary evidence before them? Clearly literature itself did not begin in places where Romance languages were used just because Romance languages started to be deployed for literary purposes, since literature in Latin had been around for over one thousand years. And to what extent should material intended for oral performance, or transitioning from an oral to a written tradition, be considered "literature," when it is still inflected perhaps by popular, oral transmission?

Furthermore, Romance languages at the time that interests us here were centuries away from becoming the national and institutionalized languages they were to become at various points subsequently: French not until after 1300; Castilian and Portuguese not until the late fifteenth century; Italian not until the nineteenth century. Meanwhile Catalan, Occitan, and many varieties of Italian peninsula languages were relegated subsequently to the status of regional languages or dialects despite the prestige they had enjoyed as literary languages in the Middle Ages. The prestige of Occitan poetry, for example, was such that Catalan and Italian speakers learned to compose in it and it was widely imitated in French, German, and other languages; similarly, there was a sophisticated and flourishing literature in Catalan in the later Middle Ages.

In any case, Romance languages were more fluid and mobile in the twelfth and thirteenth centuries than they are today, with key early witnesses often coming from peripheries rather than centers and, perhaps as a consequence of this, displaying a range of apparently indeterminate "hybrid" linguistic forms. The *Roland* and Guilhem IX are a case in point. If the *Roland* is, as French literary history was to cast it in the nineteenth and much of the twentieth century, not just "the first great monument of French literature," but also the French national epic, then it is somewhat paradoxical that the earliest and most authoritative surviving manuscript was produced in England and written in the form of French used in England at the time (often called Anglo-Norman), not in continental French.

French here is less the language of the French nation than that of a Norman diaspora (which includes, as well as England and Normandy, Sicily, southern Italy, and the Crusader States in the eastern Mediterranean). Guilhem IX, on the other hand, was one of the most powerful noblemen in Europe. In all likelihood his main power base was Aquitaine and therefore linguistically firmly Occitan, but he was also Count of Poitou and is known to have held court in Poitiers. Various linguistic features of his poetry have been identified as characteristic of the Poitou or even as Gallicisms.

While both the language of Poitou and the idiosyncratic linguistic features of Guilhem's poetry are still a matter of scholarly debate, it is clear that his poetry does not quite conform to the elegant Occitan koine that was to be used almost uniformly by troubadours from 1150 (modelled on, but not identical to, Occitan as spoken in the Limousin). Linguistically Guilhem's lyrics are as much outliers as the *Roland*, but the key point here is that like the *Roland* they promote an ideology that has transnational currency, in this case associated with the amorous rather than heroic activities of the chivalric class ("courtly love" in modern scholarship), an ideology that was from the outset associated with Occitan poetry, just as epic heroism was associated with French.

Finally, should we privilege text or manuscript in our account? As we will see, the status of both the *Roland* and Guilhem IX's lyrics looks different depending on whether we focus on what modern scholarship hypothesizes about the texts as they may have been composed in the decades around 1100, or on the manuscript evidence that affords us only indirect access to these authorial versions, since it is inevitably later and offers a more complex and less clear-cut picture both of the texts and of their inaugural status.

Further questions arise if we ask what we mean by literature in the first place. Etymologically literature connotes writing and/or being formed with letters. For some the *Roland* is always going to be but a reflection of a lost performance of a long narrative song that evolved as part of an oral, not a written tradition, in which case the notion of literature in itself may be misplaced if "literature" is understood as necessarily entailing writing. Similarly, troubadour lyrics were intended as oral performances, and the role of writing in their composition (particularly for the early troubadours) has been disputed. Some have argued that initially early troubadour lyrics were composed and circulated orally, whereas others have argued for the use of writing from the outset, at least in transmission, in the form of "song sheets." Arguments in favor of the literary qualities of the *Roland* and Guilhem's lyrics on the grounds of their structure and/or prosody, while convincing in my view, are nonetheless subjective, so I would prefer here to dwell on two qualities that may be viewed as symptomatic of literature that are more susceptible to empirical scrutiny: on the one hand a relation to writing and on the other a preoccupation with textual fabrication.

This last is key because whatever we think of how these texts were voiced (and maybe "vocality" is a more useful notion than "orality"), key to literary endeavor is surely the defamiliarization of everyday spoken language and the creation of a marked discursive space that is set apart from everyday speech. The use of verse may be crucial to this (which of course is also characteristic of song), as is, as well, the development of a recognizable form and lexis associated with a particular ethos (in other words genre).

It has become axiomatic of modern scholarship on the *chanson de geste* (medieval French epic poetry) at least to acknowledge its origin in oral culture and traditions. In the 1960s and 1970s some critics went further, making analogies to modern surviving oral epic traditions, performances more than written texts, suggesting that surviving early chansons de geste were but reflections of these lost performances. Later twelfth- and thirteenth-century chansons de geste may have accrued more literary qualities as a tradition of preserving these stories in writing grew, particularly in "cyclical" manuscripts that drew sequences of chansons de geste about a single character into a linear narrative, but the repetitions and formulas characteristic of the earliest examples, rather than being "poetic" or a feature of "literary style" in the modern sense, are rather primarily mnemonic and an index of orality. Yet whatever its origins the *Chanson de Roland* challenges us to think about what a chanson de geste actually is precisely in relation to writing. Two points should be borne in mind here.

First, literacy in the Middle Ages was necessarily acquired through a Latinate, usually clerical education, that was reserved for only a small minority, which means all writing bore a relation to Latin and was the preserve of an elite. Secondly, while literature was therefore the preserve of an elite (which it almost certainly was in the Middle Ages and usually is), this does not necessarily mean that only a *literate* elite had access to written texts, since texts were read aloud to groups, performed in the case of lyrics, and the audience thereby were interpolated into what Brian Stock (1983) has called a "textual community."

The word *geste* in Old French is famously polysemic: it can mean an action or sequence of actions, a story or a legend, or a dynasty or family. In the *Chanson de Roland*, which narrates the heroic death of Charlemagne's (fictional) favorite nephew, Roland, his companion Oliver, and Charlemagne's twelve peers at the Battle of Roncevaux in the Pyrenees, the word occurs five times:

> Ço dit li quens: "Jo n'en ferai nïent;
> Deus me cunfunde, se la geste en desment!"
>   (Whitehead 1946, 787–88)

> (Thus speaks the count: "I shall do no such thing;
> May God confound me if I taint my family's name!")
>   (Gaunt and Pratt 2015, 787–88)

> Dist l'arcevesques: "Nostre hume sunt mult proz.
> Suz ciel n'ad home, plus en ait de meillors.
> Il est escrit en la geste Francor
> Que vassals ad li nostre empereür."
>   (Whitehead 1946, 1441–44)

> (The archbishop said: "Our men are very brave.
> There is no king on earth with more or better warriors.
> It is written down in the Frankish annals
> That our emperor has excellent vassals.")
>   (Gaunt and Pratt 2015, 1441–44)

> Ço dit la geste e cil ki el camp fut—
> Li ber Gilie, por qui Deus fait vertuz—
> E fist la chartre el muster de Loüm.
> Ki tant ne set ne l'ad prod entendut.
>   (Whitehead 1946, 2095–98)

(Thus state the annals and an eyewitness to the battle,
The noble Giles, for whom God performs miracles,
And who made the charter at the monastery of Laon.
If you don't know this, you have not understood properly.)
    (Gaunt and Pratt 2015, 2095–98)

Il est escrit en l'ancïene geste
Que Carles mandet humes de plusurs teres.
    (Whitehead 1946, 3742–43)

(It is written in the ancient annals
That Charles summons his men from many countries.)
    (Gaunt and Pratt 2015, 2742–43)

Ci falt la geste que Turoldus declinet. (Whitehead 1946, 4002)
(Here ends the ancient tale that Turoldus relates.)
    (Gaunt and Pratt 2015, 4002)

I quote here from my own translation but well remember how my cotranslator and I agonized over how to render *geste* in English. Thus, while we followed scholarly consensus in the first occurrence by taking *geste* to be a reference to Roland's family, it is equally possible to see Roland having a quasi-Gidean moment here in which he, as a character in a narrative, seems aware that he is destined to be a character in a narrative-to-be and feels he must stick to a preordained story if he is not to thwart his destiny. An alternative translation would then be "May God confound me if I contradict (or belie) the story." Charlemagne has just told Roland that he will leave half his army with him as they retreat from Spain over the Pyrenees, rightly fearing betrayal at the hands of Ganelon, Roland's stepfather and Charlemagne's brother-in-law, but Roland impetuously refuses as he *already knows* it is his destiny to play a particular part in a geste of which he will be the hero, which requires that he face Saracen hoards against impossible odds.

In all the other instances, the meaning of *geste* as "story" clearly predominates. It is striking, however, that in two of these examples geste is explicitly a *written* account and that in a third the geste is mentioned in close proximity to "the charter at the monastery of Laon," which is undoubtedly a written text. In further, quasi-Gidean, *mises en abîme* the substance of the *Geste Francor*, of the geste that proclaims the story that confirms what an eyewitness said and subsequently had written down, and of the *ancïene geste* is identical with the substance of the very text we are reading (or hearing). The *geste* or "ancient tale" the mysterious figure Turoldus ends in the last instance is therefore not just a tale, but in the light of the previous examples by implication a written text. One might also note in this final line of the poem the use of the Latin declension for his name and the unusual verb *declinet*, on one level (as we translated) "to end," but on another "to decline" in the sense of "to decline" grammatically.

Turoldus has been variously seen as a *jongleur* (or minstrel), the poet, or a scribe. Of course, we shall never know which now, but it is striking that this final line of the poem retrospectively insinuates a veneer of Latinity while using a word that implicitly references writing and the written, therefore literary, organization of narrative material.

This suggests a preoccupation with form and structure. The *Roland*'s exploitation of both has been used to underline alternatively its supposed oral features *and* its "literary" qualities. Some point to the fact that the climactic confrontation between the dying Oliver and Roland and Roland's death scene occupy the midpoint of the text, showing it deliberately has a symmetrical structure; others see this more as an accident of oral *remaniement* (reworking), suggesting that an earlier version ended with Charlemagne's return to collect the bodies of his massacred rearguard (about three quarters of the way through the surviving text) and that the so-called Baligant episode, in which Charlemagne defeats a newly arrived Muslim lord and takes revenge for the death of Roland on Ganelon, is a more recent addition. Some use the celebrated *laisses similaires*, in which an action seems to be repeated three times in three *laisses* or strophes by being narrated three times in very similar, but not identical terms, as evidence for the "oral" and formulaic quality of the text, but for others, their poise and lyricism make the whole text "poetry," freezing a particular moment in time, and thereby defamiliarizing the spoken language to create a marked (and highly elegiac) discursive space.

It is perhaps to state the obvious that regardless of the *Roland*'s origins it was clearly a written text to the extent that it *was* written down and that had it not been copied, we wouldn't know about it at all. While other medieval versions of the *Roland* are available in scholarly editions, the version that is always taught and widely reproduced (and which I have been citing) is the so-called Oxford *Roland*, so called because it survives only in a manuscript held in Oxford, Bodleian Library, Digby 23, which is an extraordinary literary object on a number of counts. First, while the dating of both texts and manuscripts for this period is necessarily imprecise, the manuscript itself seems to date from the first half of the twelfth century, which means the text was copied only a few decades after its composition in this form, at most forty to fifty years later. This relatively small chronological gap separating text and surviving manuscript is the exception rather than rule for this period. Second, Digby 23 is one of just a handful of manuscripts containing "literary" texts in French that have survived from the first half of the twelfth century. Third, its handwriting and *scripta* are unmistakably Anglo-Norman, and as far as we know the manuscript never left the British Isles. The manuscript is small and the handwriting sometimes irregular. Its meagre appearance and less than polished execution led some scholars to posit it was a so-called *manuscrit de jongleur* (minstrel's manu-script), intended as an *aide-mémoire* for performance, but the very notion of a minstrel's manuscript now has little credibility.

How was a minstrel to afford parchment, and if his job was to perform orally transmitted narratives based on mnemonic techniques and improvisation, why would he need a written copy? A few other surviving manuscripts from this period—with both Latin and vernacular texts—with a similar appearance and format to Digby 23 seem to have been made in and for monastic environ-ments. Furthermore, at an early stage (but we don't know when), the *Roland* was bound together with another twelfth-century manuscript (possibly from France), a copy of Calcidius's *Timaeus Platonis*. While it would be injudicious to make any assumptions about Digby 23's copy of the *Roland* based on this later (though still medieval) confected codex, rather than being something a minstrel toted in his knapsack, the Digby 23 copy of the *Roland* is more likely to have been made for a learned, literate, and literary public.

In some senses its literary qualities are brought all the more sharply into relief by its uniqueness, not just codicologically (being one of only a very few manuscripts like this with a text in Romance to survive), but also textually. Traditional philology tells us that seven manuscripts and three fragments of the *Roland* survive, though no other manuscript transmits the version of the text found in Digby 23. Other manuscripts transmit versions that are reworked from a source close to Digby 23, but not identical to it. The closest to the Oxford *Roland* is found in Venice Marciana Fr Z 4. This thirteenth-century Italian manuscript offers the only version apart from Digby 23's to use as-sonance rather than rhyme at the end of the line, and up to Roland's death it follows the Oxford *Roland* fairly closely, though its French is highly inflected by Italian forms. It is also, however, over six thousand lines long, expanding the narrative by paying more attention to the traitor Ganelon and to Oliver's sister Aude, betrothed to Roland, focusing thereby less exclusively on battle and the dynamics of counsel scenes. Not all the manuscripts of the subsequent rhymed versions are materially complete, but these texts seem to date from the late twelfth century, with surviving manuscripts dating from the thirteenth and fourteenth centuries, and they range in length from between six thousand and eight thousand lines, largely through a further expansion of the narrative in relation to Ganelon and Aude. While just a couple of manuscripts are Northern French, several more are Italian.

Thus, however iconic the *Roland* was to become for French literary history in the modern period, its dissemination in France seems, based on the surviving material evidence at least, to have been slight, and it seems to have had more traction as a written text in French (in whatever form) elsewhere. Furthermore, its dissemination overall is slight in absolute terms compared to that of some medieval French literary texts: thus while to compare the dissemination of the *Roland* to that of the *Roman de la Rose* (thirteenth-century; over three hundred manuscripts) is not to compare like with like, at least some twelfth-century texts seem to have been far more fortunate in their take up by posterity, Benoît de Sainte-Maure's *Roman de Troie* for example (ca. 1160; over sixty manuscripts). And while medieval French texts such as these are far from stable in transmission (before Dante's *Commedia* only sacred and some classical texts were copied exactly), they are less frequently subject to the wholesale *remaniement* (or reworking) that early texts like the *Roland* or some lyrics undergo. Fluke survival of a masterpiece in a single manuscript is hardly unprecedented (think of *Beowulf* for example) and indeed is part of the mystique of some epic poems, but the fact is that despite its modern reputation, the Oxford *Roland*'s posterity in the centuries that immediately followed its composition was meagre.

Of course, we know from iconography, references in other texts, and onomastics that the legend of Roland was everywhere from the tenth century onward, and while this points to multifaceted popular traditions that underpin the Oxford *Roland*, the very uniqueness of this particular written version is evidence not simply for it being the reflection of an oral tradition, but rather on the contrary for its literariness. And yet it survived in only one rather poor-quality manuscript, and though the version it transmits was clearly of interest, in that it formed the basis of other versions, it was not considered by the poets who set about reworking it or by other scribes (at least on the basis of surviving evidence) to be of sufficient value to transmit as it was other than in the exceptional Digby 23. This most precious of literary masterpieces might therefore easily not have survived at all, and there is no sense in the material culture that has transmitted it to us (whether directly or indirectly in the form of reworkings) of the inaugural status it has been accorded in modern times.

Guilhem IX's small lyric corpus has no overt reference to writing, but that he partakes of a literary culture seems clear both historically and from the lexis of his poetry:

Ben vuelh que sapchon li pluzor
D'est vers si.s de bona color
Qu'ieu ai trag de mon obrador,
Qu'ieu port d'ayselh mestier la flor,
Et es vertatz,
E puesc en trair lo vers auctor,
Quant er lassatz. (Eusebi 2003, 6:1–7)

(I indeed want everyone to know that this verse, which I have brought
forth from my workshop, is of good color, for I carry the flower in this
craft, and this is the truth, and I can call this verse as my witness, once
it is bound up.)

Vers is the generic term for song for the first few generations of troubadours.
The thirteenth-century prose *vida* (literally "life" or biography) of the mid-
twelfth-century troubadour Peire d'Alvernhe (the earliest to be mentioned
by Dante) states that until his lifetime all troubadour lyrics were *vers* as the
distinction between *canso* (love song, courtly love lyric) and *sirventes* (satirical
or political song) had not yet emerged. Its origin and meaning has been much
discussed by scholars, but the most likely explanation is that the term derives
from Latin *versus*, which means simply "verse" in classical Latin, but which in
the Middle Ages was also used as a technical term in music to denote either
an addition of new text to an existing melody, or the addition of new melody
and text to a sequence. One crucially important center for medieval music in
France, the Abbey of St. Martial in Limoges, seems to have had a particular
significance for troubadour lyric in that some early troubadour lyrics adopt
forms that are highly reminiscent of some of those recorded at St. Martial
from the late eleventh century onward, with some troubadour melodies also
showing the influence of Latin sequences from St. Martial.

One cannot, of course, assume that Guilhem IX uses the term *vers* in-
tending a direct allusion to the Latin term *versus* as used at St. Martial, but
St. Martial was one of the most important abbeys in Guilhem's domain,
and its musical culture would not have been unknown in adjacent centers
like Poitiers. My point is that whatever his own level of Latinity, and there
is no reason to assume he did not know Latin, Guilhem is part of a milieu
that is steeped in Latin literary culture: he is also, for example, known to
have had (sometimes adversarial) contact with Robert d'Abrissel, founder
of Fontrevault.

The very idea of the *vers* may therefore evoke, perhaps sardonically, a
term from church (and therefore learned) musical culture, and other terms

used here in the first stanza of "Ben vuelh" may also be semantically enriched through knowledge of Latin and Latin textual culture: *color, flor, auctor*. Saying a poem is "of good color" may be evocative of Horace's celebrated analogy between poetry and painting in his *Ars poetica*, and one might then wonder in the light of this if *flor* is also an allusion to the flowers of rhetoric. *Auctor* may mean "author" or "authority." In this instance, the latter meaning is clearly intended, but "authors" or "authorities" were by definition (ancient) written authors and authorities, evoking thereby Latin written texts. Guilhem's move is a bold one: whereas ancient written authority is usually summoned as witness to some universal, often theological truth, here his own vernacular *vers* or song is witness to his own poetic prowess.

Equally dominant in this stanza is the semantic field of craftsmanship: *obrador, mestier, lassatz*. Guilhem's poem emerges from a "workshop"; he has a *mestier*, which is to say a profession, trade, or craft; and his poem is going to be "bound up," "laced," possibly woven. Implicit in all this is a comparison to other poets. For if Guilhem is the best in his *mestier* or craft, then he is not the only one exercising it. The "first troubadour" was not alone then, but the first among peers, and therefore already working in a tradition, even if the work of his peers does not survive. Later in the tradition, weaving, painting, carving, plaining, polishing, smoothing, gilding, and filing all become metaphors not so much for poetic composition itself (*trobar*) as for the work the poet invests in making his song as formally perfect as possible, and for style, whether the aim is smooth transparency, or challenging hermeneutic opacity and difficulty, which often goes hand in hand with a harsh or unusual soundscape and the cultivation of rare, fiendishly arcane rhymes.

Yet the formal complexity of some troubadour poetry is not arid ornament. For a troubadour, being a wordsmith is intrinsic to the refinement and sincerity required of the courtly lover. As Guilhem puts it in "Pos vezem de novel florir":

> Del vers vos dic que mais ne vau,
> Qui be l'enten, e n'a plus lau,
> Que.l mot son faitz tug per egau
> Comunalmens,
> E.l sonetz, ieu meteus m'en lau,
> Bos e valens. (VII, 37–42)

(I tell you that the verse is worthier and praised more when it is well understood, for the words are all fashioned evenly, and the tune, I take pride in this, is good and valuable.)

In a pact typical of later troubadour poetry, Guilhem posits a discerning audience capable of appreciating the refinement and craftsmanship of his poetry. My translation perhaps emphasizes craftsmanship unduly here by translating *faitz* ("made") as "fashioned," but this is suggested by the insistence on craft elsewhere in Guilhem's small corpus and by the frequency with which he himself uses the formula *farai un vers* as an exordial phrase ("I will make a vers": three times in ten poems) or the related phrase *fait ai lo vers* ("I have made the *vers*"). He thus insists on the act of making, perhaps echoing the use of *facio* by Latin poets. *Per egau* ("equally") and *comunalmens* ("commonly" or "all the same") are equally challenging to translate accurately and succinctly: Guilhem may be referring to the predominance of the "a" rhyme (four times in six lines with the rhymes then "all the same"), to homogeneity of sound, or even to how the stanzaic structure of the lyric requires replication. Whatever his precise meaning, our attention is being drawn to the words of the lyric being no simple spontaneous or artless outpouring. The emphasis on making or fabrication is no less apparent in the pride taken in the relation between lyric and melody. This, in a poem where the poet says he is required to maintain the *aizimens* (12, "rules" or "conventions") of others to obtain joy and to be *obediens* (30, "obedient") to others to succeed in love, evinces a highly controlled amorous and poetic culture, governed by convention.

If "Pos vezem de novel florir" is apparently a sincere love song, "Ben vueill que sapchon li pluzor" turns into a scabrous joke, in which gaming metaphors are used initially to narrate how the poet's lady is not at all impressed by his failure to rise to the occasion, only to conclude by how vigorously he was eventually able to play the game because the third of his dice was loaded (50–62). Does the bawdy intent, explicitly or implicitly sexual in exactly half of Guilhem's surviving lyrics, make them any the less literary? On the contrary, lyrics like "Ben vueill que sapchon li pluzor," or "Companho, farai un vers . . . covinen" (in which Guilhem invites his audience to advise him to choose between two horses, who have different qualities in the saddle, and who turn out of course to be two women), or "Farai un vers pos mi sonelh" (in which a first-person narrator pretends to be deaf and dumb in order to gain the confidence and sexual favors of two ladies who are delighted to have found a man who can't kiss and tell) all parody to some extent the higher register and more refined tone of courtly lyric. They therefore emerge from and rely on a literary register and literary practices for their comic effects.

Guilhem's status as first troubadour fascinates critics endlessly, and the historical Guilhem seems in his lifetime and in the following decades to have enjoyed a reputation as a larger-than-life figure who enjoyed parties, as a womanizer (who disgraced himself several times with high-profile affairs, divorces, marriages of questionable validity, and even abductions), and as a statesman who played for high stakes, but who did not always win, largely because he was not always the best of strategists. His reputation is to some extent reflected in the late thirteenth-century *vida* devoted to him:

> Lo coms de Peitieus si fo uns dels majors cortes del mon e dels majors trichadors de dompnas, e bons cavalliers d'armas e larc de domnejar; e saup ben trobar e cantar. Et anet lonc temps per lo mon per enganar las domnas. Et ac un fill, que ac per moiller la duquessa de Normandia, don ac una filla que fo moiller del rei Enric d'Engleterra, maire del re Jove e d'en Richart e del comte Jaufre de Bretaingna.

> (The Count of Poitou was one of the most courtly men in the world and one of the greatest deceivers of ladies, and he was a good knight at arms, generous in his courting of women; and he was skilled at composing poetry and singing. And he went around the world for a long time in order to dupe ladies. And he had a son, who married the Duchess of Normandy, with whom he had a daughter who was the wife of King Henry of England, mother of the Young King and Sir Richard and of Count Geoffrey of Britany.)

This short text illustrates neatly an early apprehension of the reciprocal relationship the troubadour tradition posits from the outset between *trobar* (composing poetry) and *dompnejar* (courting women), though with a twist, as being courtly, and therefore possibly being a troubadour at all, is equated with deceiving women.

But more importantly for my purposes, the vida proposes for the first time a genealogy that was to be fundamental to later literary history of the courtly tradition. Guilhem, we are told, was the grandfather of the great Eleanor of Aquitaine (d. 1204), who married first Louis VII of France (in 1137), then Henry Count of Anjou (in 1152), who quickly became Henry II of England (1154, d. 1189). Eleanor, the vida tells us, was mother of that paragon of chivalric values Henry the Young King (d. 1183) and of Richard the Lionheart (d. 1199). The vida does not tell us that she was allegedly also the patroness of authors of courtly romances and that her daughter by her first marriage to the King of France, Marie de Champagne (d. 1181), was patroness to the great French author of courtly romances Chrétien de Troyes, no less, but the message is nonetheless clear: the high point of courtly culture in the later twelfth century, according to this brief paragraph—and modern literary history—has a direct line of contact with its point of origin.

The historical authenticity of vidas, however, is uneven. They were composed to introduce authorial collections of lyrics in thirteenth-century Italian song books. Some are highly accurate, others telescope historical facts, and others still seem to extrapolate biographical information from the lyrics they were written to introduce. This vida is transmitted in two "twin" manuscripts: Paris Bibliothèque Nationale fonds français 854 and 12473, often referred to as *chansonniers I* and *K*, both late thirteenth-century Italian manuscripts from the Veneto that derive quite closely from the same source in that they share common errors, sequences of lyrics, and so on. These two manuscripts are an important source for the vidas and *razos* (short prose narrative texts that offer explanations for the production of individual lyrics). While these are the only two manuscripts with lyrics attributed to Guilhem that habitually have vidas to introduce the poets' works, several others with works by him that have collections of vidas in a separate section (Paris Bibliothèque Nationale, fonds français 1749, New York Pierpont Morgan, 819 and Paris Bibliothèque Nationale, fonds français 22543, *chansonniers E, N*, and *R* respectively) do not include Guilhem's vida. This vida is therefore not only brief, but marginal to the tradition as a whole. Indeed, in each of the two manuscripts, it introduces just one lyric, the congé, and is buried in the middle of the codex (f. 142v and f. 128r respectively). Chansonniers often give pride of place to troubadours they deemed to be significant for the quality and authority of their work (for example the later twelfth-century troubadours Giraut de Borneil or Peire d'Alvernhe). Some of these very same troubadours attracted Dante's attention, and some lyrics by some troubadours survive in more than ten manuscripts with some of their most successful lyrics surviving in more than twenty. By comparison Guilhem IX's lyrics and Guilhem himself seem therefore to have attracted little attention from thirteenth- and fourteenth-century scribes and compilers. Even to say that Guilhem's lyrics survive in nine manuscripts is a little misleading as a gauge of their success, as four of these transmit only one lyric and in three of these it is the same one, the congé. Only four manuscripts have more than two lyrics, with one manuscript transmitting eight (nine if you count one that modern scholars agree is falsely attributed, Paris Bibliothèque Nationale, fonds français 856, the vast *chansonnier C* from Occitania, which generally transmits a large number of *unicae* or otherwise unknown lyrics), another six (*chansonnier E*), and another curiously repeating a sequence of five in almost exact reverse order (*chansonnier N*). So all in all Guilhem and his corpus are rather shadowy presences in the manuscript tradition. Furthermore, troubadour manuscripts almost always attribute lyrics individually to poets by means of a rubric. Barring one instance of misattribution of one lyric to another early troubadour, Jaufre Rudel, the rubrics to the corpus we attribute today to Guilhem IX simply identify the author as "lo coms de peitieus" or some orthographic variation thereon, but they do not say which Count of

Poitou, and there are in fact several possibilities, Guilhem's son for example (also called Guilhem, d. 1137) or even Richard the Lionheart. It is therefore at least possible that the information and genealogy with which the brief vida concludes was suggested to its author by the attribution in rubrics he found in his source: he had to choose a plausible Count of Poitou and he chose Guilhem IX. And whereas one of the two manuscripts with the vida offers a visual representation of Guilhem as a knight on horseback, perhaps an attempt to represent his high rank and chivalric prowess, the other offers a far more generic minstrel-like figure (see figures 11.1 and 11.2).

None of this necessarily makes the identification incorrect, but it does make Guilhem IX an even more spectral presence in the manuscript tradition.

I have sought to illustrate the extent to which, in the case of both the *Roland* and Guilhem IX's lyrics, their inaugural status, so crucial to modern literary history, went largely unnoticed and unremarked in the medieval written record. My intention, however, is not to suggest that they do not deserve the importance they have been accorded. Assuming the lyrics attributed to "lo coms de Peitieus" in the chansonniers are in fact by Guilhem IX, they seem to have exercised considerable influence over the troubadours of the next generation, active in the 1130s and 1140s (Jaufre Rudel, Marcabru, Cercamon). Two of these troubadours (Jaufre and Marcabru) exercised a significant influence on the subsequent tradition, Jaufre largely through two highly successful songs and Marcabru through a large, widely imitated, and varied surviving corpus. A version of what we know as the Oxford *Roland*, as we have already seen, was incorporated into subsequent versions, and incorporation is a form of imitation.

Both the *Roland* and Guilhem seem therefore to have founded a practice that was seen as worth continuing. The *Roland* and Guilhem's lyrics were therefore both consecrated as art by the generations immediately following, even if they subsequently sank back into obscurity. They also certainly deserve their position in literary history on aesthetic grounds. Yet in addition they mark a fundamental shift (and therefore a beginning of sorts) in terms of orientation. Prior surviving material is almost all religious (in fact hagiographic), with the exception being the fragment of the translation of Boethius into Occitan, which is learned.

The term "secular" should be used with caution since all aspects of medieval life and culture were shot through with religious thought and belief, but on the other hand both the *Roland* and the lyrics of Guilhem IX are preoccupied with a range of issues that are not primarily religious, even if a Christian framework is taken for granted: heroism and bravery, loyalty and male bonding, treachery in the *Roland*; sex and love, poetics, and feudal rivalry in Guilhem IX's lyrics. This is also an important part of what leads to their being perceived as "literature" in the

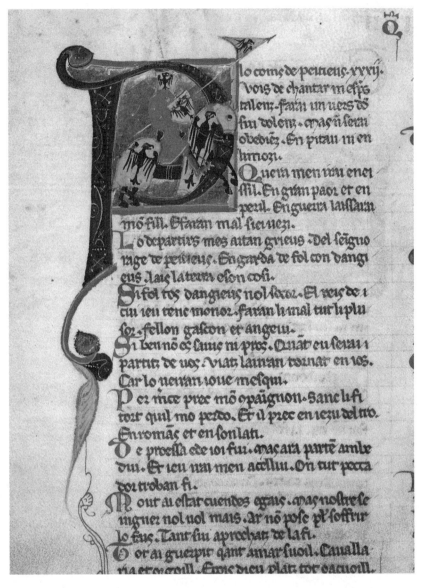

11.1. Detail of manuscript BnF fonds français 854 (Occitan *chansonnier* I), f. 142v. Paris, Bibliothèque nationale de France, Paris.

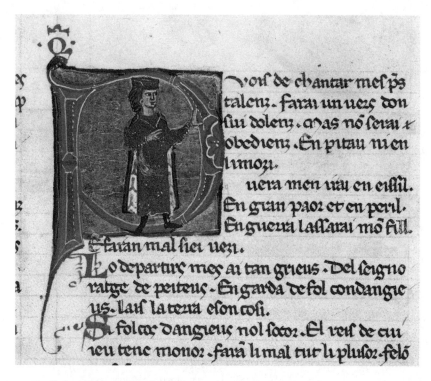

11.2. Detail of manuscript BnF fonds français 12473 (Occitan *chansonnier* K), f. 128r. Paris, Bibliothèque nationale de France, Paris.

modern period: they mark for us (even if this was not considered so significant at the time) the point at which, on the one hand, a form of textual composition broke sufficiently away from a Latinate religious framework, while remaining in a relation to it, to be legible as "literature," while, on the other, emerging from vernacular performances to be written down.

I want to conclude, however, by suggesting that perhaps we are looking in the wrong place for the beginnings of literature in Romance languages. I began by mentioning the Strasbourg Oaths, which are embedded in a Latin chronicle and announced as being in *romana lingua* as opposed to another, parallel set of oaths, sworn *in teudisca lingua*, that is in German (cited from Ducos, Souter and Valette 2016, 112):

Cumque Karolus haec eadem verba romana lingua perorasset, Lodhuvicus, quoniam major natu erat, prior haec deinde se servaturum testatus est:

"Pro Deo amur et pro christian poblo et nostro commun salvament, d'ist di in avant, in quant Deus savir et podir me dunat, si salvarai eo cist meon fradre Karlo, et in aiudha et in cadhuna cosa si cum om per dreit son fradre salvar dift, in o quid il mi altresi fazet et ab Ludher nul plaid nunquam prindrai, qui meon vol, cist meon fradre Karle in damno sit."

Quod cum Ludhovivus explesset, Karolus teudisca lingua sic haec eadem vera testatus est:

"In Godes minna ind in thes christianes filches ind unser bedhero gehalmissi. . . ."

Sacramentum autem quod utrorumque populus, quique propria lingua, testatus est, romana lingua sic se habet:

"Si Lodhuuigs sagrament que son fradre Karlo iurat conservat, et Karlus, meos sendra, de suo part, non l'ostanit, si io returnar non l'int pois, ne io ne neuls cui eo returnar int pois, in nulla aiudha contra Lodhuuuig nun li iu er."

Teudisca autem lingua:

"Oba Karl then eid then er sinemo bruodher Ludhuuuige gesuor geleistit . . ."

And when Charles had repeated the same declarations in the Romance language, Louis, since he was the oldest, swore the first to obey them:

"For the love of God and for Christendom and our common salvation, from this day onwards, as God will give me the wisdom and power, I shall protect this brother of mine Charles, with aid or anything else, as one ought to protect one's brother, so that he may do the same for me, and I shall never knowingly make any covenant with Lothair that might harm this brother of mine Charles."

When Louis had finished, Charles repeated the same oath in the German language:

"For the love of God and for the sake of Christian people and for the sake of both of us . . ."

And the oath both their peoples swore, each in their own language, is thus in the Romance language:

"If Louis keeps the oath that he has sworn to his brother Charles, and Charles, my lord, on the other hand breaks it, and if I cannot dissuade him from it—neither I nor anyone that I can dissuade from it—then I shall not help him in any way against Louis."

And in the German language:

"If Charles obeys this oath which he has sworn to his brother Louis . . ."

Nithard's *De dissensionibus filiorum Ludovici pii*, written between 842 and 843, therefore not long after the oaths were taken, is (naturally) in Latin and narrates the quarrelsome relations of the three sons of Louis the Pious, Charlemagne's son. The oaths themselves concern the pact made by Louis, king of the East Franks (Germans), with Charles, king of the West Franks (French), against their brother Lotharius. According to the text, Louis takes his oath in Romance while Charles takes his in German; in other words each oath is taken in the language of the opposing army, implicitly so all can understand. This gives the impression that Nithard—himself a member of the imperial family—is recording what they actually said (rather than a Latin transposition). But, of course, it is easy to forget that the oaths as recorded in this Latin text are unlikely to be exactly what was actually said when the oaths were sworn, however short the chronological gap between the composition of the text and the events it describes. Rather the oaths are a *representation* of what they said, particularly when mediated through the tenth- or eleventh-century manuscript that is the only surviving witness of Nithard's text. *Romana lingua* here is thus the object of representation within a Latin text.

Much ink has been spilled on the reasons for the oaths being sworn in the vernacular and on what the linguistic forms found in the oaths may tell us about the state of the languages in the ninth century. It used to be suggested that the vernacular was used because the brothers had insufficient Latin, but Rosamund McKitterick (1991) persuasively argues this is highly implausible given the levels of education of Carolingian princes. The vernaculars were more likely deployed, rather, so that the opposing armies may understand the oaths, even if this is only by implication and as dramatized by Nithard.

Regardless of the reason, the oaths are significant not only because they give us insight into the state of the language for a period when we have little other concrete evidence, but also because they play a key role in codifying for the first time a written form of a Romance language. Yet the focus has invariably been on the oaths as historical documents, and maybe this is to miss something crucial about the context in which they are embedded. In a recent revisionary rereading, Bernard Cerquiglini has sought to set the oaths in this broader context—Nithard's chronicle—rather than abstracting them from it (precisely as the earliest instances of written French) as so often happens when they are scrutinized by Romance philologists (including Cerquiglini himself in previous publications, as he freely admits). For Cerquiglini (2018), historians and philologists alike "reduce" Nithard's "literary monument to the status of a document" (20), his point here being that *De dissensionibus filiorum Ludovici pii* is a crafted and engaged, racy and well-paced, often implicitly eyewitness narration that seeks to persuade its readers of a particular point of view, with the oaths being a key element in Nithard's quest for verisimilitude, and therefore persuasiveness. For Cerquiglini this text therefore meets all the criteria for being "literature." The further significance of this insight is that French literature does not owe its existence to the prior existence of writing in French in documents, a common view according to which the protoliterary and then more properly literary endeavors of the poets of the *Séquence de Sainte Eulalie*, the *Vie de Saint Léger*, the *Vie de Saint Alexis, Gormont et Isembart*, and then the *Roland*, were possible only because French had already been written down for nonliterary purposes. Rather the genesis of written French is a result of literary endeavor in the first place:

> Les quelques lignes non latines qu'il ose confier au parchemin prennent valeur et sens au sein d'une oeuvre et par un imaginaire: Nithard est le premier écrivain de langue française. C'est dans la littérature que surgit cette langue, née sans doute de quelque malheur intime, cénotaphe d'un destin. (119)

> The few lines not in Latin that he dares to set down on parchment have value and meaning when set in the context of a work by an imaginative writer: Nithard is the first writer in the French language. This language arises from literature, born no doubt of some personal unhappiness, cenotaph of destiny.

This is a beguiling and dramatic, if somewhat Romantic proposition, that seems to suggest that a language like French can see itself as a language (or at least see itself as a high-status language) only once it has a literature, but it persuasively highlights the importance of the retrospective framing of certain writing practices as literature for literary traditions to come into being. Cerquiglini is misleading on one count, however. The language Nithard represents here for the first time is not "the French language," or at least not yet, but rather *romana lingua*, the language of a more heterogeneous group of peoples than the term "French" implies.

Further Reading

Asperti, Stefano. *Origini romanze: Lingue, testi antichi, letterature*, 2006.
Careri, Maria, Christine Ruby, and Ian Short. *Livres et écritures en français et en occitan au XIIIe siècle: Catalogue illustré*, 2011.
Gaunt, Simon, and Sarah Kay, eds. *The Troubadours: An Introduction*, 1999.

Meneghetti, Mari Luisa. *Le Origini delle letterature medievali romanze*, 1997.

Stock, Brian, *The Implications of Literacy: Written Language and Models of Interpretation in the Eleventh and Twelfth Centuries*, 1983.

Zumthor, Paul. "Document et Monument: A propos des plus anciens textes de langue française," *Revue de Sciences Humaines* 970 (1960): 5–19.

German

JOEL LANDE

The Swedish Academy's decision to award Herta Müller the Nobel Prize for literature in October 2009 was met with broad enthusiasm. There was little doubt that her harrowing narratives of European totalitarianism, sensitive portrayal of human suffering, and laconic style made Müller a worthy recipient of the world's highest literary prize. When the spokesperson for the Swedish Academy, Professor Peter Englund, was interviewed after the announcement, he made passing mention of an unusual aspect of her biography: Müller was born to a German-speaking minority in Romania, but since 1987 she had been living in Berlin. Englund's characterization of Müller as a German writer was and is uncontroversial: she lives in Germany, almost all her writing is in the German language, and her novels consistently focus on the German-speaking minority in Romania. And yet the fact that Müller could be identified in this way reveals quite a bit about the literary tradition to which she belongs. To pick out Müller as a German author does not speak solely to her language, citizenship, or place of residence. It picks out a bit of each of these but without identifying any of them as the defining feature. Particularly in the literary domain, German has some fuzziness built into it.

This is not new. From the very earliest stages of its development, "Deutsch" has been a language spoken across central Europe. "Deutschland," meanwhile, referred to much more than the federal republic known in English today as Germany. Well into the latter half of the nineteenth century, the term applied to the entire community of speakers of German. For centuries now, German literature has been shaped by a territorial entanglement, encompassing disparate groups and stretching across political borders. Long before the two major wars of the twentieth century fundamentally redrew the boundaries of European nation-states, German literature was more closely associated with the concept of a people and culture than with a state or principality.

In fact, German literature arose in regions that now belong to a host of different nations. In addition to Germany, Austria, and Switzerland, there were German speakers in what is now the Czech Republic, France, Hungary, Italy, Latvia, Poland, Slovenia, and more. For this reason, it has long been common to refer to the German people as a nation bound together by a culture (the term of art is "Kulturnation"), rather than as a political body. The geographical extension of German literature also means that it has been enlisted on the behalf of multiple different nation-building projects—from the establishment of a unified German state in the nineteenth century, through the Nazi period, and again in the communist German Democratic Republic. The sheer multiplicity of these projects should caution us against identifying German literature with any single political entity. Indeed, it would be a mistake to think that Herta Müller's identification as a German writer points to some contemporary postnationalist ethos. From the broader historical perspective, there is nothing anomalous about it. So, too, it is not at all unusual that Müller has authored books in Romanian as well as German. Across the German-speaking world, polyglotism is rather the rule than the exception.

to refer to the German people as a nation bound together by a culture (the term of art is "Kulturnation"), rather than as a political body. The geographical extension of German literature also means that it has been enlisted on the behalf of multiple different nation-building projects—from the establishment of a unified German state in the nineteenth century, through the Nazi period, and again in the communist German Democratic Republic. The sheer multiplicity of these projects should caution us against identifying German literature with any single political entity. Indeed, it would be a mistake to think that Herta Müller's identification as a German writer points to some contemporary postnationalist ethos. From the broader historical perspective, there is nothing anomalous about it. So, too, it is not at all unusual that Müller has authored books in Romanian as well as German. Across the German-speaking world, polyglotism is rather the rule than the exception.

Another dimension of Müller's receipt of the Nobel Prize deserves highlighting. The award came soon after the publication of the novel *Atemschaukel* (*The Hunger Angel*, 2009), by far her most successful literary work. Müller's novel appeared with one of the most visible literary presses in Germany (Carl Hanser Verlag) and was glowingly reviewed, within a few short months, in nearly every major German newspaper. Although the Swedish Academy had recently defended itself against accusations of eurocentrism, it decided in early October to award her the Nobel. In all likelihood, the decision grew out of the extraordinary enthusiasm surrounding Müller's novel. The prize meant not just approximately $1.4 million for Müller, but also a level of international acclaim that would lead to translations into dozens of languages, and scores of public appearances, as well as a place on the bookshelves of readers within and beyond the academy.

In this anecdote, one can see the outlines of a literary enterprise that involves more than just authors and their published works. Beyond the surface appearance of Herta Müller's recognition as one of the great writers of the twenty-first century, a vast network of factors is at work: languages, publishing houses, bookstores, readers, reviews, critiques, prizes, universities, and more. Listing these is not meant to diminish the magnitude of Herta Müller's accomplishments as an author. Rather, it underscores the fact that Müller's great international success was secured through her participation in a broader nexus of institutions and activities. In the anecdote, that is, one can see what one might call a literary ecosystem in action.

To look for the origins of German literature entails looking for the processes that brought this ecosystem into existence. It means tracking down the factors that conspired to form a literary enterprise capable of reproducing and thereby transforming itself up to the present day, such that German literature can be

said to have both a distinctive history and a distinctive present. This ecosystem—in terminological shorthand, modern German literature—did not begin
to take shape until quite late: the eighteenth century, to state the most basic
claim of this chapter. As it happens, the idea that German literature was late on
the scene is a commonplace with roots in discussions that took place already
in the eighteenth century. Between around 1730 and the turn of the nineteenth
century—in perhaps more familiar terms, between the early Enlightenment
and Romanticism—it was standard for German writers to complain that they
lagged behind the other European lands, particularly England and France.
Whether justified or not, this anxiety fed into a large-scale effort to establish a
German literature on a par with those of other European tongues. Meaningful
differences emerged over the century between the make-up of German literature and its counterparts, and these differences gave the modern German
literary ecosystem its unique mold.

Putting an encompassing literary context at the forefront of the following
discussion comes at a cost. It delimits the sort of literary beginning at issue in
this chapter. In particular, it sweeps into the background at least two landmark
historical moments, both of which could have provided a legitimate point of
entry for an account of how German literature began. The first falls around
1200, during the reign of the Hohenstaufen (1138–1250), when a rich and varied
body of lyric poetry known as the *Minnesang* arose in the Danube region and
a cleric from the city of Passau composed the heroic *Nibelungenlied* (*Song of
the Nibelungen*). This epic, along with the great romances by figures including
Hartmann von Aue, Gottfried von Strassburg, and Wolfram von Eschenbach,
are artful testaments to European chivalry. Around the same time, there also
emerged a vibrant and singular literature of religious women in Latin and the
vernacular, most prominently the prophetic visions and mystical revelations
of Hildegard of Bingen and Mechthild of Magdeburg.

The second watershed moment began in 1457, when Johann Gutenberg
published the Mainz Psalter, the pioneering book made with movable type.
The printing press was essential to Luther's translation of the Bible into German as well as to the spread of Protestantism across northern Europe. It was
on this religious and media-historical basis that the major writers of the seventeenth century gained a foothold. Beginning in the early decades of the century
with the scholar and poet Martin Opitz, a surge of new German lyric poetry
and tragic drama came onto the scene. The spiritual trials of the Thirty Years'
War and its aftermath found expression in the province of Silesia, located in
what is now Poland, which gave rise in the mid- and late seventeenth century
to an original school of poets, including the great tragedians Andreas Gryphius
and Daniel Caspar von Lohenstein as well as the two lyric poets Christian von

Hoffmannswaldau and Paul Fleming. And this is to say nothing of the innovative exploration of the picaro genre of the novel by Hans Jakob Christoffel von Grimmelshausen in his *Simplicissimus* and its sequels, which appeared in print starting in 1668.

The incompleteness of these lists is sure to cause consternation to some literary historians; the claim that they are not where German literature gets its start all the more so. And indeed some consternation is justifiable, given how common it is to speak of medieval and baroque German literature, not least in the large body of scholarly research on both periods.

The decision to set down the milestone in the eighteenth century is motivated by the conviction that, while it would be possible to reconstruct the literary ecosystems of the thirteenth and seventeenth centuries, they would not resemble the one of today. In focusing on the eighteenth century, the following account is thus avowedly rooted in the present: it surveys pivotal factors in the creation of what we now understand as German literature. Advocates of medieval and baroque literature should take solace in the fact that one of the factors that speaks in favor of focusing on the eighteenth century is that this period made a foundational contribution to the codification of premodern German literature as a heritage worth editing, printing, reading, imitating, and thus keeping alive.

A helpful framework for understanding the revolutionary character of eighteenth-century developments can be found in a remark made by Madame de Staël in her intellectual ethnography of the Germans first published in 1813. Reflecting on the differences between the German and other European literatures, she claims, "German literature is perhaps the only one that began with criticism; everywhere else criticism came after the masterpieces, but in Germany it produced them."[1] De Staël encourages us not only to pay attention to the intertwinement of literary criticism and literary creativity, but also to consider the generative role of theoretical and practical reflections in the formation of imaginative literature in the German language. Although de Staël was familiar with little beyond the works by figures like Friedrich Schiller and Johann Wolfgang von Goethe, whom she visited at the end of 1803, her observation captures a deep truth about the formative role of literary criticism over the previous decades.

A key area of critical debate concentrated on the German language, the very element of literature. During the eighteenth century, great progress was made in resolving the regionally colored differences that had historically characterized the language into a single standard grammar and orthography. What eventually became known as High German was established within two broader processes: the effort to establish rules for how the German language works, on the level both of the individual word and of the sentence, and the aspiration to create a literature of world-historical rank. While the second point will come into sharper focus later, it is worth outlining the factors that cemented the categorical difference between writing in a dialect and writing in High German—a difference that also had a lasting impact on the shape of German literature, as when Johann Peter Hebel wrote poetry in Alemannic around 1800 or when H. C. Artmann composed lyric in the Viennese dialect during the twentieth century. In fact, it was the codification of High German that transformed the use of dialect into a charged form of literary expression.

While a familiar *idée reçue* would have it that Luther's translation of the Bible, a project begun in the 1520s, was decisive for the emergence of modern German, the emergence of a standardized German and its replacement of Latin as the dominant language in scholarly and literary contexts was a more protracted and multifaceted process. Important sites of activity were the so-called language societies (*Sprachgesellschaften*), which between approximately 1600 and the mid-eighteenth century aimed to improve and promote the native tongue. In addition to composing verse poetry, members of language societies also penned treatises on the theory and practice of German grammar, rhetoric, and poetics. Patriotic panegyrics on the German language were a mainstay among major German scholars from the humanist Martin Opitz at the beginning of the seventeenth century to the polymathic genius Gottfried Wilhelm Leibniz at its end. One of the greatest figures in this lineage is the scholar Justus Georgius Schottelius, whose *Complete Work on the German Language* (*Ausführliche Arbeit von der deutschen HaubtSprache*, 1663) remained influential into the nineteenth century. Schottelius analyzed the origins of German words, proposed morphological paradigms, and prescribed syntactical rules with the goal of promoting High German ("die HochTeutsche Sprache"). His primary ambition was to create a superregional version of the German language for use in political and scholarly contexts. This effort formed part of a broader shift in humanistic reflections on language across Europe, in the course of which the idiosyncratic structures of vernacular languages became genuine objects of scholarly interest, thereby expanding the scope of grammatical study beyond Latin.

While Schottelius's treatise was immensely successful within the scholarly community, giving rise to a cottage industry of epigonal texts, fundamental issues remained unresolved. For one, his attempt to carve out a form of High German unmoored from the conventions of a single regional dialect and instead based on comparison and inference did not meet with universal approval. Equally importantly, whatever impact Schottelius had among fellow humanists, German writing remained for the duration of the seventeenth century a hodgepodge of orthographic, morphological, and syntactic practices. It took more than another hundred years for the German vernacular, begun with Luther, to achieve its characteristically modern level of standardization and uniformity.

One figure in particular spurred on the effort to overcome the Babel of German dialects: a professor from Leipzig named Johann Christoph Gottsched. His *Grundlegung einer deutschen Sprachkunst* (*Groundwork of the German Verbal Art*, 1748), which was the culmination of over two decades of work on the subject, had hygienic and patriotic dimensions. In line with the seventeenth-century writers before him, one of his chief ambitions was to elevate the standing of the German people among their European counterparts. This was not a political project organized under the umbrella of a German state. Instead, patriotism took shape in the eighteenth century, in Gottsched's writings and those of many others, as the effort to foster a sense of shared identity rooted in more local forms of community, each of which contributed to a regionally fragmented but culturally unifiable German people. Characteristic of Gottsched's specific brand of patriotism was his belief that the creation of a bona fide High German demanded the expulsion of supposedly extrinsic elements, from Latin vocabulary to French turns of phrase. This aspiration to linguistic purity, built around the distinction between native words and foreign ones, actually has had a long and distinguished career, from the comprehensive *German Dictionary*, begun by Jacob and Wilhelm Grimm in 1838, to the lexicography of today.

For the formation of High German, Gottsched's use of the language spoken and written by educated people from Saxony (more precisely, the Meißen region of Saxony) was of decisive importance. That is not to say that he adopted it wholesale. Instead, Gottsched spent great effort on identifying contaminating elements in Saxon, including errant verbal forms and infelicitous syntactic constructions. Gottsched's treatise was written for what he called his "contemporary critical times."[2] That is to say, his treatise does not just outline the correct rules and forms, but also compiles spurious constructions and common solecisms, rebuking the misconceptions of forerunners and contemporaries. Language reform thus fit within the epoch-making critical ("kritisch") project, the contours of which shall emerge into sharper relief below.

The triumph of Gottsched's model, meanwhile, is visible in the strong resemblance between his proposals and the High German used today. Its success was owed in no small part to broader educational reforms that included an interest in making it easier to learn to read and write German. In many ways Gottsched's mantle was assumed by the language reformer and lexicographer Johann Christoph Adelung, who authored treatises on grammar (1782), style (1785), and the history of the German language (1806), as well as a multivolume dictionary (1774–86). Like others before him, he made the case for the Upper Saxon dialect, arguing that it enjoyed the greatest prestige and had achieved the highest level of refinement in ethical life (*Sitte*) as well as the arts and sciences. Adelung's writings are particularly revealing for their interlacement of language and literature. In the essays he wrote on High German, orthography, and literature for his short-lived periodical, *Magazine for the German Language,* Adelung treats all three as part of the general enterprise of improving taste (*Geschmack*), one of the most hotly debated concepts at the time. In Adelung's hands, it signaled his belief that only sweeping social transformation could improve German language and literature. On this basis, he denied that individual authors could alter the linguistic landscape or even contribute singlehandedly to the cultivation of High German, since literary authors are but expressions of the overarching characteristics of their age and its taste, not a vanguard capable of actively shaping it. This dimension of Adelung's reflections on High German solicited vehement disagreement from the prominent satirist, novelist, and critic Christoph Wieland, who argued that real progress in establishing High German required the progressive contributions of great literary authors—in the contemporary parlance, geniuses.[3]

The difference between these two viewpoints—literature as downstream from the civilizing process or literature as shaping it—grew out of two distinct ways of thinking about reform. Adelung's approach was ultimately continuous with the rule-based approach that Gottsched had inherited from the early modern scholarship on poetics, rhetoric, and grammar. As we shall see shortly, Gottsched in fact attempted something quite similar in the literary domain. Wieland's rejection of this standpoint, by contrast, involved the assertion not only that progress can be had only step by step, through the interventions of signal authors, but also that its course cannot be anticipated or precipitated. While Adelung's approach to High German influenced the burgeoning pedagogical reforms, his views on literature had, already in the 1780s, ceded pride of place to paradigms closer to Wieland. In other words, what proved successful for the establishment of the German language—standardization—was ultimately jettisoned as the modern conception of German literature took shape.

In order to understand how notions of the literary work and authorship shifted in the latter half of the eighteenth century, it is best to consider the webwork of reform efforts to which the High German project contributed. In the first half of the eighteenth century, the same Gottsched who played a pioneering role in shaping the modern German language also made a case for a uniform and rule-governed literature akin to the ones found among peer European nations and, more importantly, in the mold of the ancient Greeks and Romans. Gottsched's perch at the university in Leipzig, where he taught subjects ranging from poetics to metaphysics, allowed him to disseminate his ideas in hubs of intellectual activity from Zurich to Berlin as well as among the younger generation gathered at the university. His service as leader of a local learned society (*Sprachgesellschaft*), meanwhile, granted him access to a hospitable local audience and to publication organs for reaching more distant ones. In the course of the 1730s and 1740s, he engaged in vigorous, sometimes vituperative debate with scholars across the German-speaking world, most famously with his Swiss colleagues Johann Jakob Bodmer and Johann Jakob Breitinger.

Despite the hostility that eventually emerged between the professor from Leipzig and his Swiss colleagues, all three shared a sense of moral purpose. All three also promoted their ideas in small-scale periodicals and large-scale treatises that served as much to outline fundamental tenets as to assess recent publications. As their penchant for rule-based literary composition fell into disfavor during the latter half of the eighteenth century, these two publication vehicles remained essential components in the German literary environment. Indeed, early eighteenth-century reformers set an important precedent for later developments by utilizing criticism as a means to give momentum to and modify the direction of literary praxis.

Gottsched's *Versuch einer Critischen Dichtkunst vor die Deutschen* (*Attempt at a Critical Poetics for the Germans*), first published in 1730 and then revised and expanded three times over the following decades, grew out of the desire to put literature on a philosophical footing and to model it after traditional poetic and rhetorical categories. Hewing rather closely to rhetorical categories like *aptum* and *decorum*, his treatise seeks to teach writers to craft works in accord with prescribed rules and to train readers to judge existing ones against them. As a way of lending his rule making the veneer of authority, Gottsched included as the introduction to his treatise a translation and commentary of Horace's *Ars Poetica*. Gottsched regarded Horace's poem as a congenial model for his own reform project owing to his conviction that the Roman poet lived at a time when the "number of bad poets" must have been as great as in contemporary Germany.[4] Indeed, he casts his own attempt to cull the poetic rules from vaunted ancient and modern authorities as an echo of Horace's own harkening back to Greek models. At the same time, Gottsched supported his rather dry poetic rules with the philosophical ideas of his contemporary Christian Wolff, particularly when he tried to outline a procedure for creating a literary object out of a true moral proposition. Some contemporaries and essentially all the later generations were repelled by this formulaic approach as well as by the underlying belief that literature is but a circuitous route for rendering moral precepts more directly available through reason. Gottsched's Swiss contemporary Breitinger, meanwhile, established an alternative approach with greater longevity: he rooted the production and evaluation of literary works in the sensuous effects of words and the freedom of the imagination. Breitinger argued that literature is not bound to imitate the world as it is, but instead may create virtual worlds that are uniquely capable of moving the passions and affording the reader or listener the pleasurable experience of beauty. In Breitinger's text one can observe one of the earliest attempts in the German corpus to separate off literature from other forms of discourse, thereby introducing the notion that it has standards as well as effects unlike any other form of human thought or expression. Perhaps the most important outgrowth of Breitinger's poetics is G. E. Lessing's *Laocoon* from 1766, a text that has, until today, influenced reflection on the differences among artistic media. With exceptional acuity and deep humanistic learning, Lessing spells out differences between literary and imagistic modes of representation and then uses these differences to elaborate standards of propriety for each.

As these examples make clear, the systematic shape of eighteenth-century literary criticism was closely connected to its practical purpose. Criticism was, first of all, a way to improve the contemporary conventions among writers. Good evidence of this can be found in the structure of Gottsched's treatise, with its division between an abstract examination of the poet's ideal character and of poetic imitation, on the one hand, and the elaboration of its constitutive genres, on the other. The latter half was particularly geared toward effecting immediate change. To take Gottsched's most cherished genre, the chapter on tragedy couples an abstract account of the genre's elementary features and governing precepts, with an assessment how the various European traditions, including German, have either succeeded in or failed to embody them. This second part, which was repeatedly revised and expanded between about 1730 and 1750, tracks recent developments and expresses abiding dissatisfaction with the halting progress in German letters. Gottsched sought to redress the deficit of proper German-language plays in a series of anthologies that he edited. In the six volumes entitled *The German Stage* (*Die deutsche Schaubühne*, 1741–50), Gottsched enlisted his wife as a translator and author, and he recruited a younger generation of writers to contribute new dramatic compositions. The anthologies, comprising primarily comedies and tragedies in the mold of the Greeks and Romans, were meant as a resource that writers and theatrical troupes could use to create a dramatic literature deserving of the name. Even though later generations abandoned Gottsched's stalwart classicism, many shared the sense that an overhaul of the German stage demanded more than a change in audience preferences and acting conventions; it was especially important to furnish the stage with a battery of worthy texts. While early theatrical reforms pushed a standard of generic purity that bore no lasting literary fruit, the years after 1750 saw attempts to stake out a middle ground between the traditional comedy-tragedy dyad, from the comedic personnel of bourgeois tragedy to the near-tragic pathos of sentimental comedy. Both of these genres had fairly short careers; both were modeled after recent trends in English and French. At the same time, a number of the greatest German plays from later decades, from Lessing's *Nathan the Wise: A Dramatic Poem* to Heinrich von Kleist's *The Battle of Herrmann: A Drama*, used generic subtitles that avoid the opposition between comedy and tragedy but instead inhabit a more neutral ground. Indeed, one might argue that the competition between classicizing and non- or anticlassicizing trends is one of the most powerful generative forces driving the emergence of German literature.

There is a second practical dimension to eighteenth-century literary criticism that deserves emphasizing. Its significance can be discerned in the use of the term "critical" to describe much of the writing about literature in the age. Beginning with Gottsched's *Critical Poetics* and Breitinger's similarly titled treatise from ten years later, the term referred to a strategy for producing commentary on poetic works with the goal of cultivating the ability to recognize their perfections and imperfections. While Gottsched maintained an interest in spurring on writers, the critical project broke with the early modern tradition in primarily directing its efforts at readers. Unlike the rhetorical and poetic handbooks that emerged from within the Latinate Republic of Letters (*Gelehrtenrepublik*), early eighteenth-century criticism offered praise and blame for the purpose of cultivating the standard of taste in an aborning public. Not coincidentally the German loanword *Publikum* first emerged as a hotly debated term in the 1760s, becoming the subject of diatribes, essays, and even treatises (by among others Bodmer, F. J. Just, Klopstock, J. G. Hamann, J. G. Herder). By speaking to an audience of readers, literary criticism began to differentiate itself as an independent sphere of observation. In fact, entire journals appeared on the market devoted exclusively to reviewing recent publications.

The most ambitious of these, the aptly titled *Allgemeine Deutsche Bibliothek* (*Universal German Library*), had its first run in 1765 and continued printing until 1803. Its professed goal was to provide a comprehensive discussion of the previous year's publications, not simply in order to announce what has been produced, but also to highlight excellences and shortcomings. During this period, the literary review developed conventions distinct from the sort of neutral and informative reviews of recent publications that filled the natural scientific journals of the same period. It is important to notice that, while historians can now identify the authors of many of the literary reviews, almost all of them were first published anonymously. Journals thus allowed for the interchange of observations about contemporary literature, positive as well as negative, while avoiding the controversies that might have come with clear authorial attribution. In the course of the eighteenth century, literary writers began to write knowing that critics were looking over their shoulders, and readers began to read knowing what critics thought. Within this marketplace of books and critical reflections, there was just as much to be learned from literary failures as from literary successes.

While the effort to improve German letters through publications and criticism was in most respects inward looking, it did not mean that the Germans cut themselves off from the outside world. On the contrary, the gates were opened in the mid- and late eighteenth century to an unprecedented flood of translations. The publisher Friedrich Nicolai speaks in his novel *The Life and Opinions of Sebaldus Nothanker* (vol. 1, 1773), a text chock-full with reflections on the literary scene of the time, of "translation factories" where books are being produced like linens or stockings, but with even less care than textiles get.[5] The novel goes on to describe a menagerie of industrious laborers populating the market with books from English, French, Italian, and Spanish: translators that devote their entire lives to translation, ones with scholarly pretensions, ones that translate for relaxation, ones that want to be recognized as original authors.

Strangely enough, at least from today's perspective, the thirst for new books from abroad was so unquenchable that many translations were made on the basis of a previously existing translation from a third language, most often, from a French translation of an English text. For example, the first German version of Jonathan Swift's *Gulliver's Travels* was made on the basis of a French rendering—not because the translator could not read English, but rather because he found the French version more elegant. That being said, many literary writers from the eighteenth century were also avid translators, including Luise Gottsched, Lessing, J.M.R. Lenz, Wieland, Schiller, and Goethe, to list just a few of the most distinguished names. At least for this venerable group of writers, translation was more than a means to supply readers with fresh material; in fact, none of their translation projects was driven by commercial or utilitarian motives. Far more important was the desire to edify readers and to furnish writers with valuable literary models. The translation boom, it bears emphasizing, was part and parcel of the critical project, as the enclosed lengthy introductions often make clear. Not only do they spill lots of ink pointing out the flaws and celebrating the virtues of translated books, but they also sometimes mention parts they have chosen to improve or excise altogether.

The translation boom speaks to one of the organizing distinctions of the literary ecosystem that emerged over the course of the eighteenth century. To wit, there was widespread interest in figuring out how much the development of a literature of rank should rely on culture-internal versus culture-external resources. Closely related to the opposition between classicizing and anticlassicizing trends in eighteenth-century literature, there was a tension between those who thought that it best to ennoble German literature by drawing on vaunted ancient or contemporary European models and those who advocated the use of local conventions. Whereas early Enlightenment figures like Gottsched held fast to the idea that imitating the ancients (and those who have best imitated them: the French) was decisive for establishing a German literature, the second half of the century became increasingly skeptical about wholesale cultural transfer. For example, Lessing famously challenged the belief that French theater provided a good model for German writers, instead championing the English tradition as closer kin and a potentially more fruitful object for imitation. And yet he also intensively studied the theories of tragedy advanced by Aristotle and Corneille, in addition to his contemporary Diderot. Lessing's foundational corpus of literary and critical writings amounts to the first instance of the literary cosmopolitanism that characterized many of the great writers from the second half of the eighteenth century. Counterintuitive though it may seem, his interest in the broader European context, both in his translations and in his original works, was deeply informed by his belief that German literature must speak to the idiosyncratic make-up of the German people. In the words of his peer Justus Möser, "In my opinion we must get more from ourselves and from our soil than we have hitherto done, and use the art of our neighbors, at the most, insofar as it serves our idiosyncratic products and their culture."[6]

There was a profound conceptual innovation underlying the tension between what one might call endogenous and exogenous methods for creating a literature. Whereas the rhetorical and poetic tradition of the early modern period had typically thought of literature in the singular, outlining uniform rules applicable in every time and place—Gottsched's *Critical Poetics* can be thought of as the swansong of this tradition—a new sensitivity to cultural difference became palpable over the latter half of the eighteenth century. Literature was rethought as something deeply rooted in the character of a nation or people, with its own conventions and standard of taste. The conceptual basis for the transformation is legible across a broad swath of European texts from the eighteenth century. Nationalism was emerging as a powerful political framework; the repercussions of this epoch-making transformation could also be felt in aesthetic and literary discussions. One representative example from the German-speaking world is Friedrich Justus Riedel's *Theory of the Beautiful Arts and Sciences* (*Theorie der schönen Künste und Wissenschaften,*

1767/1774), which argues that assessments of literature and art must be made in light of "the national character [*Nationalcharakter*] and, in general, the circumstances" that shape local ways of thinking and doing, because "every people has national sources [*Nationalquellen*] out of which judgments about the good and the beautiful flow."[7] The important point is that Riedel recognizes cultural difference as coloring almost all aspects of social life, including "religion, conventions, traditions, prejudices, . . . their pride, their character, their language, their form of government, their knowledge [*Kenntnisse*], and a hundred other points." In advancing these claims, the author picks up on a mode of argumentation that had caught on just a few years earlier.

Although the concept of a nation would later take on a stronger political valence, in the mid-eighteenth century it primarily figured in attempts to compare peoples and cultures. Concern with the concept of a national character had, to be sure, been spurred on by the Pan-European conflicts of the Seven Years' War (1756–63). Equally important was the popularity of the French philosopher Baron de Montesquieu's massive tome *De l'esprit des lois* (*The Spirit of the Laws*, 1748), which was quickly translated and widely read in the German-speaking lands. In the wake of Montesquieu, there was an explosion of interest in delineating the relative advantages and shortfalls of the European peoples, including in their legal and governmental systems. Figures like Riedel projected these arguments about national specificity onto the literary domain, arguing that a properly German literature must express the unique features of its culture.

The indecision over whether to look inside or outside German culture in order to improve its literature is nowhere clearer than in a project launched by the Bavarian government in the first decade of the nineteenth century to create a so-called Nationalbuch (National Book). Although the latter half of the eighteenth century had seen a proliferation of literary anthologies, the commissioner of education for the Ministry of the Interior, Friedrich Niethammer, developed the idea of a government-sponsored volume that could serve as the "foundation for the universal education of the nation."[8] Niethammer decided to recruit the cooperation of the prominent poet, translator, and scholar Johann Heinrich Voss as well as of the most venerated literary figure of the day, Goethe. The goal in Niethammer's mind was to create a book that could serve as the "foundation for the universal education of the nation [*Grundlage der allgemeinen Bildung der Nation*]."

The fascinating proposal that Niethammer sent to Voss and Goethe is rooted in his firm belief that a volume of "national classics" could provide a center of gravity for a nation that lacked political unity or a capital city. Niethammer's text is remarkable not only for its faith in the nation-building power of literature, but also for Niethammer's confidence that the Germans possessed a corpus of texts that could possibly be for the Germans what "Homer was for the Greeks." As throughout the latter half of the eighteenth century, nation here means the German speakers—by contrast with the English or French or Spanish. The goal of figures like Niethammer was to foster a shared identity, cutting across the long-standing divisions between estates, not to create the sort of political entity embracing all German speakers that became the subject of intense debate later in the mid-nineteenth century.

Though he eventually opted to forgo participating in the project, Goethe took it seriously enough to write a programmatic essay that he sent to Niethammer and to develop a schema of proposed contents. His essay is remarkable for many reasons, including its categorical rejection of a restrictive conception of the texts to be included in what he retitled a "Lyrical Folk Book" (*Lyrisches Volksbuch*). In addition to the exclusive focus on lyric poetry—most likely due to ease of memorization and the amenability to oral declamation—Goethe also transforms the book into a volume primarily meant for less educated social groups. Goethe rejects the exclusive focus on texts originally written in German, instead arguing that no nation can "make the claim to absolute originality" and that, over time, "foreign goods have become our property." With a cosmopolitanism that anticipates his later meditations on world literature, Goethe suggests that the German people will benefit most from the study of the finest poems from all literatures. Indeed, in his schema, Goethe even goes so far as to say that such a collection of literary works could assume an importance for the coalescence of the German people akin to the role historically played by the Bible.

By the first decade of the nineteenth century, in other words, there was little doubt that German literature had a history. The sense that there was a literature to be spoken of was no doubt bolstered by the radical expansion of the book market over the course of the eighteenth century. To get a sense of the dynamic nature of the historical moment, it is worth considering a few statistics. For the Easter book fair in Leipzig, the number of announced publications rose from 755 in 1740 to 2,569 in 1800. During the same period, the number of publishers rose from approximately 150 to 500. While about the same number of Latin and German books were published in 1700, by the end of the century the portion of Latin text had shrunk to well below 20 percent. Equally important, the genres of literary writing underwent significant shifts, especially during the latter half of the century: while the Gottscheds died in the 1760s with a paltry collection of six novels in their library, all but one belonging to Luise, three hundred new ones appeared in 1800 alone. Of these, an increasing number were original German compositions. Friedrich Blanckenburg's *Theory of the Novel* (*Versuch über den Roman,* 1774) heralded the rise of a new genre that could serve as a medium for exploring the "feelings and deeds" of the individual.[9] In the very same year that Blanckenburg championed the possibility that the novel could provide a sort of national glue, analogous to the role Homer's epics had played in ancient Greece, only now focused on human interiority rather than collective political events, Goethe published the first international best seller in the German language, *The Sorrows of Young Werther* (*Die Leiden des jungen Werther,* 1774/1787).

The rise of the prose novel, whose predominance is so characteristic of modern literature, was all but inevitable. Indeed, while epic and tragedy had long counted as the most profound literary genres, the Romantic Friedrich Schlegel put Goethe's *Wilhelm Meister's Apprenticeship* (*Wilhelm Meisters Lehrjahre,* 1795–96) on a par with the French Revolution as a signature of the age. For Schlegel the novel embodied his double project—described in the 116th fragment of his journal *Athenäum* as "progressive universal poesy"—of dissolving all boundaries between the traditional genres and also between human life and the literary work.

This explosion of the novel profited immensely from the growing pool of female readers. That said, most reading at the time was voiced and conducted in small groups of men and women; the sort of solitary and silent reading that we now take for granted was still *in statu nascendi.* While the leisure time required for reading was still more readily available to aristocratic women, there is good evidence that women from the so-called middle estates were becoming avid readers. Indeed, the number of publications specifically geared toward women—for example, in collections bearing titles like the *Frauenzimmer Bibliothek* or *Allgemeine Damenbibliothek*—is indicative of a decisive transformation in the make-up of the German reading public during the latter half of the eighteenth century.

These anthologies specifically geared toward women contributed to the emerging conviction that a shared literary tradition could help foster common knowledge, common values, and a common national self-image. Literature was progressively rethought as a culturally unifying force. By the closing decades of the eighteenth century, there was little doubt that German literature was worthy of being collected, curated, and studied. This belief relied on an important historical innovation: the sense that the past could be transformed into a collective heritage and thereby speak to the present. By the turn of the nineteenth century, in short, a new form of consciousness was being born, a literary memory that could be mobilized in educational and artistic projects. A powerful index of this is the sudden interest in the German-language texts from the Middle Ages that we now recognize as classics. One can see the

process taking shape in the 1730s and 1740s, as Bodmer, Breitinger, and Gottsched began collecting medieval works and championing their importance.
In 1758–59, the two Swiss scholars published the most extensive compilation
of medieval lyric (Minnesang), the so-called *Codex Manesse* or *Große Heidel-
berger Liederhandschrift*, to which they attached a glossary and commentary.
They also republished the eleventh-century verse epic known as the *Annolied*,
which focuses on religious and political events in the city of Cologne. The re-
verberations of their collecting and editing can be felt in the many publications
by one of Bodmer's students, Christoph Heinrich Myller, who in the course of
the 1780s published the *Nibelungenlied*, Wolfram von Eschenbach's *Parzifal*,
Gottfried von Strassburg's *Tristan*, and Hartman von Aue's *Iwein*.

Beyond the reissuing of texts, the eighteenth century also started to see
earlier German literature as a resource for artistic inspiration. Sometimes this
took the form of imaginative rewritings, as in the case of the verse fables of
Reynard the Fox (adapted from French into German in the twelfth century),
which Gottsched translated into modern German prose, before it was transformed into a dark verse epic by Goethe in the wake of the French Revolution. Similarly, about a decade after Bodmer and Breitinger republished the
medieval Minnesang, a collective of aspiring poets known as the Göttinger
Hainbund (Grove League of Göttingen), began to compose poems modeled
after the medieval songs. Contemporary German literature was thus inserting
itself within a national lineage that was, at the time and largely by virtue of
such deeds, coalescing into a recognizable heritage.

As part of this process, ambitious authors also recognized creative potential
in seminal moments in German cultural history that had hitherto not played
much of a literary role. Perhaps the most prominent exponent of this trend
was Goethe, whose canonical works such as *Faust*, as well as many less widely
known ones including ballads and plays, drew on the late medieval and early
modern periods. Among the most ambitious literary authors from the years
around 1800 that fit within this paradigm, two deserve special mention. Friedrich Schiller spent a good chunk of the 1790s working on his grand *Wallenstein*
trilogy, which recounts events from the Thirty Years' War with meticulous detail, providing a panoramic image of society, from lowly soldiers to the military
elite. Two of Heinrich von Kleist's greatest works, the drama *Kätchen von
Heilbronn* and the novella *Michael Kohlhaas*, harken back to events from the
Middle Ages and the age of the Reformation respectively. Dozens of similar
texts by less well-known authors were composed in the closing decades of
the eighteenth century. But one related phenomenon deserves special attention. During the very same years, there emerged a prominent interest
in oral genres from folk songs to folk tales. The collection and republication

of such forms was motivated by the belief that their lack of a straightforward authorial source, together with their informal patterns of circulation, make them a uniquely direct expression of the German nation and its idiosyncratic character.

At the same time, the surge of interest in oral forms testifies to the capacity of literature to integrate its (nonliterary) antecedents. The increased visibility of writing led to a revaluation, even fetishization, of orality. One need only think of the Ossian craze across Europe—within the German context, most famously memorialized in Goethe's *Werther* and in an essay by J. G. Herder—to see how infectious the idea of an archaic oral poetry proved. There can be little doubt that the imagination of an ancient bard—whether Gaelic as in the case of Ossian, or the more familiar figure of Homer—played a pivotal role in the conception of literature around 1800, particularly in British and German Romanticism. The success of this project is most visible in the collections of fairy tales by the Grimm brothers, compiled and reedited between 1812 and 1858, and still anthologized today.

The burgeoning interest in oral forms provided a powerful counterpoint to one of the most consequential developments of the late eighteenth century: the rise of the author as an aesthetic, juridical, and economic entity. Strange as it may seem today, for most of early modern and modern European history, authors did not have the final say over their works. Whereas during the early modern period the sovereign disposed over publication privileges, in the closing decades of the eighteenth century copyright laws slowly gave authors control over their work. Before that, authors sold their works to a publisher, who reaped whatever profits were to be had. In the absence of enforceable copyright laws, successful works were quickly pirated and reprinted, particularly outside of what is now northern Germany, where most of the major publishers were located. But as authors began self-publishing, creating subscription services, and challenging the rampant reprinting by publishers who had not paid for the privilege, a reorientation of the relationship between the author and the work began to take shape. The contentious process that led to the recognition of the author's property and personal rights transformed literature into a form of writing that was at once singular and nonreproducible and, at the same time, a commodity that could be sold, purchased, and owned.

The emergence of German copyright was accompanied by a sea change in the conception of authorship and the literary work. This is especially visible in the abandonment of the idea that the author is but a conduit or mediator of literary expression, a model traceable from the Homeric poems through the early modern rhetorical and poetic traditions. In the closing decades of the eighteenth century, the author was rethought as an independently creative instance, productive of unique and proprietary utterances. Simultaneously, the reconception of the literary work as a singular object with a distinct authorial source raised some heavy-duty issues. Philosophers ranging from Immanuel Kant to Johann Gottlieb Fichte and literary authors from Klopstock to the Romantics were troubled by the question whether a work of literature consists of its printed pages, or if it is a more ethereal substance connected to the author's individual spirit (the term of art was "Geist" or "geistig"). The literary work became at once a product among others, freely circulating in the marketplace, *and* one restricted by its original production in the mind and pen of the author. And once authors could no longer rely on lump-sum payments from publishers, they had to become more market savvy, drawing their salary directly from book sales. In the course of these developments, authors began to rely on success in the marketplace for livelihood and fame, rather than falling back on patronage relationships or other forms of social status.

This reconfiguration of the relationship between the author and work went hand in hand with what one might call the invention of the literary career. Indeed, in the course of the eighteenth century, it became increasingly important to read a text in light of where it fell within the author's biography. While this practice first began to gain traction in the middle of the eighteenth century, its crucial importance as a hermeneutic tool was unmistakable by its end. In his *Gespräch über die Poesie* (*Conversation on Poetry*, 1800), Friedrich Schlegel powerfully describes the aesthetic and conceptual differences between different phases of Goethe's career—a bold gesture, to be sure, considering that the great poet was still alive and had some of his most productive years still ahead of him. The recognition of an author's biography as a condition of reading and interpretation meant that works could now be appreciated because of how they embody the exuberance of an author's youth or the sagacity of old age. As the product of a human being whose career unfolds over time, literary works became increasingly appreciated for the traces they bore of the vicissitudes and errancies in the arc of a human life.

Goethe himself embraced this viewpoint, even going so far as to spend the final decades of his life on a massive autobiographical project and devoting great energy to preparing a complete edition of his own works. Despite the gift of an exceptionally long life, he was unable to complete the latter project before his death in 1832. Goethe bequeathed his estate to the Grand Duchess Sophie von Oranien-Nassau, who supported the publication of an edition of unprecedented scale: 143 volumes. Given the magnitude of Goethe's achievement, and the importance he had already assumed in German letters during his lifetime, it is perhaps no surprise that his estate also sponsored the first literary archive in the Germany, an idea first advanced by Wilhelm Dilthey in

1889. Dilthey's proposal is crucial for a number of reasons. For one, it is striking evidence of how the author figure became the primary point of orientation in literary and cultural-historical investigation. The archive was conceived around the belief that all of Goethe's hitherto unpublished jottings, schemas, and drafts were of genuine consequence. Dilthey also asserted that the archive could serve as a monument to the newly established German nation, whose political unity had been achieved but a few years earlier in 1871.

There is a temptation to interpret Dilthey as the inevitable culmination of the eighteenth-century endeavor to make literature into an instrument for fostering cultural unity, now cast as an instrument for securing and enriching political unity. But such an approach ignores the fact that, even at the moment of its birth, modern German literature was more than a national-political project. To give but the most prominent example, Goethe himself repeatedly denounced cumbersome conceptions of national literature. Not only did his cosmopolitan take on the National Book challenge the viability of a German literature rooted exclusively in a single linguistic tradition, but he also proclaimed that the age of national literature was over and a new phase of world literature (*Weltliteratur*) had begun.

Equally importantly, the enlistment of the literary tradition in the name of the nation-state was a short-lived and always-partial project. At the same time that Dilthey devised a literary archive that could be a pillar of the nascent German nation-state, there was an unforeseen explosion of creativity in Austro-Hungary, exponents of which count among the most eminent denizens of European modernism: Hugo von Hoffmansthal, Rainer Maria Rilke, Franz Kafka, Robert Musil, and others still. The idea of German literature as the sole property of a unified German state was a catastrophic and imperial but brief one. By 1945, it was over. This outcome underscores the tension that has always existed between the singular concept of German literature and the political multiplicity that has always characterized its people.

Further Reading

Blackall, Eric. *The Emergence of German as a Literary Language*, 1979.

Bosse, Heinrich. *Autorschaft ist Werkherrschaft: Über die Entstehung des Urheberrechts aus dem Geist der Goethezeit*, 1991.

Kiesel, Helmut, and Paul Münch, ed. *Gesellschaft und Literatur im 18. Jahrhundert: Voraussetzungen und Entstehung des literarischen Markts in Deutschland*, 1977.

Lande, Joel. *Persistence of Folly: On the Origins of German Dramatic Literature*, 2018.

Martus, Steffen. *Werkpolitik: Zur Geschichte kritischer Kommunikation vom 17. bis ins 20. Jahrhundert mit Studien zu Klopstock, Tieck, Goethe und Goerge,* 2007.

Schlaffer, Heinz. *Die kurze Geschichte der deutschen Literatur,* 2013.

Watanabe-O'Kelly, Helen, ed. *The Cambridge History of German Literature,* 2000.

Weimar, Klaus. *Geschichte der deutschen Literaturwissenschaft bis zum Ende des 19. Jahrhunderts,* 2003.

Wellbery, David, ed. *New History of German Literature,* 2004.

Russian

MICHAEL WACHTEL

The Russian literary tradition is a product of the modern age, and not simply in the sense of the standard opposition of antiquity versus modernity. It is a recent phenomenon even in comparison to other modern European literatures (e.g., English, French, German, Italian, Polish). The belatedness of Russian literature is the result of numerous historical factors, including the geographical breadth of Russia itself, the xenophobia bred by such vast distances, the limited extent of literacy, and more than two hundred years of the "Tatar yoke" (from the thirteenth to the fifteenth centuries). However, the single most significant obstacle to literary tradition was the Russian Orthodox Church, which until the eighteenth century stifled most forms of secular and even religious culture. In the West, religion was often a catalyst to cultural and artistic development, with monastery libraries serving as the model for the first universities. Within the Roman Catholic Church, religious thinkers like Thomas Aquinas and the Jesuits championed reason and thus philosophy in the broadest sense. In contrast, the Russian Orthodox Church emphasized memorization over inquiry, fearing the human intellect as a potential source of heresy and apostasy. The Orthodox Church sought to instruct the populace through images rather than words; hence the rich tradition of icon painting, which had no correlate in verbal art.

Histories of Russian literature invariably begin with the medieval period. However, this period can be understood as the beginning of the Russian literary tradition only if literature is defined in the narrowest sense, as any word that is committed to paper—or, more precisely, to parchment. Even within this limited definition, it would be difficult to argue for the medieval period as the beginning of Russian literature because the language used was not Russian, but rather what is now called "Old Church Slavonic" or—depending on one's linguistics and politics—even "Old Bulgarian." The creation of an alphabet can be dated to the ninth century. It was the work of Cyril (hence the word "Cyrillic") and Methodius, two monks who sought to translate holy texts from Byzantine Greek into a language that could be understood by the Slavs in Moravia. Whether Cyril and Methodius were of Greek or Slavic origin is disputed, but to call them Russian would be anachronistic, since the concept of Russia as a distinct location or even ethnicity did not exist at the time.

The word "Russian" did exist, though its meaning was vague: "Originally the terms *Rus'* and *Russian* referred specifically to the Norsemen, but from the eleventh century on, they came to denote Slavic-speaking Christian inhabitants of Eastern Europe without any regard to their ethnic origin, be it Slavic, Scandinavian, Finnic, Baltic, or Khazar."[1] At the end of the tenth century—the exact year is usually given as 988—inspired more by political considerations than religious epiphany, Prince Vladimir declared Orthodoxy to be the official religion of a loosely united land of Eastern Slavs, the center of which was Kiev. (This is sometimes known as "Kievan Rus," a term coined by nineteenth-century historians.)

The existence of a written language was essential for disseminating holy writ. Over the next few hundred years, numerous texts were produced in this "church" language, almost all of which were translations of the Gospels and the liturgy, the only texts familiar to most believers in the early centuries of Slavic Christianity. Precise numbers are revealing: only twenty of the fifteen hundred surviving parchment manuscripts from the eleventh to the fourteenth centuries are not concerned with religion.[2] Once again, there is a thorny issue of nomenclature in regard to the language used in these texts. As Alexander Schenker notes: "Depending on the local political situation the terms *Old Russian*, *Old Ukrainian*, and *Old Belarussian* have been applied to essentially the same body of texts."[3] Regardless of what we call this language, it must be emphasized that the range of texts it produced was extremely limited. While Eastern Orthodoxy in Byzantium (much like Christian culture in the West) was steeped in the traditions of antiquity, Kiev's approach to Orthodoxy was narrow and pragmatic. In the words of D. S. Mirsky: "The study of rhetoric, dialectics and poetry, of the Trivium and Quadrivium, of all the 'humaniora,' never penetrated into South Slavia, Georgia or Russia, and only those forms of literary art were adopted which were considered necessary for the working of the national Church."[4]

The few literate people in the Slavic lands were primarily engaged in copying religious texts. There was no tradition of exegesis, nor was it encouraged. To the extent it was deemed necessary, interpretation of the holy texts was borrowed from preexisting Byzantine sermons. In this regard, it is worth noting that well into the eighteenth century, literacy in Russia was acquired by painstakingly working through sacred texts and committing them to memory. As Victor Zhivov writes: "The basic means of learning language was reading 'po skladam' ('by syllables'). The procedure was strictly regimented and considered sacred. It began and ended with prayer and was seen as a kind of

introduction to Christian life. The special importance of correct and comprehensible reading was conditioned by the fact that the failure to follow the rules
of reading could, from the point of view of Eastern Slavic bookmen, lead to
heretical error."[5]

In the 1660s, patriarch Nikon convinced Tsar Alexis that the centuries-old
Church Slavic translations of the Bible should be reviewed, compared with the
Greek source texts, and corrected insofar as it was philologically warranted.
(A similar project had been undertaken in the West by Erasmus more than a
century earlier, but with less extreme consequences.)

From the perspective of the twenty-first century, the changes that resulted
from this process were relatively minor. They did not involve fundamental
questions of doctrine, but simply individual words, the spelling of names (admittedly, one of those names was "Jesus"), and in some cases specific church
rituals. And yet these reforms set in motion a schism that was never to be
resolved. The Old Believers rejected any change to the holy writ. For them,
this text was not a translation, but the direct word of God, and it was heresy
to alter even a syllable of it. They were no less horrified by the changes to
centuries-old ritual. Given that Byzantium had fallen (for its sins, as far as
the Old Believers were concerned), there was no reason to take Greek religious practice as a model for anything. Fleeing systematic persecution, the
Old Believers withdrew into their own communities, refusing to recognize
the authority of the patriarch and in some cases preferring self-immolation
to submission to what they saw as the kingdom of the Antichrist. This rapidly
escalating conflict led to the creation of a powerful text invariably regarded
as a masterpiece of Old Russian literature: the eventful and stylistically rich
autobiography of the Archpriest Avvakum, an uncompromising Old Believer.
Modeled in places on hagiography and written to inspire loathing of the reforms, Avvakum—who would ultimately be burned at the stake for his beliefs
and intransigent character—inveighs against the hypocrisy of the Orthodox
officials while extolling the virtue of the traditional Orthodox Church.

On the one hand, this historical episode demonstrates why Russians have
traditionally both respected and feared the written word. On the other hand,
it shows why a creative literary tradition was so slow to take root in Russia.
It is hardly surprising that in the centuries preceding the schism there was so
little imaginative literature.

The church encouraged only three genres in Old Russia, all of which were
undertaken by monks (usually anonymous), and all of which had Byzantine
models: homiletics (sermons), hagiography, and history (chronicles). Each
of these follows its own set of rules and thus can be understood as a distinct
tradition; the chronicles, moreover, were a secular tradition. Yet it would be

difficult to view any of them as the beginning of Russian literature, at least in the sense of *imaginative* literature. These texts were written for purely didactic or explanatory purposes. They were written in prose, not in verse, which is generally the starting point of literary traditions. And while the authors—like any authors—concerned themselves with rhetoric and style, their works lacked what Roman Jakobson would call a "poetic function." Most importantly, insofar as these genres played any role in the modern Russian literary tradition, it was marginal.

In the vast expanses away from the cities and from the ecclesiastical authorities, folklore developed freely, providing a creative outlet from time immemorial. Knowledge of this subject is limited, since folklore collecting did not occur systematically in Russia until the nineteenth century, after similar activity had begun in western Europe. Nonetheless, what has been recorded reflects a wealth of genres: heroic poems, wedding songs, funeral laments. As oral genres, these works cannot be understood as the origin of the literary tradition. However, folklore does enter into the literary canon in the Romantic period, when folk creativity, initially spurned by both the church and the secular poets, was suddenly valued as an outpouring of native wisdom.

"The Lay of Igor" (also known as "The Song of Igor's Campaign") presents an especially complicated case in any discussion of Russian literary tradition. This mysterious prose text of about three thousand words was written in a language usually called "Old Russian." The subject of the work is a disastrous Russian defeat that took place in 1185, and all signs point to the work being composed shortly after that event. The text clearly draws on some sort of secular epic tradition; it uses many tropes (metaphor, hyperbole) as well as poetic devices (alliteration, euphony), but it also includes references to East Slavic folklore. It is impossible to establish whether the author was acquainted with foreign models or simply with a Russian tradition that has disappeared without a trace. As Vladimir Nabokov writes: "Soviet historians are as helpless as earlier Russian scholars were to explain the striking, obvious, almost palpable difference in artistic texture that exists between The Song and such remnants of Kievan literature as have reached us across the ages. Had only those chronicles and sermons, and testaments, and humdrum lives of saints been preserved, the Kievan era would have occupied a very modest nook in the history of medieval European literature; but as things stand, one masterpiece not only lords it over Kievan letters but rivals the greatest European poems of its day."[6] Nabokov's assessment echoes a passage by Aleksandr Pushkin (1799–1837), widely, if inaccurately, considered the father of modern Russian literature: "Unfortunately, we do not have an ancient literature. Behind us lies a dark steppe and above it looms a single monument: 'The Song of Igor's Campaign.'"[7]

So what prevents us from giving pride of place to "The Song" and declaring it the beginning of the Russian literary tradition? The primary reason is that this work, though probably celebrated in its day and known to some extent even into the sixteenth century, fell into oblivion. Its rediscovery in an ancient manuscript collection in the 1790s created a sensation. From that point on it was translated into modern Russian by several major poets and exerted an influence on numerous others. The fact that the sole manuscript—itself an obviously flawed copy dating from the fifteenth or sixteenth century—was reduced to ashes during the Napoleonic invasion of Moscow, less than two decades after its rediscovery, has led to two centuries of claims and counterclaims about the authenticity of the work. However, even if its provenance as a work of the twelfth century is accepted, the history of its reception makes it difficult to view "The Song" as a point of origin. One may regard this situation as being akin to "Beowulf" in the English tradition, but "The Song" is a much shorter work, and, whereas "Beowulf" can be related to other works of Old English, "The Song" has no comparable context in Russian; it is unique.

To quote Pushkin once again: "Our literature arose suddenly in the eighteenth century just like the Russian gentry class, without ancestors and genealogy."[8] Though this judgment is too peremptory, it is essentially correct.

Modern Russia is usually considered the creation of Peter the Great, the energetic reformer who ruled as a ward from 1682—and independently from 1694—until his death in 1725. The changes he introduced, largely adaptations of Western models and institutions, redefined every aspect of Russian life, including religion, social life, warfare, and the arts. Peter's innovations were announced abruptly and apodictically, and they were executed immediately, if at times unenthusiastically. In certain important respects, however, he was following the policies of his late father, Tsar Alexis.

The case of theater is revealing. Alexis had begun his reign in 1645 with the traditional Russian distrust of the arts. While even his own father's wedding had permitted celebratory performances by balalaikas and *skoromokhi* (Russian mummers, a folk tradition that survived in spite of church disapproval), Alexis banned all these sinful entertainments at his own wedding, allowing only church hymns. However, twenty years later, after the death of his first wife, he remarried, this time to a woman who was not only literate, but even culturally sophisticated, having been raised in the house of the head of the foreign office. Under her influence, Alexis seems to have softened. To celebrate the birth of his son (the future Peter the Great), he even ordered a private theater to be built and lavished enormous resources on it. He himself commissioned the first play, based on the book of Esther. The resulting performance, which lasted ten hours, utterly enthralled the tsar. While that premiere was performed only for the royal family, Tsar Alexis later insisted that his nobles also attend.

So can we call this the beginning of Russian drama? For several reasons, we cannot. As Simon Karlinsky explains: "The theatrical experiment of Tsar Alexis, interesting as it was historically, remained little more than a private whim of the monarch. His subjects either did not know of the performances or regarded them with sullen hostility. The surviving plays, written for Alexis by Germans in German and then translated into Russian, are not a part of the Russian literary tradition."[9]

Curiously, this experience would repeat itself in the age of Peter the Great. During his travels abroad, Peter encountered flourishing theatrical traditions and, with his usual impulsiveness, decided that Russia should follow suit. While away at war, he ordered that a theater be constructed on Red Square, a move designed to horrify traditional sensibilities. Despite attempts at sabotage, the theater was built within a year, again at considerable expense and featuring intricate sets and stage machinery. Yet like the theater of his father, Peter's foray into drama failed to make a mark on Russian culture. Karlinsky writes: "The venture was the most unmitigated disaster in the history of Russian theater. . . . With all the encouragement and subsidies Peter lavished on it, his theater lacked three basic and mutually dependent ingredients essential for any theatrical undertaking: there were no Russian plays, no suitable literary language into which foreign plays could be translated, and hence no interested audience."[10] In short, the existence of an appropriate performance space did not ensure the existence of a theatrical tradition. Peter could control his subjects, force them to participate in various activities, but he could not will a literary tradition into existence. Peter's theater produced plays from the western European repertoire (including Gryphius and Molière), but once rendered into what Karlinsky aptly calls a "hybrid of archaic biblical style and equally archaic legalese," they became utterly incomprehensible to an audience that was in any case unfamiliar with the very concept of secular culture.

Similar "false starts" can be found in the sphere of poetry. Once again, the emergence of poetic activity can be traced to the reign of Alexis, Peter's father. Under this tsar, Russia occupied Belorussia, since the fourteenth century a part of the Catholic Polish-Lithuanian Commonwealth, though constantly threatened by its eastern neighbor. In 1656, on a visit to this newly conquered territory, Alexis was greeted by the verses of a local monk known to posterity as Semeon Polotsky (Simon of Polotsk). Polotsky had studied at the main Slavic Orthodox seminary in Kiev, which under Polish influence had introduced poetics as a part of the curriculum. In 1659 Polotsky and his students made a trip to Moscow, where they announced their presence with another poem to the tsar and his family. Polotsky clearly made a good impression. In 1663 he was permanently installed in Moscow, eventually becoming both court preacher and tutor to the tsar's son Fedor, whose brief reign as Fedor III—he died at age twenty-one—was marked by an enlightened interest in the broader world. Polotsky also inevitably became involved in politics, since his time in Moscow coincided with the schism. Sharing the cosmopolitan and imperial tastes of the modernizers, Polotsky came out strongly in opposition to the Old Believers.[11]

Among Polotsky's achievements as a writer was the introduction of syllabic poetry, which took root in Russia and continued unabated for about eighty years. Was Polotsky the beginning of the Russian literary tradition? Such a claim has been made, but it would have to include significant caveats. The authors of the most recent history of Russian literature note that some scholars "speak of Polotsky as the 'progenitor of Russian poetry'. We might turn the claim around by asking: How can a Ruthenian churchman immersed in the Latin and neo-Humanist literary arts, positioned between Catholicism and Orthodoxy, writing in Church Slavonic syllabics, and whose major works were never published, be said to relate to any native tradition, whether past or future?"[12]

Polotsky was an outsider in all respects. He was not a native speaker of Russian (which was by this point a language distinct from Ukrainian, Polish, and Belorussian [Ruthenian]), and his poetics clearly draw on the syllabic poetry that defined Polish verse. Having reaped the cultural benefits of European humanism, the Poles had already established a rich literary tradition. Jan Kochanowski (1530–84), in Czeslaw Milosz's words, "undoubtedly the most eminent Slavic poet until the beginning of the nineteenth century,"[13] had composed a Polish rhymed psalter that served as the model for the same project of Polotsky. Syllabic poetry, which is based on isosyllabic poetic lines, was common to all Slavic—and Indo-European—cultures. (There are no surviving specimens of "proto-Slavic," but the language and versification have been reconstructed by historical linguists.)[14] It may thus be safely assumed that there is nothing about syllabic verse contrary to the nature of the Russian language.[15] However, the fact that Polotsky's lines featured a mandatory feminine cadence—a stress on the penultimate syllable of each line—shows indisputably that this was a Polish import. The Polish language has fixed stress on the penultima; a feminine cadence is thus unavoidable, unless a line concludes with a monosyllabic word. In contrast, the Russian language does not have fixed stress. If Russian syllabics had arisen independently, there would have been no need for each poetic line to conclude with a pattern of a stressed syllable followed by an unstressed one. That this seemed "natural" to Polotsky is a clear indication that he did not appreciate the rhythmic possibilities of Russian.

A still greater problem that Polotsky encountered was the lack of a literary language. Though a vernacular Russian language now existed, it was not used in writing. By the seventeenth century the written language, created centuries earlier for religious and liturgical purposes, had become divorced from the language in daily use. In 1696, the German Pietist, diplomat, and linguist Heinrich Wilhelm Ludolf published (in Oxford) his *Grammatica Russica*, the fruit of an eighteen-month stay in Muscovy in 1693–94. As he explained: "loquendum est Russice & scribendum est Slavonice" (Russian should be used for speaking and Slavonic for writing). The full extent of such diglossia remains a contested subject, but Ludolf's basic claim is supported by extant poetic texts.[16] In short, some legal texts seem to reflect elements of the vernacular, but these elements had no place in poetry, which continued to be written in a church language that was hundreds of years old. What this meant for any literary pursuit was that, if authors wished to create imaginative literature, they were forced to do so in an archaic language that was familiar solely from church services and thus unable to express most actions, ideas, or emotions characteristic of everyday life.

As the example of Peter the Great's theater indicates, literary tradition cannot be created ex nihilo. It requires time to educate a generation of writers, to develop a literary language, and to cultivate an audience. But within fifteen years after Peter's death, this had happened. That this process was achieved so quickly is largely due to a triumvirate of talented poets who took advantage of the new cultural openness: Antiokh Kantemir (1709–44), Vasily Trediakovsky (1703–69), and Mikhailo Lomonosov (1711–65). In terms of personality and education, these towering figures of Russian culture differed profoundly from each other, but they had one essential thing in common: they all spent a considerable amount of time in the West. Their experiences brought them into contact with a culture that they wished to emulate. Their poems, largely modeled on Western works that themselves were already thirty to seventy years old, begin what can truly be called the modern Russian literary tradition.

Kantemir was himself not Russian. His father was a Moldavian prince who fled to Russia. The family spoke Italian and modern Greek at home. Thanks in part to his excellent education, he was appointed a diplomat to London in 1732—when he was a mere twenty-four years of age—and to Paris six years later. He became friendly with Voltaire and Montesquieu, translated important French philosophical works into Russian, and, more importantly, composed a series of original Russian satires using any number of Western models (Horace and Juvenal as well as Boileau and Italian and Polish poets). Throughout his satires, Kantemir used a language that reflected contemporary spoken Russian. He furnished these poetic texts with copious footnotes, in which he explained his numerous references to Greek mythology and even some common figures of speech. These notes make clear just how little a Russian writer of his time could assume from his readership; the most obvious conventions and references were dutifully explained. Despite concerted efforts, Kantemir was unable to publish his works in Russia. During his lifetime, they were known in manuscript to a very small circle of readers. Their first publication was posthumous, in French translation and without the footnotes, which were presumably unnecessary for readers familiar with Western poetry.

Trediakovsky's route to western Europe was different. Born in Astrakhan, in southern Russia near the Caspian Sea, and educated there by Capuchin monks at a Jesuit college, he learned Latin and became familiar with Western humanistic culture at a young age. He later studied at the Slavo-Greco-Latin Academy in Moscow (an institution founded in the late seventeenth century under the influence of Kievan monks, thanks to the relative freedom of Peter's reign) and then spent four years abroad, attending lectures in The Hague and in Paris. After returning to Russia, he first made his name as the translator of Paul Tallement's 1663 novel *Voyage de l'isle d'amour* (*Voyage to the Island of Love*). Though the church reprimanded Trediakovsky for his translation's baleful influence on Russian youth, the court was enthralled. Trediakovsky was appointed a member of the Academy of Sciences, an institution founded by Peter the Great that was at this point peopled almost exclusively by Germans. He shared the fruits of his considerable erudition in the form of numerous translations from the French (in prose and verse) as well as in original poetry and treatises on poetry. A passage from Trediakovsky's introduction to his 1730 Tallement translation gives a clear sense of how quickly both the literary language and the literary sensibility were changing. Trediakovsky asks his readers forgive him for translating not into "Slavonic" ("slavenskim iazykom") but rather into Russian ("russkim slovom"). He gives three reasons for his decision to do so. "First, the Slavonic language is a church language, whereas this book is secular. Second: the Slavonic language at the present time is very obscure, and many who read it do not understand it; but this book is about *sweet love*, for which reason it should be comprehensible to everyone. Finally, which may seem to you the most simple reason, but which is for me the most important: the Slavonic language today sounds harsh to my ears, although earlier I not only wrote in it, but even spoke it with everyone."[17] Tallement's novel contains poems interspersed with prose, and Trediakovsky's translations were among the first love poems to be published in Russia.[18] This was more than five hundred years after the genre first flourished in Western literatures.

Mikhailo Lomonosov, the son of a wealthy peasant fisherman, had a more modest education than Kantemir and Trediakovsky. Raised in the far north of Russia, where he learned literacy from a local parish priest, he eventually made his way to Moscow and St. Petersburg, studying both human and natural sciences. Coming from peasant stock, Lomonosov faced considerable administrative obstacles in the hierarchical world of Petrine Russia. Only with great difficulty was he able to enroll in institutions of learning, but he was resourceful and made the most of his opportunities. In 1736, he and two other students were dispatched to Germany to study mining. Lomonosov found time to educate himself in the natural sciences broadly, as well as in philosophy and literature. He also began to write poetry. In 1739 he composed his "Ode on the Taking of Khotin," in which he celebrated a recent Russian victory over the Turks. He transparently based this work on a 1718 ode that Johann Christian Günther had devoted to a German victory over the Turks. Lomonosov's poem, sent from Germany to the Academy of Sciences in St. Petersburg, was a landmark in eighteenth-century Russian literature and, as we shall see, a turning point in the history of Russian poetry. In an accompanying essay on Russian versification, he polemicized with Trediakovsky, who had sought to reform syllabic versification by making its rhythms somewhat stricter. Lomonosov did not feel that there was anything worth reforming; there was no point in tinkering with the old system; one needed to reject it entirely and start anew. "Our poetry is only beginning," he insisted.[19] Returning to Russia soon thereafter, Lomonosov became a member of the Academy of Sciences, where he was entrusted by his German colleagues with the teaching of Russian poetry. Quarrelsome by nature, he entered into a series of increasingly nasty disputes with Trediakovsky, to the detriment of both. Despite periods of great success, both Trediakovsky and Lomonosov died in penury.

As pioneers, Kantemir, Trediakovsky, and Lomonosov benefited from a confluence of factors that had radically changed Russian culture. The first was a conscious redirection from above, a monarch who weakened the church's pervasive influence and opened the society up to Western ideas. This turn to the West brought with it sweeping changes, including an acceptance of secular culture, which itself introduced the possibility of imaginative literature in a range of genres. The 1730s and 1740s witnessed widespread poetic activity as well as the appearance of poet-theoreticians who wrote prose works to explain the "rules" of poetic composition and establish a hierarchy of genres. Among the many reforms of poetic language (lexicon, syntax, spelling), the entire system of versification changed.

The Petrine reforms not only enabled literary production; they also brought about significant changes in the dissemination of literature. Printing presses were no longer the monopoly of the church. Books, initially in the form of translations, began to appear in unprecedented quantities. Peter personally involved himself in all aspects of the book trade, from the question of what to translate, to the quality of the translations, to the means of production.[20] In his lifetime, admittedly, few Russian books were literary in nature. They were primarily devoted to practical subjects like history, law, engineering, and especially what was known as "military science." Still, Western literary texts slowly began to appear, especially works with strong moral or didactic qualities (e.g., Aesop's Fables, a perennial favorite). The Academy of Sciences, a Petrine project that came into being only in the year of the monarch's death (1725), was able to publish its own books, which were not subject to church censorship. These books were printed in a new "civil" alphabet, which distinguished them from the church script, now exclusively the realm of the ecclesiastical. Trediakovsky's notorious Tallement translation, for example, was subsidized by Russia's ambassador to France and published by the Academy of Sciences.[21]

It is likewise revealing that, when Trediakovsky, Lomonosov, and Alexander Sumarokov (a younger contemporary, who was to become the first major Russian playwright) published three different poetic translations of one and the same psalm—rendered in different meters and strophic forms—it was published not by the synod typography, but by the Academy of Sciences. This was presumably viewed as an aesthetic experiment rather than a religious project. Psalm translation was to become a major genre of eighteenth-century poetry, but it was neither sponsored nor published by the church.

With Lomonosov and Trediakovsky, the profession of Russian writer came into being. Until this point, writing had been merely an avocation, something done in addition to one's primary duties and outside of one's primary identity. Given the limited spread of literacy, however, eighteenth-century Russian writers could hardly expect to earn a living through the sale of their works. The social structure allowed them only two potential sources of income: the church, which continued to look skeptically at most forms of creative endeavor, and the court, which was becoming increasingly Europeanized and thus supportive of the arts. A patronage system arose, which encouraged poets to compose panegyric poetry—traditionally called "solemn odes"—on signal events, whether military or domestic (coronations, weddings, birthdays, etc.).

This was hardly unprecedented in literary history: it goes back at least as far as Pindar. Trediakovsky had pioneered the solemn ode in Russia by using Boileau's "Ode on the Taking of Namur" (1693) as the model for his own "Ode on the Taking of Danzig" (1734). Read side by side, Trediakovsky's poem seems at times a direct translation, with Russian toponyms and proper names substituted for the French originals. He leaned heavily on Boileau also in terms of form. The French poem was written in stanzas of ten lines with a distinctive rhyme scheme (a quatrain of alternating rhyme, followed by a couplet, followed by a quatrain of ring rhyme), with each line composed of seven syllables.

French poetry is always syllabic, just as Russian poetry—though influenced by Polish practice rather than French—had been syllabic for almost a century. Trediakovsky retained Boileau's distinctively rhymed ten-line stanzas but used nine-syllable rather than seven-syllable lines.

Lomonosov's Khotin ode in many respects followed Trediakovsky's example and was no less derivative than Trediakovsky's Danzig ode. It was written in ten-line stanzas with the same rhyme scheme that Boileau and Trediakovsky had employed. In this case, Lomonosov had modeled the form, the overall structure, and much of the specific imagery on Günther's poem. He likewise borrowed Günther's versification, but insofar as Russian poetry was concerned, this represented his most radical innovation. Since Lomonosov was living in Germany rather than France, he had grown accustomed to syllabo-tonic verse, which is based not on the number of syllables per line, but on metrical feet, the regular alternation of stressed and unstressed syllables. By writing his poem in iambs, Lomonosov in one stroke did away with more than seventy years of poetic practice. Equally innovative was Lomonosov's importation of masculine rhyme, used in consistent combination with feminine rhyme. The fact that one poem could undo such a lengthy tradition suggests that this tradition was not terribly firm to begin with. And indeed, the alacrity with which syllabic verse was forgotten is astonishing. In the space of a few years, syllabic poetry disappeared from the repertoire of Russian poets. After a few brief attempts to modify syllabic verse to bring it closer to syllabo-tonics, even Trediakovsky recognized that Lomonosov's reform had won the day. Like everyone else, he began to write syllabo-tonic poetry, even returning to his previously published syllabic poems and revising them in accordance with the new system.

Scholars still debate why Lomonosov's reform of versification was so successful, but whatever the reason, it is difficult to overstate its significance in the history of Russian literature. Syllabo-tonic poetry has dominated Russian poetry ever since Lomonosov introduced it. And while additional prosodic forms have coexisted with it, such as accentual (tonic) verse since the early twentieth century and free verse in the post-Soviet period, syllabo-tonic verse has never been displaced. Equally important for the present discussion is that fact that, since the advent of syllabo-tonics, not a single effort was made to revive syllabic poetry. That chapter of Russian literary history came to an abrupt and complete end. Vladislav Khodasevich was speaking for many poets when he wrote (in emigration in 1938): "The years have chewed from memory / Who fell at Khotin and why / But the first sound of the Khotin ode / Was our first cry of life."[22] It is likewise revealing that Pushkin and his contemporaries were familiar with Lomonosov's poetry—even if it was not congenial to their own work—yet they were barely acquainted with the syllabic poetry of Kantemir and Trediakovsky. In 1816, Pushkin's elder contemporary Konstantin Batiushkov wrote a prose piece called "An Evening with Kantemir," in which he lauded Kantemir and even cited a passage from his verse. But Batiushkov's primary interest in Kantemir was as an urbane cultural ambassador to Paris, who admitted to Montesquieu that "the Russian language is in its infancy."[23]

Both Lomonosov and Trediakovsky were scholars as well as poets, which is to say that, in addition to their verse, they wrote treatises about the aims and methods of poetry. Both were significantly influenced by European neoclassicism, which presumed a set of rules that, if followed faithfully, would produce good poetry. The precise rules for Russian poetry had yet to be established, but both Trediakovsky and Lomonosov had no doubt that this was a task they must resolve. Once again, Lomonosov's views proved to be the more influential. Borrowing as usual from earlier writers (in this case Quintilian), Lomonosov formulated a theory of poetic language based on three styles. The high style was drawn from Old Church Slavonic words no longer in common usage, but nonetheless understandable: completely obscure words in Old Church Slavonic were rejected altogether. This lexicon, with its solemn liturgical associations, served as the ideal vehicle for elevated genres like the ode and the tragedy. The middle style relied on words common to Old Church Slavonic and Russian. Because these words were in everyday use, but not devoid of elevated associations, they were deemed appropriate for "delicate" genres such as the verse epistle, idylls, and love poetry. One might recall in this context the above-cited comments of Trediakovsky on why he translated Tallement's novel about love into "Russian" rather than "Slavonic." A low style, which drew maximally on words in common usage that did not have Church Slavonic elements, was reserved for genres such as epigrams, fables, and (prose) comedies.

It is interesting that there is no place in Lomonosov's scheme for loan words from western European languages. For all his formal dependence on Western models, Lomonosov viewed the Russian lexicon as sacrosanct. Indeed, he argued that Russian was in this respect the true heir to Greek and thus superior to the Latinate languages of western Europe. The influence of "Gallicisms" would become a factor in the Russian literary language only after Lomonosov's death; it is especially pronounced in the literature of the late eighteenth and early nineteenth centuries.

According to Lomonosov's influential theories, the more elevated the genre, the less familiar it should sound. In addition to the Slavonic lexicon, Lomonosov's odes displayed complicated syntax, a "thick" and barely pronounceable—and thus distinctive—sound texture, and elaborate tropes (e.g., zeugmas, striking similes and metaphors, unexpected personifications). These factors combined to create a poetic language that sought to move readers—or listeners—emotionally rather than convince them through logic and syllogism.[24]

In terms of their poetic practice, Lomonosov and Trediakovsky concentrated their efforts on the "high" genres. These were prestigious and in demand, either directly commissioned or likely to be rewarded by a patron. They showed less interest in the "lower" genres, which were therefore more hypothetical then real. At times the sole examples of certain genres are found in the theoretical texts, leading one to surmise that they were composed less as self-standing works of literature than as models for future writers to emulate.

Modern Russian literature is often considered the creation of Alexander Pushkin (1799–1837). There is some justification for this claim, since Pushkin set the standard that subsequent poets would measure themselves against. However, Pushkin's work is by no means a point of origin; it is thoroughly embedded in the literary culture of the eighteenth century. Though he would redefine the hierarchy of genres and the lexical register of Russian poetry, his favored meters are iambic, and his high regard for genre as such makes him an obvious heir to his eighteenth-century predecessors. Gavrila Derzhavin (1743–1816) deserves special mention in this context, as many elements of his poetry anticipate Pushkin. It is telling that in *Eugene Onegin* (chapter 8, stanza 2), Pushkin proudly recalls a scene from his schooldays, when he recited his poetry before an elderly but approving Derzhavin. Pushkin generally eschewed the high style, preferring a middle style more in keeping with the elegy, which comes to replace the ode as the favored genre of the early nineteenth century. Still, Pushkin does not hesitate to take advantage of that high style when the genre or theme demands it. And while the lexicon and verbal texture of his verse cannot be mistaken for Lomonosov's, only rarely does his versification stray beyond the limits of what Lomonosov defined. Pushkin created a poetry of unprecedented imaginative richness by reconciling the legacy of the French Enlightenment with European Romanticism (including the Romantic rediscovery of Shakespeare). Yet his work would be unthinkable without the experience of Russia's eighteenth-century poets, whom he drew on selectively, but consciously.

It bears emphasizing that Russian prose, though synonymous with Russian literature for many Anglophone readers, is a late development, as it is in most national literary traditions. Until the middle of the nineteenth century, prose occupies a place at the bottom of the hierarchy of genres. Pushkin published his first short stories in 1830, more than fifteen years after publishing his first poem, and his prose works—though no less inventive than his verse—show him experimenting with various generic possibilities, seeking an appropriate place for fiction in his creative world. His prose, like his poetry, draws on Western sources but has an obvious stylistic affinity with the stories that Nikolai Karamzin had pioneered in the late eighteenth century, when he was transplanting Western prose genres to Russia.

It seems appropriate to summarize our discussion before reaching some conclusions about the Russian literary tradition and its place among modern European traditions. Historians routinely begin their accounts of Russian literature as early as the eleventh century, but it is only in the eighteenth century that we find a combination of cultural and social factors propitious to the development of a literary tradition. While individual works that could be understood as literary (depending, of course, on one's definition) predate this flowering of literary culture, they cannot be seen as a meaningful point of departure for future writers. For example, Avvakum's autobiography displays a colorful Russian style and a distinctive worldview, but, as Čiževskij notes: "as a writer he was unable to create a school, even among his followers."[25] From the point of view of tradition, his work is like the proverbial tree in the forest that falls unheard. Avvakum himself drew on hagiographical traditions, as would Dostoevsky and Tolstoy. However, to insist that the medieval vitae are therefore the starting point of the Russian literary tradition would be a hollow argument. For one thing, modern Russian literature was established independently of such writings. Eighteenth-century poets, not to mention Pushkin's generation in the early decades of the nineteenth century, evinced no interest in hagiography. For another, Tolstoy and Dostoevsky—regardless of their own religious beliefs and personal didactic aims—completely reconceptualized this genre, using it as one of many elements in a heterogeneous secular literary culture. The "Song of Igor's Campaign," its artistic qualities notwithstanding, is likewise an unsatisfying point of origin, as its disappearance for centuries meant that it could influence writers only at a point when Russian literary culture had already been firmly established.

Finally, one could point to the almost hundred-year history of Russian syllabic verse, which was indeed a continuous tradition. Yet the fact that the advent of syllabo-tonic poetry obliterated this tradition suggests that it was a false start rather than a prehistory. However talented these poets may have been, they were handicapped in their aspirations by the absence of a literary language and by the lack of anything beyond handwritten copies to disseminate their work. These factors severely limited the poets' contemporary impact and hampered their subsequent reception.

One may fairly wonder why scholars have so assiduously studied Old Russian literature while largely ignoring the more voluminous production of the seventeenth century. Especially surprising is the energy that Soviet scholars invested in the study of Old Russian literature, given that its pronounced religious character ran contrary to the country's strict atheism. Vladimir Kuskov, whose 1977 *History of Old Russian Literature* was deemed sufficiently reliable to be translated into English (in the Soviet Union), tried to explain away this stumbling block: "Old Russian books were stored and copied primarily by monks; naturally they were less interested in preserving or duplicating secular texts. This no doubt helps to explain the fact that the overwhelming majority of surviving Old Russian works are religious in character."[26] This argument is specious; Kuskov's suggestion that there was a significant body of secular literature ignored by the monks overlooks the fact that, beyond the church, there was almost no literacy in Russia. Hence one struggles to imagine who would have been composing this supposedly suppressed secular literature.

The primary reason that the Soviets focused on Old Russian literature and not on seventeenth-century Russian literature seems to be one of status. Antiquity confers authority. By placing the origins of Russian literature in the eleventh or twelfth centuries, Russians could claim a privileged place for themselves among modern European literatures. After all, even the Germans and French could point only to the twelfth and thirteenth centuries as the beginning of their respective literary traditions. Of course, with the possible exception of "The Song of Igor's Campaign," Russian literature had nothing of the quality of the French and German medieval Romances and lyric poetry. And in terms of quantity the situation was even less flattering: the brevity of "The Song" cannot be compared to the large number of extant Western medieval masterpieces.

With each ensuing century—at least until the nineteenth—the comparison of Russian and Western literary production became increasingly unflattering. While the Renaissance unfolded in western Europe, Russia was overrun by the Tatars, who did nothing to further Russia's intellectual development. In Pushkin's words, "The Tatars did not resemble the Moors [in Spain]. Having conquered Russia, they did not give it algebra or Aristotle."[27] To claim the seventeenth century as the origin of Russian poetry would be still more embarrassing, as its verse was indisputably borrowed from neighboring Poland and Belorussia. Russian national pride could grudgingly accept a western European origin for its literary tradition, but it was loath to admit a cultural dependence on its Slavic neighbors.

Such quarrels belong to the sphere of cultural politics and national psychology rather than literature and aesthetics. If we turn dispassionately to the material itself, we can see that the Russian example beautifully illustrates how quickly a literary tradition can compensate for its belatedness. In a period of less than one hundred years, Russia managed to assimilate five centuries of Western literary development. To a great extent, this transformation was achieved by translation—of texts, of genres, of styles. And translation remained central to Russian literature. It is a remarkable fact of Russian poetic culture that the vast majority of major poets—from Pushkin to Pasternak—were also serious translators.

Once models were available, Russians quickly learned to develop them. When Karamzin traveled to Germany in 1789, he astonished his hosts by declaiming Russian poetry. After one such recitation, the writer Karl Philipp Moritz remarked: "Perhaps the time will come when we will study Russian. But for this to happen you will need to compose something magnificent."[28] This sentiment elicited a sigh from Karamzin. However, a mere ten years later Pushkin was born, and in his brief lifetime he created numerous "magnificent" works—as inventive as anything being written in western Europe. And even if Europeans were slow to recognize Pushkin's brilliance, by the end of the century Russian novelists were taking Europe by storm. Dostoevsky defined Pushkin's genius as a "responsiveness to everything," and this could easily be extended to the whole of modern Russian literature.

The international success of the Russian literary tradition demonstrates that cultural accomplishment is not a matter of being the first, but of creatively adapting and remaking what has already been accomplished. Osip Mandel'shtam would call this his "blessed inheritance," the poet's right to ignore his immediate "neighbors" and enter into a dialogue with poets of different eras and nations.[29] Through their reception of western European predecessors and contemporaries, Russian authors created a literary tradition of rare distinction and unusual distinctiveness.

Further Reading

Dixon, Simon. *The Modernization of Russia 1676–1825*, 1999.
Franklin, Simon. *The Russian Graphosphere, 1450–1850*, 2019.
Gudzy, N. K. *History of Early Russian Literature*, translated by Susan Wilbur Jones, 1949.
Levitt, Marcus C. *Early Modern Russian Letters: Texts and Contexts*, 2009.
Likhachev, Dmitry, ed. *A History of Russian Literature: 11th–17th Centuries*, 1989.
Miller-Gulland, Robin. *The Russians*, 2009.
Mirsky, Prince D. S. *A History of Russian Literature from the Earliest Times to the Death of Dostoyevsky (1881)*. 1927.
Reyfman, Irina. *Vasilii Trediakovsky: The Fool of the "New" Russian Literature*, 1990.

Silbajoris, Rimvydas. *Russian Versification: The Theories of Trediakovskij, Lomonosov, and Kantemir*, 1968.

Vinogradov, V. V. *The History of the Russian Literary Language from the Seventeenth Century to the Nineteenth*, a condensed adaptation into English with an introduction by Lawrence L. Thomas, 1969.

PART IV

Modern Geographies

Each of the literatures discussed in this volume thus far arose in an age before the birth of the modern nation-state. A surprisingly small number of the chapters in this book actually deal with a language and literature that is today also associated with a culture and polity, which has made it largely unnecessary to point out that thinking in terms of "national literatures" is a relic of a relatively small window in political and cultural history. Nonetheless, it is worth emphasizing the historically anomalous nature of the claim that literary traditions, even ones from the distant past, find their proper place in the nation-building projects that dominated the nineteenth-century political landscape.

The literatures discussed in part 4 have been shaped by the emergence of the modern nation-state, albeit in often uncomfortable and dissonant ways. The examination of their genesis and their developmental rhythm reveals that these literary traditions arose under conditions of colonial expansion and domination, and gained currency outside the well-weathered cultural categories that so many of the foregoing chapters fall under. No chapter among the following four exemplifies this terminological challenge so clearly as "world literature," which first appeared as a category in the years around 1800 and, ever since, has promised an alternative to the confines of the national-literature model. As Jane O. Newman points out in the final chapter in this book, "world literature" has long been a contested concept, at least since Erich Auerbach's 1952 essay "The Philology of World Literature," and has picked up steam over recent decades. Auerbach's foundational essay announces the need for a method that can highlight the diversity of singular literary traditions that is the truly universal human heritage. The idea of world literature has also played a decisive role in attempts—often economically motivated—to amass a reservoir of texts with transnational appeal. Indeed, publishers have labored to create a marketplace for books ostensibly belonging to the nebulous field of world literature, and many authors of international acclaim have taken to crafting books for that very same niche. World literature has also become central to more conceptually ambitious efforts to carve out a form of literary understanding that reveals our shared humanity. As with so many concepts, the extension of world literature cannot be decided once and for all; its astonishing success in the twentieth century is, rather, a testament to the economic and scholarly attempts to find lines of flight that cut across linguistic and cultural boundaries and that can reconfigure the landscape of readers and writers.

Although the other chapters in this section are similarly concerned with umbrella concepts that resist straightforward definition, they collectively show how the colonial enterprise that began around the turn of the sixteenth century altered the relationship between literary expression, culture, and territory. In other words, these literatures arose out of the confrontation between societies—confrontations that were characterized by violent domination and shot through with racial prejudice. And yet they also gave rise to new forms of observation, struggles for authorial voice, ways of reimagining the past, sub-communities of literary expression and audience. Latin American literature in the Spanish language was, for example, initially shaped by a colonial elite that sought not just to speak to readers on the Iberian Peninsula about their firsthand experiences as explorers and conquerors, but also to report about novelties—from pineapples and hammocks to native religious practices, as Rolena Adorno points out. Early Spanish writers were deeply concerned with establishing their authority as protagonists in the act of colonial expansion and with claiming their moral superiority over the natives, which Europeans ultimately took as license to subjugate natives of the New World. In almost no time at all, early Latin American literature became a creole enterprise as the native and colonial Spanish populations intermixed. Various retellings of stories about Spanish "explorers" lent an exaggerated, almost mythic aura to what were once historical accounts. Only in the nineteenth century, as the wars of independence detached South American nations from the Spanish Empire, were these early texts codified as an independent Latin American literature, even though they were written by European colonialists who addressed a remote audience in Spain.

The relationship between author and audience that shapes the Latin American context has striking resonances in colonial Africa. Focusing particularly on a Swahili text that was cherished by natives and canonized by British authorities, Simon Gikandi draws out a fundamental tension between the colonial desire to establish an authoritative text, representative of a local culture, and the irregular patterns of circulation traced by the eighteenth-century poem *Al-Inkishafi*. Moving between Arabic and Latin scripts, wrested from the hybrid linguistic and religious culture along the East African coast, and implanted in a comparatively homogeneous colonial setting, *Al-Inkishafi* represents the colonial desire to uncover precolonial texts that could be celebrated as classical Swahili literature. As with Latin American literature, the consolidation of a colonial library depended heavily on the activities of a cultural elite—in this case, the exchanges between a rarified group of Swahili speakers and European orientalists. In addition, Christian missionaries sought to expand their horizon of religious influence onto the African continent and thereby contributed to the violent and asymmetrical relationship between colonialist and colonized. Much as the Spaniards viewed natives with an indiscriminate gaze, the colonial authorities had little awareness of the regional and dialectic differences among various Omani groups.

While nineteenth-century attempts to canonize Swahili and Latin American literatures were shaped by the desire to retrospectively establish an independent tradition, the beginnings of African American literature are best characterized as the struggle of Black Americans for agency and the capacity to participate in the broader social and political world. Within the scope of this volume, the case of African American is, therefore, unique: it refers less to the effort to identify an independent literary tradition than to the attempt to stake a claim to the sort of personal authority White Americans took for granted. Douglas Jones highlights that these developments were inflected by Christianity, especially by the belief in equality before God. And yet equality did not mean overlooking entrenched racial differences and imbalances but was instead bound up with the felt need to craft a distinctively Black sense of self. Although early Black writers adopted narrative, poetic, and dramatic forms from the White literary culture around them, access to publication venues, often through unprecedented acts of entrepreneurship, created the means for Black authors to establish their authorial voice and create a sphere where texts could circulate among Black writers and readers.

Each of these four chapters is thus positioned at the interstices of cultures. Of course, this is true of all the traditions examined in this book, but in these four case studies in particular the confrontations and appropriations that form literary beginnings were distinctively uneven and often characterized by violence and subjugation. The ways in which European expansion, including its depravities, has shaped the modern period stands in stark, sometimes problematic contrast to the universalizing gestures that often characterize the modern conception of literature.

Latin American

ROLENA ADORNO

There are many Latin American literatures, and the one examined here is that of the Spanish language. Portuguese-language literature is another, and the literature of Brazil has its own rich history and development. What is "Latin" about both of them is the language of ancient Rome, from which their vernaculars developed. The term "Latin America" was invented by the French in the mid-nineteenth century when they set out on their failed attempt to rule Mexico and establish an empire in the Western Hemisphere. Quickly taken up by Spanish American politicians and intellectuals, "Latin America" became a way for them, like the French, to set themselves apart from Anglo-America. These were the decades immediately following the Latin American Independence era, which spanned the 1810s and 1820s.

In the aftermath of the successful wars of independence from Spain, Spanish American poets, essayists, and critics collected and published the works of their predecessors and peers. Taking a Pan-American approach, the Venezuelan-born Andrés Bello and the Argentine Juan María Gutiérrez bridged Enlightenment learning and Romantic aspirations in pursuit of literary and political expression. Desiring to establish an American poetic tradition, Gutiérrez published a landmark anthology, *América poetica* (1866–67), choosing as its opening salvo Bello's poem "Alocución a la poesía" ("An Address to Poetry") (1823), which beckoned Poetry to the New World's shores. Spanish-authored works were also drawn into the fold. The Chilean bibliophile José Toribio Medina (1852–1930), for example, selected the great Spanish epic poem by Alonso de Ercilla *La araucana* (*The Araucaniad*) (1569, 1578, 1589) as one of the foundational texts of the Chilean national literary tradition. The Spanish chronicles of discovery and conquest in the Americas, reedited and published in eighteenth-century Madrid by Andrés González de Barcia to celebrate the past glories of Spain, provided the new Latin American republics in the nineteenth century with modern editions of writings on which they grounded their nascent literary traditions.

In the mid-twentieth century, academic writers, most notably the Dominican Pedro Henríquez Ureña (1884–1946), looked back to the Spanish colonial era to explain the Latin American literary cultural tradition. His *Literary Currents in Hispanic America* (1945) was presented as the Charles Eliot Norton Lectures at Harvard for the academic year 1940–41, and there he laid out the topics and tropes by which he identified the literature of Spanish America, devoting a third of his work to the colonial period, which allowed him to take a broad view, unencumbered by the interests of nationality or nationalism. Some of Latin America's most prominent poets and writers of fiction also took a long look back, contemplating the earliest writings from and about the Americas and their pre-Columbian civilizations. Pablo Neruda's *Canto general* (*General Song*) (1950) and Octavio Paz's *Piedra del sol* (*Sunstone*) (1957), two of the greatest achievements of twentieth-century Latin American poetry, did so allusively. In fiction, Miguel Ángel Asturias's *Leyendas de Guatemala* (*Legends of Guatemala*) (1930), Rómulo Gallegos's *Canaima* (*Canaima*) (1935), Alejo Carpentier's *El reino de este mundo* (*The Kingdom of This World*) (1949), Gabriel García Márquez's *Los funerales de la Mama Grande* (*Big Mama's Funeral*) (1962), and Carlos Fuentes's *Terra Nostra* (*Terra Nostra*) (1975) stand out. Carpentier (1904–80) and García Márquez (1927–2014) have been the most influential. Carpentier theorized the beginnings of Latin American literature, first with an emphasis on the world of nature, the "marvelous real" (*lo real maravilloso*), later with an emphasis on history. Both merged in Latin American magical realism, the greatest novelistic expression of which is García Márquez's *Cien años de soledad* (*One Hundred Years of Solitude*) (1967).

With this brief sketch as background, it is time to examine how the early writers of Spanish America saw themselves. This meant establishing their own authority, be it political, moral, broadly cultural, or strictly literary. First came those sixteenth-century Spanish-born writers who told the tales of conquest and, by their narrations of events, engaged in the debates about the Spanish claims on the Indies, its lands, peoples, and resources; some of them addressed the debates about how to carry out the Christian mission of evangelizing the native peoples. Prose took the lead, but poetry emerged too, from the popular Spanish ballads (*romances*) and folk tunes (*villancicos*) sung by conquistadores to the apogee of New World epic poetry with Alonso de Ercilla's princely *La araucana*. By the seventeenth century, writers born in America appeared, and they included the first generation of writers of indigenous heritage as well as American-born authors of Spanish descent (Spanish creoles). Poetry took new baroque flights of the imagination and also brooded darkly on the world, whose failings could be mitigated only by biting humor. In both poetry and prose, native American traditions also came to play a small but significant role.

On this imaginary "map" of literary exploration, Christopher Columbus (1451–1506) charted the original course. He announced the existence of the

Americas (although he thought he had arrived at the easternmost reaches of Asia) in his imperfect, acquired Spanish. In his "Letter of Discovery," as it has been called, he set forth the agenda of the topics that would be repeated, transformed, challenged, and inverted over the following centuries. He also drew a map. It consisted of a single, jagged line representing the coastline of an island. He wrote in a few names that he had chosen for this "Asian" archipelago, calling the island "La ispañola" (Hispaniola) to honor his royal Spanish sponsors. He added the name "Cibao," which he understood to be the natives' reference to what he hoped would be Cipango (Marco Polo's name for Japan) and the untold riches of the East. This map was pregnant with possibilities; it evoked all the people and resources that might be there, imagined and unseen. It anticipated the story of the earliest days of Latin American literature in Spanish.

Columbus wrote to the Spanish court of Ferdinand and Isabella from offshore in the Canary Islands in mid-February 1493, adding a postscript upon reaching the port of Lisbon a month later (*Letter of Columbus Announcing the Discovery of America* [1493] 1959). In the Canaries, Columbus reflected on his impressions, experiences, hopes, and expectations. He used the term *maravilla* (marvel) to describe Hispaniola, its navigable rivers, and the timorousness and generosity of its people. The sparkling sunlight of the natural world greatly impressed Columbus in his three-week stay on the island, and in it he saw a return to a prelapsarian paradise—a paradise peopled by natives who, he assured his courtly readers, would serve the Christian monarchs gladly.

He reported that he found neither idolatry nor human sacrifice, but he speculated that idolaters could be found in neighboring islands and that, for their sins, they rightly could be taken as slaves. His expectations, from his readings, included the legendary race of Amazons. Although he did not see any, he gave assurances that such fearsome women were to be found a few islands away. He reported that he found no monsters, but that he had heard of people who ate human flesh, and that elsewhere, farther away still, human babies were born with tails. (The startling ending of García Márquez's *One Hundred Years of Solitude*, in which the last member of the patriarchal Buendía line is born with a pig's tail, can be seen as a silent, ironic homage to this earliest Spanish report from the Americas.)

On his second voyage (1493–94) Columbus assigned a Catalan friar of the Order of St. Jerome, Fray Ramón Pané (ca. 1475–98?), to live with the natives on Hispaniola to learn about their religious beliefs for the purpose of replacing them with Christine doctrine. Thus Fray Ramón authored the first book written in the Americas by a European, *An Account of the Antiquities of the Indians* ([1498] 1999), which was first published in 1571 in Italian. (Its Spanish-language manuscript is lost.) Pané's approach was opposite that of Columbus.

Pané made no bones about admitting the difficulty of communication with the Taínos. He was the most forthright of all the early writers in confessing that doubt, and he wrote that, because the Taínos had no written language, they were unable to give trustworthy accounts of their ancestral knowledge; furthermore, they did not agree on its substance so it was impossible for him to write it down in an orderly fashion. He feared, in fact, that he had set down last things first and first things last, and that what he had written was altogether of little use. Pané's account nevertheless contains precious firsthand knowledge about the Taínos prior to their eventual extinction owing to conquest violence, forced labor, and disease.

Other early writers tended to acknowledge only indirectly the difficulty of communication with native communities. Álvar Núñez Cabeza de Vaca (ca. 1485–92 to ca. 1559) was one of them. He wrote the account of his sojourn across the breadth of North America, from Florida to Texas to Mexico (1528–36), in the aftermath of the failed Pánfilo de Narváez expedition of 1527 to conquer and settle the area surrounding the rim of the Gulf of Mexico (*The Narrative of Cabeza de Vaca* [1542] 2003). Although Cabeza de Vaca portrayed himself as a key protagonist of events, he allowed that communication with native groups was possible over such a vast domain thanks to the Black African slave Estevan. (Cabeza de Vaca refers to Estevan as "Estevanico," which was the diminutive form used for social inferiors, or simply as the Black man, *el negro*.) In the cross-continental liminal zone where the hierarchy of White man over Black could not prevail, Estevan guided his three Spanish companions overland from the eastern Texas coast to that of western Mexico. After long years of habitation among the native peoples of the Mexican gulf coast area, Estevan achieved this ten-month, cross-continental trek, Cabeza de Vaca wrote, by using gourds as talismans to communicate with native groups. Although Cabeza de Vaca does not mention that Estevan's Blackness was likely to have been his most potent magical sign, his recognition of the African slave's talismanic powers demonstrates his awareness of their efficacy.

Cabeza de Vaca also took into account native tales of magical transformation such as that of "Mala Cosa" (Bad Thing), which seems to have been a classic example of the trickster figure. (The trickster figure was a creator and destroyer without reference to divinity, and some of its earliest forms were found in ancient North America.) Cabeza de Vaca wrote that the natives told him that some fifteen years earlier Mala Cosa had appeared and performed acts of bodily mutilation, making incisions and pulling out the entrails of his victims, who were later restored to health. The natives told Cabeza de Vaca that when they performed their ritual dances, Mala Cosa would appear, sometimes dressed as a man, other times as a woman, and that he could hurl a straw hut into the air and then crash it to the ground. Cabeza de Vaca said he found the tale of Mala Cosa and his feats laughable—until he and his companions saw the scars of the healed incisions. Explanation failed him.

In most of the early writings, however, explanation was too readily forthcoming. Two narrative principles were typically at play. One is the blurred distinction between the factual and the fictional, and the second is the problem of first-person narration, when the narrator is both protagonist and reporter. The case of "Gonzalo Guerrero" illustrates both. The name "Gonzalo Guerrero" is enclosed in quotation marks because the flesh-and-blood existence of such an individual was invented from hearsay and gossip that eventually morphed into "fact" and historical canonization. The frequency with which such phenomena occurred, and the fame that the figure "Gonzalo Guerrero" has enjoyed—not least in Tzvetan Todorov's *The Conquest of America* ([1982] 1984)—invite further consideration.

The problem for the Spanish in the 1530s and 1540s was to explain their repeated failure to conquer the Yucatan Peninsula. "Gonzalo Guerrero" is the story of a shipwrecked Spanish sailor, reinvented as a Maya warlord, that offered an appealing explanation. In 1534 Hernán Cortés (1485–1547) recalled that, when on route to conquer Mexico in early 1519, he was told about a shipwreck survivor who had failed to appear when Cortés and his men had picked up on the island of Cozumel (not far from today's Cancun) the shipwrecked Spanish captive Jerónimo de Aguilar. (With Doña Marina, aka La Malinche, who had been captured and baptized at Coatzacoalcos on the Mexican Gulf coast, Aguilar acted as interpreter for Cortés's negotiations between the Spanish and the natives of Mexico all the way from Veracruz to Mexico-Tenochtitlan and for long afterward.) Attempting to recall the name of the shipwreck survivor who had failed to appear in 1519, Cortés called him "Morales" and suggested that the fellow did not want to rejoin the Spanish because he was "painted like an Indian, his ears were pierced, he was married to an Indian woman, and had children by her." Two years later, in 1536, a Spanish veteran of the Yucatan campaigns referred vaguely to such an individual by a different name.

This shadowy figure was nevertheless featured in published historical accounts. He appeared in the *General y Natural Historia de las Indias* (*General and Natural History of the Indies*) ([1535, 1547] 1851–55) by the Spanish naturalist and historian Gonzalo Fernández de Oviedo (1478–1557); Oviedo gave him the name of "Gonzalo." A decade later, in his *General History of the Indies and Conquest of Mexico* (1552), the Spanish historian Francisco López de Gómara bestowed on "Gonzalo" the surname of "Guerrero," which means, appropriately, "warrior." The tale unfolds further. In his *History of the Conquest of New Spain* ([1550s–84] 2008), the Spanish foot soldier and conquest veteran

Bernal Díaz del Castillo (ca. 1495–1584) supplied an additional protagonist: the nagging, haranguing, Maya wife of "Gonzalo." Bernal Díaz also provided the couple's mixed-blood (mestizo) children, thinking, no doubt, of some of his own. A staunch defender of the Spanish military conquests in America, Bernal Díaz viewed as silly the Venetian glass trading beads that expeditions carried to impress and use as barter with the natives. In Bernal Díaz's deft handling, the baubles become children's playthings. Dramatizing the figure of "Gonzalo," Bernal Díaz recreates the scene of the Spanish shipwreck survivor–cum–Maya warlord's refusal to join his countrymen: "Gonzalo" instead asks them to admire his handsome children and give them the green glass beads as toys, as gifts from his homeland.

From a phantom Castilian shipwreck survivor vaguely recalled twenty years after the fact to a Maya warrior who was a doting father and had an out-spoken wife, the saga of "Gonzalo Guerrero" shows how the historical became literary—and how the literary morphed into the historical—in the hands of the early writers of Latin America. On one hand, twentieth-century Anglo- and Latin American academic historians, citing sources such as those here named, have attributed to "Gonzalo" the responsibility for the Spaniards' repeated defeats. On the other, two more recent twentieth-century writers have "dis-covered" accounts that they claim are bona fide, authentic autobiographies of "Gonzalo." But they are diametrically opposed: In one "Gonzalo" is a fearsome Maya warlord; in the other, a pacifist and Spanish loyalist. The many lives of "Gonzalo Guerrero"!

The invented Gonzalo's penning of his own, albeit contradictory, memoirs, illustrates a second principle. It shows that one of the burdens of the early writers was the tension created by being both protagonist and reporter of the events narrated. Bernal Díaz, for example, complained that Hernán Cortés (1485–1547) exaggerated his feats to such a degree that his written accounts (*Letters from Mexico* [1519–26] 1986) made it seem that he had conquered Mexico singlehandedly. At the same time, Bernal Díaz understood the need for self-promotion. This was because histories such as his, like the writings of Cortés, grew out of their first-person accounts of ancestral and personal deeds (*relaciones de méritos y servicios*), which they used to seek recognition and reward from higher authorities. Acknowledging the difficulty of being a truthful, modest witness of one's deeds, Bernal Díaz recounts a conversation with two readers of his in-progress manuscript who chided him for praising himself too much. Bernal Díaz retorted that, since the Spanish writers of the conquest histories had not given the ordinary conquistadores their due, and if he did not sing his own praises, who would? Passing clouds in the sky, birds on the wing?

If the matter of authorial self-promotion was on the table, so was the di-
lemma of how to offer forthright descriptions of never-before-seen sights and
the wonders of New World nature. Bernal Díaz memorably recalled his first
view of the magnificence of the great Aztec capital of Mexico-Tenochtitlan.
He was amazed, he wrote, at the sights that seemed to come from the enchantments of chivalric legend or the tales of *Amadis of Gaul* ([1508] 2003), and
some of his fellow soldiers had even wondered, he said, if what they saw was
a dream. Here Bernal Díaz expressed the failure of his powers of description,
seeing things never before heard of, never before seen, nor even dreamed.
But he made reference to the visionary enchantments of the books of chivalry
not because he thought he was reliving them (which has become one of the
unexamined commonplace interpretations about his experience), but rather
because he needed a reference point, common to himself and his faraway
readers, that would allow them to imagine what he could not describe. Indeed,
he cautioned, although the number of battles about which he wrote because
of having participated in them might *seem* to his readers to be exaggerated or
fantastic à la *Amadis*, they were, he assured his readers, all true.

In his study of New World nature and its inhabitants' inventions, Oviedo
was overwhelmed by the variety of phenomena for which there were no Old
World antecedents. So to convey his own observations, he drew pictures, and
those line drawings were reproduced as woodcuts in his *Natural History of
the West Indies* ([1526] 1959) and his *General and Natural History of the Indies*
(1535, 1547). He made a sketch of the pineapple fruit because he knew that
the Spanish term "piña" (pine cone, pine nut), which he used to identify it,
badly missed the mark. He suggested that its prickly exterior required that it
be picked up with a towel or a handkerchief, but that its reward was the sweet
taste of its fruit and its marvelous scent. Another example: He drew a picture
of the scaly crested iguana. It was delicious to eat, he said, but was it aquatic
or terrestrial? The church, Oviedo opined, would have to determine if its flesh
could be eaten on Roman Catholic fast days. Finally, his lively drawing of the
woven hammock, of which his drawing appeared both in his *Natural History*
of 1516 as well as in his *General and Natural History* of two decades later, depicts a Taíno invention that was, in his view, a remarkable instance of human
ingenuity and a fine innovation in sleeping comfort, certainly on the tropical
island of Hispaniola.

All this suggests that one of the first challenges of the early writers was
to find ways to portray and interpret, verbally or graphically, their observations and experiences of Spain's New World. The greatest object of debate
and interpretation, always present even when not mentioned, was its native
peoples. Figure 14.1 provides a tableau that makes it possible to bring two of

14.1. Fray Bartolomé de las Casas, 1484–1566. *Narratio regionum Indicarum per Hispanos quosdam devastatarum verissima*, 1598. Beinecke Rare Book and Manuscript Library, Yale University.

the foundational, enduring writers of early Spanish America sharply into focus. This image graphically depicts an event in the Spanish conquest of the island of Hispaniola that occurred probably in 1503 or 1504.

Its full-throated pictorial rendering accompanied the debates over the legitimacy of Spain's New World conquests and the rights to sovereignty over its native peoples. The events depicted were narrated in *A Short Account of the Destruction of the Indies* ([1552] 1992) by Fray Bartolomé de las Casas (1484–1566), the Dominican friar and activist preacher who advocated for better treatment of the indigenous peoples (and, ultimately, for Spain to abandon its claims to the Indies altogether). Also rendered in precise detail in a water-color drawing prepared to accompany a French translation of *A Short Account* in 1579, the composite scene reproduced here appeared in print as a copper engraving in Las Casas's account, published in Frankfurt by Theodor de Bry in Latin and German translations of 1598 and 1599.

The site is the Caribbean island of Hispaniola; it was Spain's first administrative headquarters in the Americas and served as its Caribbean "launching pad" for all successive expeditions. The engraving depicts Taíno islanders crying out and trying to escape from being burned alive in a dwelling set ablaze. Its fires are tended by two men, one dressed in tatters carrying a sheaf of straw; the other—smaller and younger—struggles with a load of kindling wood. Dressed in courtier's garb, he is perhaps the page of the commander who, similarly dressed, presides over the scene. The other focal point is the lifeless corpse of a half-clad woman, wearing a crown and hanging from a tree. In the distant background, naked Taínos plead for their lives as thundering Spanish horsemen, lances unsheathed, pursue them. The Spanish commander is Nicolás de Ovando; the men being killed in the fiery holocaust are the island's native lords, and those pleading and fleeing in the background are their compatriots. The hanging corpse depicts Anacaona, the once-powerful queen of the island principality of Xaraguá.

Las Casas's and Oviedo's interpretations of the events represented in this scene illustrate the polemical, polarizing tendencies of the writings of the early postconquest era. In *A Short Account of the Destruction of the Indies*, Las Casas describes these events as a massacre of innocents who had, in fact, aided the Spanish in their colonizing efforts. Queen Anacaona had welcomed to her domain Columbus's brother Bartolomé Colón and, later, the royally appointed governor Ovando. Las Casas wrote that, for her natural nobility, she deserved the finest treatment from the Spaniards but instead was "honored" by them by a public hanging. In his *General and Natural History of the Indies*, Oviedo took the opposite view: Anacaona and her people had plotted against the Spanish and aimed to entrap and vanquish them; thus, in a strike of retribution executed preemptively, the Spanish achieved the desired result, pictured here.

Both Las Casas and Oviedo characterized Anacaona as a powerful sovereign; for Las Casas, she was generous, prudent, and noble, undeserving of death; Oviedo portrayed her as libidinous, corrupting her people with her own immorality instead of tending to their moral betterment. To make his point, Oviedo compared her to Semiramis, the ancient legendary Assyrian Babylonian queen who ruled after her husband's demise, just as Anacaona reigned after the death of her husband, Caonabó. According to Oviedo, Anacaona's condonation of men and women living indiscriminately together in arrangements that Oviedo could compare only to those of barnyard animals, not to mention Anacaona's indiscriminate "sleeping around" with Spaniards, meant that she deserved to be hanged. Las Casas made his literary comparisons in the language of the Christian gospel: the metaphors were sheep (= innocent natives) and wolves (= greedy, devouring Spaniards), and the substance of his missionary theory came from the gospel; Jesus advised his disciples that, if the people they encountered did not wish to receive them, they should shake the dust from their feet and leave them in peace. (This was Las Casas's theory of peaceful, voluntary conversion.) Oviedo's learned literary comparisons came from his early years of service at princely Italian courts, and his acquaintance there with the newly available classics of ancient Western tradition that prompted him to cast a jaundiced eye on ancient (and modern) paganism and its customs.

Las Casas and Oviedo agreed on one thing: the importance of the Taíno institution of the *areíto*, which meant "to sing, dancing" or "to dance, remembering." The oral, choral areítos had their counterpart in the popular oral traditions of Spanish poetry that came to America with the conquistadores and missionaries. The romances (ballads) and the villancicos (rustic country tunes) of fifteenth-century Iberia arose in opposition to the long-resident cultures of Islam, and they were imported into the Americas under the same banner. The romances celebrated military heroism and the triumph of Christian warriors over their Muslim enemies and lamented the ill-fated loves between Christian warriors and Muslim maidens. The villancicos promoted and proclaimed the adherence of the popular classes to the miracles of the Christian faith.

Together, the romances and villancicos made it possible for reflective Spanish observers to appreciate the significance, if not the substance or detail, of the autochthonous traditions. These included the areítos of the Taínos, the *tocotines* of the Nahuas of the Central Valley of Mexico, and, in the Quechua-speaking Andes, the *arawi* that sang of remembered historical deeds and the longings of love that were later transformed into melodies of Christian devotion in the colonial church.

Las Casas and Oviedo understood the areíto's role as the keeper of native historical tradition. Las Casas admired the areítos' synchronized precision of performance, in which three or four hundred men would dance, each man's arms on the shoulders of the adjacent dancers while, in a separate group, Taíno women danced with the same rhythm and order. In addition to historical remembrance, Las Casas added, the areíto was employed to tell folk tales and sing work songs, as when the women grated the casaba roots from which they made their bread. He recalled that the areíto was later adapted for devotional use. Whenever a newly created oratory or chapel featured an image of the Virgin Mary, the Taínos, he wrote, kept it clean and tidy, decorating it with their banners of woven cotton and making it a site for the performance of their areítos. Oviedo compared the areíto to popular choral-and-response dances that he had seen in Spain and in Flanders, where they were also performed by separate groups of men and women.

The evocative expression "to dance, remembering" also suggests the voices raised in song in the Spanish ballads. These, in turn, had been revolutionized by the presence of a new voice of poetry in Spain, the Castilian poet-soldier Garcilaso de la Vega (1503–36). In sonnets, songs, and pastoral eclogues, Garcilaso took up imported Italianate poetic meters and transformed them into new ways of expressing thought and emotion in lyrical compositions in Spanish. The significant event for the development of Spanish-language poetry in early Latin America was the publication in 1543 of Garcilaso's lyric poetry, which swiftly traveled to Spain's American viceroyalties (*Poems* [1543] 2009). In the meantime, the popular Spanish balladeers kept up the *romancero* traditions, and the cadences of the old villancicos were renewed in the church's efforts to evangelize the native peoples through the use of *loas* and *autos*; these were short dramatic pieces in verse that, when performed in indigenous languages, were intended to inspire native communities to convert to Christianity.

The poet Garcilaso's courtly dictum "taking up now the pen, now the sword" (*tomando ora la pluma, ora la espada*) became a watchword for his Spanish and Spanish creole followers in America. One was the already-twice-mentioned poet Alonso de Ercilla y Zúñiga (1533–94), the author of the most famous epic poem in the Spanish language, *La araucana*. Ercilla honored the poetic legacies of Vergil, Tasso, Lucan, and Ariosto, but he considered the poetry of Garcilaso to be his most significant inspiration. *La araucana* was a literary triumph that immortalized the valiant Araucanian peoples while at the same time acknowledging Spain's historical failure to conquer them. Ercilla's reputation as a poet was earned by his creation of Araucanian heroes and heroines, whose nobility of character he proclaimed and defended, as well as by his meditations on the devastating human costs of the conduct of endless war. There were no more fated heroes than Ercilla's sublime creation of the Araucanian warrior Lautaro and his beloved Guacolda. Lautaro and Guacolda dreamed the same dream of doom on the eve of his demise in battle against the Spanish. In this brief but moving portrait, Ercilla honored the gods of love and war as Garcilaso had done before him.

Garcilaso de la Vega's other great successor in the Americas was El Inca Garcilaso de la Vega (1539–1616). Born Gómez Suárez de Figueroa, El Inca Garcilaso was the son of an Inca noblewoman and a Spanish captain. He took the name of his Spanish father Garcilaso de la Vega and, with it, that of his revered ancestral namesake. El Inca Garcilaso used as the subtitle for his translation of the Neoplatonist dialogues of León Hebreo, *La traducción del Indio* (*The Translation by the Indian*) (1590); adding the honorific "Inca," he debuted his pen name El Inca Garcilaso de la Vega. He did the same in his history of the Spanish conquest of Florida, *La Florida del Inca* (*The Florida of the Inca*) (1605). Although seldom read today, the *Diálogos de amor* (*Dialogues of Love*) allowed El Inca Garcilaso to meditate on the challenge of reconciling the learning of biblical heritage with that of ancient Greece, and merging Platonist allegorical thought with systematic Aristotelian logic. It was, no doubt, his "rehearsal" for the equally formidable challenge that he would face in attempting to reconcile Andean Inca and Judeo-Christian religious cultural traditions in his magnum opus, *Royal Commentaries of the Incas* ([1609, 1616] 1966).

El Inca Garcilaso was the master of the written word and one of the most eloquent stylists of the Spanish language in his era. Using the methods of philology, he defended the brilliance of Inca civilization on the basis of his native knowledge of Quechua, and he proudly proclaimed himself a mestizo, turning the racializing (in effect, racist) accusation into a source of personal honor. Sent to Spain at the age of twenty, El Inca Garcilaso lived the rest of his life in Andalusia. (He is buried in a chapel of the Cathedral of Córdoba, formerly its magnificent mosque.) Never permitted to return to his Peruvian homeland, he cherished in memory his indigenous American heritage. One of his most memorable portraits is that of his Inca uncle Cusi Huallpa. Garcilaso recalled that when he, as an adolescent youth, lamented the death of another Inca relative, his uncle Cusi Huallpa bit his tunic in rage at the innocence (ignorance) of his mestizo nephew, whom he accused of being, because of mixed race, complicit in the betrayal of the Incas of which the deceased relative (*auca*, enemy) was also guilty. Race mattered, El Inca Garcilaso emphasized, and the complexities of blood and blood loyalties were frequently confounding.

Another member of this postconquest generation from viceregal Peru was Felipe Guaman Poma de Ayala (ca. 1535–60 to ca. 1616). Guaman Poma, whose totemic names mean "falcon" and "lion," was ethnically Andean; his home territory was not Inca Cuzco but rather the central Andes of Peru south of Huamanga (today's Ayacucho). Recruited by church officials as a youth and taught the Spanish language, Guaman Poma's charge was to identify the practitioners of traditional Andean religion and denounce them in support of the church's local campaigns to "extirpate idolatry." Coming to understand the difference between traditional Andean shamans and those opportunists— "false shamans," he called them—who exploited traditional Andean beliefs for personal gain, Guaman Poma took up the pen to denounce them and especially the Spanish colonialist exploiters who, he argued, were bringing the Andean race to ultimate destruction through violence, forced labor in the mercury and silver mines of Castrovirreina and Potosí, and miscegenation. Guaman Poma's artistic talent was nurtured by the Mercedarian missionary Fray Martín de Murúa, for whom he worked, drawing more than one hundred pictures, before setting out to write his own chronicle, *El primer nueva corónica y buen gobierno* (*The First New Chronicle and Good Government*) ([1615] 2009).

Guaman Poma dedicated his manuscript book to King Philip III of Spain, requesting that it be printed and kept "in the archive of heaven as in that of earth." The work consisted of a four-hundred-page polemical account of ancient and conquest-era Peruvian history (*New Chronicle*) and an eight-hundred-page memorandum (*Good Government*) offering extensive, detailed plans for the civil and ecclesiastical reform of the Spanish colonial regime in Peru. The work was not published in its own time, but it survived, no doubt because of its dynamic, full-page line drawings, all four hundred of which had been created by the author. The manuscript book has formed part of the royal collections of the monarchs of Denmark since the 1660s, when a Danish diplomat, a Hispanophile and ambassador to the Roman Catholic court of Spain, presented it to his king, Frederick III (r. 1648–70) of Denmark.

Like El Inca Garcilaso, Guaman Poma offers many examples of the complexities of blood and ethnic loyalties. Among Guaman Poma's repeatedly mentioned protagonists was one Don Juan Capcha, a low-born Andean elevated to high status by the ignorant Spanish administrators whose interests he served. Thanks to that support, Guaman Poma wrote as he drew the repugnant Capcha's portrait, Capcha was always dressed in the clothes of a Spanish courtier. Wealthy and powerful, he intimidated the Andean peasants beholden to him, took bribes from local Spanish administrators, and masqueraded as a devout Christian. Guaman Poma portrays him, literally, "with a drink in each hand" and a cask of Spanish wine and a clay vessel of fermented Peruvian corn liquor (*chicha*) at his side. But the larger picture Guaman Poma created was of his shock on arriving in 1615 at Peru's viceregal capital of Lima. The devastating, upside-down social order that he witnessed prompted him to add a new chapter to his already-sewn manuscript book. He called it "Camina el autor" ("The Author Journeys"), and in it he exposed all the ills he found in the colonial city and on the roads that led to it. The city of Lima in 1615 was, in Guaman Poma's depiction, the apogee of a baroque chaos of mixed alliances and multilayered treacheries.

Another prominent colonial city of that era, a dependency of the Peruvian viceroyalty, was Santa Fe de Bogotá in today's Colombia. The year 1638 marked the first centenary of its founding, and, for that occasion, one of its Spanish creole sons, Juan Rodríguez Freile (1566–ca. 1640), wrote a work titled *Conquista i descubrimiento del Nuevo Reino de Granada* (*Conquest and Discovery of the New Kingdom of Granada*). The reversal of the sequence "discovery and conquest" referred to the area's sixteenth-century settlement in a nearly bloodless conquest while the discovery of its fabled gold (the myth of El Dorado) had yet to be realized. (It was, in fact, the "discovery" that, to this day, has never been made.)

Two nineteenth-century manuscript copies of the work were labeled "El carnero," and it has been published since the 1920s under that title. The nineteenth-century manuscripts' owners knew that "El carnero" referred to "dressed and tanned sheepskin" and that its synecdochic referent was the cherished record books of Old Castile in which the privileges and properties of its citizenry were listed. The Independence-era residents of Bogotá honored that heritage because, as prestige-seeking creoles in the 1820s, they knew that proving Spanish lineage was paramount, whether they were Spanish loyalists or in favor of independence.

Rodríguez Freile studied the municipal archives of the century-old city and discovered the deceptions—private peccadillos of love and jealousy with severe public consequences—on which the city's history had been built. One of his tales is the much-anthologized episode of Juana García, a mulatta diviner who intuited the adulterous betrayal by a faraway Spanish creole husband in Santo Domingo of his (also adulterous) Spanish creole wife back home in Santa Fe de Bogotá. The mulatta Juana was also the clairvoyant source of the announcement that two of the New Kingdom's first government officials, who had been sent back to Spain to be punished for their civic and sexual crimes, had drowned at sea. When knowledge of Juana's prescience was discovered, she was punished by the Inquisition for witchcraft and exiled with her mixed-race daughters from the city. She protested for being scapegoated: Santa Fe's finest Spanish creole ladies were the guilty ones! Rodríguez Freile shows that the consequences of attributable crime (including "witchcraft") were uncommonly harsh for the city's underprivileged, mixed-race subjects. He does not, however, place the blame for his society's dysfunction on the likes of Juana García. In a lapidary sentence Rodríguez Freile concluded that the fortified quarters of viceroys and governors could not keep out the temptations of amorous passion: "while royal appointments are made by the king, human nature has much broader jurisdiction." Although this prose work has been called a jocular and joyous "New World Decameron," Rodríguez Freile wove its salacious episodes into sobering narrations in which the personal passions of lust or greed by royal and ecclesiastical officials brought about the economic and moral ruin of the already old New Kingdom.

Rodriguez Freile ended his work with a resounding paraphrase of Psalm 109 in which he beseeched the Almighty to punish Bogotá's corrupt aristocratic Spanish governors, asking that they be forced to serve tyrants, be condemned in every tribunal, and see their children become wandering beggars and perish, extinguishing their lineage for once and all time. García Márquez's conclusion to *One Hundred Years of Solitude* echoes this prophecy as the novel's narrator proclaims that races condemned to a century of solitude do not have a second opportunity on this earth. (In a twist of his own lapidary sentence, the new Nobel laureate in literature, at the end of his acceptance speech in

Stockholm in 1982, asked that races condemned to a century of solitude be given that second chance.)

The chiaroscuro of the seventeenth century gave rise to the spectacular as well as the sordid. Built on the ruins of the fabled Mexico-Tenochtitlan immortalized by Bernal Díaz del Castillo, the viceregal capital of New Spain witnessed glittering baroque civic occasions. One, the installation of a new Spanish viceroy, took place in November 1680. It is remembered because Carlos de Sigüenza y Góngora (1645–1700) and Sor Juana Inés de la Cruz (1648–95) were its memorialists. Sigüenza and Sor Juana were friendly interlocutors and sometime intellectual rivals, and their literary personalities step out of the pages of their works. As authors they were united in their common use of hyperbolic literary expression and adherence to the symbolic doctrines of interpretive prefiguration. Both were assigned the task of creating ceremonial triumphal arches for the investiture of the new viceroy, and their choices of topic paint the Hispanic baroque of the Americas in vivid, Old and New World colors.

Supported by his studies of the Aztec historiographic tradition, Sigüenza made its war god Huitzilopochtli into the heroic human leader of the historical migration from Aztlán in western Mexico to Anáhuac, the "land on the edge of the water" of Lake Texcoco where Mexico-Tenochtitlan had been founded. Sigüenza's "mirror of princes" was printed in his *Teatro de virtudes políticas que constituyen a un príncipe: Advertidas en los monarcas antiguos del Mexicano Imperio* (*A Display of the Civic Virtues That Comprise an Exemplary Prince, Notice of Which Is Given by the Ancient Monarchs of the Mexican Empire*) (1680). There he recounted the occasion of the viceroy and vicereine's formal arrival, for which Sigüenza's triumphal arch soared some ninety feet into the air. Atop it stood a live performer, a Nahua maiden in native costume. Her task was to welcome the royally appointed viceroy and his consort, then turn around on the twelve-foot-wide ledge on which she stood. Her task, from this precarious position, was to recite the poetic conclusion of their welcome. The seventeen-stanza panegyric was the concluding poetic encomium of Sigüenza's composition that praised the pagan princes of the Aztec dynasty as the "Phoenixes of the West" (*Fenizes del Occidente*).

Not construed simply as esoteric reminders of a lost past, the pagan Aztec princes who had presided over wars of ritual human sacrifice became, in Sigüenza's bold formulation, the models of ethical conduct for the new Spanish viceroy to emulate. Sigüenza's *Teatro* blended the treatises on the education of Christian princes, the Jesuit tendency to honor antecedent cultural traditions, and his own brand of creole patriotism into a composition that pulled together all the branches of ancient and modern learning. These included Bernal Díaz's chronicle of the conquest of Mexico, the works of European

Renaissance mythographers, the church fathers, Alciato's *Emblematum liber* (*Book of Emblems*), and, from the native Aztec hieroglyphic tradition, the name and place glyphs of the Mexican monarchs whose dynastic reigns he had studied in the Mexican codices.

Sor Juana chose as her theme the Roman sea god Neptune to honor the viceroy's aristocratic title, Marqués de la Laguna, literally, "marquise of the lagoon." *Neptuno alegórico* (*Allegorical Neptune*) (1680) was the published memoir of her ephemeral ceremonial creation. But after he learned about Sor Juana's homage to the Marqués de la Laguna as Neptune, Sigüenza's creole cultural patriotism went to work: To prevent ancient Roman myths being recognized as the source of America's most ancient traditions, Sigüenza took a page from the philosophical speculations of Athanasius Kircher's *Oedipus Aegyptiacus* (*Egyptian Oedipus*) (1652–54). The Mexican creole author proclaimed that the ancient Mexicans descended from Naphtuhim, the founder and ruler of ancient Egypt who was the son of Misraim (or Egypt), who was, in turn, the son of Ham and therefore the grandson of Noah. Sigüenza thus argued that Egypt was the origin of all natural wisdom and religion and that ancient Mexico was its ultimate heir. With this sleight of hand, Sigüenza reduced the Roman sea god Neptune from a primary into a secondary position as a patriarch of the native peoples of the Americas.

Sor Juana, however, also paid homage to Mexico's pre-Columbian civilization. Her eloquent and often piquant poetic voice was accompanied by her remarkable ear for language, and this was captured in her composition of *tocotines* in Nahuatl. The *tocotín* was an Aztec choral dance, and its name was possibly an onomatopoeic representation of its rhythms. Often forming part of longer lighthearted Spanish colonial compositions called *ensalada* or *ensaladilla* in reference to the mixture of fresh vegetables whose flavor was enhanced by the addition of salt (*sal*), Sor Juana included tocotines among the dozens of songs that she composed in various languages, even African Congolese, to commemorate the glories of the Infant Jesus, the Virgin Mary, and the church's saints. Paying homage to the autochthonous Nahua heritage and inventing the name "the God of the Seeds" (*el Dios de las Semillas*) as an alias for the Aztec war god Huitzilopochtli, she turned a Nahua ritual in Huitzilopochtli's honor into the centerpiece of a didactic, versified prelude (*loa*) to her dramatic representation of the mysteries of the faith (*auto sacramental*) titled "Divine Narcissus" (*Poems*, [1689] 1985, 89–127). In it she referred obliquely to Huitzilopochtli and directly to the feast of Teocualo, for which a life-size statue of the Aztec god was sculpted from cereal grains; it was first reverenced, then consumed, by all the classes and castes of the pre-Columbian Nahua community in attendance. Sor Juana's syncretic loa was a spectacular literary-allegorical synthesis that metamorphosed a rite of Nahua paganism into the preannouncement of Christianity.

Sigüenza y Góngora was a thoroughly baroque thinker of his era, and if, on one hand, he pursued scientific investigation in his astronomical studies, he was also taxed with producing New Spain's annual astrological predictions. He was among the first to study the pre-Columbian past of ancient Mexico and Mexican chronology for their own merits, rather than learning about them for the purpose of destroying them. He was also an intellectual who retained his belief in miraculous events even as he ordered (and his request was fulfilled) to have his corpse dissected for the purpose of advancing medical science.

Sor Juana was heralded in both Spains, old and New, as the "Tenth Muse" (*la décima musa*). This was the epithet that announced the publication in Madrid of the first gathering of her works, which consisted of sonnets, songs, and sacred and profane theatrical pieces (*Poems*, [1689] 1985). It appeared in 1689 under the title *Inundación castálida*, in homage to the sacred spring dedicated to the Muses at the foot of Mount Parnassus. But make note: Sor Juana's "spring" was not a trickle but rather a flood (*inundación*).

Sor Juana's literary legacy has endured, and two of her works are still read today: her imperishable poem "Primero sueño ("First Dream") (1692), and her defense of women's pursuits of intellectual interests "Respuesta a Sor Filotea" (*The Answer*) ([1691] 1994). "First Dream" (excerpted in *Poems*, 1985, 71–77) catalogued her imagined intellectual ascent, when all bodily functions were stilled, to pursue and reach the pinnacle of human knowledge. In her poem Sor Juana failed in this secular journey of the human spirit, but the quest has long endured. Not a mystical poet, Sor Juana wrote compositions that combined her cerebral inclinations with a gift for poetic language that was nourished by three sources: the classics, the great sixteenth-century renovation of poetry in Spain, and the rhythm and rhyme of the spoken languages she heard around her. More accessible to a wide readership today is *The Answer*. Viewed as a protofeminist declaration insofar as Sor Juana defended her right to read, study, and write, it provided a learned catalog of women from ancient to (her) modern times whose often autodidactic examples she "merely," tongue in cheek, emulated. "First Dream" and *The Answer* are among the most universally admired texts of the Hispanic baroque, and her poetry, in particular, is considered to be the culmination of the poetic revolution that began with the Castilian poet Garcilaso de la Vega more than a century earlier.

This tour of colonial cities, begun with Guaman Poma and Rodríguez Freile, ends on a note anticipated by them. Sigüenza y Góngora's celebration in 1680 of lost Aztec princes was followed, a decade later, by his "Alboroto y motín de Mexico del 8 de junio de 1692" ("Riot and Mutiny in the Mexican Capital in 1692") (1692). It recounted a riot of thousands of the viceregal capital's underclasses, most prominently Nahuas, due to a food shortage. They stormed the seat of Spanish power in Mexico-Tenochtitlan, burning its buildings and creating one of the first significant uprisings against Spanish colonial rule in the Americas.

Less dramatic in presentation but more corrosive in effect were the daily practices that inspired the versified accounts by witness-interpreters of Lima, the capital of the viceroyalty of Peru called "the City of Kings" because its foundation in January 1535 fell near the feast day of the Adoration of the Magi. These antitriumphalist views of the colonial city portrayed not the immediate terror of urban riots but rather the more subtle, daily damage to human dignity and enterprise caused by the chicanery and corruption of its Spanish creole inhabitants and their native- and mixed-race collaborators.

Two urban poets from the viceroyalty of Peru fill the air with the cacophony of their city's argot in satirical verse: Mateo Rosas de Oquendo (ca. 1559–1621) and Juan del Valle y Caviedes (1645–98). Separated by nearly a century, Oquendo's *Sátira hecha por Mateo Rosas de Oquendo a las cosas que pasan en el Pirú año de 1598* (*A Satire Composed by Mateo Rosas de Oquendo about the Things That Are Happening in Peru in 1598*) and Juan del Valle y Caviedes's *Diente del Parnaso* (*The Tooth or "Bite" of Parnassus*) (1689) tell in verse the story of the Peruvian viceregal capital. Rosas de Oquendo unmasked the pretentiousness of Lima's residents in local street speech as well as in a learned literary idiom; his targets were adulteresses and adulterers, pimps, prostitutes, and rogues of all sorts. Even libidinous oldsters did not escape his pen, and he threw all ages, classes, and castes into the mix.

Toward the end of the seventeenth century, Valle y Caviedes offered greater poetic range. His "Parnassus's bite" took a hunk out of the hide of pseudo-professionals, physicians and healers who replaced, in peacetime, the invading, weapon-wielding conquistadores of old. These peacetime destroyers were part of a larger picture: the immigrant Castilians who came to the Peruvian viceroyalty to make their fortunes while remaining unwilling to appreciate and nurture the resources by which climate, flora, fauna, mineral wealth, and the labor of the natives sustained them. With silent kudos to Oviedo's naturalist studies and Sigüenza y Góngora's scientific interests, Valle y Caviedes recommended the modern approach of medical science—observation and experiment—to replace the outmoded learning that scholasticism represented. In homage to the great Spanish baroque work Francisco de Quevedo's *El Parnaso Español* (*The Spanish Parnassus*) (1652), Valle y Caviedes's "Parnassus's bite" attempted to end the outmoded ways of a now-decadent urban world and to project a future that he could imagine but not achieve. "Parnassus's bite" concludes this transoceanic, inter-inland, and transcontinental trek.

This imaginary map unfolds no further, but if it did, it would lead again to the polymath Andrés Bello (1781–1865), who was mentioned at the outset of this essay. He was one of the Latin American intellectuals who bridged the era that embraced the end of Spanish colonialism and the early decades after Latin American Independence. At age twenty he accompanied Alexander von Humboldt on his exploration of Venezuela's Mount Ávila; at age thirty he joined a compatriot, the Independence-era military general Simón Bolívar, in London; together they sought British recognition of the Americanist cause, and Bello served as Bolívar's private tutor.

After nearly twenty years in exile in London, Bello took Chilean citizenship and settled in Santiago, where he and his colleagues founded the University of Chile (1843). Bello also played a central role in the creation of the Chilean Civil Code (1853), which became widely influential throughout South America. Understanding the Spanish language to be central to the task of fomenting cultural unity among the Spanish American republics, he wrote a Spanish grammar "for use by the Americans" (*Gramática de la lengua castellana destinada al uso de los Americanos*) (1847). He promoted the advancement of learning on all fronts, both to "germinate the fertile seed of liberty" and to pursue "the noble, vast, and difficult task that the love of homeland has placed upon us" ("la tarea noble, vasta i penosa, que nos ha impuesto el amor a la patria" [Bello, *La Biblioteca americana*, 1823, 1:viii]).

Like Columbus's enigmatic, single-line map of Hispaniola's coastline, Bello's pronouncements conveyed high hopes and bold aspirations. Whereas Columbus had sought the riches of the East, Bello's "Cibao" would be found in America's active pursuit of the arts and sciences: the development of its natural and physical sciences, the cultivation of its arts, and the writing of its history. In this light, two of Bello's most prominent interlocutors, Simón Bolívar and the Mexican creole Independence-era thinker Fray Servando Teresa de Mier (1763–1827), provide relevant testimony. Bolívar expressed the conviction that Las Casas's A *Short Account of the Destruction of the Indies* of 1552 should be taken as a foundational document in the creation of an independent America, and Mier published afresh Las Casa's *Short Account*—in London in 1812, in Philadelphia in 1821, in Mexico City in 1822, and possibly in Puebla, Mexico, that same year—with the same purpose in mind. Thus the earliest writings from and about Spanish America were given new life, new meanings, and new importance at the time of Latin American Independence. And so they have endured to the present day.

Further Reading

Casas, Bartolomé de las. *A Short Account of the Destruction of the Indies*, [1552] 1992.

Columbus, Christopher. *Letter of Columbus Announcing the Discovery of America*, [1493] 1959.

Cortés, Hernán. *Letters from Mexico*, [1519–26] 1986.

Díaz del Castillo, Bernal. *The History of the Conquest of New Spain*, [1550s–84] 2008.

Guaman Poma de Ayala, Felipe. *The First New Chronicle and Good Government*, [1615] 2009.

Juana Inés de la Cruz, *The Answer*, [1691] 1994.

Juana Inés de la Cruz, *Poems*, [1689] 1985.

Núñez Cabeza de Vaca, Álvar. *The Narrative of Cabeza de Vaca*, [1542] 2003.

Oviedo y Valdés, Gonzalo Fernández de. *General y Natural Historia de las Indias*, [1535, 1547] 1851–55.

Oviedo y Valdés, Gonzalo Fernández de. *Natural History of the West Indies*, [1526] 1959.

Pané, Ramón. *An Account of the Antiquities of the Indians*, [1498] 1999.

Todorov, Tzvetan. *The Conquest of America*, [1982] 1984.

Vega, Garcilaso de la. *Poems*, [1543] 2009.

Vega, Garcilaso de la, El Inca. *Royal Commentaries of the Incas, and General History of Peru*, [1609, 1616] 1966.

15

African

SIMON GIKANDI

When it comes to African literary history, the question of when, how, and why literature emerged has always been vexed, complicated by a set of competing literary centers, a multiplicity of languages, and the overdetermining role of European colonial cultural and language policies. Of all the continents of the world, Africa has perhaps the most languages; it has competing timelines when it comes to when and how literature emerged; there is confusion about what is considered distinctively African in terms of literary expression; and there is uncertainty about how this literature fits into both old and new categories of world literature. If one asked scholars of African literary history how the literature they study emerged, one would most likely get one of two answers.

The first one—the most dominant—is that African literature emerged when Africans began to write in the major European languages, or to transport European genres, especially the novel, to the field of the dominant African languages. The novel is considered central to this version of African literary history because, of the major genres, it is the one assumed not to have antecedents in precolonial Africa, meaning that we can trace its movements in time and space from its assumed European center to the colonial periphery. In this situation, disputes about the beginnings of African literature tend to revolve around periodization: Should we locate the emergence of African at the beginnings of the first half of the twentieth century when Africans started producing a self-conscious literature in the European languages, or should we to go further back in time and trace the emergence of literary genres in African languages in the nineteenth century?

The second response to the question of how African literature emerges is popular among scholars of oral literatures and writing before 1900. For members of this group, a preoccupation with beginnings seems misguided because, they argue, African literature is as old as any other literature, and evidence of this can be found in old oral epics and praise poetry, and in the existence of traditions of writing in ancient African languages such a Ge'ez, Swahili, and Arabic with its numerous Ajami scripts. Preferring a longue durée approach to African literary history, scholars in this tradition insist that the critical issue is not the flow of literature from Europe to Africa, but the existence of alternative, non-European centers for African literary production. Shifting the center, they argue, leads to a different conception of cultural and linguistic flows. Instead of tracing African literary beginnings in London or Paris, we engage literature in its multiplicity of unexpected encounters: ancient Egyptian literature is connected to that of ancient Greece; Geez, the language of classical Ethiopian literature, is located within the expansive orbit of Eastern Christianity; and Arabic literary traditions form an important bridge between eastern Africa, Asia, and the Levant.[1]

Still, there is one area in which these divergent responses meet: confronted by the diversity of languages and literary traditions in Africa, literary historians have often been tempted by the desire to subject this literature to a process of periodization and system of classification that mirrors literary histories elsewhere. The challenge of explaining a diversity of literatures and languages under the category of a singular African literature is simply how to reconcile the multiple geographies and histories that determined the emergence of literature with the errantry of writing—its refusal to respect boundaries. What this situation seems to demand is a method that is attuned to the bifurcated nature of the history of literature in Africa, one that recognizes that while the structures and institutions in which African literature emerged seemed fairly homogenous, this homogeneity was itself at odds with the heterogeneity of the literature produced. In other words, to understand the emergence of literature in Africa one must simultaneously acknowledge and explain the homogenizing impulse of colonialism and the existence of forms of literature that resisted this impulse or seemed to be at odds with it. It is only by exploring the tension between these two movements that we can understand how the emergence of African literature was both similar to, and different from, the other traditions discussed in this volume.

In this chapter, I will start with a discussion of the emergence of African literature at the interstices between the power and authority of colonial institutions and the desires of an African elite that turned to literature as a mode of self-expression and self-determination. Here, we will see how the cultural processes that led to the emergence of literature in other traditions—questions of literacy, the rise of a reading public, the culture of print, and problems of translation—accounted for the beginning of a literature in Africa as it did in many parts of the world. I will then turn my attention to literary traditions that predated colonialism and hence seemed at odds with dominant assumptions about a literary history predicated on periodization. My focus will be on one particular tradition (Swahili) and one of its canonical texts (*Al-Inkishafi*), which I hope to read as paradigmatic examples of how literature emerged in a cultural and linguistic space defined by divided literary inheritances (African and European) in a rapidly changing cultural geography. Neither the Swahili language nor *Al-Inkishafi* are singular or exceptional in African literary history. There are other examples of African writing that preceded colonialism, including Hausa literature in Arabic script, and Amharic and Somali literatures. My focus, however, is not on the unique histories of these traditions or their unique claims; rather I'm interested in the reinvention of a precolonial literary tradition under colonialism and what this reformulation means for our thinking about literary beginnings.

Literature in the Interstices

In spite of the many debates that have surround it since its inception, the identity of African literatures in European languages does not present problems of what Edward Said has called "the lore of beginnings."[2] This is a corpus that was conceived within the structures of European literature, its institutions of criticism, and its dominant genres. In fact, for most of the long twentieth century, the fortunes of this literature were tied to colonial institutions, including the Christian mission, the school, and the university college. For this reason, it developed in close affinity to European literary movements and a European-centered pedagogical project promoted through selective colonial schools. In spite of its legitimate claim to be African, this literature was written to be read and interpreted within the institutions and protocols that emerged in Europe in the eighteenth century.

With few exceptions (the most notable example is the Nigerian writer Amos Tutuola), pioneers of African literature in European languages were heavily influenced by the major literary trends of the twentieth century. Léopold Sédar Senghor, a prominent poet before he became the first president of Senegal, was one of the founders of the Negritude movement, which, aligned with surrealism, was one of the most significant poetic responses to the crisis of European society before and after the Second World War. Chinua Achebe, author of *Things Fall Apart*, perhaps the most widely read African novel, discovered modernism when he went to study English literature at University College, Ibadan, in western Nigeria, opened in 1949 as a branch of the University of London. Wole Soyinka, the winner of the 1986 Nobel Prize in Literature, studied modern drama at the University of Leeds before being apprenticed at the Royal Court Theatre in London in the late 1950s.

One might expect writing in African languages to have been different, but here, too, the institutional European idea of literature lay beneath the surface of a discourse intended to elaborate and celebrate African experiences and cultures. The most prominent writers in African languages—Daniel Fagunwa in Yoruba, Thomas Mofolo in SeSotho, and Sol Plaatje in Tswana, to cite a few examples—were products of Christian missions. It is here that they encountered the texts and writers who were to serve as models for their writing—the King James Bible, Shakespeare, John Bunyan, and, yes, Maria Corelli. In spite of continuous and unending debates about the politics of language in Africa and the insistence by writers such as Ngugi wa Thiong'o that African literatures in European languages are "Afro-European" rather than African, the line that separates these two linguistic traditions is thin.[3] For in the end, debates about language choice in Africa are troubled and complicated by the fluidity of the category of literature itself. Consider this: for a long time, texts that we now assume to be pioneer African novels, works such as Mofolo's *Moeti oa Bochabela* (*Traveller to the East*), first published in 1907, or Ephraim Casely-Hayford's *Ethiopia Unbound* (1911), were not conceived as such by their authors; rather, they were assumed to be fables or allegories fashioned after John Bunyan's *Pilgrim's Progress*.

When it comes to Africa, then, the story of the beginnings of literature is about not simply the emergence and consolidation of a corpus, but also the reinvention of texts and their domestication within a new sphere of the literary. The emergence of a new literary sphere, which was chaperoned by colonial administrators and missionaries often working in tandem, would lead to the quick homogenization of what had hitherto been distinctive literary traditions. The writing down of oral literatures and traditions, an activity popular with newly literate subjects, meant their subjection to colonial orthographies built on the standardization of different dialects. What came to be known as Yoruba literature, for example, was expressed in one dialect—that of Oyo—which Anglican missionaries had decided was the new standard. Once the orthography had been standardized, all aspects of Yoruba creative writing were required to fit into an authorized phonetic structure. In addition, the idea of literature that took hold among the newly literate Africans was built on a repertoire of texts made available or indeed authorized by the mission schools. Irrespective of language or region, the King James Bible, Bunyan's *Pilgrim's Progress*, and the plays of William Shakespeare would become the foundational texts of African literature in the British territories. Later, the literary bureaus set up by the colonial governments in East Africa and Rhodesia would dictate the rules of what was assumed to be good writing to aspiring African writers.[4] This explains why, in spite of their linguistic diversity, African literatures published in the nineteenth century and the first half of the twentieth century share so many characteristics.

But the story of the emergence of African literature is also about textual errantry, and this can be found not so much in oral traditions that are mistakenly believed to have been untouched by colonialism, but in the life of texts that predate the European idea of literature introduced by colonial institutions. Produced in alternative religious traditions and competing centers of power, texts written in Arabic or Ajami in the Hausa Islamic centers of Kano and Kaduna or the Swahili sultanates on the East Africa coast could not easily be subjected to the homogenizing impulse of colonialism. And since this literature had emerged outside the literary sphere defined by the Christian mission or the colonial school, it could not be accounted for by the literary histories that colonial agents were constructing. Texts produced outside the culture of colonialism could not, however, escape the systematizing impulse of colonialism because the centers of culture that had authorized them in the first place were steadily being undermined by colonial authority. Situated at the interstices of the old and new order, these texts take us right to the heart of what Denis Feeney has identified as a central, if not the central, problem in explaining the emergence of a literary tradition—the question of what it means to think of literature as "contingent and unpredictable to the highest degree."[5]

If there is one compelling reason for keeping contingency at the center of debates about African literary history, it is that however admirable they are, the works that seek to classify or categorize African literature tend to replicate, rather than resist, the homogenizing impulse of colonialism and hence sacrifice the heterogeneity of literary texts and the cultures that produced them. At the same time, however, an appeal to heterogeneity cannot evade the historical circumstances that made systematization and institutionalization essential to the meaning of literature in a public sphere that was overdetermined by colonialism. How does one read contingency and systematization in the same register? Perhaps one way of doing so—the one I have adopted in this chapter—is to focus on the history, circulation, and reception of a central text that predated colonialism yet came to be repositioned in the colonial library as a classic. One such text is *Al-Inkishafi*, variously translated as the "catechist of the soul" or "the souls awakening," written by Sayyid Abdalla Bin Ali Bin Nasir and published on the East African coast sometime in the early nineteenth century (see figure 15.1).[6]

On Contingency and Textual Hybridity

Al-Inkishafi has a complex identity: It is a Swahili poem written in an Arabic Ajami script. It was conceived and written in the Sultanate of Pate, which, though located on the East African coast, was governed by an Arab elite. It is a

15.1. Abdallah ibn 'Alī ibn Nāṣir. al-Inkishafi (MS 380548a). Handwritten manuscript, in blue ink, on ruled paper. William Hichens Collection, SOAS, University of London.

text with a distinctly Islamic religious identity. And it is a text, which in its lifetime, moved from being a religious work to a literary classic that was read and valued for its poetics rather than homiletic identity. My discussion here will focus on how *Al-Inkishafi* was transformed from being a merely religious text in the Islamic dynasties of the northern coast of Kenya into a classic of Swahili literature, central to teaching and thinking at the major centers of European orientalism, most notably the School of Oriental and African Studies (SOAS). Reflecting on the transportation of this text from one cultural sphere—and reading public—to another will help us understand the fundamental relationship between the designation of a classic and the problematic of beginnings and to ask, once again, the question Edward Said asked in *Beginnings*: "Is there a privileged beginning for a literary study—that is, an especially suitable or important beginning for a literary study—that is wholly different from a historical, psychological, or cultural one?"[7]

The surprising thing about *Al-Inkishafi* is that it did not have to work hard to acquire its status as a classic or as a beginning point in Swahili literature. Indeed, at a time when the supposed absence of writing was considered to be a mark of the continent's backwardness, *Al-Inkishafi* was one of a very limited set of African works accorded the status of a classic both by European philologists and their native informants. What accounted for this early canonization? There is no doubt that the allure of the text arose from its mysterious history: Who was the author of the poem? When was it written? Was it written as primarily a religious text or a contribution to the world of Arabic letters? As missionaries and colonial philologists sought answers to these questions, a literary history emerged to consolidate *Al-Inkishafi*'s standing.

Certain issues were settled quickly: It was established that the author of the poem was Sayyid Abdalla Bin Ali Bin Nasir (1720–1820), a member of a Hadhramaut family who had settled on the East African coast at the beginning of the seventeenth century. According to William Hichens, a colonial government officer and the editor of an authoritative edition of the poem published in 1936, Sayyid Abdallah came from a family that claimed direct descent from the prophet Muḥammad. In 1600, one of Sayyid Abdallah's ancestors, Sheikh Abubakar bin Salim, described as "a sage and poet of fame," had sent his two sons to East Africa to help the Sultan of Pate push back a Portuguese onslaught on the Lamu Archipelago (see figure 15.2).[8]

Sheikh Abubakar's sons stayed and established a branch of the Sayyid dynasty on the island of Pate off the north coast of present-day Kenya, where they became governors, custodians of the Islamic faith, and patrons of Afro-Arabic cultural life. Continuing the tradition of his Arabic ancestors, Sayyid Abdallah became a prominent poet and lived to witness the fall of the Sultanate of Pate, which was defeated by the Mazrui dynasty of Mombasa in 1814. No specific date for the composition of *Al-Inkishafi* exists, but the poem seems to be contemporaneous with its manifest subject—the defeat and destruction of the Pate dynasty—so it was probably written between 1810 and 1820. However, the dating of the poem is complicated by claims made for an earlier version of the poem, the so-called *Kingozi* original supposedly written at the beginning, rather than end, of Sayyid Abdullah's life.

While scholars have established who the author of *Al-Inkishafi* was, and we have a general idea when the text was written, none of these can account for the status the poem was to acquire at the end of the nineteenth century and the beginning of the twentieth. For one, given the existence of early Swahili texts, including Fumo Liyongo's *Utenzi wa Liyongo*, which dates to the thirteenth century, it is hard to claim that *Al-Inkishafi* is the oldest or even most popular text in the tradition. Furthermore, the dating of Swahili literature has always been enigmatic; instead of providing clear timelines or histories of texts, dates in the Swahili literary tradition are reminders of gaps and discontinuities. It is said, for example, that Swahili literature first emerged around 1000 CE with the introduction of the Arabic script to the East African coast, but the oldest texts in the tradition are dated to the beginning of the sixteenth century, almost five hundred years later, and there are periods when no texts seem to exist. This has led some historians of Swahili literature to conclude that "Kiswahili poetry cannot be dated."[9] Indeed, a curious fact of Swahili literary history is that few texts are recorded between 1500 and 1700, the momentous period

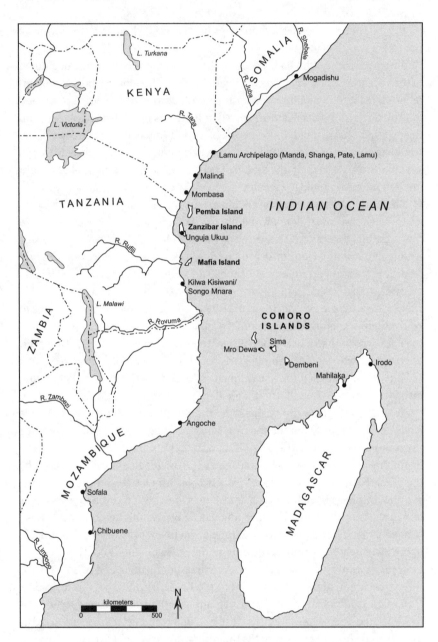

15.2. The Swahili Coast. Courtesy of Dr. Stephanie Wynne-Jones and Dr. Jeffrey Fleisher, Rice University.

of the Portuguese invasion of the East African coast and resistance against it. Although *Al-Inkishafi* is the rare early Swahili poem in which there seems to be a concurrence between the text and the historical event, we cannot be certain about its exact dates.

The identity of the poem is further complicated by a number of factors related to its location in a hybridized culture on the East African coast. Not only is *Al-Inkishafi* a poem produced by a member of the Hadhramaut elite at the end of the Pate dynasty; it is also a Swahili poem written in Arabic script.[10] For this reason, the poem has been caught in a long-running debate on whether it—and Swahili literature in general—is Arabic or African in origin and character. What has been at issue here is not ethnicity, but the relationship between ordinary and literary language. For while the structure and grammar of the Swahili language is derived from the Bantu family of languages that are dominant in central, southern, and eastern Africa, it has tended to borrow some dominant and familiar poetic styles—mostly metrical forms—from the Arabic and Persian traditions. The visible presence of these borrowings would lead some scholars, most prominently Jan Knappert, to argue that Swahili culture was "essentially Oriental, not African, in its material as well as it its spiritual aspects" and that Swahili literature became more "oriental" as it evolved because writers using the Arabic script found that it was not "suitable to represent Swahili sounds" and hence turned to Persian and Urdu traditions to enrich the phonemic nature of their poetry.[11]

Both of these views, which were highly contested in the 1960s and 1970s, have been undermined by recent work in linguistic archeology and a reexamination of the use of the Ajami script used to produce Swahili literature before 1900. Exhaustive research in the origins of the Swahili language has repudiated racial theories about its orientalism and concluded that it has "the typological characteristics of a Bantu language."[12] And in his extensive research on Swahili literature in the Ajami script, John Mugane has shown that confronted by the inability of Arabic to carry sounds that were prominent in Bantu languages but absent in Arabic, Swahili developed a script that would represent what was missing in Arabic (2015, 182–83). In essence, Mugane concludes, the "inadequacy of the Arabic script presented an opportunity for writers of Swahili to be creative, as their predecessors had been in their oral adaptation of foreign words" (2015, 184).

New research has, however, not entirely quarantined *Al-Inkishafi*—and Swahili literature in general—from the colonial and postcolonial politics of language, especially those revolving around the meaning of dialect. Like other old Swahili texts, *Al-Inkishafi* emerged in a context in which the ruling Afro-Arab dynasties on the East African coast were associated with linguistic formations that claimed to be exceptional. The Pate dynasty was associated with what is popularly known as the Kiamu or Kipate dialect; their Mazrui rivals in Mombasa were associated with Kimvita; and the Omani dynasty in Zanzibar used, and promoted, Kiunguja, which became the language of trade and missionary work from the East African coast to the eastern Congo. While the differences between these Swahili dialectics were perhaps not objectively significant, they came to be associated with three different centers of power. What this meant, among other things, was that the social standing of a text depended on the dialect in which it was written and the power of the dynasty associated with it. With the defeat of Pate in the early nineteenth century, the Kiamu dialect retreated from the centers of power to be replaced by Kimvita, the dialect of Mombasa under the Mazruis; when the Mazrui dynasty was defeated by the British in the late nineteenth century, the authority of the Swahili language shifted to Zanzibar where, with the help of Protestant missionaries, Kiunguja became ascendant.

There is one final point to make about the identity of *Al-Inkishafi*: while the work was written in poetic form, following strictly prescribed prosodic conventions, the identity it claimed and wanted to affirm was not that of poetry in our modern understanding of word; it was essentially circulated as a purely homiletic work; and, closely identified with the Islamic tradition of its author, it was "designed to instruct its hearers and to secure their moral improvement."[13] The opening verses of the poem perform a mandatory invocation that puts the poetic work in the hands of God as it were:

BISMILLAHI naiqadimu
hali ya kutunga hino nudhumu
na AR-RAHMANI kiirasimu
basi AR-RAHIMI nyuma ikaye

(In the name of God
I set out to write this poem
I write first He is merciful
And He is compassionate)[14]

The author of the poem worked under an assumption, common in Arabic literature, that the act of writing was the textualizing of sacred scripture and that poetry was "inextricably entangled with religion" and "determined by pious or hieratic interests."[15] In this context, the value and popularity of *Al-Inkishafi* would depend on its religious intention. As Hichens put it in his introduction to the 1939 edition and translation of the poem, "manuscript copies of the Inkishafi are treasured by many Swahili households, and the Inkishafi is well known to and is frequently quoted in theological discussions by the literate section of Swahili society" (8).

Nevertheless, the identity of the poem changed considerably as it made its way into the colonial library. The most significant of these changes was that as it became identified as a classic of Swahili literature, *Al-Inkishafi* began to be valued and interpreted as a literary work in the European sense of the word. In short, the poem moved from a community of readers—and sphere of judgement—that was theological in nature to one defined by European literary conventions about literature and its reading public. The things that made the poem distinctly Swahili—the use of four lines with three rhymed, for example—could not be captured in translation. Indeed, as I will show in the last sections of this chapter, attempts to translate the poem were only reminders of its untranslatability. And yet *Al-Inkishafi* continued to be classified as a classic—if not the classic—of Swahili literature.

The Reinvention of Literature

There is no doubt that *Al-Inkishafi* was venerated in precolonial Swahili circles. We have evidence of this from some of the earliest accounts by the European missionaries and colonial agents who sought to promote it as a classic at the end of the nineteenth century and beginning of the twentieth century. In his introduction to C. H. Stigand's *A Grammar of Dialect Changes in Swahili*, the Reverend W. E. Taylor, the first translator of the poem into English, described *Al-Inkishafi* as "a great, if not the greatest, religious classic of the race."[16] This view was confirmed by Hichens in his introduction to his 1939 edition and translation of the poem: it is considered "one of the many classic works of Swahili authorship in a field of literature which extends over a period of at least seven centuries, and which touches upon every conceivable theme and mood within the pale of Swahili experience" (Hichens [1939] 1972, 41).

Building on the veneration of the poem by Muslim religious scholars, Hichens went on to edit and translate it into a standard edition, complete with notes and commentaries, and thus secured its identity as a literary text—and a classic—in the European sense of the word. According to Hichens, *Al-Inkishafi* was one of the first complete Swahili texts to be prescribed for the Swahili diploma at the Department of African Studies at the School of Oriental and African Studies at the University of London (SOAS). Writing after Hichens, Lyndon Harries, a scholar of Swahili at SOAS, expressed skepticism about the early attention given to *Al-Inkishafi* by European scholars who described it as the greatest Swahili poem without making comparison to other works in the tradition. For Harries, the most that could be said about *Al-Inkishafi* was that "it was a very good example of poems of its kind."[17] He was, however, quick to concede that it was hard to displace *Al-Inkishafi* from the position it occupied in Swahili society because of the esteem in which the poem was held by "the people with the most influence and perhaps the best judgement."[18]

With the publication of Hichens's text, *Al-Inkishafi* was traveling on two parallel tracks. On one hand, the poem continued to play a scriptural role for Swahili Muslims. On the other hand, Christian missionaries and philologists, building on the veneration of the text among Muslim scholars, adopted it to play multiple roles in the evolving colonial library—to serve as the building block for classical Swahili texts, to the cultural achievements of the gifts of the Swahili as "a race," and to bring together two elites—European oriental-ists and African Muslims—in the work of remaking society. In an ironic twist, *Al-Inkishafi* bestowed cultural power on a defeated Swahili elite because, as native informants, they endowed the text with the aura that attracted European scholars to it. This was the testimony given to Hichens by Sheikh Mbarak Ali Hinaway, the liwali of Mombasa in the 1930s, and one of the most influential representatives of Omani interests in colonial East Africa:

> The leading Muslim theologists in East Africa have greatly valued the poem; and it was the practice of some not only to memorise the whole of it, but to carry copies of it with them. The learned Sayyid Ali bin Abdallah Jamalillail, the uncle of Sayyid Saleh bin Ali, the erudite and celebrated theologist of Lamu, used always to carry a copy of the *Inkishafi* in his pocket; and another learned and respected theologist and jurist, Sharif Sayyid Mansab bin Ab durrahman, who died in March 1922, and who, himself a poet of distinction, was unrivalled in his knowledge of archaic Swahili, used to know the whole poem by heart, and he was in the habit of reciting verses from it during con versation and lectures. (Hichens [1939] 1972, 8)

As in the case of Latin literature in the late Middle Ages, the survival of *Al-Inkishafi* and its availability for European scholars depended on an educated elite, which, to borrow Erich Auerbach's words, "by its interest, its understand-ing, and its wealth made possible the continued existence of literature."[19] In this context, it would be a mistake to see the reinvention of texts such as *Al-Inkishafi* as a purely colonial affair. The authority of Hichens's philological project—his definitive ascription of an author to the poem, for example—relied heavily on what he considered to be the "consensus of Swahili opinion" (Hichens [1939] 1972, 13). Indeed, by the beginning of the twentieth century, persons of high rank in Swahili society, most of them of Arab origin, had become important gatekeepers of Swahili classical texts and cultures, using their dual connection to the Arabian Peninsula and the colonial system to validate texts or to reposition them in the colonial library.[20] Hichens, a seminal figure in the collection, editing, and archiving of Swahili texts, would not have undertaken this task without the active participation of these native informants. Indeed, an often forgotten aspect of Hichens's edition of the *Al-Inkishafi* was its reliance on the work of Mohammad Kijuma, a Lamu poet and one of the most distinguished copyists of Arabic literature in Swahili.

There is, however, no doubt that the turning point in the remaking of *Al-Inkishafi* as a literary text was the insertion of colonial language politics and modern (eighteenth-century) European ideas about literature into debates about culture in East Africa. It is not by accident that although *Al-Inkishafi* had been known at the beginning of the nineteenth century, it did not enter what we may now call the field of world literature until the end of that century and the beginning of the twentieth century. Also, it is not accidental that the text's rise to prominence was part of a sustained effort by missionaries and other colonial philologists to systematize African languages and translate African texts. One of the many ironies in the history of the poem is that it first became literature in the hands not of Islamic scholars, but of Christian missionaries, many of them products of the German philological tradition associated with Carl Meinhoff. The Church Missionary Society, the most active Protestant group in East Africa, recruited most of its missionaries from Germany, and many of them were educated in German Romantic theories of language. With this education and background, argues Sara Pugach, "a transnational Protestant community" was sent to Africa with firm ideas about the relationship between language and racial groups.[21]

Protestant missionaries in East Africa shared Meinhoff's strong view that the cultural achievements of a people could be judged from the complexity of their languages; they also believed that language, more specifically phonology, was the key to understanding colonial subjects as a precondition for their conversion into Christianity. This was the point stated by the Reverend Johann Ludwig Krapf, the author of the first grammar of the Swahili language published in Tubingen in 1850:

> Now it appears to me an important fact, that, as the Arabic language prevails in the North and North East of Africa, so the Suaheli presents in the South East the key to the interior of this continent. Consequently the herald of the Gospel in this quarter stands in need only of one language, by the instrumentality of which he can master in a short time all the dialects spoken

from the line down to the Cape of Good Hope. So wonderfully simple are the leadings of Divine Wisdom, to bring about the greatest results, when it suits her purpose at the fulness of time.[22]

For Krapf and other missionaries, Swahili occupied a strategic linguistic role because it was part of a group of African languages with a common root and could hence reach the widest audience possible. In this spirit, Krapf undertook the task of translating the Gospels of St. Luke and St. John into Swahili and of developing a dictionary of the language. The publication of Krapf's *Dictionary of the Suahli Language* in London in 1882 was an important landmark in the incorporation of Swahili into nineteenth-century debates on language and identity.

What did this European intervention mean for already existing African literatures? For one, while Swahili literature had up to this point functioned as an appendage to a larger religious project, it now had a dictionary, a grammar, and textual translations consolidating its claims to be literature. In the formal colonial period, which began with the partition of Africa at the Conference of Berlin (1884), and within the ideologies of religious conversion initiated by missionaries beginning in the first half of the nineteenth century, texts such as *Al-Inkishafi* would come to be incorporated into the European idea of literature as it had evolved since the eighteenth century. Once it had been proclaimed to be a classic, the poem attracted translators; and in the process of translation, the diverse interests of the colonizer, the missionary, and the oriental philologist converged sometimes in unexpected ways.

Consider, for example, the earliest translation of the poem: Described as "a Recension and Poetic Translation of the Poem *Inkishafi*, a Swahili *Speculum Mundi*," Taylor's translation of the northern version of the poem was significantly published as an appendix to a volume entitled *A Grammar of Dialect Changes in Swahili* published in 1915 by C. H. Stigand, an officer and adventurer in the British colonial expeditionary force in East Africa and the Sudan. Some of the missing stanzas in Taylor's rendition were supplied by Professor Alice Werner, a distinguished German orientalist at SOAS in 1932. The translation of the poem was the beginning of what would turn out to be a cumulative philological project—and the textualizing impulse—that was to continue into the postcolonial period. It would create the condition for Hichens's edition in 1939, which would, in turn, lead to James de Vere Allen's popular translation in 1977.

Why did colonial philology favor texts such as *Al-Inkishafi*? There is no obvious answer to this question, but it is highly probable that finding themselves among a people ostensibly without writing, colonial philologists tended to gravitate toward—and privilege—those with texts. Werner, who was to play a significant role in the institutionalization of Swahili studies at SOAS, summarized the thinking behind colonial textual preferences in 1918:

> Swahili stands alone among the Bantu languages in possessing a literature, which originated before the people came in contact with Europeans and has probably been in existence for several centuries. The Arabs, who settled on the east coast of Africa from the seventh century onwards, brought with them their alphabet and their prosody; and their descendants who, intermarrying with the daughters of the land, evolved the Swahili language, have preserved both to this day, though not without modifications.[23]

Since texts coming out of Muslim communities could be located easily within a tradition of Arabic and Persian poetry, philologists had ready tools for discussing these texts. The association of writing in East Africa with Arabic had two long-term consequences. First, as Mugane has shown in detail, there was the unfortunate assumption that an Arabized Swahili was superior and a marker of "prestige, power and piety."[24] Secondly, the Arabization of Swahili led to the acceptance of the grammar of orientalism—and its racial assumptions—as an essential paradigm for understanding *Al-Inkishafi*. The poem was being chaperoned into the canon by scholars with deep orientalist training or inclinations. Taylor, an Oxford-educated classicist and Anglican minister, came to Swahili through the study of classical Arabic; Werner was a German-trained scholar of oriental philology; and Hichens was a colonial administrator with a particular fondness for the East African coast. Orientalism seemed to give the text a space in which it could claim affinities with a tradition that was already exalted in European colonial circles.

Standardization and Translation

Still, we have to address a question I raised earlier: Why did European philologists, who had many more compelling options before them, come to promote *Al-Inkishafi* as the classic work of Swahili literature? Was the designation of the poem as a classic an acknowledgment of its value or an archiving gesture, one prompted by the need to have a Swahili text that would display the orientalist style favored by European philologists? One way of addressing these questions is to note that *Al-Inkishafi* was a classic first and foremost in an antiquarian sense: The work existed as an incomplete text and in multiple versions; it hence appealed to scholars because it demanded reconstruction to a mythical original; the text also demanded a mastery of its religious context and ontology. For James de Vere Allen, readers "who wish to gain the maximum from this poem must try to interpret it from within the cultural context in which it was written. . . . To do this fully it is necessary to steep oneself in the text of the Koran and its teachings, if not, indeed, in the experience of the Islamic religion itself" (5). The deep religious context of the poem gave it an opacity that demanded a particular training in interpretation.

Ultimately, the aura that now surrounds *Al-Inkishafi*, indeed what makes it the defining text of Swahili classical literature, would come from an unexpected direction—the colonial desire to standardize language. As missionaries and colonial administrators adopted Swahili as the language of evangelization, trade, and governmentality, they found it necessary to standardize its dialects in order to make it more portable across the East African region. Toward this end, the missions and colonial government set up language boards in both Kenya and Tanganyika to explore ways in which a common orthography and grammar would be constructed in a context defined by tension between the dialect of the north, which now encompassed the dialects spoken in Kenya and that of the south, which now referred to the dialects spoken in Zanzibar and the Tanganyika mainland.

At a meeting held under the auspices of the East African Language Board in Mombasa in 1928, a meeting attended by none other than Meinhoff, missionaries and colonial education officers decided to adopt the dialect of Zanzibar as the standard Swahili. The political motivations for standardization would be debated for a long time; but its literary consequences would soon become apparent.[25] Supporters of the Zanzibari dialect, mostly government officials, supported it because of its assumed connection to everyday language; advocates of the dialect of the north, mostly missionaries, argued that it was the language most associated with literary culture; the former won the argument and local scholars left out of it could only lick their wounds.

The standardization of Swahili had an unexpected twist: the Swahili of Zanzibar acquired dictionaries and grammars and was instituted in schools and government offices; with the active involvement of the postcolonial government of Tanzania under President Julius Nyerere, a notable translator of Shakespeare, Kiunguja, the Swahili of Zanzibar, became the language of the academy, the media, and governance. Simultaneously, Kiamu and Kimvita, the Swahili dialects of the north, including the language of *Al-Inkishafi* became, as it were, dead languages. These northern dialects could no longer be used in schools or government offices; it was no longer fashionable to produce literature in them. At the same time, these dialects—now that they were considered dead—were endowed with the aura of a classical literary language. Like Greek and Latin before them, the ostensibly dead dialects were the languages that elevated a work such as *Al-Inkishafi* into a classic.

The Swahili elites of the north coast were obviously not happy with a standardization of the language that favored their Zanzibari rivals, but there is no evidence that they went out of their way to oppose it. They seemed to acquiesce to the idea that a language that had been designated as both dead and classical had its advantages. For Swahili elites, the designation of a work such as *Al-Inkishafi* as a classic did not mean that it was a text that had been rendered obsolete or one whose identity had been locked in time; rather, what they saw was a poem that was being reinvented within the new domain of the colonial and postcolonial library and thus being endowed with a new lease of life and renewed authority.[26]

A key element in the reinvention of *Al-Inkishafi* was its repositioning as part of a new culture of reading associated not with the mosque, as had been the case in the past, but with the modern school. Literacy was not new among the Swahili, and so long as one could read the Arabic script, texts such as *Al-Inkishafi* could be studied by those who had access to a manuscript or copy. With colonization, however, the sphere of reading changed in dramatic ways: the Arabic script was superseded by the Latin one; Swahili texts written in Arabic now needed to be translated into Swahili in the new script; the printing of books made them available to those who could read, irrespective of class and rank. Ironically, this remapping of literature could not have taken place without the support of the Arabic-speaking elite in the centers of Swahili culture.

Why did leading Swahili religious scholars need a classic, or encourage colonial philologists to produce one for them? And why were they keen to help in what might appear, on the surface, to be the desacralization of homiletic texts? Here, as in other colonial situations, native elites were keen to attach themselves to European philological projects as a way of imagining scriptural alternatives to colonial culture. More significantly, Swahili elites needed to secure and hold on to texts that had recently been reinvented as ancient and classical because they saw them as invaluable cultural depositories, evidence of the existence of an important precolonial culture. If literary texts seemed to acquire an inordinate value among Swahili elites, it was because they assumed, as did other native elites across the British and French empires, that literature could function as an authentic representation of a past that had disappeared.

Al-Inkishafi lent itself well to this last role because, as the following two verses illustrate, Sayyid Abdallah's manifest theme was the disappearance of a world that had once been great, but has now been reduced to ruins:

49. Nyumba zao mbake ziwele tame;
makinda ya popo iyu wengeme.
Husikii hisi wala ukeme;
zitanda matandu walitandiye. (Hichens [1939] 1972, 80)

(Their once bright houses are now empty
young bats hang from the rafters
One hears no whispers or sounds
only spiders crawling on the beds.)

50. Madaka ya nyumba ya zisahani,
sasa walaliye wana wa nyuni.
Bumu hukoroma kati nyumbani;
zisiji na koti waikaliye. (Hichens [1939] 1972, 80)

(Niches that used to house porcelain
have become nests for baby birds
Owls screech throughout the house
And birds of ill-omen dwell inside.)

Like the images that define Pate today, the poem was to function as an allegory of ruined past (see figure 15.3).[27]

Ironically, the work of mourning or lamentation would allow the once querulous Swahili groups to find a common identity in the moment of their defeat and cooption into the colonial system. Thus, while the manifest subject of the poem had been the defeat of the Sultanate of Pate by the Mazruis of Mombasa, it would circulate along the Swahili coast as a work of common suffering. The distinguished Kenyan scholar Alamin Mazrui recalls reading the poem to his father, Al-Amin Bin Ali Mazrui, the chief kadhi of Kenya colony during World War II when the poem was conceived as an allegory of the destruction of all empires:

I was first introduced to *Al-Inkishafi* in the course of World War II. I was a child, newly literate in Swahili. My father followed the news of the war closely. Sometimes I read out a report aloud to him from a Swahili newspaper. The news included death and destruction in distant lands; and hunger and shortages in East Africa. But I also remember being asked to read out *Al-Inkishafi* aloud to him during the same period. Were ancient civilizations about to collapse in the wake of Hitler's war? Were villages being

15.3. The ruins of an old house on Pate Island. Lamu Archipelago, Kenya. John Warburton-Lee Photography / Alamy Stock Photo.

depopulated already? Were the mighty about to fall? Was Hell entering everyday life?[28]

Moving beyond its immediate historical context and situation of enunciation, the poem would create new reading publics. In this context, translation—or more specifically, disputes about translation—would come to play an important role in the emergence of Swahili and other African-language literatures.

Let me then turn to the stanza of the poem I used to illustrate its elegiac quality. First, the original as reproduced in Taylor:

> 51. Madaka ya nyumba na zisahani; sase walaliye wana wa nyuni
> Bumu hukoroma kati nyumbani; zisiji na koti waikaliye. (Taylor 1915, 77)

Then his translation:

> The niches in their rows still with porcelain incrust
> Do furnish each feathered fowl with a roost;
> Here snoreth the brown owl, here gathereth most
> Red-dove, or green-dove, to mate and to pair. (Taylor 1915, 102)

Taylor, a Protestant missionary, would instinctively turn to the language of the King James Bible—and the iambic pentameter—striving to bring the poem as close as possible to what he assumed was an emergent Christian reading public. In contrast, Hichens, the colonial administrator and orientalist, preferred a literal translation, one that would, as he put it in his introduction, render "the original Swahili as closely word for word or line for line as syntactical and idiomatic difference between the two languages and the considerations of rime and metre permit" (35). The result was a robust, "Miltonic" rendering of the poem:

> Where once in wall-niches the porcelain stood,
>   now wildling birds nestle the fledgling brood;
> The omened owl hoots 'midst the solitude,
>   and, faring there, strange wild-fowl make complain. (81)

R. Allen was conscious of what he called "the insuperable difficulty of sound" in translation and "the curious twists and cunning alliteration" (R. Allen 1946, 244) in *Al-Inkishafi*, so his version sought to capture the feel of the poem rather than its literal meaning:

In their niches for porcelain nestle young
>   birds
owls hoot in their chambers, and birds of
>   ill omen. (248)

Harries, the Swahili language expert at the School of Oriental and African Studies, provided a transliteration of the poem from its Swahili Arab script and avoided what he considered to be "the turgid and rather bombastic style favored by Hichens" (Harries 1962, 91):

The wall-niches for porcelain in the houses   are now the resting-place for nestlings   owls hoot within the house mannikin birds and ducks
>   dwell within. (Harries 1962, 99)

And in his 1977 translation, James de Vere Allen, who had all these previous translations available to him, kept Taylor's and Hichens's iambic pentameter but gave up on the rhyme:

Where once in wall-niches the porcelain stood
Are now the ragged nests of wild birds.
Owls hoot in the solitude of the ruined halls
And quail and gamebirds scuttle and cry below.
>   (J. de V. Allen 1977, 66)

In all these cases, the task of translating *Al-Inkishafi* was made much more complex by the technical demands of Swahili verse and "the different, and sometimes immensely diverse and enigmatic generic categories or forms."[29] This was particularly the case with rhyme. *Al-Inkishafi* belongs to a category of Swahili poetry called *utendi*, a form with three rhyming (AAA) lines and a fourth nonrhyming line. Whether to use a rhyme scheme or not was the first choice translators of the poem had to make. Here were the possibilities and perils. In choosing to use an iambic pentameter and couplets that were familiar to a nineteenth-century English reading public, Taylor had made his translation familiar to an audience brought up on the King James Bible and Shakespeare, but his version sounded archaic; eager to reproduce the Swahili rhyme scheme in English, Hichens and R. Allen had produced a version that was, to borrow Harries's terms, "too rhapsodical" (89); and by dispensing with the rhyme scheme altogether, James de Vere Allen had also given up the formulas that secured the identity of *Al-Inkishafi* as a Swahili poem in the *utendi* tradition.

Conclusion

The continuing debates about the translation of *Al-Inkishafi* can lead us to draw some general conclusions about the emergence of African literature at the interstices of local and colonial interests. Let us note, for example, that none of the translators discussed above, or even the major commentators on the poem who came after them, worried too much about the question of the original. Of course, translators were aware that the poem had circulated in copies written on scrolls, and that these had been revised over time. In his notes, for example, Taylor provided a long list of the native authorities and scholars who procured the text for him and the revisions they had made. He also noted the verses that were missing in this text, verses that were restored by Werner in 1932, relying on a copy provided by Kijuma, the Lamu poet. Many of the editors and translators of *Al-Inkishafi* assumed that their primary task was to produce a collated text, which, after accounting for variations and recensions, would become a reliable basis for translation.

In undertaking the remarkable task of reconstructing the text, colonial philologists seemed untroubled by the fact that the native informants who were providing the original, revising it, or simply providing commentary were also, perhaps unwittingly, engaged in acts of translation. For although it is possible that all copyists assumed that their task was to provide a faithful transcription of the originals, there was not one but two or three existing versions of the poem located in different parts of the region. And, of course, the copyists had to bring their own dialect and understanding of the Swahili language to bear on their work. Confronted with the existence of several versions of the poem, European translators started by insisting on the originality and stability of the copy that they possessed or to which they had access. Translators of *Al-Inkishafi* from Swahili to English were motivated by the belief that either the preceding versions had fallen short of a restored original—a vulgate as it were—or that the work of translation had misrepresented the structure and grammar of the Swahili to make the poem fit into English conventions or serve the interests of missionaries and colonial philologists. Whatever the mode they adopted, translators could not escape the tension between three things: the original *Al-Inkishafi*, or a version of it; Swahili literary conventions; and the English poetic norms familiar to their real and implied audience. In this sense, the emergence of African literature has to be located at the intersection of the contingent, namely the unexpected historical process that dislocated old texts from their native traditions and placed them in the liminal zone between audiences and constituencies and the demands of a totalizing colonial library.

Literature would hence emerge in a cultural and linguistic space defined by divided literary inheritances (African and European) in a rapidly changing cultural geography.

Further Reading

Abdulaziz, Mohamed H. *Muyaka: Nineteenth Century Swahili Popular Poetry*, 1994.

Allen, J.W.T. *Tendi: Six Examples of a Swahili Classical Verse Form with Translations and Notes*, 1971.

Knappert, Jan. *Four Centuries of Swahili Verse: A Literary History and Anthology*, 1979.

Mazrui, Ali Al, and Alamin M. Mazrui. *Swahili State and Society: The Political Economy of an African Language*, 2011.

Middleton, John. *The World of The Swahili: An African Mercantile Civilization*, 1994.

Mugane, John, *The Story of Swahili*, 2015.

Nurse, Derek, and Thomas Spear. *The Swahili: Reconstructing the History and Language of an African Society, 800–1500*, 1985.

Wynne-Jones, Stephanie, and Adria LaViolette, eds. *The Swahili World*, 2018.

African American

DOUGLAS JONES

Students and first-time readers of eighteenth- and early nineteenth-century African American writing are very often bewildered by the paucity of strong antislavery dissent they encounter in the texts. Lucy Terry's "Bars Fight" (1746), which scholars recognize as the first literary work by a Black person in British North America, memorializes a Native American attack on White colonists in Deerfield, Massachusetts, in a ballad form. The poem makes no mention of Terry's birth in Africa, probable transportation on the Middle Passage, experience as chattel, or resistance to her condition. Hence, its formal properties and narrative concerns in no way align with the emphasis on "fugitive" aesthetics and politics that scholars today recognize as central to African American literature.[1] Jupiter Hammon, who in 1760 became the first African American poet to publish his work and attain something of a wide readership, would seem to be a more auspicious candidate to satisfy these readers' assumptions since he wrote about slavery in several of his works. But Hammon's Calvinist faith disposed him to construe the institution of slavery as God's design and thus beyond human denunciation. In fact, Hammon late in life refused manumission and sued his master to stay enslaved. Although one finds in Phillis Wheatley's poetry and letters strands of an antislavery posture, her seeming support for race-based chattel slavery as a conduit of Christian conversion as well as her high esteem for English Renaissance and neoclassicist (especially Augustan) poetics frequently undermine her oppositionality. Even David Walker's jeremiadic *Appeal* (1829, 1830), which champions armed resistance to slavery and Black self-determination, ultimately espouses a sort of Jeffersonian republicanism as the ideal form of government. This is all the more ironic, if not self-defeating, since Walker regarded Thomas Jefferson's racialized political theory as the greatest philosophical impediment to full Black inclusion in the American polity. As these major texts suggest, early African American literary writing participates in a broader effort to achieve recognition not only as modern subjects but as full contributors to and beneficiaries of the era's many sacred and secular revolutions.

It took until the middle of the nineteenth century before systems of thought that markedly fulfill contemporary expectations acquired a foothold in African

American cultural theory and practice. The conditions that engendered this conceptual sea change were legion, but the most crucial was the establishment of autonomous free Black communities throughout the United States. These communities' steady growth in population and influence from the Early Republic era through the 1850s also governed the evolution of African American literature's origins—an evolution, this essay seeks to show, unfolding in three phases each of which projected a new emphasis for readers: testimony, rhetoric, and belletrism. The emergence of one did not mean the absence or even decline of another; there is certainly, say, belletristic intentionality and excellence in Wheatley's poetry. Yet the demographic concentration of free Black persons in cities and the social coteries it engendered (e.g., mutual relief associations; fraternal organizations; education institutes; library companies and literary societies) created the conditions, and evoked for writers and critics the necessity, for particular effects their writings should generate and exhibit. In other words, as enslaved and free Black persons' collective relationship to power shifted, so, too, did their view of the purpose of literature.

The first writers sought to assert their presence among religious and social networks that were local and often majority White (testimony); the next generation, buttressed by Black institutional and communal support, took the propriety of their authorial voice for granted and conceived of the literary as a vital front in their crusades for large-scale social change (rhetoric); finally, a small but influential cohort of writers emerged in the mid-1850s who stressed the importance of literary autonomy and the pleasures of reading and writing in and of themselves (belletrism). The texts this essay examines to offer an account of these developments are by no means exhaustive, but they do typify the assumption of (narrative) authority, sociopolitical preoccupations, and formal interventions that distinguish the origins of African American literature. I pay particular attention to the fact that early Black writers did not always focus on White institutions and readers they very often recognized but refused the sway of developments in contemporaneous Anglo-American literature. As a result, the most well-known and frequently studied literary production from the era, the slave narrative, is largely absent from what follows.

Testimony: Evangelical, African, and American

The practical beginnings of African American literary writing stem from the cultural and theological formations of eighteenth-century American evangelicalism. Swept up in ecstatic revivals and fiery worship services that preached equality before God and thus the possibility of eternal salvation for every person, regardless of his or her earthly station, enslaved and free Black persons heeded the evangelical call to *testify*, that is, to bear witness to their conversion, confess their transgressions, and celebrate their deliverance from the wages of sin. Not only did they testify as revivalists and congregants, but many did so in ecclesiastical offices such as exhorters, lay ministers, and clergy. In 1748, for example, a slave exhorter of Fourth Church (Congregationalist) of Ipswich, Massachusetts, named Flora appeared before her congregation to confess to some unnamed "Temptation and Sin" in order to "Restore me to your Charity and Fellowship and the Privileges that I have Forfitted [*sic*], by my Fall." Flora's reinstatement into this community of believers depended on a performance of shame and contrition grounded in an ethic of egalitarianism, not in her identity as Black, enslaved, and woman. In its formal and informal settings, evangelicalism offered its most downtrodden adherents opportunities to regard themselves as equal contributors to their religious communities. Because evangelical culture demanded public testimony, persons like Flora acquired not only affective and spiritual awakening but also an *expressive* one: even in the most humbling and humiliating circumstances, they still maintained the standing to receive a full hearing from their coreligionists.

The habits of body and mind Black evangelicals cultivated in worship quickly became the point of departure for their more secular pursuits, as Old Light antirevivalists, slave masters, and racial conservatives feared. The production of cultural forms and objects that corresponded to their New World experiences was one of the most pressing of those pursuits, and they discerned the prominence that authorities in the church and out of it accorded to writing. (The minister of Flora's church transcribed and maybe wrote parts of her confession and archived it among his and the church's papers.) Thus, the advent of African American authorial subjectivity emerged when, under the sway of evangelicalism, enslaved persons and their descendants perceived in themselves the authority to write for the same reasons White persons did. They discerned in Anglo-American literary culture a worthwhile set of practices with which to reflect on affects, ideas, and encounters beyond the sacred domain. To be sure, the earliest African American literary texts almost invariably attest to God's power and the propriety of Christian virtues, but they also offer evidence of the ways in which their authors and publics understood their worldly identities. What it meant for them to be "African" and "American" were among this corpus's foremost subjects of testimony.

Far more than a signifier of racial difference, "Africa" signifies in the earliest African American writing the achievements and potentialities of Black civilizations as well as their native and diasporic subjects. Two dominant paradigms emerge: stadialism and Ethiopianism. The stadialist approach positions indigenous Black societies in the first stages of cultural development, and the lack of Christianity is almost always the primary reason. Phillis Wheatley's oeuvre offers the most evocative expression of Black stadialism in the era. She called her "native shore" (i.e., western Africa) "the land of errors and *Egyptian* gloom" and (in)famously celebrated God's "mercy" for delivering her "from my *Pagan* land" to a land where one "May be refin'd, and join th'angelic train." In letters of support for proselytizing missions, she writes of an "Africa [that] is perishing with a Spiritual Famine," of "the thick Darkness which broods over the Land of Africa; and the Chaos which has reign'd so long"; only the "divine Light" of Christianity that "Europe and America have long been fed" will redeem her "benighted Country," she argued. Black Christians like Wheatley understood themselves as something other than African, not White but part of "th'angelic train." (She declined invitations to serve as a missionary in Africa, citing an "Asthmatic complaint," refusal to leave her "British & American Friends" including her dying mistress, and the strangeness of the land and its people.) To testify to one's differences from Africans past and present, then, was to claim one had progressed to a higher stage of historical development; however implicitly, such testimony also recognized slavery as the vehicle for this progression. Indeed, as a theory of New World peoples and of personhood, stadialism deems slavery an ineluctable, requisite, even advantageous institution in the evolution of world history.

Ethiopianists denounced stadialism's proslavery drift and its underlying interpretations of Africa. They regarded the enslavement of Africans as a scourge, neither necessary nor beneficial, that Europeans devised to satiate their avaricious and lecherous appetites. It was not an institution that revealed God's mercy but one that would precipitate God's retribution on its perpetrators and God's favor on its victims. Ethiopianist writers legitimated their prognosis not only in Psalms 68:31—"Princes shall come out of Egypt; Ethiopia shall soon stretch out her hands unto God"—but more importantly in a comparative historiography that regards the feats of African civilizations as equal to, sometimes greater than, those of Europeans. (This conclusion is what distinguishes Ethiopianism as such, not the citation of Psalms 68:31. The verse became a mantra of sorts in texts about race and slavery in the long nineteenth century, with writers across the ideological spectrum adducing it to various ends.) Prince Hall, who founded Black Freemasonry in Boston in 1784, was the most authoritative Ethiopianist in this phase, and his writings established a far different line of Africanist thought than Wheatley's. In Hall's two "Charges" to the African Lodge, for example, he extols Africans who were at the forefront of shaping Judaism and Christianity as well as the architectural, intellectual, and moral deeds of Freemasonry. "Jethro, the Ethiopian" was chief counselor to Moses on matters pertaining to government and justice; thus, Mosaic law is ultimately an African production, Hall suggests. Solomon, the Freemason's "Grand Master," "was not asham'd to take the Queen of Sheba [an Ethiopian by Hall's account] by the hand, and lead her into his court . . . and there converse with her on points of masonry. . . . He gave her the right hand of affection and parted with love." Such intimacies reveal Africa's centrality to the making of world-historical achievements. These and similar mythologies that recur in Ethiopianist writing do more than celebrate Africa and its peoples: they regard the best of European civilizations as built on African ones.

Notwithstanding the racial genealogy Hall posits that affirms Black persons throughout the world as legatees of glorious African pasts, he believed the plight of African Americans was largely distinct from that of contemporary Africans. The bulk of his concern was the very particular needs of Black persons in and around Boston, and he relied on modern democratic procedures like petitions to state legislatures and street demonstrations to press for change. (Even his interest in voluntary emigration to Africa was about addressing the problems of being Black in Boston first and foremost.) Hall's couching of local interests in the republican idioms of the early national United States instantiates how the first African American writers imagined what it meant to be "American": it was to be part of a locality with access to broader (i.e., national) discursive resources that one shares with others from myriad localities, but his or her respective commitments and issues are largely distinct from theirs. Jupiter Hammon did not regard the religious and social networks in and around New York City that he wrote for part of the same public of Wheatley's in Boston. Without the infrastructure to foster modes of identification and structures of affinity across regions, these were essentially local writers who knew themselves as "American" only insofar as the term was a proxy for a community (and at its most extreme, a city) that adopted facets of American nationalist ideology.

The exemplary text of this stance is Richard Allen and Absalom Jones's *A Narrative of the Proceedings of the Black People, during the Late Awful Calamity in Philadelphia, in the Year 1793: And a Refutation of Some Censures, Thrown upon Them in Some Late Publications* (1794), perhaps the first Black-authored texts to obtain federal copyright. Former enslaved persons who purchased their own and family members' freedom and went on to become Founding Fathers of African American religio-institutional life, Allen and Jones wrote *A Narrative* to debunk claims of Blacks' criminality, ineptitude, and cruel disregard for human life during the yellow fever epidemic that devastated Philadelphia in 1793. Their primary target was Mathew Carey's aspersions in his pamphlet

A Short Account of the Malignant Fever, Lately Prevalent in Philadelphia: With a Statement of the Proceedings That Took Place on the Subject in Different Parts of the United States (1793), a popular compendium that went through several editions within its first two years in print. The evidence of Black ministrations Allen and Jones provide refute Carey's portrayal of the Black community as rife with profiteers and thieves. Not only did African Americans brave contagion to nurse the sick and bury the dead in greater proportional numbers than their White counterparts did, but they made tremendous financial sacrifices for which they were still waiting indemnification. Following embedded numerical calculations Allen and Jones conclude, "We do assure the public, that all the money we have received . . . has not defrayed the expense of wages which we had to pay to those whom we employed to assist us." Furthermore, *A Narrative* describes the tremendous human cost of Blacks' service, which certainly would have astonished many of their White readers who believed, following contemporary scientific opinion, that Black persons were largely immune to "this terrible malady"; rather, "the bill of mortality for the year 1793 . . . will convince any reasonable man that will examine it, that as many coloured people died in proportion as others" who came into contact with the disease. That Allen, Jones, and African Americans stayed to help their city and fellow Philadelphians, White and Black, was their most cutting rebuke of Carey because, as they made sure to note, "Mr. Carey . . . quickly after his election [to help lead relief efforts], left them to struggle with their arduous and hazardous task, by leaving the city." Although Allen and Jones rarely launch sallies as direct as this one, the overarching aim of *A Narrative* was to settle scores (and accounts) that concern Black Philadelphians qua Philadelphians. The forms of civic engagement, sacrifice, and selflessness they detail constitute a definitively local republicanism. The "Americans" their testimony signifies is composed of the personages and political economy of Philadelphia and its environs.

Rhetoric: "But Let Us Promote Ourselves"

Allen and Jones conclude the *Narrative* with a series of addresses to three distinct constituencies: slave owners and their apologists; free and enslaved Black persons; and White abolitionists. Taken collectively, the coda diverges in both substance and style from the rest of the text: not only does it rely on oratorical techniques and heuristics to make its appeals, but the audience for those appeals extends far beyond Philadelphia. "An Address to Those Who Keep Slaves, and Approve the Practice," for example, calls on its addressees to imagine themselves as modern-day Pharaohs who incense God by enslaving

Africans, modern-day Israelites. The use of Exodus to portray modern slavery was ubiquitous in African American cultural production before the twentieth century, most notably in the spiritual "Go Down, Moses." Allen and Jones, who invoke the biblical story in all three sections of the coda, use Exodus to project a *general* condition of Black life in the United States that African Americans over the next few decades came to understand as one they shared regardless of locality or region: the institution of slavery left the enslaved vulnerable to the whims of their owners, regardless of how depraved or barbaric, while free Blacks endured a complex of civic disenfranchisement, economic privation, race-based exclusion, and fundamental degradation. That Allen and Jones's *Narrative* signals the provenance of this collective consciousness is no mere coincidence: they were at the center of the very sort of institution building that made its formation possible.

Allen and Jones were founders of the Free African Society in Philadelphia, a mutual aid association dedicated to the betterment of Black persons and their communities. Such organizations sprouted up in the late eighteenth and early nineteenth centuries across the north as well as in parts of the south and the west. Corresponding to, and sometimes directly out of, the voluntary association movement all-Black churches emerged; in some cases, they banded together with other congregations, refused White ecclesiastical authority, and formed independent and incorporated denominations such as the African Methodist Episcopal Church, for which Allen served as the first bishop. Black-led institutions offered fellowship, respite, and the capacity to commune interpersonally and imaginatively with others in allied associations across the country. The formation of print culture networks, which circulated everything from devotional materials like hymnals and sermons to poetry and reports on the affairs of the day, was vital to the establishment of these ties. Print enabled African Americans, especially cultural and economic elites, to develop the corporate national identity that we would now call "Blackness." They homed in on structures of political and social simultaneity, that is, their existing at the same time and enduring the same existential conditions, however dispersed geographically. It was an understanding of the collective of Black persons grounded in blanket, race-based forms of oppression and consequent aspirations for their people, not any sort of organic or essential racialism.

The literary-textual culmination of their efforts was the establishment of the African American press, which began with *Freedom's Journal* in 1827. *Freedom's Journal* and a great many antebellum Black-controlled newspapers enjoyed national and international circulation. Within its pages, readers found accounts, commentary, and debate concerning such major issues as abolitionism, the colonization movement, and struggles for full citizenship. These newspapers also hosted *intraracial* discussions, forums such as advice columns and letters to the editor that allowed Black contributors and readers to engage each other on topics and in terms the broader society did not dictate. If Black newspapers aimed "to plead our cause [because for] too long have others spoken for us," as the editors of *Freedom's Journal* famously declare in their introductory column, then a crucial audience of their enterprise were African Americans themselves.

The ways in which these newspapers attuned themselves to the production and circulation of intraracial dialogues instantiated how Black writings in this phase calibrated their rhetorical appeals to account for differently racialized readers with varying responsibilities. Even the most fervently antislavery works that demand full citizenship for African Americans usually direct part of their focus to Black communities, calling on their denizens to take on particular behaviors, collective habits, and political stances. The most notable text in this corpus is David Walker's *Appeal in Four Articles; Together with a Preamble, to the Coloured Citizens of the World, but in Particular, and Very Expressly, to Those of the United States of America*. Walker, who served as a distribution agent and writer for *Freedom's Journal*, rebuked his "brethren" for "*glorying* and being *happy* in such low employments [as bootblack]; for if we are men, we ought to be . . . looking forward with thankful hearts to higher attainments than *wielding the razor* and *cleaning boots and shoes*." Although these sorts of exhortations might reflect bourgeois condescension toward the poor and working classes, they were only one strand of a discursive Black public sphere that embraced voices from all segments of the community it served.

Consider the work of Walker's mentee, Maria Stewart. Stewart was born free in Hartford, Connecticut, in 1803, became an orphan at age five, then was raised by a minister's family for the next decade. She later married the shipping agent and outfitter James W. Stewart, who was also a veteran of the War of 1812. The Stewarts were part of Boston's tiny, close-knit Black middle class that also included Walker. When Walker published the first edition of his *Appeal* in September 1829, he may have used James Stewart's shipping business and contacts to smuggle the text southward. With her husband's death in late 1829 and Walker's death the following year, Stewart underwent a profound conversion experience and pledged her life's work to African Americans' spiritual growth and social improvement. In 1831 and moved by this call to service, she visited the offices of the newly established radical abolitionist newspaper the *Liberator* and submitted to its editor William Lloyd Garrison a manuscript containing religious meditations and political essays. Garrison was so impressed with Stewart's writings that he "not only gave [her] words of encouragement," as he put it, but in his "printing office put [the] manuscript into type, an edition of which was struck off in tract form, subject to [Stewart's] order." Garrison made a sizable portion of the manuscript available to readers of the *Liberator* because he published one of its essays, "Religion and the Pure Principles of Morality, the Sure Foundation on Which We Must Build," in the October 8 issue of that year.

Like all of Stewart's essays, "Religion and the Pure Principles of Morality" extols virtues such as ambition, comity, integrity, and reliability that comport with the behavioral norms that (White) middle-class paradigms deemed respectable. Yet Stewart aimed to prove those resources were not anathema to Black persons, as dominant notions of African-descended personhood maintained. Her unswerving confidence in Black achievement often led her to bracket the effects of slavery and race-based disenfranchisement, at times problematically so, but this rhetorical framing worked to persuade African Americans that their potential for excellence and virtue was equal to that of their White counterparts. In "Religion and the Pure Principles of Morality," she recognized there were but "few to promote [African Americans'] cause, none to encourage their talents," yet maintained they should "not let [their] hearts be any longer discouraged; it is no use to murmur nor to repine; but let us promote ourselves and improve our talents. . . . But 'I can't,' is a great barrier in the way. I hope it will soon be removed, and 'I will,' resume its place." However fanciful this notion might seem, antebellum African Americans, from the elite to everyday persons, advocated such a posture because they believed it was the most direct way to better their lives and, as a result, foster the conditions that would make substantive structural changes in the American polity possible.

To be sure, Stewart severely criticized those extracommunal forces that inhibited African Americans' ambitions, but she was even more relentless in her insistence there were actions Black households and communities refused to perform that would drastically improve their material conditions and elevate their standing in the broader polity. She told African American mothers it was their task to "create in the minds of [their] little girls and boys a thirst for knowledge, the love of virtue, the abhorrence of vice and the cultivation of a pure heart." To ensure the continued development of Black children beyond "good housewifery" in the home, Stewart called on them to raise money for their communal schools. "Let every female heart become united, and let us raise a fund ourselves," she implored the Black women of Boston, "and at the end of one year and a half, we might be able to lay the corner stone for the building of a High School, that the higher branches of knowledge might be enjoyed by us." The Black-established school is one of the institutional pillars of Stewart's conception of the most excellent Black community; the other is Black-owned and -operated businesses. She writes, "Unite and build a store of your own. . . . Fill one side with dry goods, and the other with groceries. Do you ask where is the money? We have spent more than enough for nonsense, to do what building we want." Not only would these businesses provide the foundation for Black economic prosperity, they would also provide African Americans dignified, self-affirming employment, which Stewart argued was virtually impossible in contemporaneous labor markets. She urged her readers to "look at our young men, smart, active, and energetic, with souls filled with ambitious fire. . . . They can be nothing but the humblest laborers, on account of their dark complexion; hence many of them lose their ambition, and become worthless." Young Black women were even more vulnerable to the negative consequences of "continual drudgery and toil," Stewart argued, because the best they could ask for were "lives as house-domestics, washing windows, shaking carpets, brushing boots, or tending upon gentlemen's tables"; unlike their "fairer sisters, whose hands are never soiled, whose nerves and muscles are never strained," young Black women never had occasion "to improve [their] mental and moral faculties." Rather than wait for White Americans to welcome their Black counterparts into all segments of the workforce, which seemed far off in Jacksonian America, Stewart enjoined Black communities to create work opportunities that would propel their members to "rise above the condition of servants and drudges."

These sorts of cultural and social entreaties became a dominant topos in African American literary culture from the early 1830s through the Civil War. African Americans engaged literatures of self-determination and its role in the production of common good with more regularity than the much-better-known-and-theorized slave narratives that overshadow other forms of Black literary production in the era. They came across such writing in a variety of formats, from newspapers and books to treatises and pamphlets, and in a variety of forms, from poetry and narrative to history and homily. Advancements in technology and transportation as well as a broader culture of reprinting made the dissemination of texts easier and more affordable for a relatively impoverished population; so, too, did the boom in the number of library companies and literary societies that African Americans formed and joined. Although these institutions often prioritized literature of national or international distinction, they also served as hubs for members to write and read each other's writings. Lyric poetry, religious devotions, and encomiums to historical figures were among the most popular forms they authored and circulated among themselves for peer criticism. The societies also encouraged members to write essays on political and social issues that concerned the condition of free and enslaved Black persons. One of the most pressing and recurring issues they and African American writers in general took up was voluntary emigration from the United States.

From the founding of the American Colonization Society (ACS) in 1816, when the project of collective Black resettlement first achieved institutional force, antebellum African Americans almost universally rejected schemes that would move them to colonies or nations in West Africa, Haiti, or elsewhere. Their refusal turned on two interrelated calculations: one, the ultimate objective of the ACS was to rid the nation of *all* free Black persons, which would only entrench slavery; and two, the United States was theirs by birthright and by labor, for it was their toil and blood that had built the country into an economic and geopolitical power. These judgements held for the next several decades, but the increasing social and political exclusion African Americans endured during that time—most notably, the abrogation of the franchise from nearly all Black men by amendments to state constitutions in the 1820s and 1830s as well as the repercussions of the Fugitive Slave Law of 1850—convinced more African Americans than ever before that they would never achieve full citizenship, let alone be welcome as equal participants and beneficiaries in the nation. "The color of the blacks is a badge of degradation," the intellectual and novelist Martin R. Delaney proclaimed in 1854, "acknowledged by statute, organic law, and the common consent of the people. . . . We propose for this disease a remedy. That remedy is Emigration. This Emigration should be well advised, and like all remedies, to remove the disease from the physical system of man, skillfully and carefully applied, within the proper time, directed to operate on that part of the system whose greatest tendency shall be, to benefit the whole." Delaney's epidemiological metaphor signified the increasingly widespread belief that virulent racism is endemic to the United States; the autobiographical allusion it contains, which many of his readers would have recognized, made its impact even more forceful: Delaney trained in medicine and was accepted into Harvard Medical School in 1850, only to be kicked out along with two other students a month into their studies because they were Black.

Delaney argued the Canadas could provide "temporary relief, especially to the fleeing fugitive," but was ultimately untenable for permanent resettlement because the Canadas are "destined to come into the United States." Instead, the "West Indies, Central and South America are the countries of our choice" because "among the earliest and most numerous class who found their way to the new world, were those [of] the African race." Since they descended from the same racial line or "stock," to use the language of mid-nineteenth-century race science as Delaney would, African Americans and the populations of the West Indies and Central and South America would be able to integrate with little difficulty, notwithstanding their significant cultural, linguistic, and temperamental differences. Delaney's racialist emigrationism was foundational to the development of racially separatist, Black nationalist ideologies that became far more determinative in African Americans' literary practice (and social movements) later in the century and over the first two decades of the twentieth. Although scholars rightly situate Delaney's iconoclasms as forerunners of strands of Black radical thought, it would be a mistake to let his stature obscure other significant contemporaneous advocate-theorists of voluntary emigrationism.

One of these figures is Mary Ann Shadd (Cary), who was the chief proponent of Black resettlement in Canada in the early 1850s and, in this regard at least, Delany's rival. Raised in a household that supported and perhaps served as a stop on the Underground Railroad, Shadd moved to Canada West (now Ontario) in 1851 to get beyond the reach of American slavocracy. There, she joined a budding a community of free Blacks and fugitive slaves and started and edited the *Provincial Freeman*, which was the official newspaper of the Provincial Union, an antislavery benevolent organization. Shortly before starting the *Provincial Freeman*, which ran from 1853 to 1857, Shadd published *A Plea for Emigration; or, Notes of Canada West, in Its Moral, Social, and Political Aspect: With Suggestions Respecting Mexico, West Indies, and Vancouver's Island, for the Information of Colored Emigrants* (1852). The organization of Shadd's pamphlet—a set of "notes" on all manner of subjects ranging from climate and topography to political economy, law, and socioreligious institutions—evokes Thomas Jefferson's *Notes on the State of Virginia* (1785), as many of her readers would have noticed. Black critics regularly designated Jefferson's *Notes* as the greatest literary hindrance to abolitionism and full Black citizenship. A good deal of early African American writing responds directly to Jefferson's charges of Black constitutional deficiencies, the most noteworthy example being David Walker's *Appeal*; other texts, like Shadd's *Notes*, are subtler in their retorts. Besides its structure, *Notes* recalls Jeffersonian racialism in its "Introductory Remarks" when outlining African Americans' plight in the United States: "The [Black] people are in a straight—on the one hand, a pro-slavery administration, with its entire controllable force, is bearing upon them with fatal effect: on the other, the Colonization Society, in the garb of *Christianity* and *Philanthropy*, is seconding the effects of the first named power, by bringing into the lists a vast social and immoral influence, thus making more effective the agencies employed." Just as Jefferson's *Notes* influenced the form and content of her *Notes*, the ideas and institutions he espoused continued to shape the American polity—Jefferson owned, traded, and sold hundreds of slaves, and he was proponent of colonizing free(d) Black persons. Her most scathing takedown of Jeffersonianism was her plea for Black emigration to a British territory. Unlike "Africa, Mexico, or South America," western Canada lacked "hostile tribes to annoy the settler, or destroy at will towns and villages with their inhabitants: the strong arm of British power would summarily punish depredations made, of whatever character, and the emigrants would naturally assume the responsibility of British freeman." The nation Jefferson projects in the Declaration of Independence failed to materialize, Shadd suggests, and the brief course of the history of the United States had revealed a "British jurisdiction" was the setting that promised life, liberty, and the pursuit of happiness to the most persecuted and exploited.

Belletrism: "I Presume When We Blacks Get a Literature . . ."

Jeffersonian America was not Shadd's only target. However indirectly, her *Notes* also repudiates those who called for Black self-determination and uplift such as Walker and Stewart as well as the abolitionists and moral reformers who made interracial appeals in a variety of literary forms, most notably the slave narratives. In fine, emigrationist writers believed these constituencies were wasting their time and talent. The ideological wrangles, reform movements, and political programs that define this phase of early African American writing all, in one way or another, respond to some version of the question "What shall be done with Negroes?" For some contemporaneous critics and observers, however, this emphasis on racial problem solving and the sort of textual formats African Americans writers frequently used to carry out this work (e.g., newspapers, pamphlets) retarded the development of an African American *literature*, a collection of written works that not only warrants distinction for its aesthetic excellence but also for its distinctive expression of Black racial self-consciousness. African American writers had yet to develop enough of this *mentalité*, the argument held, because they were too responsive to larger social issues and thus always someway sympathetic to White benefactors, detractors, and their respective tastes.

One of the most forthright and thorough commentaries to that effect is an 1853 essay in *Frederick Douglass' Paper* (*FDP*) by a correspondent writing under the penname Dion. Dion opened his text with an acknowledgment of the renown White historians, novelists, and poets had achieved over the previous few decades—this was the period scholars call the American Renaissance— but "deeply regretted" that "colored American literature exists only, to too great an extent, in the vast realm of probability." Dion adduced the work of enslaved and free Black poets as well as abolitionist orators to buttress his "hopes of the coming literary glory of colored Americans," but, notably, he does not include the slave narrative among his evidence. This absence is all the more conspicuous because, by the time of Dion's writing, several of the most popular slave narratives had already captivated readers on both sides of the Atlantic, including those of William Wells Brown (1847), Josiah Henson (1849), Sojourner Truth (1850), and Frederick Douglass (1845), who, after all, published Dion's essay in his newspaper. For Dion and like-minded critics, the genre of the slave narrative was too beholden to the formal demands of abolitionist editors and the narrative expectations of northern White readers. He also singled out the practice of writing in "the narrow limits of pamphlets or the columns of newspapers" as a hindrance to the production of a literature because these "ephemeral caskets . . . entail the destruction of the gems which they contain." What Dion calls for, in sum, is the production of Black belles lettres in large-scale formats like the novel that was about, for, and by African Americans and conceptualized as such.

Ironically enough, Black belletrism first sprouted in the very "ephemeral casket" that printed Dion's essay: *FDP*. (The first African American–authored novel, *Clotel; or, The President's Daughter* [1853], was published only a few weeks after Dion's essay, but William Wells Brown wrote *Clotel* primarily for White British readers and is hardly belletristic in intent or effect.) Douglass established *FDP* in 1851 as the successor to his *North Star* and a marker of his embrace of political abolitionism. The four-page periodical most often reserved its first three pages for news, commentary, and editorials, and its last page for advertisements and literary material ranging from poetry and critical essays to serialized fiction and reprinted work from American and British authors. That Douglass dedicated nearly a quarter of the cash-strapped *FDP* for literary matters demonstrates the aspiration to foster a Black readership in two senses. It would, first, become the foundation for the sort of African American literary enterprise that Dion envisioned and, second, help create the sort of racial self-consciousness necessary for writers and readers to regard themselves as producers of a distinctive literature.

No writer in *FDP*'s roster was more instrumental in this effort than James McCune Smith. Multilingual, radical abolitionist, and the first professional African American physician, McCune Smith remains best known for his introduction to Douglass's second autobiography, *My Bondage and My Freedom* (1855). McCune Smith's critical and literary output extends well beyond this piece, however. From 1837 to 1838, the *Colored American* newspaper published extracts from the journal that he kept while studying in and traveling throughout Europe earlier in the decade; in 1844, he wrote an important statistics-based essay challenging figures and findings of the 1840 US Census that suggested slaves' mental and physical constitutions were healthier than those of free African Americans. But it was the character sketches, chronicles of urban life, and cultural criticism that McCune Smith wrote as the New York correspondent for *FDP* that positioned him in the vanguard of the Black literary scene of the 1850s, the most prodigious and excellent decade of African American writing before the New Negro Renaissance of the 1920s and early 1930s. Consider his review of Elizabeth Greenfield's March 1855 concert at the Broadway Tabernacle in New York City. He insisted Greenfield, who was known as the "Black Swan" because her singing rivaled that of the internationally renowned "Swedish Nightingale" Jenny Lind, was the embodiment of a Black splendor and majesty that refuted the popular notion that Black persons are inherently and inescapably barbaric and doltish; she was a cultural producer African Americans should claim as one of their own, living evidence they possessed gifts worth contributing to world culture. But McCune Smith does not make any of these claims plainly. Rather, he elevates the diction, protracts the sentence, and strives for a kind of philosophical posture that might match the aesthetic majesty and politico-cultural heft of Greenfield's performance. He writes, "Having selected as her aim the divinest of Arts that are the richest endowments of nature and the most prolonged and arduous culture, it was but a light thing for her to meet Prejudice face to face and crush it." Here and throughout the essay, McCune Smith's writing works to activate in the reader some affective aspect of its subject *and* exceed that subject by deliberately calling attention to itself *as writing*: his review is both performative and an act of performance.

Such interactions between performativity and performance structure McCune Smith's writing practice—a practice that his readers and editor, Frederick Douglass, often described as too arcane, abstruse, and prolix. To be sure, McCune Smith's prose is not facile or readily intelligible, but the formal, syntactical, and linguistic experimentation that alienated his antebellum audience was McCune Smith's attempt to model a new way of writing slave and free Black life that diverges from the modal conventions of contemporaneous genres of Black writing, especially political disquisitions, religious meditations, reform tracts, and the slave narrative. Despite the quirks and innovations he brought to bear on the essay form, the cultural and sociological concerns that riveted McCune Smith were firmly in the mainstream of mid-nineteenth-century (African) American thought. This seeming tension reflected the ways in which McCune Smith sought to inspire acts of forgetting and acts of remembrance: forgetting the static, shallow subjectivities that emerged from prevailing literary genres and modalities, but remembering the imaginative, gritty, and vexed resources that sustained Black persons struggling within and against slavery's ramifications. The conceptual synchrony at play here worked to engender the readerly enlightenment and pleasure that McCune Smith and his cohort wanted for his (Black) readers.

The notion of *play* was foundational to the project of early Black belletrism, and no essay better elucidates its dynamics than McCune Smith's "The Critic at Chess" (1855). "The Critic at Chess" retells an afternoon meeting between McCune Smith and newspaper editor and abolitionist Philip Bell. In a sumptuous drawing room in Donadi's on Broadway and over coffee, the two men engage in a spirited conversation about Alfred, Lord Tennyson's "Charge of the Light Brigade" (1854), the poem's originality (or lack thereof), and its relative metrical and philological merits. Bell introduces the subject, expressing his admiration for the prosody of Tennyson's poem, especially the famous refrain "Cannon to the right of them, / Cannon to the left of them, / Cannon in front of them / Volleyed and thundered"; to this McCune Smith responds, "Flat Burglary!" McCune Smith explains that the metrics, rhyme scheme, and rhythm that give Tennyson's poem its distinctive movement and musicality come from a Congolese chant that slaves incanted to steel themselves during the Haitian Revolution. Bell goes on to imagine a scenario in which the chant inspires six million slaves "away down in the sunny [US] South" to mount an insurrection and "send the affrighted slave owners . . . [to] rush away North faster than they did from St. Domingo." McCune Smith calms down the heated Bell, and they begin a game of chess and ultimately alter Tennyson's poem to mock fellow abolitionists.

Several scholars have considered how McCune Smith breaks down and exposes the fallacies of racial hierarchies in this and other essays. But what most interests me are the formal mechanics of the "The Critic at Chess," specifically its dramaturgical structure, which intimates the sort of literary daring and virtuosity necessary to the production of an African American literature of the sort Dion and other members of the Black intelligentsia envisioned. The piece reads as a sort of closet drama, with marked dialogue, dramatis personae, and directions that outline entrances, exits, and other sorts of stage business. McCune Smith plays Communipaw, and Bell plays Fylbel. Of course, McCune Smith and Bell *are* Communipaw and Fylbel, respectively, since these are the pseudonyms each man published and appeared under in *FDP*. McCune Smith wanted to foreground the theatrical aspect of this particular meeting and, crucially, his writing of it. He establishes the mise-en-scène and the relationship between it, him, and Bell at the beginning of essay. Then, Bell speaks for the first time, quoting the first two lines of "The Charge of the Light Brigade." He concludes, "Isn't that fine, Doc—Communipaw, I mean?" At this point, it is clear "The Critic at Chess" is a performance text because the typography of a conventional script comes into focus. In this way, McCune Smith attempts to orient how one approaches the text and, more importantly, evaluate the performances therein. That is, he does not want us to read for documentary or realist effects; rather, he encourages us to appreciate the essay's aesthetic distinctions: namely, the intellectual virtuosity of Communipaw (the character) and the belletristic excellence of McCune Smith (the writer).

Communipaw's dazzling erudition and the essay's writerly merits contribute to the broader performance the essay stages: McCune Smith's *sprezzatura*. In his 1528 *The Book of the Courtier*, Italian Renaissance thinker Baldassare Castiglione defined sprezzatura as a "certain nonchalance" the courtier must perform, an act "that shall conceal design and show that what is done and said is done without effort and almost without thought." Castiglione believed sprezzatura brought "grace," "charm," and therefore favor to the courtier. Scholars credit Philip Sidney for establishing the importance of sprezzatura within English poetics and social mores, and the practice reemerged in the Victorian era as a personal virtue. The University of Glasgow–educated McCune Smith was well aware of the cultural capital that sprezzatura accrued, and positioning himself as an arbiter and conduit of high Victorianism was both a political strategy and an expression of individual exuberance. This posture instantiated McCune Smith's distinct contributions to the culture of Anglophilia that permeated Black public culture in the 1840s and 1850s. "The Critic at Chess" frames his literary-historical analysis of Tennyson's "The Charge of the Light Brigade," but in Communipaw's reclamation of a Congolese chant as source material for the poem's prosody, the essay suggests that the brand of Anglophilia McCune Smith and similar-minded African Americans fashioned was not an ingratiation to White sociopolitical elites and their lifestyles. Rather, early Black belletrist writers understood English cultural achievements as one of many sets of conceptual and symbolic matrices to take up publicly, and for the collective benefit and intellectual betterment of their own readers.

Put differently, the strands of Anglophilia in McCune Smith's writings mark his attempt to give rise to forms of Black personhood and literary subjectivity that were absent from contemporaneous print culture. He did not simply depict these new men and women in his texts; more importantly, he hoped they would emerge from *reading* such texts. He imagined "The Critic at Chess" would engender for its (Black) reader the same feelings of heady excitement that Communipaw and Fylbel experienced, thus prompting the reader to accept ludic and unfamiliar ways of thinking and doing Black life. That he was one of the two most educated African Americans in the period did not dissuade him from believing that all persons, including slaves, were capable of the cultural poise and intellectual aplomb he and his cohort exemplified—and he had direct evidence to prove his point: namely, James McCune Smith, who was born enslaved and lived as such for the first fourteen years of his life. McCune Smith and other Black belletristic writers of the 1850s insisted on narratives of African American life that were deeply at odds with those that circulated in the antebellum public sphere. Made possible by the pioneering testimonies and rhetorical interventions of earlier enslaved and free Black writers, the project of a discernably African American literature Black belletrists craved and initiated in the 1850s signaled the advent of a racial self-consciousness that set new aims and possibilities for African-descended writers in the United States.

Further Reading

Brooks, Joanna. *American Lazarus*, 2003.

Clytus, Radiclani. "Visualizing in Black Print: The Brooklyn Correspondence of William J. Wilson aka 'Ethiop,'" *J19: The Journal of Nineteenth-Century Americanists* 6, no. 1 (2018): 29–66.

Cohen, Lara Langer, and Jordan Stein, eds. *Early African American Print Culture*, 2012.

Ernest, John. *Liberation Historiography*, 2004.

Jones, Douglas A. "Slave Evangelicalism, Shouting, and the Beginning of African American Writing," *Early American Literature* 53, no. 1 (2018): 69–95.

McHenry, Elizabeth. *Forgotten Readers*, 2002.

Peterson, Carla. *Doers of the Word*, 1995.

Rael, Patrick. *Black Identity and Black Protest in the Antebellum North*, 2002.

Smith Foster, Frances. "Genealogies of Our Concerns, Early (African) American Print Culture, and Transcending Tough Times," *Early American Literature* 45, no. 2 (2010): 347–59.

Warren, Kenneth. *What Was African American Literature*, 2011.

World Literature

JANE O. NEWMAN

How does world literature begin? That is the question. But it is not a simple one. Indeed, before we can even begin to answer it, we must understand how this question's key terms have conventionally been used and consider deploying them in new ways.

Helgesson and Vermeulen state that "World Literature" is a "polysemic term."[1] So is "beginning." In the spirit of this volume, I address "beginning" first.

The word "begin" has its roots in Old English and Old High German *beginnan*, "to attempt, undertake." So understood, it suggests intentional agency. Indeed, one of the term's traditional meanings is, as Edward Said famously asserts in his book about "beginnings," "something one does."[2] From here, he quite logically continues that "beginnings" are never "ideal types" (4), but, rather, contingent, human, and historical (only "origins are divine," xiii, Said explains). Yet precisely in this historicity, beginnings are also more than just individual acts. Indeed, in their very inaugural character, they are also always "something one thinks about" (xi), a "problem to be studied" (13) in terms of what came before and what ensues. The subtitle of Said's book—*Intention and Method*—points to this second sense of "beginning" as a method (from Greek: *metá + 'odós*, a "way through"), a way of classifying a "beginning" as a "beginning" "after the fact" (29). This second kind of intentional act involves thinking about how to think about something as a "beginning."

World literature can likewise be thought of in dual fashion. That is, even if, as Helgesson and Vermeulen point out, there have been "multiple ways in which world literature" has been said to "come" "to be" (1), and in full recognition that the term's "meaning and substance . . . differ, sometimes sharply, depending on who is using it" (2), David Damrosch can accurately describe the two most common deployments over the "two decades" of its most recent ascendancy (ca. 2000 to 2020) in ways that echo Said. Damrosch writes that world literature is, on the one hand, a "body of primary texts," and, on the other, a "field of study."[3] It is thus both a set of contingent, historical works and the mostly academic theorization of how to talk about them. Interestingly, when understood in the first instance as a list of "representative texts,"[4] "world literature" has as often been used (even by non-Western scholars; see Damrosch 2020, 280–85) as a "code word" for a canon of "Western" "masterpiece" or "milestone" texts (Damrosch 2020, 293, citing Dieter Lamping) as it has been assumed to refer to representative "regional" authors (Damrosch 2020, 286) and to the very many traditions and "different world[s] of literature" of non-Western, non-Anglophone "world literature" (Mani 2017, 236) whose heterogenous, so-called peripheral worlds of origin are located beyond an allegedly homogenized cosmopolitan "core." In both cases, this first way of talking about world literature assumes that it is what we might want to call global writing, past and present, whether (varying Rebecca Walkowitz) these texts are *born worldly* and intended by their authors for a broader world (or in any case nonlocal) market, or as they circulate widely beyond their origins as material objects (and as multiple versions thereof in translation) across multiple platforms after they leave their authors' hands.[5] Both neo-Latin humanist texts during the Renaissance[6] and what Walkowitz calls the "born-digital works" of the twenty-first century that, "self-published and irregularly updated," "appear in multiple languages and multiple versions of language at the same time" (2015, 131), would be relevant examples here.

In the second instance, however, when world literature—like Said's "beginnings"—is defined as a "problem" rather than as a set of texts, it becomes an object of reflection on the conditions whereby some selection of these texts has come to be designated by the term.[7] Here, world literature always already is and continues to be "made, not found" (Helgesson and Vermeulen 2015, 1) as the result of debates among multiple theorists and critics from Goethe, Gervinus, Posnett, and Meltzl to Apter, Casanova, Damrosch, and Mufti.[8] In this case, world literature "begins" when it is "institutionalized" (from Latin: *in + statuo*, set up, establish) as a Saidian "problem to be studied" in the countless anthologies, companions, and sourcebooks published by Norton, Princeton, Routledge, and Wiley, for example, that, complementing earlier volumes, began appearing at breakneck speed in the late twentieth and early twenty-first centuries when schools, colleges, and universities (mostly in the Anglophone world) moved into a more global curricular moment. This version of world literature refers to the discipline that comments on and theorizes the criteria of inclusion and exclusion used to decide what counts as such rather than to any subset of individual works, in other words. Principles of selection and strategies of embrace are the central objects of discussion.

It would be a daunting task (and exceed the limits of the current volume) to provide an inventory of all the texts across history and linguistic traditions that world literature in the first sense comprises in order to track in a judicious and inclusive way which generation of such texts was the first or when and where and how each began and circulated. Walkowitz argues that there have been world literary novels since *Don Quixote* and *Pilgrim's Progress*, for example. Initially their "circulation" was relatively "slow" and "regional." But in the early twenty-first century, the number of texts expressly written for a global market and the speed with which they are translated and distributed are "historically unprecedented" (2015, 20–22), which means that even she can deal only with representative examples—and this in only one genre. Likewise, countless models of ways to address the "problem" of world literature and when it began have been proposed; which of these can be claimed to have come first has been the subject of much research and sometimes contentious debate. In light of the sheer plethora of texts and approaches that both of these versions of world literature contain, mere itemization cannot adequately account for how they begin in either of the two senses of the term indicated above in any way than goes beyond mere inventorying, which while claiming to be objective, would necessarily position itself as some form of polemic.

Given the impasse with which the two ways most often used to discuss the beginnings of world literature present, it might seem counterintuitive to propose understanding how world literature begins anew by reaching back to the work of a scholar often dubbed as one of the founding "fathers" of debates about the term, namely, Erich Auerbach (1892–1957), in his frequently cited "The Philology of World Literature" (1952). There, Auerbach argues that world literature might more properly be understood less as an inventory of texts and more as a way of thinking about how to read them. However, even as he uses more or less Saidian categories to distinguish between the two kinds of world literature noted above, Auerbach is resolute about respecting both the individuality of all texts and the heterogeneity of the canon as he develops a method that yokes them together.[9] He argues that world literature begins each and every time any reader engages with any given text by means of what he elsewhere calls a "hermeneutic," or "understanding," "philology" (a "verstehende Philologie").[10]

What does this mean? It means that the project of world literature begins anew each and every time the "understanding" historical tradition, period, or reader uses philology to grasp the meaning of the individual "understood" textual document of *another* historical tradition, period, or people, and, in so doing, allows the reader to discern in the text the representation of the "world" of the "human condition" that all humanity shares. When the philology of world literature is understood to begin in this way, it aligns with the role that philology plays in the work of the maverick eighteenth-century Italian scholar Giambattista Vico (1668–1774), about whom Auerbach wrote his entire life.

Referring to a single mid-twentieth-century theorist of world literature, namely, Auerbach, as a master theoretician of a new way of understanding how world literature writ large begins of course risks falling into the trap about which Djelal Kadir warns us if we treat a single scholar as a prosopopoeia personifying a field.[11] Understanding Auerbach's way of thinking with Vico about how and where world literature begins nevertheless allows us to go beyond the practices of either dueling inventory taking or cunning methodological invention, indeed, beyond thinking of world literature either as a kind of literary Tower of Babel beset by a disorderly confusion of linguistically disparate texts or as an act of corralling all the literatures of the world together by means of some only notionally universal approach. That Auerbach himself famously claims in his essay "The Philology of World Literature" that the key to developing a successful philology of world literature is to find a good "place to begin" (*Ansatzpunkt*) suggests the suitability of his model for our purposes here. In what follows, I sketch in more detail the challenges that the term "world" has presented in debates about both the texts that might count as world literature and academic discussions of the field before turning to Auerbach's reading of Vico.

Where Is the World of World Literature?

In his *What Is a World? On Post-colonial Literature as World Literature* (2016), Pheng Cheah emphasizes what he perceives as the shortcomings of most "recent theories of world literature" when they are descriptive and place "literary texts" "in a reactive position" whence they can do no more than "map flows of literary exchange across national boundaries and through global circuits." The critique is relevant for both of the ways world literature has most often been defined, as discussed above. With his "normative" (i.e., nonlocal) definition of "worlding" that goes beyond this cartographically based principle, Cheah proposes that literature can "exert" "force" in the world rather than being merely produced by or reflective of it.[12] His challenge has a formidable tradition of definitions of the "world" in world literature to take on. It is a tradition that many scholars assume began with Johann Wolfgang von Goethe (1749–1832) in 1827 when he famously remarked to Johann Peter Eckermann (1792–1854) that "the epoch of world literature (*Weltliteratur*) was at hand." The claim was followed not too many years on by Karl Marx (1810–83) and Friedrich Engels's (1820–95) equally famous assertion that in the place of the "old wants," or desires, of nations for only their own literary heritages and national traditions of texts, "new wants" had arisen, particularly among the bourgeoisie.[13] In both cases, the emergence of world literature is linked to the timetables of modernization and the circulation of commodities and thus tracks with developments in an extraliterary world. Synchronizing world literature's beginnings with socioeconomic and subsequently also with political and ultimately ideological ones in this way robs literature of the ability to begin or to do any work on its own, as Cheah notes.

Helgesson and Vermeulen helpfully sort through the generations of theorists from Goethe to Damrosch and methods, such as the more recent turn to "translation studies, book history, and the sociology of literature," whose logics are rooted in this kind of extratextual overdetermination of world literature, using categories first developed by Raymond Williams in their grouping of "residual," "dominant," and "emergent" individuals and approaches (Helgesson and Vermeulen 2015, 3–13, here 8). Mani's examination of the specific tradition out of which Goethe in particular arose is more granular and suggests that reducing the debates about world literature to the work of a succession of representative "founders" of spatially or geographically located canons is misleading. For example, Goethe did not occupy the anchor position even in the German tradition; both Christoph Martin Wieland (1733–1813) and August Wilhelm Schlegel (1767–1845) wrote about world literature (albeit in different ways) several decades earlier.

Likewise, methodologies such as Helgesson and Vermeulen's "emergent" "book history" have longer and more complex histories, with (in the German example) "major world literary anthologies," such as Johannes Scheer's *Bildersaal der Weltliteratur* (*Portrait Gallery of World Literature*) (1848) already on the market when Marx and Engels's *Communist Manifesto* appeared (Mani 2017, 23–24). Having set the timetable for when and where collections of world literature and the discussion of the term "first" emerged in Germany on its ear, Mani then goes on to place the very idea of single "beginnings" in question by describing a second beginning a half century later in what was by then the nation-state of Germany during the run-up to World War I.[14] Introductions to and handbooks and histories of "World Literature," explicitly so labeled, began pouring forth from Germany's presses at the time.

The first literary magazine (in Germany) devoted to publishing individual works of "world literature," the weekly *Die Welt-Literatur: Die besten Romane und Novellen aller Zeiten* (*World Literature: The Best Novels and Novellas of All Times*), for example, began a successful publishing run in 1915. While *Die Welt-Literatur* stopped appearing in 1920 after Germany's defeat, it was relaunched in 1923. Soon thereafter, Hermann Hesse published his at-the-time hugely well-known, but now virtually forgotten essay on world literature, "Eine Bibliothek der Weltliteratur" ("A Library of World Literature") (1929), which moved the discussion in a decidedly more internationalist as well as almost existentialist direction that could be read as a response to the malaise of the times. Hesse's boosterism of Farsi, Arabic, Chinese, Sanskrit, and Tibetan literatures seems to have been designed, Mani argues, to indicate how the "basic tenets of human existence find expression through language" in texts from all over the world (2017, 149). How to achieve a common vision of humanity via literature was of course very soon to be understood in more sinister ways, when *Die Welt-Literatur* was absorbed in 1934 into a Nazi-identified publishing program under the same name, suggesting yet a third moment when world literature in Germany began. The journal continued to publish until 1944 (2017, 155).

In tracing the Goethe-to-Goebbels axis, Mani's account of these several beginnings of world literature in the German tradition paints a richer and more nuanced picture than the ones that dominate the less fine-grained narratives about Goethe and other "founders" that are often scrubbed of the complex geographical and historical contexts and conditions out of which they arise. But his dislocation of the temporal narratives about such beginnings does not disturb their geographical and historical overdetermination as he remains within the confines of his chosen example—the intense pressures on the idea of "German identity" over the centuries notwithstanding. Somewhat counterintuitively, even those theorists who critique not only such Eurocentrism, but also the only apparent alternative of a larger cosmopolitanism, meet something of the same challenge. In her well-known *Against World Literature*, for example, Apter would redeem the world literature signified by a single, easily digestible set of texts crafted to suit the tastes of the emerging Anglophone market for world literature anthologies and texts from such "facile globalism" (Apter 2013, 56) by keeping specificity and the original language of each text front and center.

Calls to understand world literature as always already beginning only at the local level are fully justified as a way of resisting the reductionism of both of these formerly hegemonic versions of the world literary tradition by strategically privileging local traditions both of orature and of textuality, indeed, of all the abundant and diverse forms of literary capital that circulate outside of and beyond the Western metropole. But precisely the aptness to world literature debates of the vocabularies of domination and resistance and of periphery and core reminds us of a parallel genealogy of the logic that governs these debates.

Even in geospatially inflected narratives that privilege the local (past and present), that is, participants in the crowded world of world literary civilizations are often described as acceding to their maturity only when they represent the formation of a situated collective's identity or profile—regardless of how peripheral or resistant to that community identity they might actually have wanted to remain in the first place. When an author or text comes to be identified with the ability to claim sovereignty over her or its right to create an identity-forming tradition of texts (also oral ones) in this way, the story relies on a logic akin to what is often referred to as Westphalianism and results in the creation of a mosaic of traditions that, ever insistent on autonomy, remain uncoupled from one another, coexisting in an uneasy proximity, perhaps, but unable to see how together they form a world.[15] Moreover, this system of independent literatures and voices remains beset by the same challenges as the more literal Westphalian system of states to which it is conceptually indebted, since, while literary Westphalianism assumes an ostensibly pluralist system in which each and every sovereign republic of letters, large and small, is allegedly accorded an equal place at the table, a "great power" logic continues to shape the relation among them when it is organized by inequities of size, power, visibility, and prestige, as it so often is. In other words, only some of the world's literatures become "worldly," that is, are recognized, translated, and circulated around the globe. Perhaps worst of all, particularly when one of the more recently and newly empowered writer-participants in the rainbow pluriverse of a world literary canon does arrive on the world scene, he or she runs the risk of being constrained by presses and marketing agencies to succumb to the expectations of "ethnic nominalism," which demands that the individual author represent only a "national[ly] neutral" version of an identifiable common voice.[16] When this happens, global literatures are yoked to a specific location in the same way the "masterpiece" versions of European world literary texts are and reduced to functioning only as figureheads rather than as individual, heterogeneous instances of voice and text.

In the face of the challenges associated with the continuing Westphalianism of these debates, world literature theorists have proposed an array of alternative spatial geometries and timetables that offer an alternative to these kinds of determinisms, from David Damrosch's "ellipses," which would have world literature begin in the act of reading two or more individual and closely read world texts and traditions together, with their terms of engagement involving complex relations of genre, medium, and theme, to Vilashini Cooppan's "ghostly" repetitions and "uncanny" hauntings.[17] Still other models, including Franco Moretti's discussion of world literature as a system of "trees," "branches," and "waves" (2000, 66–67), have proposed altogether differently figured approaches designed to help track the regularities of much grander inclusionary "systems" (2000, 57) of world letters.

Such approaches challenge the notion that the world of world literature is rooted in one moment and place by arguing that it begins in and as an act of dislocation. They also suggest that it begins in reading, a claim suggestive of the very terms with which Erich Auerbach approached the question of world literature in his essay "The Philology of World Literature." Auerbach's Vichean philology of world literature offers a way out of the impasses described here.

The World of Auerbach's Vico as a Place to Begin: A Philology of World Literature

In *Death of a Discipline*, Gayatri Spivak proposes a "planetary" comparative literature as a way of thinking the beginnings of the "world" of world literature in new ways. "Discontinuous" from any one "differentiated political space" and thus nonhegemonic, this "planetarity," as Spivak calls it, is "mysterious" in its ability to transcend hierarchies of ranked difference, yet inclusive of the very differences it oversees.[18] Some fifty years before Spivak, Erich Auerbach had already defined world literature as "planetary" somewhat less mysteriously, writing in "The Philology of World Literature" (1952) that "our philological home" is "no longer the nation," but, rather, "the earth," or "the planet" (*die Erde*) ([1952] 2014, 264).

In this essay and in his posthumously published *Literary Language and Its Public in Late Latin Antiquity and in the Middle Ages* (1958), Auerbach goes on to render this planetariness quite a bit more concrete than Spivak's when he endorses a practice of "radical" historicist "relativism" designed to engage the internal complexity and poetic-aesthetic specificity of any and all particular literary texts, but always within a greater common frame; there, he defines the particular text as a marker of the "absolute essence" of an all-inclusive world literature that can "only be apprehended in its particular historical forms."[19] The subtitle of the "Introduction" of *Literary Language*, "Purpose and Method," uncannily predicts the subtitle of Said's *Beginnings*; with its focus on Vico, the chapter points to the source of the method Auerbach famously wrote that he "learned" from Vico, as he writes in "Vico's Contribution to Literary Criticism" (1958) (10). This method lies at the root of the philology he proposes in "The Philology of World Literature" and gives us access to a different kind of "world," or "Welt," namely the one that Jean-Luc Nancy has called "mondalité," which is the "worldhood," of the "whole of human relations" that all cultures share, each in its unique way.[20]

It is not surprising that the twentieth-century German Jewish Auerbach was interested in literature's capacity to offer a window onto some kind of larger world as well as insight into the entrapment of humanity in the harsh "iron cage" of modernity largely of its own making; he came of age in a Europe torn apart by World War I (studying at one point in Heidelberg and associating with circles around Max Weber) and spent much of his adult life in exile, first in Istanbul, Turkey, and then in the United States.[21] Even though they do not use the term "Westphalianism," numerous readers of Auerbach, including Aamir Mufti, Veli Yashin, and Ben Hutchinson, have underscored Auerbach's sensitivity to the world system of states that they describe as at the foundation of specifically geographically conceived threats to him and to the West that the postwar Cold War and neo-Westphalianizing era of a decolonization represented during the period when the essay was written.[22]

Auerbach does in fact refer at the opening of the essay to the vicissitudes of this located moment as both the political world and the world of literary studies were confronting them at the time. He laments, for example, the race to modernity among the world's nations as a reductive race to the same. Under the pressure of great power "Euro-American" or "Soviet-Bolshevist" alignment, he observes, "standardization" is setting in; "different cultures" have so much "begun to resemble one another" in the present moment of "fateful convergence," with its shockingly rapid "contraction" of difference, that soon only a "homogenized" world and its literary expression, a probably monolingual world literature, will "survive." In this context, Auerbach proposes a philology of world literature that would redeem individual traditions. His focus is not merely on literatures of the West, however. Born of the "perspectivism" and "historicist humanism" of Goethe's age, he writes, philology's access to "the literatures of the world" in general over the "last several millennia" has secured for us what he calls the "archive" of "records" of the "drama" of all "human beings" as they became "aware of their condition as humans." Only this existentially inclusive "archive" of the "human race" writ large can preserve the "realization of a unified vision of the human race in all its variety," including, he adds somewhat ominously, but, again, understandably in 1952, the "vision" of the "wealth of conflicts" that is our "common human fate." Each record of humanity's "fate," as we encounter it in the "history" of the "realities of the world" and in the "drama" of world literature too, "moves us" by making us "aware of who we are in the most intimate way" ([1952] 2014, 253–64). When we see "human beings" as they appear "before us in the fullness of their lives," he writes, we see in their fates our own fate playing itself out in what Cheah describes as a "specular" fashion (2016, 25) in ways that go beyond the local.

Cheah describes the version of philology Auerbach develops in "The Philology of World Literature" as based on a logic entirely different from the one that organizes the standardized (Greenwich Mean) time of Western progressivist modernity (2016, 1). Each "drama" of the human happens in its own time—as well as in its own place—and is thus neither an earlier primitive nor a later "modern" stage of humanity's unfolding; it is also both local and global at one and the same time. There is something profoundly anti- or at least un-Westphalian and permanent about the potentially infinite "profusion" of world literary cultures Auerbach describes, each of them capable of preserving its local difference without effacing or foreclosing the possibility of earlier or later generations or closing its borders to others or succumbing to a deadly agon for control within. For Auerbach, philology permits what Cheah calls the "fabrication" of something called "humanity because the philological study of the unique development of [a proliferation of] specific linguistic traditions as manifested in the world's different literary cultures can help us compose a universal history of the human spirit that underlies these literatures" (2016, 25). Cheah's use of the word "universal" here distracts from Auerbach's intense commitment to specifics, however, and to what at the very outset of his 1952 essay he calls "the great [and mutually enriching] diversity of what we do not share." What philology does, Auerbach writes, in its capacity as the "leading [synthetic] method in the humanities" that pulls all the other "arts as well as the history of religion, law, and politics" into its orbit, is to plunge into humanity's dauntingly "abundant" archive in order to disinter, in each individual and "heterogeneous" case and on the basis of any and all particular "starting points," or places to begin (*Ansatzpunkt*), "the history of the entire world" as the "history" of all "human beings."

In this essay, the world of Auerbach's world literature thus begins when we allow the place we have begun—a local tradition, a "rhetorical form," even a single "word"—"to speak" *its* world in ever expanding circles as it "illuminates areas" even "further afield" in what he calls a "radiating fashion." In this model, literature is less a product of the world than the world that begins in the literary texts that are the objects on which the philologist's eye is trained. Put another way, the world circulates in a text rather than the text circulating in the world. And every time we begin with a specific object, Auerbach argues, we begin "anew" when we find in the variable particular a "unified vision of the human race" (253–64). We thus understand both the other and ourselves in each philological act.

Initially, these kinds of claims about an act of philological understanding, or hermeneutics, that can give birth to the world we share with all humanity may seem too abstract. What is the path that leads from reading any particular literary text to an understanding of humanity's "common" fate? How can any single literary *Ansatzpunkt*, or place to begin, be said to represent the entirety of human existence? To answer such questions, one must turn to the work of the man to whom Auerbach turned as a model throughout his life, namely the philosopher of history and theorist of rhetoric Giambattista Vico (1668–1744). Sheldon Pollock writes that Vico's work offers "the closest analogue to the sort of critical philology" that Auerbach may have intended, a kind of philology that allows thick historical specificity and some larger truth not to collide, but to intersect.[23] In "Giambattista Vico and the Idea of Philology" (1936), Auerbach describes Vico's philology as a "philosophically informed philology" ([1936] 2014, 33); in "Vico's Contribution to Literary Criticism" (1958), he states that his own philological approach is based on it (10). Auerbach unpacked his understanding of Vico's insight into human culture some fifteen times over the course of his life and in several cases appears to have turned to him at precisely the times when he (Auerbach) was himself confronted with what in his lecture "Vico and Herder," which he held in Cologne in 1931, he calls the "injustice" (*Unrecht*) that "we and those close to us experience . . . on a daily basis" (11). What Auerbach sought in Vico's work was not just an explanation of this injustice's cause or impact on his local case, however. Rather, he also sought a way of understanding the permanence of such injustices as all periods and civilizations confront them in this both best and worst of all possible worlds, each in its own time and place.

Vico offers his explanation of the disturbingly consistent patterns he sees in the drama of human history in his *Principles of [the] New Science . . . concerning the Common Nature of the Nations* (1744). The title, with its emphasis on the "common nature of the nations," makes Vico's interest in what humanity shares clear. Early in his career, Auerbach completed a partial translation of this book; he was intrigued by Vico's main point there that if we really want to know what we share with other human beings, we can study only "that of which human choice is author, whence comes consciousness of the certain" (*certum*) and thus of what he calls "civil society."[24] As a result, we must leave aside the study of the "world of nature, which, since God made it, He alone knows." This world is the realm of the "true" (*verum*). In spite of the way that the distinction between the *certum* and the *verum* has been played out over and over again in Vico reception, the two realms were in fact understood by Vico himself as more or less consubstantial. In a 1922 essay on Vico, Auerbach explains how this *coincidentia oppositorum* worked, describing the "Geschichtsdrama"—the drama of history—of humanity's existence *in the world* as what Vico calls an "expression" of Divine Providence and thus of "God's will."[25] Already here, Auerbach makes it clear that Vico did not always consider this "drama" or its Providential stage director in a sanguine way. His "Man" is not just a powerful *homo faber* or the "god" of his world, in other words; he is also the producer of the "certainty" of that world's chaos.

Again, making such an observation in 1922 is not surprising; Auerbach had fought and been wounded in the conflagration of World War I (1914–18), in which a whole generation of youth across Europe had been slaughtered and which had left Germany in economic and political ruins. It is understandable that the "sublime plan" that originates in Providence was one that, if it is understood to shape the realities of human history, must include "blood and starvation, gossip and confusion, life and death." Or, Auerbach suggests, at least we hope this is God's plan, since intuiting it might allow us to "endure what is happening to us with composure." This may be what Auerbach means later in "The Philology of World Literature" when he writes that philology's task is to discern evidence of a "plan" in the records of the "history of the human race" as humanity made it, which explains why we can begin with almost any text or set of cultural remains, since we can find in it and them evidence of the baleful existence we share (255).

Understanding the details of Providence's severe plan for human history, as Auerbach understood Vico to have articulated it, is important since they lie at the heart of what he calls Vico's "hermeneutic philology," or "philology of understanding" ("verstehende Philologie"), which was itself based on the Neapolitan's other famous insight into the "corso" and "ricorso" of human history. In all his essays on Vico, Auerbach rehearses Vico's cyclical theory of history in dark detail. Each and every nation is said to move from the moment of Original Sin and some version of the Flood through the initial stages of "wild" and "primitive man" and the rudimentary social arrangements into which his fear of the elements, which he holds for divinities, drives him. This stage is followed by the development of inequitable agricultural cultures along feudal lines and the era of class struggle that results, which is followed by the founding of "free" republics to which this struggle leads. The republics then devolve into hierarchical societies based only on self-interest, and from there, on into the era when an enlightened absolute monarchy must regulate the war of all against all. This allegedly rational age itself then rapidly comes to an end, felled by its own decadence, which results in the return to a renewed primitive and barbaric state, whence the "corso" begins anew. All nations run this same Providentially decreed "course," which Vico himself describes in the *New Science* as the "rise, progress, maturity, decadence, and dissolution" of all "human civil institutions," the course that, again, finds its "recourse" in "all nations," an "infinite" number of them "throughout eternity" and always in accordance with Providence's "divine laws" (335 and 252). As dark as this account of humanity's alleged achievements may be, what Auerbach appears to be suggesting is that while Vico was reconciled to the realities of evil, he also understood Providence to be equally as committed to saving humanity overall when it allows the decline of any individual, historical civilization to serve as the basis for the next civilization's rise.

This is what Vico's own philology—his study in the *New Science* of the "corso" and "ricorso" of human history as the "eternal ideal history" that is proper to all periods and "nations" as they march out of and back into barbarism over and over again—taught Auerbach, as he writes in an essay entitled "Giambattista Vico and the Idea of Philology," which appeared in 1936, the very year the German Jewish scholar fled Hitler's Germany for Istanbul. In this essay, Auerbach addresses Vico's theory of the "senso commune" for the first time, defining it as another aspect of what "all of humanity has in common," a shared sensibility bestowed by Providence on each and every one of us as a "natural predisposition for specific forms of life and developmental paths" that are both "everywhere the same" and specific to their unfolding at any particular time and place ([1936] 2014, 30). According to Auerbach on Vico, the "senso commune" forms the basis of our ability to understand one another as subjected to the whims of Providence as the force that both shapes the details of our individual "empirical" existence in the course of history, and enables each of us to understand one another "simultaneously" and "from [our] own inner resources" (31–32). This is why we can understand, as Vico did, that the fears and reaction of the "primitives" (30) are also *our* fears as we face the momentary calm and provisional states of well-being that every society achieves, but also its and thus our ultimate and inevitable decline.

For Auerbach, philology is thus a hermeneutics, or way of reading and understanding, that relies on the "senso commune." One historical nation or period or collective succeeds in understanding the documents and artifacts of another historical nation, period, or collective in all their heterogeneous specificity as a "place to begin" when it understands both its and the other collective's common subjection in this world to Providence's intent. Auerbach writes in "Vico and the National Spirit" (1955) that philology is the tool that allows us to understand humanity's tendency, particularly in each primitive stage, to react to its fears in the face of the world's "phenomenal chaos" ([1955] 2014, 49) with the invention of myths, rituals, and social and political norms in what Vico calls "poetical" fashion, norms that soon solidify into the institutions with which we make and shape the world.[26] In addition to having arranged for the common "corso" of all the nations' recursive development into barbarism, then, Vico's Providence has *also* arranged, via the "senso commune," for all nations to be able understand all other nations' "corsi," the terrors by which they are consumed and the conflicts that hurl them through life, the provisional states of well-being and then, their ultimate and inevitable decline, as this "corso" is visible in all nations.

Perhaps counterintuitively, Vico's philological science in effect assumes an almost upbeat commonality and "community," or "Gemeinschaft," for humanity writ large—even as any given instantiation of that humanity and all of us slouch toward our end. Auerbach calls this kind of philology a "philosophical philology" over and over again—by which he appears to mean the kind of philology that, again, can discern the "entirety of the great and horrific reality of its history" that is human "history's eternal design" ("Giambattista Vico and the Idea of Philology," [1936] 2014, 34–35).

It may not have been by chance that this essay on Vico—which was, again, published in 1936 and that Auerbach may have been completing even as he was trying to find a safer berth outside of Germany—in fact opens with the question of which "discipline" the *New Science* can actually be said to belong to. We may legitimately ask whether Auerbach was thinking in that year about Vico's work here or his own, about the work that "philology" could do not only in the face of his present circumstances, but in the face of the dire plan that Providence seemed to have for humanity overall. And what is the relation of this philology to the philology he invokes as the method for understanding how world literature begins almost twenty years later in "The Philology of World Literature"? What Auerbach appears to be suggesting in both cases and thus in the dark times of Nazi Germany and a tense Cold War, respectively, is that even if philology cannot repair the grim cycle of human history's boom and bust, it can at least offer a respite from it in the form of a kind of philologically enabled empathy. In the end, he appears to argue, following Vico, that humanity will survive because of each nation's ability to understand the documents and artifacts of other nations—which nevertheless also suggests that each nation also understands and accepts that those nations' trials and tribulations will inevitably also be its own. This logic is what subtends not only Auerbach's choice of texts in his famous *Mimesis: The Representation of Reality in Western Literature* (orig. 1946; trans. 1953), but also his way of reading them as he examines at close range the immense and variegated suffering of humanity in those texts of the Western tradition that he finds "worldly" in this way and discounts other texts that keep the realities of human existence at arm's length.[27]

Philology's capacity via empathetic reading to allow readers entry not just into a historically or geographically enlarged canon, but potentially into any other and all worlds different from our own as well, is promising—even if its ability to do so is only palliative, he suggests in "The Philology of World Literature," since it cannot stop us from destroying either each other or ourselves from within (256–57). Auerbach's Vichean philology proposes a theory of world literature that explains how any individual literary text can give us access to the human world we share with others in places and times that might seem to differ radically from our own. World literature thus begins each time we read in this way.

Further Reading

Apter, Emily. *Against World Literature: On the Politics of Untranslatability*, 2013.

Auerbach, Erich. "The Philology of World Literature," 1952, in *Time, History, and Literature: Selected Essays of Erich Auerbach*, edited by James I. Porter and translated by Jane O. Newman, 2014.

Casanova, Pascale. *The World Republic of Letters*, translated by M. B. De-bevoise, 2004.

Cheah, Pheng. *What Is a World? On Post-colonial Literature as World Literature*, 2016.

Damrosch, David. *Comparing the Literatures: Literary Studies in a Global Age*, 2020.

Damrosch, David. *How to Read World Literature*, 2008, 2018.

Damrosch, David. *What Is World Literature?*, 2003.

D'Haen, Theo. *The Routledge Concise History of World Literature*, 2012, 2013.

Helgesson, Stefan, and Pieter Vermeulen. *Institutions of World Literature: Writing, Translation, Markets*, 2015.

Mani, B. Venkat. *Recoding World Literature: Libraries, Print Culture, and Germany's Pact with Books*, 2017.

Moretti, Franco. "Conjectures on World Literature," *New Left Review* 1 (January–February 2000): 54–68.

Mufti, Aamir R. *Forget English! Orientalisms and World Literatures*, 2016.

Prendergast, Christopher. *Debating World Literature*, 2004.

The Routledge Companion to World Literature, edited by Theo D'haen et al., 2012.

Walkowitz, Rebecca. *Born Translated: The Contemporary Novel in an Age of World Literature*, 2015.

CONCLUSION

All the authors in this book have, in their own way, emphasized the unpredictable and contingent nature of literary beginnings. We have seen again and again that willed efforts to found a literature never bear fruit unless they emerge from a broader network of institutions and practices. This book's investigation of literary beginnings weakens, one might say, two seemingly uncontroversial pillars of today's literary universe: the author and the book. Even though modern publication and educational practices, as well as the capitalistic marketplace, center on bound pages and the names of the people who created them, literary beginnings steer the focus to other factors. Think of the promulgation of a Korean script at the end of the fifteenth century and the ensuing attempt to found a Korean vernacular literature; or of the "Lay of Igor," the twelfth-century poem in Old Russian that has often been understood as the first literary text in the Russian tradition. As with many similar cases discussed in the preceding chapters, these first texts in what is now described as a literary heritage were not, in and of themselves, enough to shape expectations and practices in the ways required for the emergence of this heritage.

The inquiry into literary beginnings complicates familiar chronologies of literary history and challenges the idea that a literature begins with the single, chronologically identifiable literary text or event. Indeed, if the study of literary beginnings shows anything, it is that the existence and perpetuation of literature depends on factors far in excess of what any individual person or object can accomplish. The nature of this "excess," and the factors contributing to its formation, is a highly contingent affair.

What, then, is the surplus value in comparing literary beginnings? To answer this question, it is helpful to imagine an alternative book—one that presents a definition of literary beginning and then unfolds as a series of chapters devoted to the various factors that contribute to it. Would this not have been a more straightforward, less disciplinarily myopic project?

We chose not to proceed in this fashion, and for instructive reasons. The concept of literature is today applied to such a diverse array of historical phenomena, from hieroglyphics to comic books, that we doubt a definition of literary beginnings is even possible. In the absence of finely grained case studies devoted to moments of literary beginning, any speculation about what it takes for a literary tradition to gain traction itself risks spinning off into the void. In our view, if it turns out that the beginnings of ancient Chinese and colonial Latin American literature share very little, we feel all the richer for this knowledge. Viewing one tradition against the backdrop of others can draw out its unique features, highlighting the ones that were especially important to the evolutionary process and allowing us to appreciate their uniqueness or commonality. Without taking a close comparative look, it is impossible to know both how a literature came into existence *and* what is special or exciting about how it did so. The inductive procedure of this book ensures that our claims about what constitutes a bona fide literary beginning remain grounded in empirical observation.

In searching for the elements held in common by the literatures represented here, it quickly became clear to us that the concept of *literary beginning* presented a special challenge. Even where we recognize strong resemblances among literary beginnings, we realized, they do not share a single set of characteristics. The reward of comparison, in this instance, is not only a renewed appreciation of the literary traditions that we know best, but also an expanded sense of the many ways that literatures emerge and develop. However hackneyed it may sound, the capacity of confrontation between the familiar and the unfamiliar, particularly when it ends with unresolved difference, can productively denaturalize our conception of what makes up a literature.

There is also something concrete to take away from the juxtaposition of so many case studies, which one might think of in terms of visual scale. From Galileo's telescope to the personal computer, human beings have become remarkably adept at altering the size and resolution of the objects we see. Historians, including literary ones, do something similar all the time: the big picture is as important to historiography as the illustrative or anomalous episode. Comparing literary beginnings requires attentiveness to such phenomena of scaling. After all, if one views the historical landscape too closely, each literary tradition can look irreconcilably different, and viewed too distantly they can all look the same. One of our chief hopes for this book is that it will sensitize readers to phenomena of literary-historical scaling. Doing so involves *both* increasing our awareness of disciplinary parochialism *and* keeping our eyes open to the value in searching for commonalities shared by particular traditions.

One surprising result of looking at literary traditions individually rather than under a broader abstract category, as we've discovered, is that we come to see appropriation as the norm and not the exception. Tendencies to emphasize difference and singularity have their virtues, but they come to seem highly unusual against the backdrop of the traditions surveyed in this volume, which have been promiscuous in their borrowings, and in their precedents and models. Imitation is an essential element of literature, even if such imitation introduces new inflections. This has been the case ever since the first identifiable author in human history, the priestess Enheduanna, took on the task of appropriating Sumerian literature for speakers of another language, Akkadian. Our case studies demonstrate that appropriation is at the heart of culture: no culture is invented from whole cloth, and none is insular.

Once literary traditions have achieved momentum, they are sustained by means of transmission. This book has introduced a range of technologies, publishing and reading practices, and writing conventions that transmission relies on: from the scribal establishments of the ancient Near East to the widespread libraries and schools of the Hellenistic Mediterranean, and on to the panoply of the modern world's institutions, with publishing houses, universities, and school curricula featuring Dante or Shakespeare. Once again, this impression of enormous variety dwindles if we helicopter up, to a perspective from which we see that what really counts is the sheer process of curating and transmission without which no literature can survive.

Someone has to care enough about curating and preserving this material for it to endure, and the chapters in our volume consistently highlight the professional and societal investments in these processes. Above all, some sense of common cause or identity—a shared sense that something significant is at stake—appears indispensable to the perpetuation of literary traditions, even if the particular form of identification can vary enormously, from palace or temple to city, ruling class, empire or nation.

For most contemporary university students, it can be difficult to imagine forms of adherence or identification different from those of the modern nation-state, around which most university departments of literature and humanities are still organized. The comparative approach of this book allows readers to see how recent this form of identity is, and how many other ways of belonging and distancing have existed in the course of world history, and of literary history as a result.

Any act of comparison must juggle similarity and difference, and the experience of reading the chapters in this book has made us realize how stimulating and enlightening it is to be challenged to recognize both, often by trying to understand the lay of entirely unfamiliar land. The "author," for example, proved to be a surprisingly robust figure in many traditions, well before the modern period, when so many modern theorists have posited that the concept

emerged; on the other hand, some traditions dispense with the author altogether, or imagine the author function in quite different ways. The "book" is an
astonishingly late invention, and almost all literary history did just fine without
it. This recognition makes us return to the traditions we know best with a new
understanding of their contingent distinctiveness and awakens our curiosity
about the number and diversity of the world's literary traditions.

NOTES

Introduction

1. Emily Apter has trenchantly challenged "macrocomparative" concepts of world literature along these lines. See Apter 2008, 591.
2. See the exceptionally ambitious project collected in Moretti 2007.
3. Finnegan 1970 and 1992.
4. Goody 1987.
5. Pollock 2006; see also Beecroft 2015, chap. 3.
6. Beecroft 2015, 109.
7. Casanova 1999.
8. Schlegel 1981.
9. Barthes 1971, 170.
10. Jakobson 1960, 356.

Part I. East and South Asia

1. Pollock 2006.
2. Elman 2014.

Chapter 1. Chinese

1. For the origins and historical development of *wen*, see Chow 1979.
2. Lewis 1999.
3. Qiu 2000.
4. Bagley 2004. For a contrasting view, see Smith 2011.
5. Falkenhausen 1993; Kern 2007.
6. Kern 2009; Wang 1988, 1–72.
7. Wang 1988, 73–114, specifically discusses the songs devoted to King Wen.
8. I prefer the Chinese names for both Kongzi and Mengzi (Mencius), whose names became latinized only by Jesuit missionaries.
9. For the debates surrounding creation in early China, see Puett 2001; for Kongzi as the imagined author of the *Annals*, see Kern 2018.
10. Chow 1968.
11. Lewis 1999, 147–93.
12. For a fuller discussion, see Schaberg 2001, 57–95, esp. 86–95. My translation is largely Schaberg's.
13. For an account of the "Great Preface" in early Chinese hermeneutics, see Van Zoeren 1991.
14. For a discussion, see Kern 2015.
15. Kern 2010; Riegel 1997.

16. Kern 2019.
17. Owen 2006, 73.

Chapter 2. Japanese

1. Perkins 1992, 17.
2. Suzuki 2016.
3. Chin 2017.
4. For a critical history of writing and literacy in early Japan, see Lurie 2011.
5. Fogel 2013.
6. Lurie 2007.
7. Lurie 2011, chap. 4; Kornicki 2018, chap. 6. Denecke 2013, 45–56.
8. Denecke 2014.
9. Feeney 2016.
10. Wang 2005.
11. Como 2009.
12. Blum 1980.
13. Kōno et al. 2015–19.
14. Kōnoshi 1995; Cranston 1993, 53.
15. Ebersole 1989.
16. Duthie 2014.
17. Or "*wa-kan* dialectic"; Pollack 1986 and Sakaki 2005.
18. Denecke 2013, 4–10.
19. On early and medieval Chinese notions of authorship, see Li 2017.
20. Owen 2006.
21. Shields 2017.

Chapter 3. Korean

1. A modern typeface rendition of one of the longest lineage novels, which circulated in 180 manuscript volumes, amounts to twelve printed volumes, each ranging between three and four hundred pages. Kim Chinse 1987–94.
2. Zito 1997.
3. Owen 2017.
4. Lee 1975, 151.
5. Choi 2014, 856.
6. Lee 1975, 245.
7. Lee 1975, 146.
8. Lee 1975, 268.
9. Lee 1975, 146.
10. Ch'oe 1997.
11. Choi 2014, 584 and 655. On the historical and diplomatic context of the invention of the Korean script, see Chŏng 2009.
12. *Sejong sillok* 103:19b (1444/2/20).
13. Kim Sŭngu 2015, 161–87 and 292–309.
14. There are at the moment sixteen extant manuscripts of this text, which attest to its wide circulation. Among the manuscripts, there is a royal palace edition and a rental library edition. This study is based on the modern rendition of Ewha Woman's University manuscript in fifteen volumes.
15. *So Hyŏnsŏng rok* 2010, 4:372.
16. *So Hyŏnsŏng rok* 2010, 1:20.
17. *So Hyŏnsŏng rok* 2010, 1:24.

18. *So Hyŏnsŏng rok* 2010, 1:63.
19. *So Hyŏnsŏng rok* 2010, 1:41.
20. *So Hyŏnsŏng rok* 2010, 1:58.

Part II. The Mediterranean

1. Charpin 2010.
2. Haubold 2002.
3. George 2003.

Chapter 5. Greek

1. A sizable bibliography exists on the cup's fragmentary inscription, for which scholars have proposed a variety of restorations; for this, see Gaunt 2017, esp. n. 7.
2. Murray 1994, 50.
3. Here I broadly summarize the approach developed first by Milman Parry in a series of publications from the 1920s; these are conveniently collected in Parry 1971. See too Lord 1960 and 1991.
4. For this, see D'Angour 2005, 93.
5. For the discussion that follows, I draw on D'Angour 2005 and 2006, and Ford 2002.
6. For this reading, see D'Angour 2005, 103.
7. For extensive discussion, see Powell 1991.
8. Powell 1991.
9. Janko 1982, 228–31.
10. Janko 1998.
11. Powell 1988, 78; see also Powell 1991, 162–63.
12. Osborne and Pappas 2007, 134.
13. Osborne and Pappas 2007 make both these points.
14. Carruesco 2016, 85.
15. Esrock 1994.
16. For detailed discussion, see Barber 1992.
17. Florence, National Archaeological Museum 4209.
18. See Bergren 2008, 46–47.
19. Barber 1991, 382. In a kind of mise-en-abyme, cloths may themselves incorporate inwoven or embroidered letters, identifying the god to whom they are donated, the donor, and the mythological figures they display. As such, these textiles join the other "oggetti parlanti" cited so far.
20. For this, see Tuck 2006.
21. Powell 1991, 165–67.
22. Cf. the inscription on a Corinthian oil jug of ca. 670: "I am the lekythos of Tataie. Whoever steals me will go blind" (*IG* XIV 865), with Faraone 1996.
23. Here I draw on J. L. Austin's well-known account of performative speech whose enunciation effects what its contents describe. For this, see Austin 1975.
24. For the statue and inscription, see Day 2010, 33–48.
25. Day 2010, 40; Day's discussion also points to the Odyssean example that I go on to cite.
26. For discussion with earlier bibliography, see Woodard 2014, 265–66, with Langdon 1976, 18–21.

Chapter 7. Hebrew

1. Some of these works count as two or more books in the total count of twenty-four.
2. Schniedewind 2013, 3–4, 9.
3. Rollston 2006.

4. See, for example, Carr 2005 and van der Toorn 2007. For discussion of this kind of comparative approach, see Quick (2014), who cautions that the differences in the political and social development of Egypt and Mesopotamia with Israel and Judah must be taken into account.
5. See Lord 1965. In biblical studies, this approach was popularized in particular by Niditch (1996), who herself draws on the so-called Scandinavian school of biblical scholarship and its preoccupation with oral tradition and folkloristic studies. See Nyberg 1935; Nielsen 1954.
6. The emergence of the "first" alphabetic script is surely not directly documented, and consequently the date for the period of its emergence is obscure and has been subject to a range of diverse suggestions.
7. Sanders 2009, 49.
8. Pardee 2007.
9. Only a few very examples of the Ugaritic cuneiform alphabetic writing system derive from outside of the kingdom of Ugarit: seven from across the Levant (found at Beth Shemesh, Tabor, Tell Taanak, Sarepta, Tell Nebi Mend, and two from Kamid el-Loz) and one from Cyprus (Hula Sultan Teke). See Bordreuil and Pardee 1989, 362–82.
10. See Smith 2008, 47–48.
11. This suggestion comes from Laura Quick, personal communication.
12. The inscriptions of Kulamuwa (KAI 24), Zakkur (KAI 202), Barrakib (KAI 216), the inscription from Tell Fakhariyah (KAI 309), and the Kutamuwa stele from Zincirli feature written descriptions of the speaker's lifetime accomplishments in their own voice alongside images of their face and/or body.
13. Translation from COS 2:147–49.
14. Translation of this inscription has been excerpted from Pardee 2009, 53–54.
15. Weinfeld 1991, 262.
16. Greenstein 2014.
17. KAI 308 I:1.

Chapter 8. Syriac

1. Moss 2010.
2. Pollock 2009.
3. Berthelot 2018; Kosmin 2014, 254–55.
4. Debié 2018.
5. Healey 2017; Gzella 2015; Drijvers and Healey 1999; Debié 2015, 167; Traina 1996; Beyer 1986, 31–32.
6. Healey 2008.
7. Van Rompay 2008.
8. Brock 1992; Wood 2012.
9. Butts 2016, 199–201; Johnson 2015; Healey 2007; Taylor 2002; Brock 1994.
10. Balty and Briquel-Chatonnet 2000; Healey 2006.
11. Drijvers and Healey 1999, B01.
12. Van Rompay 1994; Healey 2012.
13. Gzella 2019; Healey 2008; Van Rompay 1994; Boyarin 1981.
14. Ter Haar Romeny 2005a and 2005b; Healey 2012 and 2008; Joosten 2013, 12–16, and Joosten 2017; Beyer 1986, 43–44; for Jewish Syriac inscriptions, see Noy and Bloedhorn 2004 128–32; for some caution on Edessa as the main center of Christianity in Roman Mesopotamia, see Taylor 2018.
15. Brock 2004, 167; Andrade 2020; Mengozzi and Ricossa 2013.
16. Debié 2015, 460–61 and 467–68; Zerubavel 2003.
17. Contini and Grottanelli 2005, esp. 193–95 for chronology; Lindenberger 1985; Becker 2006, esp. chap. 1.
18. Brock 1985; Sprengling 1916; Watt 1985 and 1986; Nieten 2013; another important treatment of Syriac meter is considerably later, by the Syriac scholar Severus Bar Shakko (d. 1242 CE).
19. Camplani 1998; Drijvers 1966. For Sextus Africanus, see Adler 2004 and Brock 1992, esp. 222.
20. Ephrem the Syrian, *Hymns against Heresies* 53.5 (ed. Beck 1957); I follow the translation in Sprengling 1916.
21. Griffith 2017.

22. Baumstark 1922, 39; for one of the earliest attestations of this root in Syriac with the meaning of "to dispute," see Aphrahat 6.8 (118.2 ed. Wright 1869 = 276.15 ed. Parisot 1894–1907).
23. McVey 1999; a view downplaying this innovation by Bardaisan is in Griffith 2006; see also Wickes 2018.
24. Ephrem the Syrian, *Prose Refutations* 2.223 l. 14 (ed. Mitchell 1912–21; translation 2, cv).
25. Pollock 2009, 23; Ross 2001, 145–62; Winkelmann 2007.
26. Ephrem the Syrian, *Prose Refutations* 2.221–23 (ed. Mitchell 1912–21).
27. Pollock 2009, 23; Beecroft 2015.
28. Baumstark 1933; Drijvers and Healey 1999, Am5.
29. Duval 1907, 10.
30. *Life of Rabbula* 40 (ed. Phenix and Horn 2017); Drijvers 1966, 162.
31. Ephrem the Syrian, *Hymns against Heresies* 1.16 (ed. Beck 1957).
32. Mitchell 1912–21, 2:clxxxiii and 1:162 and cix; Reeves 1997.
33. Pedersen and Larsen 2013, 123–26; Gardner 1996, 101–3; Contini 1995; Lim 1992; an early Manichaean text, the *Cologne Mani Codex*, contains a passage from a letter to Edessa by Mani (Cameron and Dewey 1979, 50–51).
34. Manichaean poetry survives in Coptic; see Allberry 1938; Wurst 1996; Säve-Söderbergh 1950.
35. Gardner 1996.
36. Griffith 2006; Fiano 2015; the later *Vita* tradition of Ephrem, chap. 31, presents the view that Ephrem's choice to write *madrāšē* was meant to counteract the influence of Bardaisan. Conversely, for the development of Syriac prose, a most influential author was Aphrahat: see, e.g., Murray 1983.
37. Ephrem the Syrian, *Hymns on Julian Saba*, 4.8–10 (ed. Beck 1972; trans. Griffith 2006).
38. Ephrem the Syrian, *Hymns on Julian Saba*, 4.8–10 (ed. Beck 1972; trans. Griffith 2006); Jacob of Serugh, *Homily on Ephrem*, 65 (Amar 1995); Wood 2012; Mengozzi and Ricossa 2013; Brock 2008; Jiménez 2017.
39. Ephrem the Syrian, *Hymns against Heresies*, 1.11 (ed. Beck 1957; trans. Griffith 2006).
40. Ephrem the Syrian, *Hymns against Heresies*, 54 (ed. Beck 1957; trans. Griffith 2006).
41. Ephrem the Syrian, *Hymns against Heresies*, 55 (ed. Beck 1957).
42. Debié 2015, 167–72; Andrade 2015.
43. *Life of Rabbula* 40 (ed. Phenix and Horn 2017).
44. Ephrem the Syrian, *Hymns against Heresies* 1.17 (ed. Beck 1957): "Bardaisan . . . , seeing that the youth longs for sweetness, through the harmony of his songs excited the passions of the youthful."
45. Brock 2003; Rigolio 2013; Arzhanov 2018.
46. For substantial improvements to this chapter, I would like to thank the organizers, speakers, and participants in the Princeton workshop, in addition to Adam Becker, Averil Cameron, Emanuel Fiano, Anthony Gelston, Simcha Gross, Sandra Keating, Yitz Landes, Barry McCrea, Alessandro Mengozzi, Michael Pifer, Ute Possekel, David Taylor, Lucas Van Rompay, and stimulating audiences in Durham, Princeton, and Oxford.

Chapter 9. Arabic

1. Cf. Schoeler and Toorawa 2009, 1.
2. [Bloch] 2002, esp. 744.
3. Cf. Pellat 1991, 603. For a detailed study on the poetry of lamentation, see Borg 1997.
4. For the following, cf. [Bloch] 2002, 745–56, 763–64.
5. For the qaṣīda, see Jacobi 1971 and Bauer 1992.
6. Bauer 1992, 268.
7. For the onager episode see Bauer 1992 and Jacobi 1971, 57.
8. For the following, see Schoeler 2006, 87–110; contrary to Zwettler 1978.
9. Bauer 1993, 135.
10. Serjeant 1983, 134ff.
11. Besides incorporating generally acknowledged research (outlined, e.g., in Watt 1977 and Paret 1983), this and the next three paragraphs are based on the seminal new investigations of Angelika Neuwirth in her book *Der Koran als Text der Spätantike* (The Koran as a text of late antiquity) and

on the Corpus Coranicum research project of the Berlin-Brandenburg Academy of Sciences and Humanities (toward a critical edition of the Koran), carried out under Neuwirth's leadership. For the following, cf. Neuwirth 2010, sections starting at pp. 280, 321, 327, 362, and 561.

12. Neuwirth 2002, 562, 563.
13. Motzki 2004, 1.
14. Juynboll 1982–89, 45.
15. Sezgin 1967, 55.
16. See Jaeger 1912, 135–37, 147.
17. Carter 1983, 119.
18. Versteegh 1993.
19. Carter 1983, 120.
20. Carter 1983, 122.
21. Versteegh 1987, and esp. 154–55.
22. Saliba 2007, 62.
23. Gutas [1999] 2005, 34 and following.
24. Gibb 1962, 66.
25. See Heinrichs 1969, 193.
26. Marzolph and van Leeuwen 2004, 1:372.

Chapter 10. English

1. Glissant 1997, 143–44.
2. But many have argued that post-Conquest writings in English demarcate a distinct English culture and nationalism. See Treharne 2012; Turville-Petre 1996.
3. Greenfield, Calder, and Lapidge 1986; Huscroft 2019, 1–14; Gneuss 2013; Campbell, John, and Wormald 1982, 20–69.
4. Graff 1987; Matthews 1999; Guillory 1993.
5. Treharne 2012; Ashe 2017.
6. Said 1975, 5.
7. Vinsauf 1967; Butterfield 2015; Wacks 2007.
8. Wallace 2019.
9. Smith 2001; Zieman 2008; Orme 2006, 53–85; Hunt 1991.
10. Butterfield 2009, 103–265; Coleman 1996; Pearsall 1992; Wimsatt 1982.
11. Roberts 1999; Fulton 1989.
12. Clanchy 1993; Knapp 2001; Wenzel 1986. This argument, and the discussion of Early Middle English manuscripts that follows, disagrees with the claim put forth in Catto 2003.
13. Minnis 1988, 9–39; Hollander 2007.
14. Shonk 1985; Minnis 1988, 94.
15. Cartlidge 1997, 250; Hill 2003; Fein 2018.
16. Tschann and Parkes 1996; Miller 1963; Turville-Petre 2003; Robinson 1980.
17. Burnley and Wiggins 2004; Fein 2016; Shonk 1985.
18. Bahr 2013; Wallace 2016; Watson 1995; Burrow 1971.
19. Machan 2006; Echard 2004.
20. Hoccleve 1999 (*Regiment of Princes*), line 4978; Lydgate 2005 (*Floure of Curtesye*), 238; Dunbar 2004 (*Lament for the Makars*), 50.
21. Lydgate 1924 (*Fall of Princes*, Prologue), line 303.

Chapter 12. German

1. De Staël 1968, 183.
2. Gottsched 1748, 5 (unpaginated preface).

3. See Wieland 1782, Adelung 1782, and Adelung 1783.
4. Gottsched 1730, 3.
5. Nicolai 1773, 91.
6. Möser 1781, 33–34.
7. Riedel 1774, 22.
8. This and all the following quotes are taken from Goethe 1907, 397–428.
9. Blanckenburg 1774, 19.

Chapter 13. Russian

1. Schenker 1995, 60.
2. Kuskov [1977] 1980, 10.
3. Schenker 1995, 74.
4. Mirsky 1924, 77.
5. Zhivov 2009, 8.
6. Nabokov 1960, 13.
7. Pushkin 1978, 7:156.
8. Pushkin 1978, 7:156.
9. Karlinsky 1985, 45–46.
10. Karlinsky 1985, 47.
11. Čiževskij 1960, 346.
12. Kahn, Lipovetsky, Reyfman, and Sandler 2018, 165.
13. Milosz 1983, 60.
14. Gasparov 1996, 6–8.
15. Gasparov 1996, 234–35, Čiževskij 1960, 414.
16. Dunn 1993.
17. Trediakovskii 1963, 26–27.
18. Klein 2008, 15–18 and 67–69.
19. Gasparov 1984, 35.
20. Marker 1985, 23.
21. Marker 1985, 51.
22. Khodasevich 1989, 302.
23. Batiushkov 1977, 37.
24. Tynianov 2019, 77–113.
25. Čiževskij 1960, 375.
26. Kuskov [1977] 1980, 10.
27. Pushkin 1978, 7:210.
28. Karamzin 1984, 46.
29. Mandel'shtam 1997, 120.

Chapter 15. African

1. Jahn 1968; Finnegan 1970; Obiechina 1975; Gérard 1981; A. Irele 1981; Andrzejewski, Pilaszewicz, and Tyloch 1985.
2. Said 1985, 43.
3. Thiong'o 1986, 70.
4. I have discussed these issues in F. Irele and Gikandi 2000, 379–97.
5. Feeney 2016, 4.
6. Textual references will be to the following translations and editions with page numbers in parenthesis after the quote: R. Allen 1946; J. de V. Allen 1977; Harries 1962; Hichens [1939] 1972; Taylor 1915, 96–105.

7. Said 1985, 6.
8. Hichens [1939] 1972, 9.
9. Mulokozi and Sengo 1995, 25.
10. For Swahili writing in the Ajami script, see Mugane 2015, 175–91; and Mugane 2017.
11. The respective quotes are from Knappert 1967, 11; Knappert 2005, 442.
12. Walsh 2018, 121.
13. J. de V. Allen 1977, 14. For "allegorical frame" of the poem, see Wamitila 2001, 20–21.
14. For the original, I work with Hichens's transcription. Except where stated, the translations are my own.
15. Swettler 1978, 3.
16. Taylor 1915, xi.
17. Harries 1962, 87.
18. Harries 1962, 87.
19. Auerbach 1965, 241.
20. For the significant role played by Sheikh-Sir Mbarak al-Hinawy, see Hirji 2012.
21. Pugach 2012, 10.
22. Krapf 1850, 9.
23. Werner 1918.
24. Quoted in Gérard 1981, 181.
25. Good discussions of the standardization debate can be found in Mugane 2015, 192–226; Whitely 1969, 79–96. See also Mazrui 2007.
26. A typical anthology of Swahili poetry will be divided between classical and contemporary poetry. See, for example, Jahadhymy 1975.
27. For allegory as the representation of the ruins of the past, see Benjamin 1998, 159–95.
28. Mazrui 2007; J. de V. Allen 1977, 9.
29. Wamitila 2001, 49.

Chapter 16. African American

1. Terry delivered "Bars Fight" orally, which is how it circulated for over a century. In 1855, editor and novelist Josiah Gilbert Holland was the first to publish the poem, doing so in his *History of Western Massachusetts* (Springfield, MA: S. Bowles).

Chapter 17. World Literature

1. Helgesson and Vermeulen 2015, 4.
2. Said 1975, xi.
3. Damrosch 2020, 268.
4. Mani 2017, 243.
5. Walkowitz 2015.
6. On the intricacies of the large number of Latin texts circulated during the Renaissance, when vernacular languages were on the rise, see Burke 2007.
7. Franco Moretti was one of the first theorists to characterize world literature as a "problem" rather than as a set of texts. Moretti 2000, 55.
8. For a detailed account of the reception of the Goethean concept, see Nichols 2018.
9. The parallels are not surprising, yet the influence obviously goes the other way. Said and his first wife, Maire, first translated Auerbach's "Philologie der Weltliteratur" (1952) as "Philology and *Weltliteratur*" in 1969. My new translation of this essay as "The Philology of World Literature" appeared in Auerbach 2014. Auerbach's work is a major reference point for Said from the early *Beginnings* (1975) to the founding text of postcolonial literary studies, *Orientalism* (1978), to one of his last books, *Humanism and Democratic Criticism* (2004); Said's foreword to the fiftieth-anniversary republication of Auerbach's *Mimesis* (orig. 1953; 2003) appears as chapter 4 of the 2004 volume.

10. Auerbach [1936] 2014, 34. In what follows, all citations to Auerbach's essays may be found in Auerbach 2014.
11. Kadir 2011, 26.
12. Cheah 2016, 5.
13. Goethe to Eckermann, 1827, cited in Hoesel-Uhlig 2004, 34. For a detailed account of the reception of Goethe's claims about world literature, see Nichols 2018. Marx and Engels are cited in Hoesel-Uhlig 2004, 51.
14. Historian Sebastian Conrad ([2006] 2010) has pointed usefully to the use of the term "world" across multiple discourses—"world war," "world literature," "world politics"—in these years (3 and 46).
15. On Westphalianism as a category of political analysis, see Falk 2002; Beaulac 2004.
16. Apter 2008, 581.
17. Cooppan 2004, 16 and 21 ("ghostly") and passim ("uncanny"); Damrosch 1995.
18. Spivak 2003, 72–73 and 102.
19. Auerbach 1958, 13.
20. Jean-Luc Nancy, *The Sense of the World*, 1993, cited in Apter 2008, 588–89.
21. Weber famously describes the "iron cage" of modernity in his *The Protestant Ethic and the Spirit of Capitalism*. See Weber 2001, 123. On Auerbach in Heidelberg, see Hacohen 2012, 601.
22. Mufti 2012; Hutchinson 2017; Yashin 2011.
23. Pollock 2009, 958n74.
24. Vico 1984, 63 and 96.
25. The quotes here are from Auerbach 1922, 249–51. My translation.
26. In *The New Science*, Vico (1984) describes the economy, morality, politics, and the social order as "poetry," as everything that is made (poeisis) by human beings.
27. For a closer examination of Auerbach's text choices and method in *Mimesis* as a performance of the world of world literature understood in this way as it is visible in the literature of the West, see Newman 2020.

BIBLIOGRAPHY

Introduction

Apter, Emily. "Untranslatables: A World System." *New Literary History* 39, no. 3 (2008): 581–98.
Barthes, Roland. "Réflexions sur un manuel." In *L'Enseignement de la littérature*, ed. S. Doubrovsky and T. Todorov, 170–77. Paris: Plon 1971.
Beecroft, Alexander. *An Ecology of World Literature: From Antiquity to the Present Day*. London: Verso, 2015.
Casanova, Pascale. *La République mondiale des lettres*. Paris: Éditions du Seuil, 1999. Translated by M. B. DeBevoise as *World Republic of Letters*. Cambridge, MA: Harvard University Press, 2004.
Finnegan, Ruth. *Oral Literature in Africa*. London: Clarendon, 1970.
———. *Oral Poetry: Its Nature, Significance, and Social Context*. 2nd ed. Bloomington: Indiana University Press, 1992.
Goody, Jack. *The Interface between the Written and the Oral*. Cambridge: Cambridge University Press, 1987.
Jakobson, Roman. "Linguistics and Poetics." In *Style in Language*, ed. T. Seboek, 350–77. Cambridge, MA: MIT Press. 1960.
Moretti, Franco, ed. *The Novel*. 2 vols. Princeton, NJ: Princeton University Press 2007.
Schlegel, Friedrich, 1981. "Georg Forster: Fragment einer Charakteristik der deutschen Klassiker." In *Friedrich Schlegel Studienausgabe*, vol. 1, edited by Ernst Behler and Hans Eichner, 192–207. Paderborn: Verlag Ferdinand Schöningh.

Part I. East and South Asia

Elman, Benjamin A., ed. 2014. *Rethinking East Asian Languages, Vernaculars, and Literacies, 1000–1919*. Leiden: Brill.
Pollock, Sheldon. 2006. *The Language of the Gods in the World of Men: Sanskrit, Culture, and Power in Premodern India*. Berkeley: University of California Press.

Chapter 1. Chinese

Bagley, Robert W. 2004. "Anyang Writing and the Origin of the Chinese Writing System." In *The First Writing: Script Invention as History and Process*, edited by Stephen Houston, 190–249. Cambridge: Cambridge University Press.
Chow Tse-tsung. 1968. "The Early History of the Chinese Word *Shih* (Poetry)." In *Wen-lin: Studies in the Chinese Humanities*, edited by Chow Tse-tsung, 151–209. Madison: University of Wisconsin Press.
———. 1979. "Ancient Chinese Views on Literature, the Tao, and Their Relationship." In *Chinese Literature: Essays, Articles, Reviews (CLEAR)* 1:3–29.

Falkenhausen, Lothar von. 1993. "Issues in Western Zhou Studies: A Review Article." In *Early China* 18:139–226.

Kern, Martin. 2007. "The Performance of Writing in Western Zhou China." In *The Poetics of Grammar and the Metaphysics of Sound and Sign*, edited by Sergio La Porta and David Shulman, 109–75. Leiden: Brill.

———. 2009 "Bronze Inscriptions, the *Shangshu*, and the *Shijing*: The Evolution of the Ancestral Sacrifice during the Western Zhou." In *Early Chinese Religion, Part One: Shang Through Han (1250 BC to 220 AD)*, edited by John Lagerwey and Marc Kalinowski, 143–200. Leiden: Brill.

———. 2010. "Lost in Tradition: The *Classic of Poetry* We Did Not Know." In *Hsiang Lectures on Chinese Poetry* 5: 29–56. Montreal: Centre for East Asian Research, McGill University.

———. 2015. "Speaking of Poetry: Pattern and Argument in the *Kongzi shilun*." In *Literary Forms of Argument in Early China*, edited by Dirk Meyer and Joachim Gentz, 175–200. Leiden: Brill.

———. 2018 "Kongzi as Author in the Han." In *The Analects Revisited: New Perspectives on the Dating of a Classic*, edited by Michael Hunter and Martin Kern, 268–307. Leiden: Brill.

———. 2019. "'Xi shuai' 蟋蟀 ('Cricket') and Its Consequences: Issues in Early Chinese Poetry and Manuscript Studies." In *Early China* 42:39–74.

Lewis, Mark Edward. 1999. *Writing and Authority in Early China*. Albany: State University of New York Press.

Owen, Stephen. 2006. *The Making of Early Chinese Classical Poetry*. Cambridge, MA: Harvard University Asia Center.

Puett, Michael. 2001 *The Ambivalence of Creation: Debates concerning Innovation and Artifice in Early China*. Stanford, CA: Stanford University Press.

Qiu Xigui. 2000. *Chinese Writing*. Berkeley: Society for the Study of Early China and the Institute of East Asian Studies, University of California, Berkeley.

Riegel, Jeffrey K. 1997. "Eros, Introversion, and the Beginnings of *Shijing* Commentary." In *Harvard Journal of Asiatic Studies* 57:143–77.

Schaberg, David. 2001. *A Patterned Past: Form and Thought in Early Chinese Historiography*. Cambridge, MA: Harvard University Asia Center.

Smith, Adam. 2011. "The Evidence for Scribal Training at Anyang." In *Writing and Literacy in Early China*, edited by Li Feng and David Prager Branner, 173–205. Seattle: University of Washington Press.

Wang, C. H. 1988. *From Ritual to Allegory: Seven Essays in Early Chinese Poetry*. Hong Kong: Chinese University Press.

Van Zoeren, Steven. 1991. *Poetry and Personality: Reading, Exegesis, and Hermeneutics in Traditional China*. Stanford, CA: Stanford University Press.

Chapter 2. Japanese

Blum, Rudolf. 1980. *Bibliographia: An Inquiry into Its Definitions and Designations*. Translated by Mathilde V. Rovelstad. Chicago: American Library Association.

Chin, Tamara T. 2017. "Colonization, Sinicization, and the Polyscriptic Northwest." In *The Oxford Handbook of Classical Chinese Literature (1000 BCE–900 CE)*, edited by Wiebke Denecke, Wai-Yee Li, and Xiaofei Tian, 477–93. New York: Oxford University Press.

Como, Michael. 2009. *Weaving and Binding: Immigrant Gods and Female Immortals in Ancient Japan*. Honolulu: University of Hawaii Press.

Cranston, Edwin A. 1993. *A Waka Anthology: The Gem-Glistening Cup*. Stanford, CA: Stanford University Press.

Damrosch, David. 2007. "Scriptworlds: Writing Systems and the Formation of World Literature." In *Modern Language Quarterly* 68, no. 2:195–219.

Denecke, Wiebke. 2013. *Classical World Literatures: Sino-Japanese and Greco-Roman Comparisons*. New York: Oxford University Press.

—————. 2014. "Worlds without Translation: Premodern East Asia and the Power of Character Scripts." In *Companion to Translation Studies*, edited by Sandra Berman and Catherine Porter, 204–16. Somerset: John Wiley and Sons.

—————. 2017. "Sino-Japanese Literature." In *The Oxford Handbook of Classical Chinese Literature*, edited by Wiebke Denecke, Wai-Yee Li, and Xiaofei Tian, 551–67. New York: Oxford University Press.

Duthie, Torquil. 2014. *Man'yōshū and the Imperial Imagination in Early Japan*. Leiden: Brill.

Ebersole, Gary L. 1989. *Ritual Poetry and the Politics of Death in Early Japan*. Princeton, NJ: Princeton University Press.

Feeney, Denis. 2016. *Beyond Greek: The Beginnings of Latin Literature*. Cambridge, MA: Harvard University Press.

Fogel, Joshua. 2013. *Japanese Historiography and the Gold Seal of 57 C.E.* Boston, Brill.

Kōno, Kimiko, Wiebke Denecke, Shinkawa Tokio, and Jinno Hidenori, eds. 2015–19. *Nihon "bun"gakushi* 日本「文」学史 [A new history of Japanese "letterature"], 3 vols. Tokyo: Benseisha.

Kōnoshi, Takamitsu 神野志隆光. 1995. *Kojiki: Tennō no sekai no monogatari* 古事記：天皇の世界の物語 [Kojiki: Tales from the world of the emperors]. Tokyo: Nihon Hōsō Shuppan Kyōkai.

—————. 2007. *Fukusū no "kodai"* 複数の「古代」 [The doubleness of "antiquity"]. Tokyo: Kōdansha.

Kornicki, Peter. 2018. *Languages, Scripts, and Chinese Texts in East Asia*. Oxford: Oxford University Press.

Li, Wai-Yee. 2017. "Concepts of Authorship." In *The Oxford Handbook of Classical Chinese Literature*, edited by Wiebke Denecke, Wai-Yee Li, and Xiaofei Tian, 360–76. New York: Oxford University Press.

Lurie, David B. 2007. "The Subterranean Archives of Early Japan: Recently Discovered Sources for the Study of Writing and Literacy." In *Books in Numbers*, edited by Lucille Chia and Wilt L. Idema, 91–112. Cambridge, MA: Harvard Yenching Library.

—————. 2011. *Realms of Literacy: Early Japan and the History of Writing*. Cambridge, MA: Harvard University Press.

Owen, Stephen. 2006. *The Making of Early Chinese Classical Poetry*. Cambridge, MA: Harvard University Press.

Perkins, David. 1992. *Is Literary History Possible?* Baltimore: Johns Hopkins University Press.

Pollack, David. 1986. *The Fracture of Meaning: Japan's Synthesis of China from the Eighth through the Eighteenth Centuries*. Princeton, NJ: Princeton University Press.

Sakaki, Atsuko. 2005. *Obsessions with the Sino-Japanese Polarity in Japanese Literature*. Honolulu: University of Hawaii Press.

Shields, Anna. 2017. "Classicisms in Chinese Literary Culture. Six Dynasties Through Tang." In *The Oxford Handbook of Classical Chinese Literature*, edited by Wiebke Denecke, Wai-Yee Li, and Xiaofei Tian, 387–97. New York: Oxford University Press.

Suzuki, Tomi. 2016. "Introduction: Nation Building, Literary Culture, and Language." In *The Cambridge History of Japanese Literature*, edited by Haruo Shirane, Tomi Suzuki, and David Lurie, 553–71. Cambridge: Cambridge University Press.

Wang Zhenping. 2005. *Ambassadors from the Islands of Immortals: China-Japan Relations in the Han-Tang Period*. Honolulu: University of Hawaii Press.

Chapter 3. Korean

Ch'oe Yong-ho, trans. 1997. "Preface to Correct Sounds to Instruct the People." In *Sources of Korean Tradition*, vol. 1, edited by Peter H. Lee, 261. New York: Columbia University Press.

Choi Byonghyon, trans. 2014. *The Annals of King T'aejo, Founder of Korea's Chosŏn Dynasty*. Cambridge, MA: Harvard University Press.

Chŏng Taham. 2009. "Yŏ mal Sŏn ch'o ŭi Tongasia chilsŏ wa Chosŏn esŏ ŭi Hanŏ, Hansamun, Hunmin chŏngŭm" [The East Asian order during the late Koryŏ and early Chosŏn dynasties, and the Chinese language, Chinese script, and the correct sounds to instruct the people in Chosŏn]. *Han'guksa hakpo* 36:269–305.

Kim Chinse. 1987–94. *Wanwŏlhoe maengyŏn* [The pledge at the banquet of moon-gazing pavilion]. Vols. 1–12. Seoul: Seoul National University Press.

Kim Sŭngu. 2015. *Yŏngbi ŏch'ŏn ka ŭi sŏngnip kwa suyong* [Composition and reception of The songs of flying dragons]. Seoul: Pogosa.

Lee, Peter H., trans. and ed. 1975. *Songs of Flying Dragons: A Critical Reading.* Cambridge, MA: Harvard University Press.

Owen, Stephen. 2017. "Key Concepts of Literature." In *The Oxford Handbook of Classical Chinese Literature (1000 BCE–900 CE)*, edited by Wiebke Denecke et al., n.p. Oxford: Oxford University Press.

Sejong sillok. In *Chosŏn wangjo sillok* [Veritable records of the Chosŏn dynasty]. http://sillok.history .go.kr.

So Hyŏnsŏng rok [The record of So Hyŏnsŏng]. 2010. Edited by Cho Hyeran et al. Seoul: Sŏmyŏng ch'ulp'an.

Zito, Angela. 1997. *Of Body and Brush: Grand Sacrifice as Text/Performance in Eighteenth-Century China.* Chicago: University of Chicago Press.

Chapter 4. Indian

Bronner, Yigal, et al. 2014. *Innovations and Turning Points: Toward a History of Kāvya Literature.* New Delhi: Oxford University Press.

Busch, Allison. 2011. "Hindi Literary Beginnings." In *South Asian Texts in History*, edited by Whitney Cox, Yigal Bronner, and Lawrence McCrea, 203–25. Ann Arbor, MI: Association for Asian Studies.

Hawley, John Stratton. 2015. *A Storm of Song: India and the Idea of the Bhakti Movement.* Cambridge, MA: Harvard University Press.

Jamison, Stephanie. 2007. *The Rig Veda between Two Worlds.* Paris: Collège de France, Publications de l'Institut de Civilisation Indienne, fasc. 74.

Mallette, Karla. 2005. *The Kingdom of Sicily, 1100–1250: A Literary History.* Philadelphia: University of Pennsylvania Press.

Novetzke, Christian Lee. 2016. *The Quotidian Revolution: Vernacularization, Religion, and Everyday Life in Medieval India.* New York: Columbia University Press.

Ollett, Andrew. 2017. *Language of the Snakes: Prakrit, Sanskrit, and the Language Order of Premodern India.* Berkeley: University of California Press.

Pollock, Sheldon, ed. 2003. *Literary Cultures in History: Reconstructions from South Asia.* Berkeley: University of California Press.

———. 2006. *The Language of the Gods in the World of Men: Sanskrit, Culture, and Power in Premodern India.* Berkeley: University of California Press.

———. 2007. *Rāma's Last Act by Bhavabhūti.* New York: New York University Press.

———. 2016. *A Rasa Reader: Classical Indian Aesthetics.* New York: Columbia University Press.

Shulman, David. 2016. *Tamil: A Biography.* Cambridge, MA: Harvard University Press.

Tieken, Hermann. 2001. *Kavya in South India: Old Tamil Cankam Poetry.* Amsterdam: Egbert Forsten.

Wilden, Eva Maria. 2014. *Manuscript, Print and Memory: Relics of the Cankam in Tamilnadu.* Berlin: de Gruyter.

Part II. The Mediterranean

Charpin, Dominique. 2010. *Reading and Writing in Babylon.* Translated by Jane Marie Todd. Cambridge, MA: Harvard University Press.

George, A. R. 2003. *The Babylonian Gilgamesh Epic: Introduction, Critical Edition, and Cuneiform Texts.* 2 vols. Oxford: Oxford University Press.

Chapter 5. Greek

Austin, John L. 1975. *How to Do Things with Words*. 2nd ed. Cambridge, MA: Harvard University Press.

Barber, Elizabeth J. W. 1991. *Prehistoric Textiles: The Development of Cloth in the Neolithic and Bronze Ages with Special Reference to the Aegean*. Princeton, NJ: Princeton University Press.

———. 1992. "The Peplos of Athena." In *Goddess and Polis: The Panathenaic Festival in Ancient Athens*, edited by Jennifer Neils, 103–17. Princeton, NJ: Princeton University Press.

Bergren, Ann. 2008. *Weaving Truth: Essays on Language and the Female in Greek Thought*. Hellenic Studies Series 19. Washington, DC: Center for Hellenic Studies.

Carruesco, Jesús. 2016. "Choral Performance and Geometric Patterns in Epic Poetry and Iconographic Representations." In *The Look of Lyric: Greek Song and the Visual; Studies in Archaic and Classical Greek Song*, edited by Vanessa Cazzato and André Lardinois, 69–107. Leiden: Brill.

D'Angour, Armand. 2005. "Intimations of the Classical in Early Greek *Mousikê*." In *Classical Pasts: The Classical Traditions of Greece and Rome*, edited by James I. Porter, 89–105. Princeton, NJ: Princeton University Press.

———. 2006, "The New Music: So What's New?" In *Rethinking Revolutions through Ancient Greece*, edited by Simon Goldhill and Robin Osborne, 264–83. Cambridge: Cambridge University Press.

Day, Joseph W. 2010. *Archaic Greek Epigram and Dedication*. Cambridge: Cambridge University Press.

Esrock, Elizabeth J. 1994. *The Reader's Eye: Visual Imaging as Reader Response*. Baltimore: Johns Hopkins University Press.

Faraone, Christopher A. 1996. "Taking the 'Nestor's Cup Inscription' Seriously: Erotic Magic and Conditional Curses in the Earliest Inscribed Hexameters." *Classical Antiquity* 15, no. 1:77–112.

Ford, Andrew. 2002. *The Origins of Criticism: Literary Culture and Poetic Theory in Classical Greece*. Princeton, NJ: Princeton University Press.

Gaunt, Jasper. 2017. "Nestor's Cup and Its Reception." In *Voice and Voices in Antiquity: Orality and Literacy in the Ancient World*. Vol. 2, edited by Niall W. Salter, 92–120. Leiden: Brill.

Janko, Richard. 1982. *Homer, Hesiod and the Hymns: Diachronic Development in Epic Diction*. Cambridge: Cambridge University Press.

———. 1998. "The Homeric Poets as Oral Dictated Texts." *Classical Quarterly* 48, no. 1:1–13.

Langdon, Merle K. 1976. *A Sanctuary of Zeus on Mount Hymettos*. Hesperia Supplement 16. Princeton, NJ: American School of Classical Studies at Athens.

Lord, Albert B. 1960. *The Singer of Tales*. Hellenic Studies Series 77. Washington, DC: Center for Hellenic Studies.

———. 1991. *Epic Singers and Oral Tradition*. Ithaca, NY: Cornell University Press.

Murray, Oswyn. 1994. "Nestor's Cup and the Origins of the Symposium." In *APOIKIA: I più antichi insediamenti Greci in Occidente; Funzione e modi dell'organizzazione politica e sociale: scriti in onore di Giorgio Buchner*, edited by Bruno D'Agostino and David Ridgway, 47–54.

Osborne, Robin, and Alexandra Pappas. 2007. "Writing on Archaic Greek Pottery." In *Art and Inscriptions in the Ancient World*, edited by Zahra Newby and Ruth Leader-Newby, 132–55. Cambridge: Cambridge University Press.

Parry, Milman, ed. 1971. *The Making of Homeric Verse: The Collected Papers of Milman Parry*. Oxford: Oxford University Press.

Powell, Barry B. 1988. "The Dipylon Oinochoe and the Spread of Literacy in Eighth-Century Athens." *Kadmos* 27, no. 1:65–86.

———. 1991. *Homer and the Origin of the Greek Alphabet*. Cambridge: Cambridge University Press.

Tuck, Anthony. 2006. "Singing the Rug: Patterned Textiles and the Origins of Indo-European Metrical Poetry." *American Journal of Archaeology* 110, no. 4:539–50.

Woodard, Roger D. 2014. *The Textualization of the Greek Alphabet*. Cambridge: Cambridge University Press.

Chapter 6. Latin

Montiglio, Silvia. 2011. *From Villain to Hero: Odysseus in Ancient Greek Thought*. Ann Arbor: University of Michigan Press.

Harris, William V. 1989. *Ancient Literacy*. Cambridge, MA: Harvard University Press.

Chapter 7. Hebrew

PRIMARY SOURCES

COS = Hallo, William W., ed. 2003. *Context of Scripture*. 3 vols. Leiden: Brill.

KAI = Donner, Herbert, and Wolfgang Röllig. 1966. *Kanaanäische und aramäische Inschriften*. 2nd ed. 3 vols. Wiesbaden: Harrassowitz.

SECONDARY SOURCES

Bordreuil, Pierre, and Dennis Pardee. 1989. *La trouvaille épigraphique de l'Ougarit*. Vol. 1. Paris: Editions Recherche sur les civilisations.

Carr, David M. 2005. *Writing on the Tablet of the Heart: Origins of Scripture and Literature*. Oxford: Oxford University Press.

Greenstein, Edward L. 2014. "Direct Discourse and Parallelism." In *Discourse, Dialogue, and Debate in the Bible: Essays in Honour of Frank H. Polak*, edited by Athalya-Idan Brenner, 79–91. Sheffield: Sheffield Phoenix.

Lord, Albert Bates. 1965. *The Singer of Tales*. New York: Atheneum.

Niditch, Susan. 1996. *Oral World and Written Word: Ancient Israelite Literature*. Louisville, KY: Westminster John Knox.

Nielsen, Eduard. 1954. *Oral Tradition: A Modern Problem in Old Testament Introduction*. London: SCM.

Nyberg, H. S. 1935. *Studien zum Hoseabuche: Zugleich ein Beitrag zur Klärung des Problems der Alttestamentlichen Textkritik*. Uppsala: A. B. Lundequistska.

Pardee, Dennis. 2007. "The Ugaritic Alphabetic Cuneiform Writing System in the Context of Other Alphabetic Systems." In *Studies in Semitic and Afro-Asiatic Linguistics Presented to Gene B. Gragg*, edited by Cynthia L. Miller, 181–200. Chicago: Oriental Institute of the University of Chicago.

———. 2009. "A New Aramaic Inscription from Zincirli." *Bulletin of the American Schools of Oriental Research* 356:51–71.

Quick, Laura. 2014. "Recent Research on Ancient Israelite Education: A Bibliographic Essay." *Currents in Biblical Research* 13:9–33.

Rollston, Christopher A. 2006. "Scribal Education in Ancient Israel: The Old Hebrew Epigraphic Evidence." *Bulletin of the American Schools of Oriental Research* 344:47–74.

Sanders, Seth L. 2009. *The Invention of Hebrew*. Urbana: University of Illinois Press.

Schniedewind, William M. 2013. *A Social History of Hebrew: Its Origins through the Rabbinic Period*. New Haven, CT: Yale University Press.

Smith, Mark S. 2008. *God in Translation: Deities in Cross-cultural Discourse in the Biblical World*. Tübingen: Mohr Siebeck.

Toorn, Karel van der. 2007. *Scribal Culture and the Making of the Hebrew Bible*. Cambridge, MA: Harvard University Press.

Vayntrub, Jacqueline. 2018. "Before Authorship: Solomon in Prov. 1:1." *Biblical Interpretation* 26:182–206.

———. 2019. "Like Father, Like Son: Theorizing Transmission in Biblical and Ancient Near Eastern Literature." *Hebrew Bible and Ancient Israel* 7:500–526.

Weinfeld, Moshe, ed. 1991. *Deuteronomy 1–11: A New Translation with Introduction and Commentary*. Anchor Bible 5. New York: Doubleday.

Chapter 8. Syriac

Adler, William. 2004. "Sextus Julius Africanus and the Roman Near East in the Third Century." *Journal of Theological Studies*, n.s., 55, no. 2:520–50.

Allberry, Charles R. C. 1938. *A Manichaean Psalm-Book*. Part II. Stuttgart: W. Kohlhammer.

Amar, Joseph. 1995. "A Metrical Homily on Holy Mar Ephrem, by Jacob of Serugh." *Patrologia Orientalis* 47, no. 1:1–75.

Andrade, Nathanael. 2015. "A Syriac Document and Its Cultural Implications for Third-Century Roman Syria." In *Syriac Encounters: Papers from the Sixth North American Syriac Symposium* (Duke University, June 26–29, 2011), edited by Maria Doerfler, Emanuel Fiano, and Kyle Smith, 239–58. Leuven: Peeters.

———. 2020. "Romans and Iranians: Experiences of Imperial Governance in Roman Mesopotamia." In *Reconsidering Roman Power: Roman, Greek, Jewish and Christians Perceptions and Reactions*, edited by Katell Berthelot, http://books.openedition.org/efr/5148. Rome: Publications de l'École française de Rome.

Arzhanov, Yury. 2018. *Syriac Sayings of Greek Philosophers: A Study in Syriac Gnomologia with Edition and Translation*. Leuven: Peeters.

Balty, Jean C., and Briquel-Chatonnet, Françoise. 2000. "Nouvelles mosaïques inscrites d'Osrhoène." *Monuments et Mémoires de la Fondation Eugène Piot* 79:31–72.

Baumstark, Anton. 1922. *Geschichte der syrischen Literatur mit Ausschluß der christlich-palästinensischen Texte*. Bonn: A. Marcus und E. Weber.

———. 1933. "Altsyrische Profandichtung in gereimten Siebensilbern." *Orientalistische Literaturzeitung* 36:345–48.

Beck, Edmund. 1957. *Des heiligen Ephraem des Syrers Hymnen contra haereses*. Louvain: Secrétariat du Corpus Scriptorum Christianorum Orientalium.

———. 1972. *Des heiligen Ephraem des Syrers Hymnen auf Abraham Kidunaya und Julianus Saba*. Louvain: Secrétariat du Corpus Scriptorum Christianorum Orientalium.

———. 1983. "Ephräms des Syrers Hymnik." In *Liturgie und Dichtung: Ein interdisziplinäres Kompendium*, 2 vols., edited by Hansjacob Becker and Reiner Kaczynski, 1:345–79. St. Ottilien: EOS Verlag Erzabtei St. Ottilien.

Becker, Adam H. 2006. *Fear of God and the Beginning of Wisdom: The School of Nisibis and the Development of Scholastic Culture in Late Antique Mesopotamia*. Philadelphia: University of Pennsylvania Press.

Beecroft, Alexander. 2015. *An Ecology of World Literature from Antiquity to the Present Day*. London: Verso.

Berthelot, Katell. 2018. In *Search of the Promised Land? The Hasmonean Dynasty between Biblical Models and Hellenistic Diplomacy*. Translated by Margaret Rigaud. Göttingen: Vandenhoeck & Ruprecht.

Beyer, Klaus. 1986. *The Aramaic Language*. Göttingen: Vandenhoeck & Ruprecht.

Boyarin, Daniel. 1981. "An Inquiry into the Formation of the Middle Aramaic Dialects." In *Bono homini donum: Essays in Historical Linguistics in Memory of J. Alexander Kerns*, edited by Yoël L. Arbeitman and Allan R. Bomhard, 613–49. Amsterdam: John Benjamins.

Briquel Chatonnet, Françoise. 2012. "Syriac as a Language of Eastern Christianity." In *The Semitic Languages: An International Handbook*, edited by Stefan Weninger, 652–59. Berlin: Walter de Gruyter.

Briquel Chatonnet, Françoise, and Desreumaux, Alain. 2011. "Syriac Inscriptions in Syria." *Hugoye: Journal of Syriac Studies* 14, no. 1:27–44.

Brock, Sebastian P. 1985. "Syriac and Greek Hymnography: Problems of Origin." *Studia Patristica* 16:77–81.

———. 1992. "Eusebius and Syriac Christianity." In *Eusebius, Christianity, and Judaism*, edited by Harold W. Attridge and Gohei Hata, 212–34. Leiden: Brill.

———. 1994. "Greek and Syriac in Late Antique Syria." In *Literacy and Power in the Ancient World*, edited by Alan K. Bowman and Greg Woolf, 149–60. Cambridge: Cambridge University Press, Rpt. 1999, in Sebastian P. Brock, *From Ephrem to Romanos: Interactions between Syriac and Greek in Late Antiquity*, chap. 1. Brookfield, VT: Ashgate.

————. 2003. "Syriac Translations of Greek Popular Philosophy." In *Von Athen nach Bagdad: Zur Rezeption griechischer Philosophie von der Spätantike bis zum Islam*, edited by Peter Bruns, 9–28. Bonn: Borengässer.

————. 2004. "The Earliest Syriac Literature." In *The Cambridge History of Early Christian Literature*, edited by Frances Young, Lewis Ayres, and Andrew Louth, 161–71. Cambridge: Cambridge University Press.

————. 2008. "Poetry and Hymnography (3): Syriac." In *The Oxford Handbook of Early Christian Studies*, edited by Susan Ashbrook Harvey and David G. Hunter, 657–71. Oxford: Oxford University Press.

Butts, Aaron M. 2016. *Language Change in the Wake of Empire: Syriac in Its Greco-Roman Context*. Winona Lake, IN: Eisenbrauns.

Cameron, Ron, and Dewey, Arthur J. 1979. *The Cologne Mani Codex (P. Colon. inv. nr. 4780): "Concerning the Origin of His Body."* Missoula, MT: Scholars.

Camplani, Alberto. 1998. "Rivisitando Bardesane: Note sulle fonti siriache del bardesanesimo e sulla sua collocazione storico-religiosa." *Cristianesimo nella storia* 19:519–96.

Contini, Riccardo. 1995. "Hypothèses sur l'araméen manichéen." *Annali di Ca' Foscari* 34:65–107.

Contini, Riccardo, and Cristiano Grottanelli. 2005. *Il saggio Ahiqar*. Brescia: Paideia Editrice.

Debié, Muriel. 2015. *L'écriture de l'histoire en syriaque: Transmissions interculturelles et constructions identitaires entre hellénisme et islam; Avec des répertoires des textes historiographiques en annexe*. Leuven: Peeters.

————. 2019. "The Eastern Provinces of the Roman Empire." In *The Syriac World*, edited by Daniel King, 11–32. London: Routledge.

Drijvers, Han J. W. 1966. *Bardaisan of Edessa*. Assen: Van Gorcum.

Drijvers, Han J. W., and John F. Healey. 1999. *The Old Syriac Inscriptions of Edessa and Osrhoene: Texts, Translations, and Commentary*. Leiden: Brill.

Duval, Rubens. 1907. *La littérature syriaque*. Paris: V. Lecoffre.

Fiano, Emanuel. 2015. "The Trinitarian Controversies in Fourth-Century Edessa." *Le Muséon* 128:85–125.

Gardner, Ian. 1996. *Kellis Literary Texts*. Vol. 1. With Contributions by S. Clackson, M. Frantzmann, and K. A. Worp. Oxford: Oxbow Books.

Griffith, Sidney H. 2006. "St. Ephraem, Bar Dayṣān and the Clash of Madrāshê in Aram." *Harp* 21:447–72.

————. 2017. "The Poetics of Scriptural Reasoning: Syriac Mêmrê at Work." *Studia Patristica* 78:5–23.

Gzella, Holger. 2015. *A Cultural History of Aramaic: From the Beginnings to the Advent of Islam*. Leiden: Brill.

————. 2019. "The Syriac Language in the Context of the Semitic Languages." In *The Syriac World*, edited by Daniel King, 205–21. London: Routledge.

Healey, John F. 2006. "A New Syriac Mosaic Inscription." *Journal of Semitic Studies* 51, no. 2:313–27.

————. 2007. "The Edessan Milieu and the Birth of Syriac." *Hugoye* 10, no. 2:115–27.

————. 2008. "Variety in Early Syriac: The Context in Contemporary Aramaic." In *Aramaic in Its Historical and Linguistic Setting*, edited by Holger Gzella and Margaretha L. Folmer, 221–29. Wiesbaden: Harrassowitz Verlag.

————. 2012. "Syriac," in *The Semitic Languages: An International Handbook*, edited by Stefan Weninger, 637–52. Berlin: Walter de Gruyter.

————. 2017. "Syriac before Christianity: Epigraphic Research in South-East Turkey." In *Syriac in Its Multi-cultural Context*, edited by Herman Teule, Elif Keser-Kayaalp, Kutlu Akalin, Nesim Doru, and M. Sait Toprak, 1–12. Leuven: Peeters.

Jiménez, Enrique. 2017. *The Babylonian Disputation Poems: With Editions of the Series of the Poplar, Palm and Vine, the Series of the Spider, and the Story of the Poor, Forlorn Wren*. Leiden: Brill.

Johnson, Scott F. 2015. "Introduction. The Social Presence of Greek in Eastern Christianity, 200–1200 CE." In *Languages and Cultures of Eastern Christianity: Greek*, edited by Scott F. Johnson, 1–122. Farnham: Ashgate.

Joosten, Jan. 2013. *Language and Textual History of the Syriac Bible: Collected Studies*. Piscataway, NJ: Gorgias.

————. 2017. "Le Diatessaron syriaque." In *Le Nouveau Testament en syriaque*, edited by Jean-Claude Haelewyck, 55–66. Paris: Paul Geuthner.

König, Jason. 2012. *Saints and Symposiasts: The Literature of Food and the Symposium in Greco-Roman and Early Christian Culture*. Cambridge: Cambridge University Press.

Kosmin, Paul J. 2014. *The Land of the Elephant Kings*. Cambridge, MA: Harvard University Press.

Lim, Richard. 1992. "Manichaeans and Public Disputation in Late Antiquity." *Recherches augustiniennes et patristiques* 26:233–72.

McVey, Kathleen E. 1999. "Were the Earliest Madrāšē Songs or Recitations?" In *After Bardaisan: Studies on Continuity and Change in Syriac Christianity in Honour of Professor Han J. W. Drijvers*, edited by Gerrit J. Reinink and Alex C. Klugkist, 185–99. Leuven: Peeters.

Mengozzi, Alessandro, and Luca B. Ricossa. 2013. "The Cherub and the Thief on YouTube: An Eastern Christian Liturgical Drama and the Vitality of the Mesopotamian Dispute." *Annali dell'Università degli Studi di Napoli "Orientale"* 73:49–65.

Mitchell, Charles W. S. 1912–21. *S. Ephraim's Prose Refutations of Mani, Marcion and Bardaisan*. Oxford: Williams and Norgate.

Moss, Yonatan. 2010. "The Language of Paradise: Hebrew or Syriac? Linguistic Speculations and Linguistic Realities in Late Antiquity." In *Paradise in Antiquity: Jewish and Christian Views*, edited by Markus Bockmuehl and Guy G. Stroumsa, 120–37. Cambridge: Cambridge University Press.

Murray, Robert. 1983. "Hellenistic-Jewish Rhetoric in Aphrahat." In *III° Symposium Syriacum 1980: Les contacts du monde syriaque avec les autres cultures*, edited by René Lavenant, 79–85. Rome: Pont. Institutum Studiorum Orientalium.

Nieten, Ulrike Rebekka. 2013. *Struktur und Metrum in den syrisch-aramäischen Psalmen und Hymnen*. Aachen: Shaker Verlag.

Noy, David, and Hanswulf Bloedhorn. 2004. *Inscriptiones Judaicae Orientis*. Vol. 3, *Syria and Cyprus*. Tübingen: Mohr Siebeck.

Parisot, Jean. 1894–1907. *Aphraatis Sapientis Persae Demonstrationes*. Paris: Firmin-Didot.

Pedersen, Nils A., and John M. Larsen. 2013. *Manichaean Texts in Syriac*. Turnhout: Brepols.

Phenix, Robert R., Jr., and Cornelia B. Horn. 2017. *The Rabbula Corpus: Comprising the Life of Rabbula, His Correspondence, a Homily Delivered in Constantinople, Canons, and Hymns*. Atlanta: SBL.

Pollock, Sheldon. 2009. *The Language of the Gods in the World of Men: Sanskrit, Culture, and Power in Premodern India*. Berkeley: University of California Press.

Reeves, John C. 1997. "Manichaean Citations from the Prose Refutations of Ephrem." In *Emerging from Darkness: Studies in the Recovery of Manichaean Sources*, edited by Paul Mirecki and Jason BeDuhn, 217–88. Leiden: Brill.

Rigolio, Alberto. 2013. "From Sacrifice to the Gods to the Fear of God: Omissions, Additions, and Changes in the Syriac Translations of Plutarch, Lucian, and Themistius." *Studia Patristica* 64:133–43.

Ross, Steven K. 2001. *Roman Edessa*. London: Routledge.

Säve-Söderbergh, Torgny. 1950. "Some Remarks on Coptic Manichaean Poetry." In *Coptic Studies in Honor of Walter Ewing Crum*, 159–73. Boston: Byzantine Institute.

Sprengling, Martin. 1916. "Antonius Rhetor on Versification with an Introduction and Two Appendices." *American Journal of Semitic Languages and Literatures* 32, no. 3:145–216.

Taylor, David G. K. 2002. "Bilingualism and Diglossia in Late Antique Syria and Mesopotamia." In *Bilingualism in Ancient Society: Language Contact and the Written Text*, edited by J. N. Adams, Mark Janse, and Simon Swain, 298–31. Oxford: Oxford University Press.

———. 2019. "The Coming of Christianity to Mesopotamia." In *The Syriac World*, edited by Daniel King, 68–87. London: Routledge.

Ter Haar Romeny, Robert B. 2005a. "Hypotheses on the Development of Judaism and Christianity in Syriac in the Period after 70 C.E." In *Matthew and the Didache: Two Documents from the Same Jewish-Christian Milieu?*, edited by Huub van de Sandt, 13–33. Assen: Van Gorcum.

———. 2005b. "The Syriac Versions of the Old Testament." In *Nos sources: Art et littérature syriaques*, edited by Maroun Atallah, 75–105. Antélias: Centre d'Études et de Recherches Orientales.

Traina, Giusto. 1996. "Archivi armeni e mesopotamici: La testimonianza di Movsēs Xorenac'i." In *Archives et sceaux du monde hellénistique*, edited by Marie-Françoise Boussac and Antonio Invernizzi, 349–63. Athens: École française d'Athènes.

Van Peursen, Wido. 2008. "Language Variation, Language Development, and the Textual History of the Peshitta." In *Aramaic in Its Historical and Linguistic Setting*, edited by Holger Gzella and Margaretha L. Folmer, 231–56. Wiesbaden: Harrassowitz Verlag.

Van Rompay, Lucas. 1994. "Some Preliminary Remarks on the Origin of Classical Syriac as a Standard Language: The Syriac Version of Eusebius of Caesarea's Ecclesiastical History." In *Semitic and Cushitic Studies*, edited by Gideon Goldenberg and Shlomo Raz, 70–89. Wiesbaden: Harrassowitz Verlag.

———. 2008. "The East (3): Syria and Mesopotamia." In *The Oxford Handbook of Early Christian Studies*, edited by Susan Ashbrook Harvey and David G. Hunter, 365–86. Oxford: Oxford University Press.

———. 2021. "Early Christianity in the Near East." In *Blackwell Companion to the Hellenistic and Roman Near East*, edited by Ted Kaizer. Oxford: Blackwell's.

Watt, John W. 1985. "Antony of Tagrit as a Student of Syriac Poetry." *Le Muséon* 98, nos. 3–4:261–79.

———. 1986. *The Fifth Book of the Rhetoric of Antony of Tagrit*. Leuven: Peeters.

———. 2018. "Syriac." In *A Companion to Late Antique Literature*, edited by Scott McGill and Edward J. Watts, 47–60. New York: Wiley Blackwell.

Wickes, Jeffrey. 2018. "Between Liturgy and School: Reassessing the Performative Context of Ephrem's Madrāšê." *Journal of Early Christian Studies* 26, no. 1:25–51.

Winkelmann, Sylvia. 2007. "Christliche Könige im heidnischen Gewand: Betrachtungen zur partherzeitlichen Herrscherikonographie der Abgariden von Edessa." In *Der christliche Orient und seine Umwelt: Gesammelte Studien zu Ehren Jürgen Tubachs anläßlich seines 60. Geburtstages*, edited by Sophia G. Vashalomidze and Lutz Greisiger, 169–86.

Wood, Philip. 2010. *"We Have No King but Christ": Christian Political Thought in Greater Syria on the Eve of the Arab Conquest*. Oxford: Oxford University Press.

———. 2012. "Syriac and the 'Syrians.'" In *The Oxford Handbook of Late Antiquity*, edited by Scott F. Johnson, 170–94. New York: Oxford University Press.

Wright, William. 1869. *The Homilies of Aphraates, the Persian Sage*. London: Williams and Norgate.

Wurst, Gregor. 1996. *Psalm Book*. Part 2. Turnhout: Brepols.

Zerubavel, Eviatar. 2003. *Time Maps: Collective Memory and the Social Shape of the Past*. Chicago: University of Chicago Press.

Chapter 9. Arabic

Ashtiany, Julia, T. M. Johnstone, et al., eds. 1990. *'Abbasid Belles-Lettres*. Cambridge History of Arabic Literature. Cambridge: Cambridge University Press.

Bauer, Thomas. 1992. *Altarabische Dichtkunst. Eine Untersuchung ihrer Struktur und Entwicklung am Beispiel der Onagerepisode*. 2 parts. Wiesbaden: Harrassowitz Verlag.

———. 1993. "Formel und Zitat: Zwei Spielarten von Intertextualität in der altarabischen Dichtung." *Journal of Arabic Literature* 24, no. 2:117–38.

Beeston, A.F.L., and T. M. Johnstone, et al., eds. 1983a. *Arabic Literature to the End of the Umayyad Period*. Cambridge History of Arabic Literature. Cambridge: Cambridge University Press.

———. 1983b. "Background Topics." In *Arabic Literature to the End of the Umayyad Period*, edited by A.F.L. Beeston and T. M. Johnstone, et al., 1–26. Cambridge History of Arabic Literature. Cambridge: Cambridge University Press.

[Bloch, Alfred.] 2002. "Alfred Blochs Studie über die Gattungen der altarabischen Dichtung." Edited by Gregor Schoeler. *Asiatische Studien* 56, no. 4:737–68.

Borg, Gert. 1997. *Mit Poesie vertreibe ich den Kummer meines Herzens: Eine Studie zur altarabischen Trauerklage der Frau*. Istanbul: Nederlands Historisch-Archaeologisch Instituut.

Carter, Michael. 1983. "Arabic Grammar." In *Religion, Learning and Science in the 'Abbasid Period*, edited by M.J.L. Young, J. D. Latham et al., 118–38. Cambridge History of Arabic Literature. Cambridge: Cambridge University Press.

Gibb, H.A.R. 1962. "The Social Significance of the Shuʿubiyya." In *Studies on the Civilization of Islam*, edited by S. J. Shaw and W. R. Polk, 62–73. London: Routledge and Kegan Paul.

Gutas, Dimitri. [1999] 2005. *Greek Thought, Arabic Culture: The Graeco-Arabic Translation Movement in Baghdad and Early 'Abbāsid Society (2nd–4th/8th–10th Centuries)* London: Routledge.

Heinrichs, Wolfhart. 1969. *Arabische Dichtung und griechische Poetik: Ḥāzim al-Qarṭāǧannīs Grundlegung der Poetik mit Hilfe Aristotelischer Begriffe.* Beirut, Wiesbaden: Franz Steiner Verlag.

Jacobi, Renate. 1971. *Studien zur Poetik der altarabischen Qaṣide.* Wiesbaden: Franz Steiner Verlag.

Jaeger, Werner W. 1912. *Studien zur Entstehungsgeschichte der Metaphysik des Aristoteles.* Berlin: Weidmann.

Jones, J.M.B. 1983. "The Maghāzī-Literature." In *Arabic Literature to the End of the Umayyad Period*, edited by A.F.L. Beeston, T. M. Johnstone, et al., 344–51. Cambridge History of Arabic Literature. Cambridge: Cambridge University Press.

Juynboll, G.H.A. 1982–89. "Ḥadīth." In *Dictionary of the Middle Ages*, 13 vols., edited by Joseph R. Strayer, 6:45–49. New York: Charles Scribner.

Latham, J. D. 1983. "The Beginnings of the Arabic Prose Literature: The Epistolary Genre." In *Arabic Literature to the End of the Umayyad Period*, edited by A.F.L. Beeston, T. M. Johnstone, et al., 154–79. Cambridge History of Arabic Literature. Cambridge: Cambridge University Press.

————. 1990. "Ibn al-Muqaffaʿ and early ʿAbbasid prose." In *ʿAbbasid Belles-Lettres*, edited by Julia Ashtiany, T. M. Johnstone, et al., 48–77. Cambridge History of Arabic Literature. Cambridge: Cambridge University Press.

Marzolph, Ulrich, and Richard van Leeuwen. 2004. *The Arabian Nights Encyclopedia.* 2 vols. Santa Barbara, CA: ABC-CLIO.

Motzki, Harald, ed. 2004. *Ḥadīth: Origins and Developments.* Aldershot: Ashgate.

Neuwirth, Angelika. 2010. *Der Koran als Text der Spätantike: Ein europäischer Zugang.* Berlin: Verlag der Welreligionen im Insel Verlag.

Paret, Rudi. 1983. "The Qurʾān. I." In *Arabic Literature to the End of the Umayyad Period*, edited by A.F.L. Beeston, T. M. Johnstone, et al., 186–227. Cambridge History of Arabic Literature. Cambridge: Cambridge University Press.

Pellat, Charles. 1991. "Marthiya." In vol. 6 of *The Encyclopaedia of Islam*, new ed., 1960–2004, 12 vols., edited by C. E. Bosworth, E. van Donzel, et al., 602–8. Leiden: E. J. Brill.

Saliba, George. 2007. *Islamic Science and the Making of European Renaissance.* Cambridge, MA: MIT Press.

Schoeler, Gregor. 2006. *The Oral and the Written in Early Islam.* Translated by Uwe Vagelpohl. Edited by James E. Montgomery. London: Routledge.

Schoeler, Gregor, in collaboration with and translated by Shawkat Toorawa. 2009. *The Genesis of Literature in Islam: From the Aural to the Read.* Edinburgh: Edinburgh University Press.

Serjeant, R. B. 1983. "Early Arabic Prose." In *Arabic Literature to the End of the Umayyad Period*, edited by A.F.L. Beeston, T. M. Johnstone, et al., 114–53. Cambridge History of Arabic Literature. Cambridge: Cambridge University Press.

Sezgin, Fuat. 1967. *Geschichte des arabischen Schrifttums.* Vol. 1. Leiden: E. J. Brill.

Versteegh, C.H.M. 1987. "Die arabische Sprachwissenschaft." In *Grundriss der Arabischen Philologie*, edited by Helmut Gätje, 2:148–76. Wiesbaden: Reichert Verlag.

————. 1993. *Arabic Grammar and Qurʾānic Exegesis in Early Islam.* Leiden: E. J. Brill.

Watt, W. M. 1977. *Bell's Introduction to the Qurʾān.* Edinburgh: Edinburgh University Press.

Young, M.J.L., J. D. Latham, et al., eds. 1990. *Religion, Learning and Science in the ʿAbbasid Period.* Cambridge History of Arabic Literature. Cambridge: Cambridge University Press.

Zwettler, Michael. 1978. *The Oral Tradition of Classical Arabic Poetry: Its Character and Implications.* Columbus: Ohio State University Press.

Chapter 10. English

Ashe, Laura. 2017. *Conquest and Transformation: The Oxford English Literary History.* Vol. 1, *1000–1350.* Oxford: Oxford University Press.

Bahr, Arthur. 2013. *Fragments and Assemblages: Forming Compilations of Medieval London.* Chicago: University of Chicago Press.

Burnley, David, and Alison Wiggins. 2004. "The Auchinleck Manuscript." http://auchinleck.nls.uk/.

Burrow, John A. 1971. *Ricardian Poetry: Chaucer, Gower, Langland, and the Gawain Poet.* New Haven, CT: Yale University Press.

Butterfield, Ardis. 2009. *The Familiar Enemy: Chaucer, Language and Nation in the Hundred Years War.* Oxford: Oxford University Press.

———. 2015. "Why Medieval Lyric?" *English Literary History* 82:319–43.

Campbell, James, Eric John, and Patrick Wormald. 1982. *The Anglo-Saxons.* Ithaca, NY: Cornell University Press.

Cartlidge, Neil. 1997. "The Composition and Social Context of Oxford, Jesus College, MS 29 (II) and London, British Library, MS Cotton Caligula A.IX." *Medium Ævum* 66, no. 2:250–69.

Catto, Jeremy. 2003. "Written English: The Making of the Language, 1370–1400." *Past and Present* 179:24–59.

Clanchy, M. T. 1993. *From Memory to Written Record, England 1066–1307.* 2nd ed. Oxford: Blackwell.

Coleman, Joyce. 1996. *Public Reading and the Reading Public in Late Medieval England and France.* Cambridge: Cambridge University Press.

Dolan, Terence. 1999. "Writing in Ireland." In *The Cambridge History of Medieval English Literature,* edited by David Wallace, 208–28. Cambridge: Cambridge University Press.

Dunbar, William. 2004. *Lament for the Makars.* In *The Complete Works,* edited by John Conlee. Kalamazoo, MI: Medieval Institute Publications.

Echard, Siân. 2004. "Last Words: Latin at the End of the Confessio Amantis." In *Interstices: Studies in Middle English and Anglo-Latin Texts in Honour of A. G. Rigg,* edited by Richard Firth Green and Linne Mooney, 99–121. Toronto: University of Toronto Press.

Fein, Susanna, ed. 2016. *The Auchinleck Manuscript: New Perspectives.* Woodbridge, Suffolk: York Medieval.

———. 2018. "All Adam's Children: The Early Middle English Lyric Sequence in Oxford, Jesus College, MS 29 (II)." In *Middle English Lyrics: New Readings of Short Poems,* edited by Julia Boffey and Christiania Whitehead, 213–26. Cambridge: D. S. Brewer.

Fulton, Helen. 1989. "Dafydd ap Gwilym and Intertextuality." *Leeds Studies in English* 20:65–86.

Geoffrey of Vinsauf. 1967. *Poetria Nova of Geoffrey of Vinsauf.* Translated by Margaret F. Nims. Toronto: Pontifical Institute of Mediaeval Studies.

Glissant, Édouard. 1997. *Poetics of Relation.* Translated by Betsy Wing. Ann Arbor: University of Michigan Press.

Gneuss, Helmut. 2013. "The Old English Language." In *The Cambridge Companion to Old English Literature,* 2nd ed., edited by Malcolm Godden and Michael Lapidge, 19–49. Cambridge: Cambridge University Press.

Graff, Gerald. 1987. *Professing Literature: An Institutional History.* Chicago: University of Chicago Press.

Greenfield, Stanley B., Daniel Gillmore Calder, and Michael Lapidge. 1986. *A New Critical History of Old English Literature.* New York: New York University Press.

Guillory, John. 1993. *Cultural Capital: The Problem of Literary Canon Formation.* Chicago: University of Chicago Press.

Hill, Betty. 2003. "Oxford, Jesus College MS 29, Part II: Contents, Technical Matters, Compilation, and Its History to c. 1695." *Notes and Queries* 50 (248), no. 3:268.

Hoccleve, Thomas. 1999. *The Regiment of Princes,* edited by Charles R. Blyth. Kalamazoo, MI: Medieval Institute Publications.

Hollander, Robert. 2007. "Dante and His Commentators." In *The Cambridge Companion to Dante,* 2nd ed., edited by Rachel Jacoff, 226–36. Cambridge: Cambridge University Press.

Hunt, Tony. 1991. *Teaching and Learning Latin in Thirteenth-Century England.* Woodbridge, England: D. S. Brewer.

Huscroft, Richard. 2019. *Making England, 796–1042.* Abingdon: Routledge.

Knapp, Ethan. 2001. *The Bureaucratic Muse: Thomas Hoccleve and the Literature of Late Medieval England.* University Park: Pennsylvania State University Press.

Lydgate, John. 1924. *The Fall of Princes.* Vol. 1, edited by Henry Bergen. Oxford: Oxford University Press.

———. 2005. "Floure of Curtesye." In *Chaucerian Apocrypha,* edited by Kathleen Forni. Kalamazoo, MI: Medieval Institute Publications.

Machan, Tim William. 2006. "Medieval Multilingualism and Gower's Literary Practice." *Studies in Philology* 103:1–25.

Matthews, David. 1999. *The Making of Middle English, 1765–1910*. Minneapolis: University of Minnesota Press.

Miller, B.D.H. 1963. "The Early History of Bodleian MS. Digby 86." *Annuale Mediaevale* 4:23–56.

Minnis, Alastair J. 1988. *Medieval Theory of Authorship: Scholastic Literary Attitudes in the Later Middle Ages*. 2nd ed. Philadelphia: University of Pennsylvania Press.

Orme, Nicholas. 2006. *Medieval Schools: From Roman Britain to Renaissance England*. New Haven, CT: Yale University Press.

Pearsall, Derek. 1992. *The Life of Geoffrey Chaucer: A Critical Biography*. Oxford: Blackwell.

Roberts, Brynley F. 1999. "Writing in Wales." In *The Cambridge History of Medieval English Literature*, edited by David Wallace, 182–207. Cambridge: Cambridge University Press.

Robinson, P. R. 1980. "The 'Booklet': A Self-Contained Unit in Composite Manuscripts." In *Codicologica: Towards a Science of Handwritten Books*, 5 vols., edited by A. Gruys and J. P. Gumbert, 3:46–69. Leiden: E. J. Brill.

Said, Edward W. 1975. *Beginnings: Intention and Method*. New York: Basic Books.

Shonk, Timothy A. 1985. "A Study of the Auchinleck Manuscript: Bookmen and Bookmaking in the Early Fourteenth Century." *Speculum* 60:71–91.

Smith, D. Vance. 2001. *Book of the Incipit*. Minneapolis: University of Minnesota Press.

Treharne, Elaine. 2012. *Living through Conquest: The Politics of Early English, 1020–1220*. Oxford: Oxford University Press.

Tschann, Judith, and M. B. Parkes, eds. 1996. *Facsimile of Oxford, Bodleian Library, MS Digby 86*. Oxford: Oxford University Press.

Turville-Petre, Thorlac. 1996. *England the Nation: Language, Literature, and National Identity, 1290–1340*. Oxford: Clarendon.

———. 2003. "Oxford, Bodleian Library, MS Digby 86: A Thirteenth-Century Commonplace Book in Its Social Context." In *Family and Dynasty in Late Medieval England: Proceedings of the 1997 Harlaxton Symposium*, edited by R. G. Eales and Shaun Tyas, 56–64. Donington, Lincs.: Shaun Tyas.

Wacks, David A. 2007. *Framing Iberia: Maqāmāt and Frametale Narratives in Medieval Spain*. Boston: Brill.

Wallace, David, ed. 2016. *Europe: A Literary History, 1348–1418*. 2 vols. Oxford: Oxford University Press.

———. 2019. "Europe: A Literary History, 1348–1418; About This Project." Accessed July 30. http://www.english.upenn.edu/.

Watson, Nicholas. 1995. "Censorship and Cultural Change in Late-Medieval England: Vernacular Theology, the Oxford Translation Debate, and Arundel's Constitution of 1409." *Speculum* 70:822–64.

Wenzel, Siegfried. 1986. *Preachers, Poets, and the Early English Lyric*. Princeton, NJ: Princeton University Press.

Wimsatt, James I. 1982. *Chaucer and the Poems of "Ch" in University of Pennsylvania MS French 15*. Totowa, NJ: Rowman and Littlefield.

Zieman, Katherine. 2008. *Singing the New Song: Literacy and Liturgy in Late Medieval England*. Philadelphia: University of Pennsylvania Press.

Chapter 11. Romance Languages

Asperti, Stefano. 2006. *Origini romanze: Lingue, testi antichi, letterature*. Rome: Viella.

Cerquiglini, Bernard. 2018. *L'Invention de Nithard*. Paris: Les Éditions de Minuit.

Ducos, Joëlle, Olivier Soutet, and Jean-René Valette. 2016. *Le Français médiéval par les textes: anthologie commentée*. Paris: Champion.

Eusebi, Mario, ed. 2003. *Guiglielmo IX: Vers*, 2nd ed. Rome: Carocci.

Gaunt, Simon, and Karen Pratt, trans. and ed. 2015. *The Song of Roland, and Other Poems of Charlemagne*. Oxford: Oxford University Press.

McKitterick, Rosamund. 1991. "Latin and Romance: An Historian's Perspective." In *Latin and the Romance Languages in the Early Middle Ages*, edited by Roger Wright, 130–45. London: Routledge.

Nagel, Alexander, and Christopher S. Wood. 2010. *Anachronic Renaissance*. New York: Zone Books.

Paden, William D. 2005. "Before the Troubadours: The Archaic Occitan Texts and the Shape of Literary History." In *"De sens rassis": Essays in Honor of Rupert T. Pickens*, edited by Keith Busby, Bernard Guidot, and Logan D. Whalen, 509–27. Amsterdam: Rodopi.

Stock, Brian. 1983. *The Implications of Literacy: Written Language and Models of Interpretation in the Eleventh and Twelfth Centuries*. Princeton, NJ: Princeton University Press.

Whitehead, Frederick, ed. 1946. *La Chanson de Roland*. 2nd ed. Oxford: Basil Blackwell.

Chapter 12. German

Adelung, Johann Christoph. 1782. "Was ist Hochdeutsch?" *Magazin für die Deutsche Sprache*, 1, no. 1:1–31.

———. 1783. "Über die Frage: Was ist Hochdeutsch? Gegen den Deutschen Merkur." *Magazin für die Deutsche Sprache* 1, no. 4:79–111.

Blanckenburg, Friedrich. 1774. *Versuch über den Roman*. Leipzig: David Siegerts Wittwe.

de Staël, Madame. 1968. *De l'Allemagne*. Vol. 1. Paris: Classiques Garnier.

Goethe, Johann Wolfgang von. 1907. *Goethes Werke*. Vol. 42/2. Weimar: Hermann Böhlau.

Gottsched, Johann Christoph. 1730. *Versuch einer Critischen Dichtkunst vor die Deutschen*. Leipzig: Breitkopf.

———. 1748. *Grundlegung einer deutschen Sprachkunst*. Leipzig: Breitkopf.

Möser, Justus. 1781. *Über die deutsche Sprache und Litteratur*. Hamburg: Benjamin Gottlob Hoffmann.

Nicolai, Friedrich. 1773. *Das Leben und die Meinungen des Herrn Magister Sebaldus Nothanker*. Vol. 1. Berlin: Friedrich Nicolai.

Riedel, Friedrich Just. 1774. *Theorie der schönen Künste und Wissenschaften*. Vienna: Christian Heinrich Cuno.

Wieland, Christoph Martin. 1782. "Ueber die Frage: Was ist Hochdeutsch? und einige damit verwandten Gegenstände." *Der Teutsche Merkur*, no. 4:145–70.

Chapter 13. Russian

Batiushkov, K. N. 1977. *Opyty v stikhakh i proze*. Moscow: Nauka.

Čiževskij, Dmitrij. 1960. *History of Russian Literature from the Eleventh Century to the End of the Baroque*. 'S'Gravenhage: Mouton.

Dunn, J. A. 1993. "What Was Ludolf Writing About?" *Slavonic and East European Review* 71, no. 2:201–16.

Gasparov, M. L. 1984. *Ocherk istorii russkogo stikha*. Moscow: Nauka.

———. 1996. *A History of European Versification*. Translated by G. S. Smith and Marina Tarlinskaja. Edited by G. S. Smith and L. Holford-Strevens. Oxford: Clarendon.

Kahn, Andrew, Mark Lipovetsky, Irina Reyfman, and Stephanie Sandler. 2018. *A History of Russian Literature*. Oxford: Oxford University Press.

Karamzin, N. M. 1984. *Pis'ma russkogo puteshestvennika*. Leningrad: Nauka.

Karlinsky, Simon. 1985. *Russian Drama from Its Beginnings to the Age of Pushkin*. Berkeley: Univeristy of California Press.

Khodasevich, Vladislav. 1989. *Stikhotvoreniia*. Leningrad: Sovetskii pisatel'.

Klein, Joachim. 2008. *Russische Literatur im 18. Jahrhundert*. Köln: Böhlau.

Kuskov, Vladimir. [1977] 1980. *A History of Old Russian Literature*. Translated by Ronald Vroon. Moscow: Progress.

Mandel'stham, O. 1997. *Polnoe sobranie stikhotvorenii*. St. Petersburg: Akademicheskii proekt.

Marker, Gary. 1985. *Publishing, Printing, and the Origins of Intellectual Life in Russia, 1700–1800*. Princeton, NJ: Princeton University Press.

Milosz, Czeslaw. 1983. *The History of Polish Literature*. Berkeley: University of California Press.

Mirsky, D. S. 1924. "Old Russian Literature: Its Place in the History of Civilisation." *Slavonic Review* 3, no. 7 (June): 74–91.

Nabokov, Vladimir, trans. 1960. *The Song of Igor's Campaign*. New York: Vintage.

Pushkin, Aleksandr. 1978. *Polnoe sobranie sochinenii v desiati tomakh*. Leningrad: Nauka.

Schenker, Alexander M. 1995. *The Dawn of Slavic: An Introduction to Slavic Philology*. New Haven, CT: Yale University Press.

Trediakovskii, V. K. 1963. *Izbrannye proizvedeniia*. Moscow, Russia: Sovetskii pisatel'.

Tynianov, Yuri. 2019. "The Ode as an Oratorical Genre." In *Permanent Evolution: Selected Essays on Literature, Theory, and Film*, by Tynianov, 77–113. Translated and edited by Ainsley Morse and Philip Redko. Boston: Academic Studies.

Zhivov, Victor. 2009. *Language and Culture in Eighteenth-Century Russia*. Translated by Marcus Levitt. Boston: Academic Studies.

Chapter 14. Latin American

Adorno, Rolena. 1996. "Cultures in Contact: Mesoamerica, the Andes, and the European Written Tradition." In *The Cambridge History of Latin American Literature*, vol. 1, edited by Roberto González Echevarría and Enrique Pupo-Walker, 33–57. Cambridge: Cambridge University Press.

———. 2011. *Colonial Latin American Literature*. New York: Oxford University Press.

Bello, Andrés. 1823. *La Biblioteca americana, o Miscelánea de literatura, artes i ciencias*. 2 vols. London: G. Marchant.

González Echevarría, Roberto. 1996. "A Brief History of the History of Spanish American Literature" and "Colonial Lyric." In *The Cambridge History of Latin American Literature*, vol. 1, edited by Roberto González Echevarría and Enrique Pupo-Walker, 7–32 and 191–230. Cambridge: Cambridge University Press.

———. 2012. *Modern Latin American Literature*. New York: Oxford University Press.

Henríquez Ureña, Pedro. 1945. *Literary Currents in Hispanic America*. Cambridge, MA: Harvard University Press.

Chapter 15. African

Allen, James de Vere. 1977. *Al-Inkishafi: Catechism of a Soul*. Nairobi: East African Literature Bureau.

Allen, R. 1946. "Inkishafi—a Translation from the Swahili." *African Studies* 5, no. 4:243–49.

Andrzejewski, B. W., S. Pilaszewicz, and W. Tyloch, eds. 1985. *Literatures in African Languages: Theoretical Issues and Sample Surveys*. Cambridge: Cambridge University Press.

Auerbach, Erich. 1965. *Literary Language and Its Public in Late Latin Antiquity and in the Middle Ages*. Translated by Ralph Manheim. Princeton, NJ: Princeton University Press.

Benjamin, Walter. 1998. *The Origin of German Tragic Drama*. Translated by John Osborne. London: Verso.

Feeney, Denis. 2016. *Beyond Greek: The Beginnings of Latin Literature*. Cambridge, MA: Harvard University Press.

Finnegan, Ruth. 1970. *Oral Literature in Africa*. Oxford: Oxford University Press.

Gérard, Albert. 1981. *African Language Literatures: An Introduction to the Literary History of Sub-Saharan Africa*. New York: Longman.

Harries, Lyndon. 1962. "Utendi wa Inkishafi." In *Swahili Poetry*, 90–102. Oxford: Clarendon.

Hichens, William. [1939] 1972. *Al-Inkishafi: The Soul's Awakening*. [London: Sheldon.] Nairobi: Oxford University Press.

Hirji, Zulfikar. 2012. *Between Empires: Sheikh-Sir Mbarak al-Hinawy*. London: Azimuth Editions.

Irele, Abiola. 1981. *The African Experience in Literature and Ideology*. London: Heinemann.

Irele, F., and S. Gikandi, eds. 2000. *The Cambridge History of African and Caribbean Literature*. Cambridge: Cambridge University Press.

Jahadhymy, Ali A. 1975. *Anthology of Swahili Poetry*. Nairobi: East African Educational.

Jahn, Janheinz. 1968. *Neo-African Literature: A History of Black Writing*. Translated from the German by Oliver Coburn and Ursula Lehburger. New York: Grove. Originally published in 1966 as *Geschichte der neoafrikanischen Literatur: Eine Einführung*. Düsseldorf: Eugen Diederichs.

Knappert, Jan. 1967. *Traditional Swahili Poetry*. Leiden: E. J. Brill.

———. 2005. *Swahili Culture*. Book 2. Lewiston: Edwin Mellen.

Krapf, Ludwig. 1850. *Outline of the Elements of the Kisuáheli Language: With Special Reference to the Kiníka Dialect*. Tübingen: Lud. Fried. Fues.

———. 1882. *Dictionary of the Suahli Language*. London: Trubner.

Mazrui, Alamin. 2007. *Swahili beyond the Boundaries: Literature, Language and Identity*. Athens: Ohio University Press.

Mugane, John. 2015. *The Story of Swahili*. Athens: Ohio University Press.

———. 2017. "The Odyssey of 'Ajamī and the Swahili People." *Islamic Africa* 8:193–216.

Mulokozi, M. M., and T.S.Y. Sengo. 1995. *History of Kiswahili Poetry A.D. 1000–2000*. Dar es Salaam: Institute of Kiswahili Research.

Obiechina, Emmanuel. 1975. *Culture, Tradition and Society in the West African Novel*. Cambridge: Cambridge University Press.

Pugach, Sara. 2012. *Africa in Translation: A History of Colonial Linguistics in Germany and Beyond, 1814–1945*. Ann Arbor: University of Michigan Press.

Said, Edward W. 1985. *Beginnings: Intention and Method*. New York: Columbia University Press.

Stigand, C. H. 1915. *A Grammar of Dialect Changes in Swahili*. Cambridge: Cambridge University Press.

Swettler, Michael. 1978. *The Oral Tradition of Classical Arabic Poetry: Its Character and Implications*. Columbus: Ohio State University Press.

Taylor, W. E. 1915. "Introduction" and "Appendix." In *A Grammar of Dialect Changes in Swahili*, vii–xi and 73–105. Cambridge: Cambridge University Press.

Thiong'o, Ngugi wa. 1986. *Decolonising the Mind*. London: James Currey.

Walsh, Martin. 2018. "The Swahili Language and Its Early History." In *The Swahili World*, edited by Stephanie Wynne-Jones and Adria LaViolette, 121–30. Abingdon: Routledge.

Wamitila, Kyallo Wadi. 2001. *Archetypal Criticism of Kiswahili Poetry: With Special Reference to Fumo Liyongo*. Bayreuth: Bayreuth African Studies.

Werner, Alice. 1918. "Swahili Poetry." *Bulletin of the School of Oriental Studies* (University of London) 1, no. 2:113.

Whitely, Wilfred. 1969. *Swahili: The Rise of a National Language*. London: Methuen.

Chapter 17. World Literature

Apter, Emily. 2008. "Untranslatables: A World System." *New Literary History* 39, no. 3:581–98.

———. 2013. *Against World Literature: On the Politics of Untranslatability*. London: Verso.

Auerbach, Erich. 1922. "Giambattista Vico." *Der Neue Merkur* 6:249–51.

———. [1936] 2014. "Giambattista Vico and the Idea of Philology." In *Time, History, and Literature: Selected Essays of Erich Auerbach*, edited by James I. Porter and translated by Jane O. Newman, 24–35. Princeton, NJ: Princeton University Press. Originally published as "Giambattista Vico und die Idee der Philologie." Rpt. in 1967 in *Gesammelte Aufsätze zur Romanischen Philologie*. Bern: Francke Verlag.

———. [1952] 2014. "The Philology of World Literature." In *Time, History, and Literature: Selected Essays of Erich Auerbach*, edited by James I. Porter and translated by Jane O. Newman, 253–65. Princeton, NJ: Princeton University Press.

———. [1955] 2014. "Vico and the National Spirit." In *Time, History, and Literature: Selected Essays of Erich Auerbach*, edited by James I. Porter and translated by Jane O. Newman, 46–51. Princeton, NJ: Princeton University Press.

———. 1958. *Literary Language and Its Public in Late Latin Antiquity and in the Middle Ages*. Translated 1993 by Ralph Mannheim. Princeton, NJ: Princeton University Press.

———. 2014. *Time, History, and Literature: Selected Essays of Erich Auerbach*, edited by James I. Porter and translated by Jane O. Newman. Princeton, NJ: Princeton University Press.

Beaulac, Stéphane. 2004. "The Westphalian Model in Defining International Law: Challenging the Myth." *Australian Journal of Legal History* 8, no. 2:181–213.

Burke, Peter. 2007. "Translations into Latin in Early Modern Europe." In *Cultural Translation in Early Modern Europe*, edited by Peter Burke and R. Po Chia Hsia, 65–80. Cambridge: Cambridge University Press.

Cheah, Pheng. 2016. *What Is a World? On Post-colonial Literature as World Literature*. Durham, NC: Duke University Press.

Conrad, Sebastian. [2006] 2010. *Globalisation and the Nation in Imperial Germany*. Translated by Sorcha O'Hagan. Cambridge: Cambridge University Press.

Cooppan, Vilashini. 2004. "Ghosts in the Disciplinary Machine: The Uncanny Life of World Literature." *Comparative Literature Studies* 41, no. 1:10–36.

Damrosch, David. 1995. "Literary Study in an Elliptical Age." In *Comparative Literature in an Age of Multiculturalism*, edited by Charles Bernheimer, 122–32. Baltimore: Johns Hopkins University Press.

———. 2020. *Comparing the Literatures: Literary Studies in a Global Age*. Princeton, NJ: Princeton University Press.

Falk, Richard. 2002. "Revisiting Westphalia, Discovering Post-Westphalia." *Journal of Ethics* 6:311–52.

Hacohen, Malachi Haim. 2012. "Typology and the Holocaust: Erich Auerbach and Judeo-Christian Europe. *Religions* 3, no. 3:600–646.

Helgesson, Stefan, and Pieter Vermeulen. 2015. *Institutions of World Literature: Writing, Translation, Markets*. London: Routledge.

Hoesel-Uhlig, Stefan. 2004. "Changing Fields: The Directions of Goethe's *Weltliteratur*." In *Debating World Literature*, edited by Christopher Prendergast, 26–53. London: Verso.

Hutchinson, Ben. 2017. "Late Reading: Erich Auerbach and the *Spätboot* of Comparative Literature." *Comparative Critical Studies* 14, no. 1:69–85.

Kadir, Djelal. 2011. "Auerbach's Scar." In *Memos from the Besieged City: Lifelines for Cultural Sustainability*, by Kadir, 19–40. Stanford, CA: Stanford University Press.

Mani, B. Venkat. 2017. *Recoding World Literature: Libraries, Print Culture, and Germany's Pact with Books*. New York: Fordham University Press.

Moretti, Franco. 2000. "Conjectures on World Literature." *New Left Review* 1 (January–February): 54–68.

Mufti, Aamir. 2012. "Erich Auerbach and the Death and Life of World Literature." In *Routledge Companion to World Literature*, edited by Theo D'haen et al., 71–80. New York: Routledge.

Newman, Jane O. 2020. "The Gospel According to Auerbach." *Publications of the Modern Language Association* 135, no. 3:1–37.

Nichols, Angus. 2018. "The Goethean Discourses on *Weltliteratur* and the Origins of Comparative Literature." *Seminar* 54, no. 2:167–94.

Pollock, Sheldon. 2009. "Future Philology? The Fate of a Soft Science in a Hard World." *Critical Inquiry* 35, no. 4:931–61.

Said, Edward. 1975. *Beginnings: Intention and Method*. Baltimore: Johns Hopkins University Press.

Spivak, Gayatri. 2003. *Death of a Discipline*. New York: Columbia University Press.

Vico, Giambattista. 1984. *The New Science of Giambattista Vico*. Translated by Thomas Goddard Bergin and Max Harold Fisch. Ithaca, NY: Cornell University Press.

Walkowitz, Rebecca. 2015. *Born Translated: The Contemporary Novel in an Age of World Literature*. New York: Columbia University Press.

Weber, Max. 2001. *The Protestant Ethic and the Spirit of Capitalism*. 1904–5. Translated by Talcott Parsons, with an introduction by Anthony Giddens. London: Routledge.

Yashin, Veli. 2011. "Euro(tro)pology: Philology, World Literature, and the Legacy of Erich Auerbach." *Yearbook of Comparative Literature* 57:269–90.

INDEX